The Political Economy of Education in the Arab World

The Political Economy of Education in the Arab World

edited by
Hicham Alaoui
Robert Springborg

LYNNE
RIENNER
PUBLISHERS

BOULDER
LONDON

Published in the United States of America in 2021 by
Lynne Rienner Publishers, Inc.
1800 30th Street, Suite 314, Boulder, Colorado 80301
www.rienner.com

and in the United Kingdom by
Lynne Rienner Publishers, Inc.
Gray's Inn House, 127 Clerkenwell Road, London EC1 5DB
www.eurospanbookstore.com/rienner

Library of Congress Cataloging-in-Publication Data
A Cataloging-in-Publication record for this book
is available from the Library of Congress.

ISBN 978-1-62637-935-0 (hc)

British Cataloguing in Publication Data
A Cataloguing in Publication record for this book
is available from the British Library.

Printed and bound in the United States of America

 The paper used in this publication meets the requirements
of the American National Standard for Permanence of
Paper for Printed Library Materials Z39.48-1992.

5 4 3 2 1

Contents

Tables and Figures

Tables

Figures

Acknowledgments

This book was made possible by the generous support of the Hicham Alaoui Foundation and was brought to fruition through the sustained intellectual, organizational, and editorial contributions of Lindsay Benstead and Sean Yom. I would like to thank them on behalf of all the authors.

—*Robert Springborg*

1

The Political Economy of Education in the Arab World

Hicham Alaoui and Robert Springborg

Why undertake yet another study of education in the Arab world? The World Bank, the United Nations Development Programme (UNDP), various bilateral aid agencies, and countless independent analysts have already produced a substantial library devoted to documenting and accounting for Arab educational performance. Moreover, there is substantial agreement in this literature that Arab educational systems are underperforming and that they suffer from a list of ailments common to most if not all of them. It is further generally concurred that while various efforts at reform, most notably those supported by external actors, may have succeeded at local levels, none have had substantial and lasting national, systemic impacts. Finally, analysts of Arab education agree that its improvement is essential if Arab countries are to diversify economies, improve growth rates, and broaden the bases of citizenship upon which more stable and effective systems of governance can be built.

The agreed upon common characteristics of Arab education are generally negative. The major exceptions are the quantitative and proportional growth of primary, secondary, and tertiary educational systems, such that enrollment rates have expanded to become about as high as those predicted by levels of gross domestic product (GDP) per capita; and dramatically improved female participation rates at all educational levels have produced a reverse gender gap, whereby more females than males are enrolled in tertiary education in most Arab countries and, in some, even at the secondary level. These growth rates have not, however, been paralleled by improvements in quality, nor have they impacted power structures within society with respect to socioeconomic

1

status, gender, or other categories of privilege and marginalization. The extensive list of indicators of lagging performance includes test results as on the Program for International Student Assessment (PISA) and Trends in International Mathematics and Science (TIMSS); inadequate commitment to STEM disciplines (science, technology, engineering, and math); lagging literacy rates, especially among females; absence of Arab universities from lists of the world's top 300; poor preparation for and inadequate linkages with labor markets; negligible economic returns from education; and lack of preparation to exercise rights and responsibilities of citizenship.

A similarly lengthy list of causes of this underperformance is also to be found in the relevant literature. Most focus on implementation issues of an administrative, financial, curricular, or pedagogical nature. Arab educational systems are viewed as being underfinanced or suffering from misallocation of funding, or both, most notably away from primary and toward tertiary education and away from teachers and toward administrators; as having inadequate, overcrowded facilities; as being overly centralized and resistant to stakeholder participation, especially by teachers, parents, and potential private sector employers; as being insufficiently student-focused in methods of teaching and learning, partly as a result of poorly trained teachers; and as preferencing religion and social studies while devaluing science, technology, engineering, and mathematics. The systemic, contextual factor that has received the most attention in explaining underperformance is that of economic inequality, which appears to have more pernicious effects in the Arab world than in most other, if not all, emerging regions.[1]

One detects in this literature and within the development assistance community both analyst and donor fatigue due to agreed diagnostics and associated treatments having had so little impact on educational policies and practices. The "supertanker" of Arab education, long steered toward creating civil servants and acquiescent citizens disempowered politically and economically, with ever more students on board, has not managed even a small course correction, much less charting a radically new trajectory to fulfill the stated, grandiose ambitions of Arab rulers to create knowledge economies, to say nothing of realizing the long-frustrated hopes of Arab populations for improved economies and polities.

Pressures to reform Arab educational systems are intensifying from both the bottom up and the top down. Popular demands for such reforms contributed to the Arab uprisings and have persisted even where those uprisings have not. In Egypt, for example, those demands were reflected by Article 19 of the 2014 constitution, which mandated the extension of free education from the primary through the secondary level, while rendering schooling compulsory through "the secondary stage or its equivalent." It also obligated the state to allocate government spending on education equivalent to at least 4 percent of GDP. None of these constitutionally mandated thresholds has yet been met. Like other Arab rulers, those in Egypt have sought to appear to respond to popular demands, while simultaneously seeking to reshape the educational system better to serve their own priorities. In so doing they have confronted the dilemma inherent in reform of all authoritarian orders, which is how to stimulate economic growth without inducing demands for political openings.

Reconciling this dilemma has become ever more problematic, not just because of increased popular demands, but also because of structural changes to the underlying political economy. Most postcolonial Arab educational systems were geared to the needs of expanding states seeking to inculcate nationalist orthodoxy among their diverse populations. Their primary vocational focus was thus the civil service, the tangible manifestation of social contracts that have underpinned these authoritarian orders and that shield graduates from international competition. Population growth, deteriorating public finances, expanding privatization, and other policy changes associated with intensifying globalization began in the late 1980s in many Arab countries to undermine the viability of educational policies harnessed to outdated, deteriorating political economies. The 2011 Arab uprisings reflected this disjunction and provided an opportunity for it to be addressed. But effecting reform in conditions of rising political demands coupled with economic stagnation is notoriously difficult.[2] In many Arab countries the result has been a patchwork of educational policies, its components reflecting reconciliations of demands with capacities, as well as the interests of different actors, including preeminently those of rulers concerned primarily with resolving the dilemma of stimulating economic growth while not expanding political demands. The net outcome has been further diversification or, less kindly, fragmentation of the overall educational system, coupled with efforts to intensify central control over its various components.

Although overwhelmingly predominant, state executives are nevertheless cross-pressured by different constituencies. Teachers and their unions constitute the most concentrated such pressure, as Merilee Grindle in this volume (Chapter 9), supported by the World Bank's recent study of Arab education and *The Economist*'s of global education, indicates.[3] Since overgrown educational ministries are staffed primarily by teachers, bureaucratic dead weight is reinforced and added to that of teachers' vocational interests and associations. Interests of publishers of educational materials, typically generated by teachers, are threatened by innovations such as computer-based learning. Added to teacher-centered resistance to reform is the general inertia that long-established, large systems create. Those involved in them, whether as producers or consumers, tend to prefer the devil they know to the one they don't. And teachers are probably right in most cases to be suspicious of the motives of top-down reformers and resentful of efforts to exclude them from educational policymaking.

In much of the Arab world, an additional factor complicating reform efforts is that educational systems engender battles between regimes and Islamists. Most regimes have managed to fully occupy the institutional high ground in government, while conceding some, typically less, strategic space within educational sectors to Islamists, whether as teachers or as schools or universities affiliated with religious organizations and institutions, of which Egypt's Al-Azhar University is the leading example. Reform of educational policies and institutions thus necessarily involves managing not only pressures from the educational establishment, at the core of which are teachers, but also reconfigurations within educational institutions of politically sensitive curricular, personnel, and other matters, including gender relations.

Executives are also cross-pressured by newly arising, frequently conflicting objectives as the old formula of preparation for public employment and inculcation of nationalism has lost its relevance, while globalization, including the provision of comparative information on educational performance, has intensified pressure for reform. The shift of vocational focus from the civil service to the private sector—the omnibus, ambitious term describing this hoped-for change being the creation of a "knowledge economy"—implies that the economy in question should be globally competitive. This in turn requires that education meet global standards, an ambitious goal that gives rise to the political dilemma of how best publicly to reconcile it with actual performance. Over the past decade or so, empirical measures of educational attainment have proliferated in numbers, types, and countries of application, thereby standardizing national comparisons while making them more precise and widely available. Virtually all empirical evidence reveals serious deficiencies in Arab states' educational attainments, by implication casting doubt on regimes' proclaimed objective to create a knowledge economy.

The Economist, for example, citing the Global Innovation Index, which measures scientific, technological, and cultural innovation, notes that "Arab states are losing the race for technological development." On the index's key subindexes of investment in human capital and knowledge and technology outputs, rich and poor Arab countries score 22 percent and 36 percent, respectively, below the levels predicted by their GDPs per capita.[4] The World Bank's 2019 study of Arab education highlighted various deficiencies that impede the creation of human capital essential to transformation to knowledge economies. Counterproductive memorization of rules, facts, and procedures in teaching mathematics and science, for example, is almost twice the international average.[5] Autonomy of teachers and indeed of secondary schools and even universities, strongly and positively correlated with performance, is according to the World Bank "very low" in the Middle East and North Africa (MENA).[6] Average time devoted to religious studies in MENA is more than twice the 5 percent average for Organization for Economic Cooperation and Development (OECD) countries.[7] Learning-adjusted years of schooling reveal that "the poor quality of education in MENA is equivalent to approximately three lost years of education."[8] On the most recent TIMSS and the Progress in International Reading Literacy Study (PIRLS)—two of the three most widespread international education assessments—"no MENA country came close to the international medians of the percentage of students reaching the low international benchmarks." Less than half of Egypt's eighth-grade students had a basic understanding of science. In Morocco just over a third of fourth-graders "reached minimum reading literacy levels."[9] While some underperformance can be accounted for by inadequate access, as for example with pre-primary enrollments in MENA being the world's lowest, most of it is due to other determinants of educational quality.[10]

Although awareness of these empirical indicators is no doubt limited within Arab publics, dissatisfaction with educational quality is widespread, as is the perception that the much-touted transformation to knowledge economies is occurring slowly, if at all. These gaps between words and deeds of rulers are likely perceived as reflecting hypocrisy, even disdain, for publics, so they entail political risks for incumbents. The shift from education as preparation for the civil service to that for private sector–led, technologically driven growth is, in sum, proving to be problematic and politically risky, to say nothing of having yet to be achieved.

Much the same can be said about difficulties of instilling national identity and political loyalty in students. It was one thing to do so when the "imperialist" enemy of the nation was obvious to all, and so a useful foil against which to homogenize the politically relevant thoughts and identities of students. It is altogether another matter when the alleged enemies are less obvious, not so inherently evil, and changing frequently. Even the notion of Arab nationalism has become problematic, especially in those countries, such as Morocco, Algeria, Sudan, and Iraq, with significant ethnic and linguistic minorities, or in Egypt, where Arabism has always competed with Egyptian identity. The combination of didactic teaching of national history and contemporary identity poses new challenges to which governments and educational systems are responding in a more diverse, if not necessarily more effective, fashion than previously. Egypt, for example, is now emphasizing the state and the nation-building roles of the military, while tribal histories assume an equivalent historiographical centrality in many Gulf Cooperation Council (GCC) countries. But none of these fallback attempts to teach students who they are is as black and white, and hence as compelling, as the anti-imperialist, nationalist fare dished out to preceding generations.

A related contextual factor of Arab educational reform is the shift from liberal to authoritarian educational models. Liberal-arts education reached its apogee in the United States with the expansion of the middle class in the wake of World War II and, as in the Arab world and elsewhere, was associated with the growth of public employment. Its obvious decline at the post-secondary level in recent years and less obviously but nevertheless also real at primary and secondary levels has traced the downward trend of public employment in the United States. The ongoing focus on STEM disciplines, computer-based learning further stimulated by the 2020 pandemic, imposition of ever greater "accountability" as measured by performance on standardized tests, the relatively high instructional costs and apparent low vocational rewards of liberal arts, and the rise of charter schools have all militated against traditional liberal education. Emphasis on STEM disciplines alone impacts methods of teaching and evaluation, tending to standardize and routinize them.

Paralleling the decline of Western liberal education has been improving educational performance in many Asian countries, including Singapore, China, South Korea, Vietnam, and others, where more "structured" methods of teaching and learning are widely assumed to be employed. Recently announced plans by Saudi Arabia and the United Arab Emirates (UAE) to introduce the study of Chinese language into their national educational curricula may reflect the appeal of that country, its political economy, and its educational methods.[11] The challenge to Western educational models can be viewed as yet another indicator of increasingly widespread belief in the relative superiority not only of putative Asian models, but also of authoritarian ones more generally, whether in politics, economics, or society. The interpretation of liberal education as but one component of a comprehensive Western model now in decline may further undermine its appeal.

Associated with the diminishing attractiveness of liberal education is privatization of education at all levels. Since 2004, global enrollment in private primary schools has grown from 10 percent to 17 percent of total students and from 19 percent to 27 percent of students in secondary schools.[12] The UAE has the highest proportion in the world of students in private schools, some 70 percent. Saudi Arabia's proportion of privately educated students increased by some 50 percent between 2007 and 2017. Vietnam has the world's fastest-growing private sector alongside the best-performing state-school system among low-income countries. Ten percent of Chinese primary and secondary students are in private schools. Education everywhere is becoming a business and, in some cases, large and financially successful. GEMS Education, based in Dubai, operates forty-seven schools, most of them in the Middle East. In the United States about a third of graduate education is now online, of which a very substantial proportion of even that offered by public universities is in fact "designed, supplied and marketed" by private firms.[13] Private charter-school enrollments in the United States grew from 400,000 students in 2000 to 2.8 million in 2015.

Privatization's main appeal to Arab governments is as in other developing regions—financial. Most privatization programs mobilize investment capital to supplement public allocations, whether in the form of schools 100 percent privately funded or in some mixed public-private form imitative of public-private partnerships increasingly popular, including within the World Bank, for construction and operation of physical infrastructure. Privatization serves other purposes as well, including globalization of national education, which in turn holds out the promise of quality enhancement, foreign-language learning, and associated gains in prestige for the nation and its government. Privatization can also improve public education by modeling new methods and providing competition. In countries with high population growth rates, the comparatively brief startup times of private schools enable them to service markets to which the public sector is slow to respond.

While Arab governments are aware of these potential benefits, most of them are also apprehensive about privatization. Fearful of autonomous activities of any sort, they worry that indirect regulatory as opposed to direct, hands-on control of education will produce fewer of the types of citizens they want and more of those they don't. This situation is analogous to that of the early stages of privatization of Arab economies as the effectiveness and appeal of socialism waned some two generations ago. Fearful of truly autonomous economic actors but keen to reap material rewards from liberalizing political economies, most Arab governments tilted economic playing fields in favor of regime insiders and their cronies. Presumably this strategy of "preferential privatization" that gave rise to crony capitalism will also be the one with which Arab governments try to square the circle of attracting private resources into education while maintaining tight control of the sector and its outputs. The regionwide growth, for example, of Dubai-based GEMS Education, might reflect the application of this strategy in various Arab countries.

Responses to the threats and opportunities associated with educational reform vary from country to country in the Arab world. In some, financial constraints are the primary concern, whereas in others, notably the oil-rich states, commitments to economic diversification are stronger drivers of educational policy. In still others, educational systems serve as battlegrounds between competing social forces, whether ethnic, linguistic, religious, or tribal, with calculations of how best to engender or preserve national coherence dominant. All Arab educational policymakers are cross-pressured by competing fears and desires as they struggle to achieve a mix of objectives that typically include cost-cutting, attracting private domestic and foreign investors, building knowledge economies, defusing popular discontent with educational services, instilling loyalty and patriotism, and bolstering the nation's image. Policy outcomes reveal the weighting of these priorities, serving as mirrors of "princes" (rulers) reflecting their interests, concerns, ambitions, and to some extent the internal divisions with which they must contend.

Causes of Arab Educational Inadequacies

The primary purposes of this volume are to investigate the constraints imposed on reform of Arab education by the political economies in which they are enmeshed, and the consequences of these limitations. Its underlying assumption is that aspects of Arab political economies now recognized as having retarded economic diversification and growth have also impeded improvements in delivery of public goods, key of which is education. The World Bank's as well as independent researchers' recent investigations of the negative economic impacts of what Douglass North and his institutional economist colleagues have termed "limited-access orders" provide a model that can also be applied to service delivery, including education.[14] Among the contributors to this volume, Ishac Diwan (Chapter 2) has played a key role in investigating the negative micro- and macroeconomic impacts of strong insider/outsider divides characteristic of limited-access orders that preference the former at the expense of the latter.[15] A key concern of this volume is thus to investigate the degree to which such divides also negatively impact educational policies.

Determining how and to what extent beneficiaries of Arab limited-access orders shape educational systems to serve their interests, both economic and political, must rely primarily on inference, as the policy process is too opaque for intentionality clearly to be discerned through public statements and positions. The profound discrepancy between the stated and actual intentions of decisionmakers characteristic of limited-access orders further shrouds their intents. Arab educational practices—whether at the broad level of favoring private over public education, or emphasizing didactic teaching of history and religion at the partial expense of citizenship and scientific/technical educations, or in the form of discrete policies, such as hosting of foreign universities, sending students abroad, or creating secondary and tertiary institutions under the direct auspices and control of ruling elites—provide indirect, if not absolutely conclusive, evidence of intentions. In this volume, Christopher Davidson (Chapter 7) explores the intentions of national decisionmakers in financing the establishment of US university branch campuses in the Gulf, while Roel Meijer (Chapter 3) reveals how the rulers of Egypt, Tunisia, and Morocco have shaped curricular materials to impart conceptions of citizenship as duties and loyalties, rather than as rights.

Comparative experience is also relevant to infer decisionmakers' intents. Merilee Grindle, another contributor to this volume (Chapter 9), has argued, for example, that innovations in Latin American education have resulted from both political reform mongering made possible by the semidemocratic nature of those political systems—hence the opportunities they provide for politicians to appeal to constituents with proposals for educational improvements—and by reasonably meritocratic civil services that generate both will and capacity for reform.[16] The Latin American example thus begs the question of educational "reform stifling" in Arab regimes and whether it is intentional and carefully managed by elites, or is more just a by-product of general authoritarianism, including the negative impacts of clientelistic rather than meritocratic civil services. It similarly raises the question of from whence reforms might come in the more closed, Arab authoritarian settings, with the most obvious possible direction being from the top down. The emphasis on creating knowledge economies and the plethora of long-term "visions" for Arab countries as mandated by their rulers and drafted by international consulting firms suggest these rulers are contemplating how educational reforms might be accomplished without disempowering or possibly even displacing themselves. Other evidence suggests that Arab insiders are trying to reshape educational systems in a fashion informed by other authoritarian states, key of which may be China specifically and the countries of East Asia more generally. Creating selective recruitment channels into political and economic elites, as the Chinese Communist Party has done, may be an attractive alternative to the difficult and politically parlous task of a broad upgrading of mass public education, as it seems to be in Egypt under Sisi, as discussed in this volume by Robert Springborg (Chapter 5). Another of the contributors, Alisa Jones (Chapter 10), reviews East Asian educational models against the backdrop of their possible relevance to Arab ones.

Educational systems, in sum, provide evidence that can be drawn upon to investigate the intentions and behavior of Arab elites, the value of that evidence being enhanced in this volume by both Grindle and Jones through comparisons between countries within the region and to those outside it. In turn, the policies Arab elites propagate can be assessed from the perspectives of their pedagogical impacts as well as those impacts' consequences for polities and economies. This inclusive approach makes it possible to better understand why Arab education continues to underperform, why it has been so resistant to reform, and what the prospects are for fulfilling proclaimed goals of reform or, conversely, for pressure from below generating irresistible demands for real change, possibly not only of education, but also of the political systems that bear heavy responsibility for its present inadequate state.

Evaluating State Performance

Institutional economists and political economists believe that three factors determine state performance—capacity, policy, and society. Of these three factors, state capacity appears to be the easiest to conceptualize and measure. Michael Mann's notion of infrastructural power—the state's ability to penetrate and effectively regulate society and thereby benefit from that interaction—is particularly relevant to educational reform.[17] He juxtaposes infrastructural to so-called despotic power, the latter of which means the state's recourse to repression to govern as opposed to reliance on broad, deep, institutionalized state-society interactions. As regards education, since its effectiveness depends heavily on beneficial classroom interactions, infrastructural power, generated by intensive, rights-embedded interactions between citizens and governments, and so also between students and teachers, is especially vital to its success. By contrast, despotic power can be employed to structure educational policy at macro levels, including seeking to shape it to discourage outsiders to challenge the powers and privileges of insiders, but is largely irrelevant or even counterproductive to vital micro-level educational processes.

Limited-access orders rely more heavily on despotic than infrastructural power, thereby reducing their capacities to deliver human services, especially education. Capacity constraints impel these states to "import" educational services, including by sending students abroad, and to concentrate educational services on selected clienteles, thus reinforcing policy-driven preferences to privilege insiders. Moreover, capacity constraints reinforce path dependency, because innovation is particularly difficult when analysis, monitoring, and other elements of assessment are weak or lacking, a problem reinforced by fear of political repercussions of policy innovation. Authoritarian control of stakeholder organizations, including teachers' unions and associations of parents, weakens state capacities to deliver educational services, because it militates against professionalism and effective, positive stakeholder contribution to policymaking and implementation.

Unfortunately, commonly used indicators of capacity and infrastructural power are primarily financial in nature, such as ratios between direct and indirect taxes, governmental revenue as a proportion of GDP, proportion of bank credit to the private sector, and so on. The indicators of capacity and infrastructural power closest to education are those that measure presence and performance of bureaucracies, the former of which are relatively easily quantified, the latter of which are not. This leaves the challenge of seeking to define, measure, and compare Arab countries among themselves and Arab to non-Arab ones along the capacity/ infrastructural power dimensions without having clear, commonly accepted indicators for them. Instead of seeking to develop such indicators—an exercise in its own right—various of the following chapters assess in mainly qualitative fashion the capacities of respective states to foster coherent, effective educational systems.

The policy contribution to state performance is less clear than is the capacity dimension, probably because it is more subjective. It seems particularly relevant for education, however, and is reasonably well researched in that field. Much of the material in this volume, drawing on a wide variety of sources, is focused more directly on the substance of educational policy than on capacity to implement it. Historical and cross-cultural models, including evolution of curricular materials, comparisons to Asia and Latin America, and the increasing Arab infatuation with authoritarian educational models, whether homegrown or imported, are examples of such educational policies. So too is consideration of educational outsourcing by the state, whether in the form of sending students abroad, privatizing primary and secondary education, or permitting or even subsidizing foreign universities to open branches, and in approaching citizenship through an emphasis on duties rather than rights. Lurking behind consideration of educational policies and linking them back to capacity for their implementation is the nature of their formation, most especially the degree to which they involve stakeholders. The greater, more institutionalized is stakeholder involvement, the stronger the state's capacity to implement resulting policies, as is evidenced in several of the country case studies, most especially that of Morocco by Florian Kohstall (Chapter 4).

Finally, some societies are easier to govern than others. Degree of societal homogeneity/fragmentation is one of the dimensions commonly measured and assessed, with somewhat mixed findings regarding the Arab world, depending on the social solidarity in question, such as whether it is ethnic, tribal, linguistic, or other.[18] From the perspective of Arab education, the societal dimension assumes particular importance regarding such issues as language diversity; societal, class, and residential cleavages; and cultural attributes including orientation toward authority, participation, and democracy. All of these societal variables are dealt with in one or more chapters here, as for example that of the challenges posed by linguistic dualism to Algerian education, examined by Adel Hamaizia and Andrew Leber (Chapter 8).

Societal constraints in limited-access orders are particularly problematical because processes and institutions that facilitate intercommunity communications and conflict resolution are weak or absent. Control is maintained through despotic, not infrastructural, power. Societal divisions are thus likely to cut through educational systems, undermining their overall coherence, as evidence of the profound impacts of inequity in Arab countries on educational performance suggests and that is documented for Tunisia by Lindsay Benstead (Chapter 6). The gender gap also poses a particularly large barrier to young Arab women seeking successful transitions from classrooms to employment. Society-wide expectations engendered by the authoritarian bargain entailed in social contracts and the broad context of rentier economies and its inherent clientelism seem also to impact educational performance, as may attitudes formed in authoritarian family and other cultural settings, topics addressed by Ishac Diwan (Chapter 2) by drawing upon data from the World Values Survey.

Assessing the impacts on educational systems of state performance resulting from their capacities, policies, and interactions with the societies they govern complements research on the impacts of limited-access orders on economies. How the divide between insiders and outsiders observed to obtain for economic actors and their performance can be applied to education is a principal concern of this volume. Unfortunately, there are as yet no established indicators that can easily measure educational insider/outsider divides and their consequences equivalent to those for economies, such as politician-businessperson connections, firm profitability, tariff protection, access to credit, and the like. Our hope is that this volume suggests dimensions for which indicators will be developed, thereby supporting improvement in the study of the political economy of reform of Arab education from being virtually entirely qualitative as at present, to at least partially quantitative.

Notes

1. Salehi-Isfahani, Hassine, and Assaad, "Equality of Opportunity in Educational Achievement in the Middle East and North Africa."

2. Luciani, "Introduction."

3. El-Kogali and Krafft, *Expectations and Aspirations;* and "A Class Apart," *The Economist,* April 13, 2019, https://www.economist.com/leaders/2019/04/13/a -class-apart. The same observation is made in the Carnegie Endowment's 2018 report on Arab Education: Muasher and Brown, *Engaging Society to Reform Arab Education,* p. 12.

4. "Arab States Are Losing the Race for Technological Development," *The Economist,* July 12, 2018, https://www.economist.com/graphic-detail/2018/07/12/arab -states-are-losing-the-race-for-technological-development.

5. El-Kogali and Krafft, *Expectations and Aspirations,"* p. 7.

6. Ibid., pp. 8–10.

7. Ibid., pp. 11–12.

8. Ibid., p. 11.

9. Ibid., p. 14.

10. Ibid., p. 23.

11. Dalay, "Why the Middle East Is Betting on China."

12. "A Class Apart," *The Economist,* April 13, 2019, p. 3, https://www.economist .com/leaders/2019/04/13/a-class-apart.

13. "A Class Apart," *The Economist,* April 13, 2019.

14. North, Wallis, Webb, and Weingast, "Limited Access Orders." For an assessment of how limited-access orders shape MENA political economies, see Springborg, *Political Economies of the Middle East and North Africa,* especially pp. 61–73.

15. Diwan, Malik, and Atiyas, *Crony Capitalism in the Middle East.*

16. Grindle, *Despite the Odds.*

17. Mann, "The Autonomous Power of the State"; and Mann, *The Sources of Social Power.*

18. Fearon, "Ethnic and Cultural Diversity by Country."

2

Democracy and Education

Ishac Diwan

When evaluating the quality of education in the Arab region, much of the focus tends to go to the relation between education and economic productivity. On the other hand, the discussion rarely focuses on the effects of education on the social and political values and behaviors of the educated, an area of keen interest in more democratic countries. This is unfortunate. The evidence uncovered in my recent research, and summarized here, is that the social and political "returns" to education, in the sense of its contribution to the formation of emancipative social and political values, are in fact dismally lower in the region than in the rest of the world. This suggests that unless education becomes more progressive in its teaching methods and curricula, it will remain difficult to foster more open, democratic, gender-sensitive, and tolerant societies in the region.

Different views have emerged in the education literature on the relation between education and political values. Early literature, focusing on Western countries, had highlighted the emancipative effects of education—that educated individuals will demand more freedoms, and will be better able to coordinate their collective action, and that as a result, countries that become more educated will tend to become more democratic.[1] Increasingly, however, the modernization thesis is being contradicted by facts on the ground in less democratic settings. The large rise in aggregate education in countries such as China, Russia, or the oil-rich countries of the Gulf Cooperation Council (GCC) has not been met with rising levels of democratization. Moreover, new studies in nondemocratic countries have started to demonstrate at the micro level that education has little or no effect on participation in political activities, such as demonstrating or voting.[2]

In this chapter I ask three empirical questions: Are more educated individuals more emancipated socially and politically in the Arab region, compared to less educated regions? If so, is this emancipation gain commensurate with that found in other regions of the world? And if not, as we find, what accounts for the lower emancipative impact of education in the region—is it culture, or policies? The second part of the chapter discusses the mechanisms in the education sector and in society that may explain the low emancipative effect of education in the region.

Building on my recent work on the topic, the first part of the chapter examines the variations of the "sociopolitical returns" of education in Arab countries, both among different groups within the region, and with those in other regions. Qualitative critiques of Arab education systems abound. The novelty of my research is that it looks at hard numbers. To do so, I use a unique database provided by the World Values Survey (WVS), which is a global opinion poll, taken every five years, that measures a broad range of political and social values in a comparative context. The WVS sixth wave (collected during 2011–2013) included twelve Arab countries. The dataset allows for the first time to compare values in many Arab countries to values around the world. Pooling the WVS fifth and sixth waves, it is possible to compare different socioeconomic groups of individuals in twelve Arab countries, and with similar groups in seventy-five non-Arab countries, including thirteen (non-Arab) Muslim-majority countries and thirteen (non-Arab) oil-producing countries.

Three main conclusions emerge from these comparisons. First, I look inside the region to ascertain to what extent the effect of education on political values compares with the effect of other traits on values—such as age, income level, or religiosity. While all these effects play a role, it turns out that the difference between the values of the educated and the uneducated (controlling for other personal characteristics) is the largest explanatory variable for differences in the value gap between the Arab region and the rest of the world. Second, the Arab world is not homogeneous. I compare sociopolitical values across the countries of the region and across generations and education levels. And third, I compare the political returns to education in the Arab world with those of several types of countries in order to find the characteristics that can best explain the observed variation. It turns out that the sociopolitical "return to education" tends to be on the low side not just in the Arab region, but also in Muslim-majority countries, and in oil-exporting countries. This may suggest that the particularity of the Middle East and North Africa (MENA) is to be dominated by both Islam and oil. However, I argue against this view, and that instead it is the lack of democracy that drives these results in these three groups of countries.

In the last part of the chapter, I discuss three mechanisms that can explain these variations. First, I argue that it is unlikely that the results are driven by the cultural specificities of the region, in particular by socio-political conservatism related to the dominant religion. Second, I argue that autocratic regimes in the region manipulate their education sectors in order to promote values of obedience and respect for authority in ways that strengthen their rule. Third, I argue that the economic interests of the educated, and the fear of sanctions by authoritarian regimes if they are perceived to back the political opposition, also play a role in preventing them from adopting emancipated political behaviors.

Empirical Investigation

While most of the global literature on the relation between education and political values has focused on civic action, I am interested in characterizing (and contrasting) a broader range of values, going from political behavior, such as voting or demonstrating, to social preferences, such as respect for authority, and to political preferences, such as being committed or not to democratic values. Behavior is more readily observable than preferences, and thus, in repressive environments, it is more prone to strategic choice than unobservable preferences. The use of several independent variables with varying degrees of observability will add an extra source of informative variation to the tests.

More precisely, I construct the following three variables from responses to sets of questions in the WVS (see appendix to this chapter for more details), normalizing all variables over the interval [0,1]:

Respect for authority. I combine responses to two questions: (1) whether "greater respect for authority is a good thing," and (2) whether "obedience" is mentioned when asked about the most important qualities children need to learn at home. The variable measures a central quality for the maintenance of autocratic rule.

Commitment to democracy (CtD). I average responses to a question that asks respondents to rank the values provided in three separate menus, where each menu includes at least one value connected to democratic environments ("people have more say in how things are done," "giving people more say in important government decisions," "protecting freedom of speech," "progress towards a less impersonal and more humane society") and one to authoritarian environments ("making sure the country has strong defense forces," "maintaining order in the nation," "the fight against crime"). This variable measures the relative preference for democratic values compared to those for "strong rule."

Civic action (CA). I use the question, Have you done any of these things, might you do it, or would you never do it under any circumstances? I average responses for signing a petition, joining in boycotts, and attending peaceful demonstrations.

Table 2.1 shows the averages (and standard deviation) of these values in the Arab region, and in the rest of the world. It is evident that while CtD is, on average, lower in the Arab region than in the rest of the world, the averages are quite similar for the other two values of civil action and respect for authority. Thus, if differences exist for these two variables, it would be in their prevalence among particular groups (such as the educated).

It is valuable to take full advantage of our large dataset, which includes variations in values across country and time, and within country, in order to explore more systematically how the relation between education and political values among different socioeconomic groups may differ when comparing the Arab world and the rest of the world. I, therefore, develop a global regression model of the individual determinants of political values, and then add regional dummy variables in several ways to fit particular explorations. The general model has the following general form:

$$PfD = aA + bB + cC + error \qquad (1)$$

where the matrix A describes individual characteristics, B is a set of country-level variables (gross domestic product [GDP] per capita, time dummies); and C describes the populations under study in various ways (dummies for Arab, Muslim, oil-exporting, and/or democratic countries, in level, or in multiplicative forms). For ease of interpretation of the resulting estimated coefficients, I use simple ordinary least squares (OLS) techniques (while recognizing that logistical models would be more adapted to the task), and all variables have been standardized.[3]

The individual controls include age (fifteen to ninety), education (coded 1–3 for primary, secondary, and tertiary), religiosity, gender, and

Table 2.1 Summary Statistics for Main Variables, World Values Survey, Wave 5 (2005–2009) and Wave 6 (2010–2014), Arab Countries and the Rest of the World

	Arab Countries			Rest of the World			All	
	Number of Observations	Mean	Standard Deviation	Number of Observations	Mean	Standard Deviation	Minimum Value	Maximum Value
Preference for democracy (PfD)	23,036	3.00	2.52	135,591	3.75	2.58	1	10
Respect for authority	21,348	4.54	3.36	125,641	4.50	3.05	1	10
Civic engagement	23,183	3.67	2.70	144,948	3.60	2.64	1	10
Age	24,507	38.27	14.21	138,431	42.30	16.84	15	99
Education	24,471	2.63	1.03	137,600	2.94	.78	1	4
Religiosity	24,574	.76	.42	138,759	.35	.48	0	1
Inc1	23,684	.18	.38	129,599	.18	.38	0	1
Inc2	23,684	.23	.42	129,599	.20	.40	0	1
Inc3	23,684	.24	.43	129,599	.28	.45	0	1

Source: World Values Survey, Waves 5 and 6. See appendix to Chapter 2 for definition of the variables.

household income.[4] Religiosity is measured relative to the values people want to inculcate in their children, in order to avoid gender biases that would arise by using frequency of attending religious services (since women are not bound to participate in the five daily prayers in Islam). Precise definitions are in the appendix to this chapter.

Variations Among Groups

I first show that much of the difference in sociopolitical values between the Arab region and the rest of the world is due to the low emancipative effect of education in the region.[5] To show this, I compare different socioeconomic groups in terms of their values, in the Arab region and in the rest of the world. The results make it clear that differences in values are largest for educated individuals.

In the base regression model (1), A now includes individual characteristics (age, education, gender, income, religiosity), B includes only GDP per capita and a time dummy, and C includes an Arab region dummy and its interaction with individual characteristics to measure possible deviations among each group from global averages.

Let's focus on the CtD value, and on what variables explain its variations within the region. Table 2.2 shows that the main ways in which the Arab world is different are, in order of importance, the effects of education, and then of age and class, which are all less emancipative with respect to CtD than in the rest of the world (as the variables have been normalized, the size of the effects can be directly compared in the regression results). A fourth factor that stands out is religiosity, because of a large compositional effect, rather than because religiosity influences values in the Arab region differentially.

The effect of education on CtD is very much muted in the Arab region (+3 percent = +10 percent − 7 percent) relative to the rest of the world (+10 percent). This means that as an individual moves from uneducated to being a university graduate, which is about four standard deviations on the education scale (see Table 2.1), their CtD rises by 40 percent globally, but only by 12 percent in the Arab world—a very large difference. Thus, as in the rest of the world, education emancipates, but it does so much less in the Arab world compared to the global experience, resulting in low national averages on CtD.

The effect of young age on CtD is smaller in the Arab region than in the rest of the world—the net Arab slope relative to age is −3 percent (−6 percent + 3 percent), compared to a global slope of −6 percent. So, for example when comparing a person in their twenties with another in

Table 2.2 Political Values and Education, Arab Region and the World:
World Values Survey, Wave 5 (2005–2009) and Wave 6 (2010–2014)

	Commitment to Democracy	Civic Action	Respect for Authority
Age	–0.06***	–0.01	–0.00
Education	0.10***	0.17***	–0.07**
Female	0.00	–0.06***	0.00
Religiosity	–0.02***	–0.03	0.08**
Income1	0.01***	–0.04**	0.01
Income2	0.02***	–0.02	0.01
Income3	0.01***	–0.01	0.00
lnGDPc	–0.33***	0.19***	–0.13**
Arab	0.11*	0.14	–0.09
Age*Arab	0.03***	–0.05**	0.04
Edu*Arab	–0.07***	–0.13***	0.14***
Fem*Arab	0.01***	–0.04**	–0.01
Relig*Arab	–0.00	–0.00	0.04
Inc1*Arab	–0.01***	–0.02	0.01
Inc2*Arab	–0.02***	–0.02	0.01
Inc3*Arab	0.00	–0.02	0.01
N	141,914	132,019	140,703
Adjusted R^2	0.10	0.12	0.08

Source: World Values Survey, Waves 5 and 6. See appendix to Chapter 2 for definition of variables.
Notes: Ordinary least squares estimates. Regression also includes time dummies (not shown).
Standardized beta coefficients. * $p < 0.10$, ** $p < 0.05$, *** $p < 0.010$.

their sixties (about three standard deviations on the age scale), holding all other personal characteristics at their global means, the young would have an excess on CtD relative to the old of 18 percent in the rest of the world, and only of 9 percent in the Arab region.[6]

The effect of religiosity is significant, negative, and similar in the Arab region and in the rest of the world, but this translates into a larger CtD gap in the region given that it is much more religious than the rest of the world (0.76 versus 0.35 on a scale of 0–1).[7]

The income effect, which is evident in the global sample, is neutralized in the Arab region, which has only a small upper-middle-class effect. In particular, the lower-middle-class group (Inc2) has a 2 percent premium on CtD in the global sample, but zero in the Arab region. Thus, while it may be that it was the middle classes that mainly supported democratic ideals during the regional uprisings of 2011,[8] they still fell short of the intensity of middle-class support for democracy observed in the rest of the world. Finally, women are found to be more pro-democracy then men in the Arab region, but not in the rest of the world, with a small differential of 1 percent.

What is the relative contribution then of age, education, class, and religiosity in explaining the Arab gap? It is possible to estimate for example that the CtD difference between an Arab (synthetically constructed) and a global youth, both highly educated and from a lower-middle-class background, is fourteen points, which can be decomposed into a differential effect related to education (seven points), age (three points), religiosity (two points), and lower-middle-class effect (two points). Clearly, the education effect dominates each of the other three effects.

These observations apply even more to the other two values examined—respect for authority and civil action—as the region-specific education effects are even more marked in these cases compared to the effects of the other individual characteristics (see Table 2.2). It is also noteworthy that these patterns are broadly similar across different Arab countries—the value gaps measured above apply to every Arab country in the sample, albeit with different intensities.[9] Moreover, my previous work suggests that these results extend to several other social values such as patriarchy, which is closely connected to authority, but also values connected to tolerance for social and religious differences. For all these values, education emancipates little in much of the Arab region, compared to other regions of the world.[10]

In sum, political values are less emancipated in the Arab region than in the rest of the world, and much of this gap can be explained by the low emancipation of the educated, at least for the sociopolitical values focused on. This is illustrated in Figure 2.1. Not only are these values lower in the Arab region than in the rest of the world, but moreover they do not rise with education as much as in the rest of the world, and as a result the values gap rises with the level of education.

Comparing Arab Countries

Arab countries are not homogeneous. This section explores their differences in terms of our three sociopolitical values. We are interested not only in average differences among these countries, but also with how much education increases emancipation, and how this relation may have changed over time.

Figure 2.2 displays the average values in the different countries for different age cohorts. The top panel shows the measure of the values for individuals with at most primary education, while the bottom panel shows the additional value—the "sociopolitical return"—for individuals with tertiary education. I have graphed values in the countries of the

Figure 2.1 Effect of Education on Values in Arab Countries and the Rest of the World, Wave 5 (2005–2009) and Wave 6 (2010–2014)

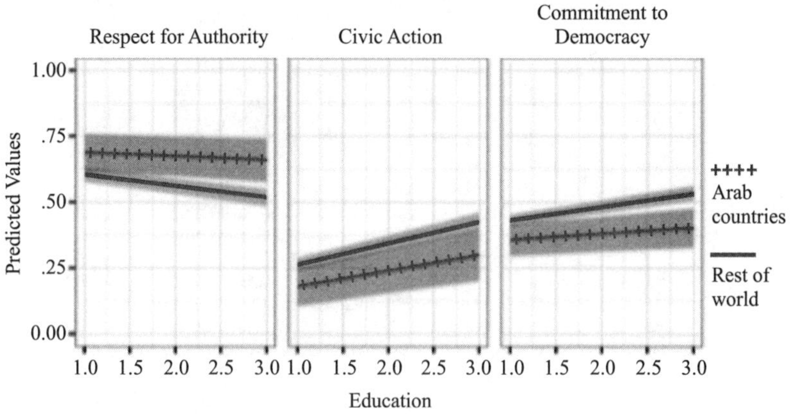

Sources: World Values Survey, Waves 5 and 6 and author's computations.
Notes: The graph illustrates the results from Table 2.2. Education is coded here as 1 for primary, 2 for secondary, and 3 for tertiary.

Arab region, as well as those in the Organization for Economic Cooperation and Development (OECD) for comparison.

For each country, the average values of the highly educated group, and of the low education group, are plotted for different age cohorts. While all the data were collected around 2011–2013, the preference of different cohorts provides some information about the past. It is well accepted in the literature that individuals develop their civic values during their formative years, between the ages of eighteen and twenty-five. To the extent that these values become fixed during a person's youth, as is generally assumed in the literature, these graphs reflect the way these values have changed over time.[11]

By comparing the graphs for the different countries and regions, three important characteristics come out. First, the political values in the Arab world are conservative among the educated, compared to the European comparator, illustrating that, as found earlier, the emancipative returns to education are very low in the region. Second, the values of the uneducated in the region tend to be similar to those of the uneducated in Europe, if perhaps a bit more on the conservative side. Thus, it is really the values of the educated that stand out as "exceptional."

Figure 2.2 Commitment to Democracy and Respect for Authority by Cohort and Education Level, OECD Countries vs. Arab Countries, World Values Survey, Wave 6 (2010–2014)

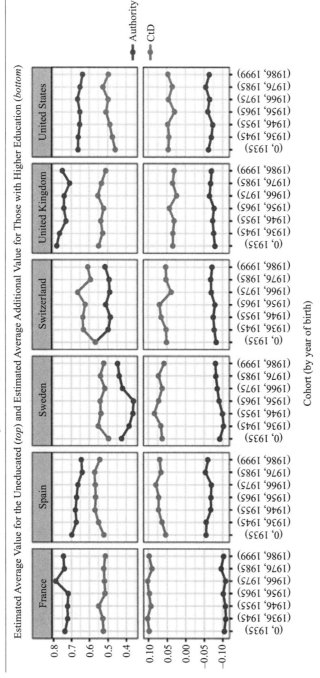

continues

Figure 2.2 Continued

Estimated Average Value for the Uneducated (*top*) and Estimated Average Additional Value for Those with Higher Education (*bottom*)

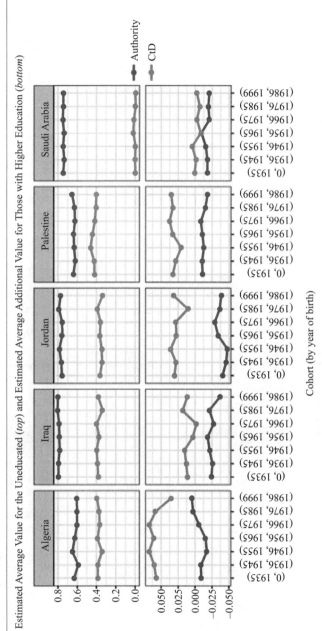

Cohort (by year of birth)

continues

26

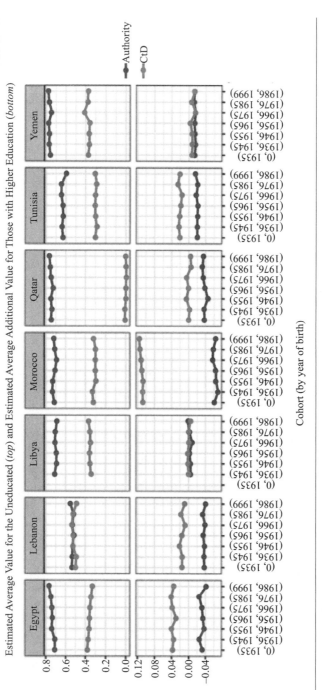

Figure 2.2 Continued

Estimated Average Value for the Uneducated (*top*) and Estimated Average Additional Value for Those with Higher Education (*bottom*)

Cohort (by year of birth)

Source: World Values Survey, Wave 6 (2010–2014).

Notes: The figures display estimates from multilevel regression models that control for education level and other variables (age, gender, relative household income, and the country's GDP per capita). The education effect is estimated randomly within each country cohort—that is, the education effect is taken to be country-specific. For each country, the top panel is an estimate of the average values for the uneducated, while the bottom panel is the average additional value for those with higher education. Values are also disaggregated by cohorts, with the dates indicating years of birth.

Third, these patterns have not changed much over time, with a few exceptions that will be noted.

In Figure 2.2, it is clear that the values of the educated tend to be very close to those of the uneducated—there is at most a four-percentage-point difference on the value scale (except for Morocco), and for many countries, much less than that. The political returns to education are high in Morocco. On the other hand, they are near zero in Libya, Qatar, Yemen, and Saudi Arabia. In the European countries, by comparison, the political returns to education tend to be large and stable, at between 5 and 10 percent. The highest return is observed in France, known for its republican education system.

Moreover, the lines in the graphs tend to be flat over cohorts in the Arab region, suggesting little change over time. A few cases are noteworthy. The data show a recent amelioration in the emancipative return to education in Iraq, but a deterioration in Algeria. In Spain, by contrast, there is a discernable emancipative trend (among those with low education for authority, and among the educated for CtD), reflecting the renovation of the education regime starting in the mid-1970s, post-Franco. This suggests that education had started to be used as an instrument of state indoctrination early in the post-independence era, a theme we will come back to in more detail later.

Islam, Oil, or Lack of Democracy?

Finally, I explore the underlying reasons for the low level of the sociopolitical returns to education in the Arab region. Is this a regional specificity correlated to particular characteristics of the region, such as the dominance of Islam, or oil production? Or is it a characteristic that the region shares with all nondemocratic countries in the world?

The comparison takes advantage of global variations in our dataset along the four dimensions: Arab, Muslim, oil exports, and democratic polity. I define countries as Muslim-majority if more than 50 percent of the WVS sample affiliates with the religious denomination—twenty-three out of seventy-nine countries covered in the sample have a predominantly Muslim population, out of which twelve are located in the Arab region, seven in other Asia, two in sub-Saharan Africa, and two in East Asia.[12] I also ask if oil exporters behave differently from the rest of the world. I use the World Bank Indicators to identify countries with more than 10 percent of GDP in oil exports in 2011 as oil producers.[13] Out of twenty-one oil producers, eight are located in the Arab region, five in Latin America, three in other Asia, two in Western countries, and three in all other regions.

I thus run regressions that include (level, and then slope) dummy variables for Arab countries, Muslim countries, oil-exporting countries, and democratic countries. As is apparent in Table 2.3, depending on which of these variables are included in the regressions, one could demonstrate that low emancipation in values is a characteristic of Arab, Muslim-dominated, or oil-exporting countries. Indeed, I find the following.

First, when I use the Arab dummy only, the Arab region has, in terms of level, political values and behaviors that are less emancipated than in the rest of the world, as noted earlier (first panel of Table 2.3). Second, when a Muslim-majority dummy is added, Arab exceptionalism weakens, as now only the value of respect for author-

Table 2.3   Effect of Arab, Muslim-Majority, Oil Export, or
Political Regime? World Values Survey, Wave 5 (2005–2009)
and Wave 6 (2010–2014)

	Respect for Authority	Commitment to Democracy	Civic Action
1. Arab	0.11***	−0.09**	−0.08*
2. Arab	0.10**	−0.04	−0.02
Muslim	−0.02	−0.08***	−0.10**
3. Arab	0.06	−0.08***	−0.03
Oil	0.10***	−0.02	−0.08
4. Arab	0.05	−0.03	0.03
Muslim	−0.05	−0.08***	−0.11***
Oil	0.13***	−0.01	−0.07
5. Arab	0.11	0.01*	0.09
Oil	0.11**	−0.01***	−0.07
Muslim	−0.04	−0.00	−0.13**
Democracy	0.09	0.32***	0.14***

Source: World Values Survey, Waves 5 and 6. See appendix to Chapter 2 for definition of variables.

Notes: Each block is from a different regression model. All regressions control for individual characteristics (age, education, religiosity, gender, income), gross domestic product per capita, and a time-fixed effect. Standardized beta coefficients. * $p < 0.10$, ** $p < 0.05$, *** $p < 0.010$.

ity appears as specific to the Arab region, and the other two are values that are more conservative in all Muslim-majority countries (and including the Arab region) (second panel). Third, if an oil dummy is added to the Arab dummy instead, the results change in a different way. Lack of democracy remains an Arab specificity, but obedience turns out to be an oil specificity, not an Arab specificity (third panel). And fourth, when the three dummies are used together, the Arab dummy loses all significance. The Muslim and oil effects now explain all the regional variation. In this view of the world, culture/religion and economic structure explain the low emancipation observed in the Arab region (fourth panel).

So, one can literally pick their results of choice, depending on which characteristic one decides to highlight. Thus, the comparative results of Diamond or Noland, showing that Arabs are exceptionally nondemocratic, or of Stepan and Robertson, showing that "Arab trumps Islam," or of Fish, showing that Muslim-majority countries have an authoritarian tendency, or of Ross, showing that "oil trumps Arab," can be all replicated at the micro level of individual opinions, using a particular structural form.[14]

What if we also control for the nature of the political regime of these countries, and in particular for how democratic they are? Here I measure the degree of democracy by the countries' Polity IV score. As a group, Arab countries have the lowest rating in the world on democracy indexes such as the Polity Index.[15] The democracy effect turns out to be very large and dominant for CtD and CA (fifth panel). Adding the Polity score to the regression eliminates the Arab region effect (with the exception of a very small and now positive effect on democracy).[16] A Muslim-majority negative effect remains for civic action. And an oil-country-specific negative effect remains for obedience. These should not be taken as proof of a form of cultural essentialism at play—rather, there are omitted structural variables that probably explain these differences, and looking for explanations for these remaining differences forms an important agenda for future research.

It is, therefore, the type of political regime that emerges as a crucial variable that explains best the variations in political values across countries. This result, it turns out, is not limited to the Arab, Muslim-majority, or oil-exporting countries. Indeed, it is quite universal: education emancipates much more in democratic than in autocratic countries in all countries of the world as shown in my recent (coauthored) work.[17]

In sum, there is nothing exceptional about the low level of individual political values among the educated in Arab countries. As in all nondemocratic countries, these values tend to be conservative. I now turn to a discussion of the reasons why this may be so.

Why Is the Impact of Education on Emancipation Low in Arab Countries?

My investigation found, using the WVS data, that the Arab region did experience a democratic demand deficit around 2008–2013. More specifically, when focusing on the Arab region in a comparative perspective, I found that the commitment to democracy values was stunted by a pro–status quo bias, which was especially strong among the educated, but which was also visible among the youth and the middle class (controlling for education). Beyond a lower preference for democracy, Arab individuals engage less in civic action, and respect authority more, when compared with similar individuals around the world. In general, family, class, state, and/or political circumstances can all influence the individual preferences of the educated. This section focuses on the different types of mechanisms that may be operating in the Arab region and that can affect the way individuals form their political preferences in ways consistent with my empirical findings.

In the Middle East area-study literature, three particular mechanisms have been advanced that can explain the emancipatory gap. First, some argue that the region's exceptionalism is due to cultural factors, and in particular its Islamic culture, which drives both a low demand for democracy and conservative individual political values. Second, work focused on education and propaganda claims that autocrats, to enhance social control, systematically use education as an indoctrination tool. Third, another branch of the regional literature has theorized the existence of an autocratic bargain between citizens and rulers, whereby the educated accept that their voices be curtailed in exchange for economic, social, and/or political advantages. Let us look at each possibility in more detail, in light of both the evidence uncovered earlier in the chapter, and the findings of the global and area-based literatures.

Culture

Individuals are subject to parental socialization efforts, with parents driven by their own moral code, as well as their interest in their children's welfare.[18] To the extent that their moral code in the region is influenced by Islam, some of the underlying religious principles would be more salient. But parents can also choose to socialize their children according to the values of the regime in place, to ensure their future success in life.

There is indeed, as cited earlier, an active debate on whether this "democratic exception" is due to a cultural bias present in Arab and/or in Muslim countries. While I do not dispute that local culture can, to some extent, affect individual preferences for a democratic order, the weight of the evidence uncovered (as shown in the results of Table 2.3) points toward a larger role for political explanations, rather than for essentialist claims.

In my data, the exceptionally weak effect of education on political emancipation predominates—in the example developed in the previous section, it explains half of the democratic gap. The cultural factor is unlikely to explain the blunted impact of education, since local culture would be expected to affect the uneducated more than the educated, who are typically more connected to global than to local values.[19] My findings do indicate one element in Arab culture that is inimical to emancipation, and that is its surplus of religiosity. But in this limited sense, the finding is that the contribution of Arab culture to the Arab democratic gap is rather small, especially when it is compared to the effect of education. In sum, the essentialist/culturalist claim is not supported by my empirical results.

Indoctrination

The indoctrination thesis is certainly appealing when one thinks of schooling in Baathist Syria or Iraq. But to what extent can one claim that such a phenomenon is at work elsewhere in the region as well? Do education systems manage to "brainwash" students, or do they simply convey signals of regime strength, and define the type of narrative that is politically acceptable to avoid repression and advance one's career? These questions remain open, and the discussion here seeks to organize a research agenda to elucidate them further.

Education can reproduce the ideological values of the regimes in place in several possible ways. It can be used as an indoctrination tool. It has been noted in the literature that the state is almost always invested in delivering education, in democratic and autocratic settings alike, which allows for direct control of the system.[20] Moreover, in most countries, states set the school curricula, and enforce its application by disciplining teachers according to particular criteria of performance. This can be done in ways to indoctrinate students in the values supportive of the regime in place. Moreover, states can indirectly influence the political preferences of the educated through selection. States control admission in schools and universities, and the provision of diplomas, and this can weed out of the system students who do not internalize what is considered by the state to be acceptable national norms and values.

A recent global literature has started to shed light on such mechanisms. In this tradition, Lott presents evidence on the prevalence of propaganda and indoctrinating institutions in all types of regimes.[21] Several recent papers based on country case studies (focused on China, Vietnam, Kenya, Egypt, and Zimbabwe) have looked at ideological differences within countries, asking in particular whether, in these autocratic and poorer countries, education causes higher levels of political participation, as it does in richer countries. A paper that manages to pinpoint precisely education as the mechanism that shapes values is that of Cantoni and colleagues, who use a change in the curriculum in certain provinces, but not others, to show that in China, the curriculum itself influences the political values of the educated.[22] More generally, in recent work,[23] I examine all countries that had transitioned from autocracy to democracy in the past three decades, using an identification strategy that allows for causal claims, and show that older cohorts educated under autocratic regimes tend to be more conservative politically than those educated under the new democratic regime (controlling for the effect of age).[24]

Coming to the regional literature, there has been some discussion about education as an instrument of indoctrination. This requires that regimes have the capacity to engage in such social engineering. This has certainly been the case in the Arab world, which has been dominated by autocratic states for the past five decades, and subjected to mass education movements since the 1960s.[25] Much of the education system is closely controlled by the state, largely through public education. There is a focus on the central role played by the education system to spread the ideology of Arab nationalism, especially through mass education campaigns in the 1960s and 1970s, in Egypt, Syria, and Iraq, and the values of conservatism and quietism in the GCC. Pedagogical methods such as rote learning in particular can encourage a respect for authority by reducing the resort to critical thinking.[26] Equally, it is also possible that the education system plays the role of a sorting mechanism, allowing only those students who show a willingness to conform to state ideology to succeed.

There is also a regional literature that connects authoritarianism, education systems, and the instrumentalization of religion for political purposes, which describes the battles between secular nationalism and religious Islam fought over school curricula in a first phase, and the subsequent Islamization of the system by the regimes in place to pacify the opposition and foster political quietism.[27]

Several interesting questions have arisen in the area-study literature that require more work. One interesting question, which echoes work done on China, is whether education manages to actually brainwash students, or whether it simply socializes them by defining the acceptable narrative, and teaching them how to pretend. Seurat's and Wedeen's work on Syria[28] suggests that people are pushed by propaganda to use the narrative of the ruling Baath Party, and that this acts as a credible signal that the regime is firmly in control. In my results, however, the fact that the educated are more prone than the uneducated to do so suggests that either indoctrination at school works better than general propaganda, or that the educated have more interests at stake to protect than the uneducated, and are thus more subject to fear of sanction.

Social or Economic Interests

Differences in individual political values in different regimes can be due to differences in their social, economic, and political interests, rather than to differences in preference per se. The focus on political *interest,* as different from preferences, arises from a recognition that the political beliefs and attitudes of the educated may differ across regime types due to the economic incentives they face. In terms of political action, the educated stand to lose their higher returns to education when open dissent is penalized.

A possibility that has received some attention in the global literature is that the educated may be more conservative because of adverse selection, to the extent that the elite's children become educated more often, and thus that students tend to come more often from pro-regime backgrounds. It is possible that the emancipation gap that I have found is overestimated, due to an elite-selection bias. But in theory, this bias could actually go in either direction, as richer students may be more conservative due to their economic interests, but they could also be more emancipated politically due to modernizing forces connected to their higher incomes.

A related possibility is that the educated have more of an interest than the uneducated to refrain from expressing dissent in repressive autocracies, because they risk losing their larger return to education.[29] Huang offers one of the rare studies that attempts to separate interests and preferences.[30] He argues that in China, propaganda acts as a credible signal of the state's hold on power, but that it does not manage to effectively brainwash the educated. In particular, he finds that students who are more aware of propaganda are not more satisfied with the government, but that they are more likely to believe that the government has a strong capacity to maintain public order, and they are consequently less willing to express dissent.

In the regional area study, the educated have been described to ascribe to an autocratic bargain, whereby they give up their political rights against economic or social advantages.[31] The interest of the educated to form an alliance with autocrats can in turn be related to several factors. Regimes have often deployed efforts to co-opt the educated, through public sector jobs, and subsidies of various sorts, as the creation of a modern middle class has been for many regimes their main legitimizing narrative. The educated have also more to lose in opposing repressive nondemocratic regimes, where the state is the main employer.[32] Moreover, in highly unequal societies, the more educated (and, therefore, richer) individuals may fear that they would be taxed more in a more democratic regime, where the interests of the less educated (and poorer) individuals become the majority view.[33] These are real possibilities. But if it was the fear of democratic governments acting to the benefit of the poor and redistributing income away from the rich that led to a low demand for democracy, we would have expected larger differences among the upper middle class and the rich, which we do not observe in my data.

Another more cultural factor that has been cited occasionally, and is more convincing, relates to the fact that in some countries, the educated elite tends to have pro-secularist social values, and they may fear that a more democratic regime would risk giving power to Islamic parties that would favor more religious and conservative values.[34]

Conclusion

The interest in understanding the political culture of Arab countries has risen among policymakers and social activists because of the failure of the popular uprisings of 2011 to deliver political change, and the political chaos that has ensued. My concern here has been about the formation of individual preferences, which must affect the possibility of success of popular uprisings. Are political values related to local culture, and thus impervious to change, or are they instead related to particular policies, or to political circumstances, that are amenable to change?

The evidence uncovered in this chapter is that the political returns to education are much lower in the Arab region than in the rest of the world, and that this emancipation gap among the educated largely explains best the region's emancipation gap relative to the rest of the world. From this perspective, the failure of Arab societies to make political progress can be directly related to the political values of the educated.

But understanding the root causes for the phenomenon uncovered here must be a crucial element in rethinking what would be the ingredients of a better future. The key question posed by the results is that of figuring out the deeper reasons shaping the low demand for democracy in Arab countries. Several possible logically coherent interpretations suggest themselves—the exception uncovered could conceptually be due to differences in culture, but also to differences in interests, circumstances, or active policies by autocratic governments to influence individual preferences. While I cannot claim that the results in this chapter completely disentangle these different reasons, they can at least help in making some informed speculations.

One hypothesis that looks quite convincing is that educated Arabs have been much less emancipated because the type education that they have received was constructed over time in ways that manufacture consent. The cultural explanation, while plausible, is less convincing. Instead, state indoctrination and socioeconomic interests seem predominant. Trying to disentangle these hypotheses further is an important agenda for future research.

The results suggest already that rather than believe that immutable culture is the main constraint to changes in values, one needs instead to focus on what can be done on the policy front. In this respect, education emerges as an area where the focus of reforms should concentrate, not just on its quality from an economic productivity perspective, but also on the social and political qualities it embodies.

In any event, that the political values of the educated stand out as particularly low in the Arab region is a deep cause for worry. The policy implications are clear. Looking at the impact of the type of education Arab youth receive on their social and political values, it will remain difficult to foster more open, democratic, gender-sensitive, and tolerant societies. There is a need to start looking more carefully at how to improve education systems in ways not just to bolster the marketability of individuals in the economy, but also, and more important, to improve their social and political impact on Arab societies, such as by fostering a sense of community, strengthening values of civic engagement, inculcating democratic principles, supporting gender equality, and promoting social tolerance.

Appendix: Definition of Variables

Respect for authority. Average of (1) Do you think it would be a good thing, a bad thing, or don't you mind? "Greater respect for authority"; (2) Mention "obedience" when asked about the most important qualities children need to learn at home.

Commitment to democracy (CtD). Uses responses to the question, "People sometimes talk about what the aims of this country should be for the next ten years. In each of the 3 menus listed below, which option you consider the most important? And which would be the next most important?" PfD is defined as the number of times democratic principles (M1: 3; M2: 2; M3: 2 or 3) are listed ahead of security interests (M1: 2; M2: 1; M3: 4).

Menu 1

> 1. A high level of economic growth
> 2. Making sure this country has strong defense forces
> 3. Seeing that people have more say about things
> 4. Trying to make our cities and countryside more beautiful

Menu 2

> 1. Maintaining order in the nation
> 2. Giving people more say in important government decisions
> 3. Fighting rising prices
> 4. Protecting freedom of speech

Menu 3

> 1. A stable economy
> 2. Progress toward a less impersonal and more humane society
> 3. Progress toward a society in which ideas count more than money
> 4. The fight against crime

Civic action. Have you done any of these things, you might do it, or would never do it under any circumstances?
- Signing a petition
- Joining in boycotts
- Attending peaceful demonstrations

Age: The numerical scope of this variable is restricted to 15–99.

Education: A 1–4 scale where 1 stands for people with no education, 2 for people with at most a primary school diploma, 3 for people who have more than primary school and less than university education, and 4 for people who have at least started a university program.

Female: Takes a value of 1 for female and 0 for male.

Income: Inc1, Inc2, and Inc3 are dummy variables related to the three first quartiles of the income distribution, respectively, relative to the group in the richest fourth quartile.

Religiosity: Whether religious faith is an important quality in a child.

Lngdpc: Logarithmic value of GDP per capita (purchasing power parity, constant 2005 international dollars) for the year in which the survey was done (World Bank Indicators).

Lnoilrent: Logarithmic value of oil rents over GDP, taken the year in which the survey was done (World Bank Indicators).

Muslim: Share of self-declared Muslims in the total population, which asks religious denomination of the respondent.

Democracy: Polity Index scores from http://www.systemicpeace.org/polityproject .html.

Notes

1. Rosenstone and Hansen, *Mobilization, Participation and Democracy in America;* Wolfinger, and Rosenstone, *Who Votes?;* Inglehart and Welzel, *Modernization, Cultural Change, and Democracy;* Inglehart and Welzel, "Changing Mass Priorities"; Dee, "Are There Civic Returns to Education?"; Verba, Schlozman, and Brady, *Voice and Equality.*

2. Huang, "Building the World-Class Research Universities"; Wang, "Are College Graduates Agents of Change?"; Dang, "Quasi-Experimental Evidence on the Political Impacts of Education in Vietnam"; Larreguy and Marshall, "The Effect of Education on Civic and Political Engagement in Non-Consolidated Democracies"; Croke, Grossman, Larreguy, and Marshall, "Deliberate Disengagement"; Blaydes, "Who Votes in Authoritarian Elections and Why?"; Friedman, Kremer, Miguel, and Thornton, "Education as Liberation?"

3. These are Algeria, Egypt, Iraq, Jordan, Kuwait, Lebanon, Libya, Morocco, Palestine, Qatar, Tunisia, and Yemen. The WVS interviews 1,000 to 3,000 individuals per country using polling methods that are meant to produce nationally representative samples. The WVS's fourth and fifth waves, collected around 2000 and 2008, only included four Arab countries.

4. Standard errors are clustered at the country level.

5. I measure income with dummies (relative to the richest group) to allow for nonlinearities.

6. The new result is not that youth in the Arab region are more emancipated compared to the elderly, but that they are less so compared to youth globally.

7. The result that education emancipates politically in the Muslim-majority countries is not new, but that it does so much less than elsewhere is. See Tessler, "Islam and Democracy in the Middle East"; and Jamal, "Reassessing Support for Islam and Democracy in the Arab World?"

8. Diwan, "Understanding Revolution in the Middle East."

9. To evaluate the country effects, the regressions have been run by replacing the Arab dummy by country dummies for each of the twelve Arab countries covered by the WVS. The regressions yield in general effects with the same signs as those in Table 2.2, when they are significant, with only a few exceptions. For the CtD value for example, age is negatively correlated with CtD, except for Palestine; education has a positive sign, except in Qatar; religiosity has a negative sign, except in Iraq and Yemen; income has a positive sign, except in Yemen. See Al-Ississ and Diwan, "Preference for Democracy in the Arab World."

10. United Nations Development Programme, *The Arab Human Development Report 2016: Youth and the Prospects for Human Development in a Changing Reality* (New York: United Nations Publications, 2016); United Nations Economic and Social Commission for Western Asia, *Social Development Report 2: Inequality, Autonomy, and Change in the Arab Region* (Beirut: United Nations House, 2018).

11. The shared predispositions of age cohorts are described as generation effects in the sociological literature. See Inglehart and Welzel, "Changing Mass Priorities"; Yates and Youniss, *Roots of Civic Identity;* and Burke and Stets, *Identity Theory.* Empirical research on political generations has produced solid findings that certain attitudes, acquired during a formative period, persist throughout life. Yates and Youniss show that the disposition to civic action is developed during individuals' formative years, and particularly through schooling, and that participation by students in community activities is a good predictor of future political participation during their lifetime.

12. Besides all the Arab countries, the countries with more than 50 percent of their population reporting following the Muslim religion in the WVS sample are Azerbaijan, Bangladesh, Burkina Faso, Indonesia, Iran, Kazakhstan, Kyrgyzstan, Malaysia, Mali, Pakistan, Turkey, and Uzbekistan.

13. These countries are Algeria, Azerbaijan, Ecuador, Iran, Iraq, Kazakhstan, Kuwait, Libya, Nigeria, Norway, Qatar, Russia, Saudi Arabia, Trinidad, Venezuela, Vietnam, and Yemen.

14. Diamond, "Why Are There No Arab Democracies?"; Noland, "Explaining Middle Eastern Authoritarianism"; Stepan and Robertson, "An 'Arab' More Than a 'Muslim' Democracy Gap"; Fish, "Islam and Authoritarianism"; and Ross, "Does Oil Hinder Democracy?"

15. Freund and Jaud, "On the Determinants of Democratic Transitions."

16. This is similar to the result in Inglehart and Norris, "Islamic Culture and Democracy." The authors control for the level of democracy and find that the only value that is "exceptional" in the Arab region is that of patriarchy.

17. Diwan and Vartanova, "Does Education Indoctrinate?"

18. Bisin and Verdier, "A Model of Cultural Transmission, Voting and Political Ideology."

19. Norris, *Democratic Deficit.*

20. Kremer and Sarychev, "Why Do Governments Operate Schools?"; Pritchett, "'When Will They Ever Learn?'"

21. Lott, "Public Schooling, Indoctrination, and Totalitarianism."

22. Cantoni, Chen, Yang, Yuchtman, and Zhang, "Curriculum and Ideology."

23. Diwan and Vartanova, "Does Education Indoctrinate?"

24. A similar test is provided in Alberto and Fuchs-Schündeln, "Goodbye Lenin (or Not?)." They show that, after unification, individuals with an East German background remained more conservative throughout their lives than those of West German origin.

25. I am not arguing here that the prevalence of autocratic regimes in the region is due to individual political values. Indeed, most political scientists do not believe that individual preferences have a great effect on whether a country ends up democratic or not; instead, democracy is believed to arise as an agreement among elites. See Przeworski, *Democracy and the Limits of Self-Government.* It may be the case that democratization is driven by changes in elite bargains, but that chances of reversals to autocracy are lower when a country's democratic culture is stronger; see O'Donnell, Schmitter, and Whitehead, *Transitions from Authoritarian Rule: Comparative Perspectives.*

26. United Nations Development Programme and Arab Human Fund for Economic and Social Development, *Arab Human Development Report 2002: Creating Opportunities for Future Generations* (New York: United Nations Publications, 2002); United Nations Development Programme, *The Arab Human Development Report 2016: Youth and the Prospects for Human Development in a Changing Reality* (New York: United Nations Publications, 2016); United Nations Economic and Social Commission for Western Asia, *Social Development Report 2: Inequality, Autonomy, and Change in the Arab Region* (Beirut: United Nations House, 2018).

27. Mazawi, "Schooling and Curricular Reforms in Arab and Muslim Societies"; Kadi and Billeh, *Islam and Education;* Doumato and Starrett, *Teaching Islam;* Faour and Muasher, *Education for Citizenship in the Arab World.*

28. Seurat, *L'Etat de Barbarie;* Wedeen, *Ambiguities of Domination.*

29. A related argument is that individuals associate democracy with regime change, which they fear because of the probable chaos that such a transition would entail, especially in environments where autocrats had worked hard at not facilitating such transitions. If this was a predominant factor, it might possibly explain the democratic gap among the lower-middle-class individuals, which can be particularly vulnerable to economic shocks, but there seems to be no particular reason why it would particularly affect the educated and the youth. See Greif and Tadelis, "A Theory of Moral Persistence."

30. Huang, "Building the World-Class Research Universities."

31. Desai, Olofsgård, and Yousef, "The Logic of Authoritarian Bargains."

32. There is country-level evidence that in electoral authoritarian regimes, more educated citizens may deliberately disengage from politics; see Croke, Grossman, Larreguy, and Marshall, "Deliberate Disengagement." Blaydes argues that the more educated understand that political opposition will be costly but is unlikely to make a difference: Blaydes, "Who Votes in Authoritarian Elections and Why?"

33. Acemoglu and Robinson, *Economic Origins of Dictatorship and Democracy.*

34. Lust, "Missing the Third Wave."

3

Citizenship in Egyptian, Tunisian, and Moroccan History Textbooks

Roel Meijer

Arab historical textbooks are mostly produced by the state and are often criticized for their authoritarian, unidimensional, and heavily biased political nature. Seldom are they written by academic historians; never are they broadly reviewed or debated by experts before publication.[1] The list of complaints is long. The Egyptian Institute for Personal Rights (EIPR) criticized Egyptian textbooks for neglecting the role of ethnic and religious minorities, workers, and women, and focusing on the "collective" of the nation.[2] Moroccan textbooks have been taken to task for their "Jacobinian" nature of imposing an Arabized, national, homogeneous, "monocultural" unity on a culturally and ethnically diverse country.[3] On the whole, Arab textbooks stand accused of hampering the development of a "historical consciousness"[4] and producing a biased master narrative of the struggle for national independence.[5] Moreover, this narrative has the goal of legitimizing the current authoritarian regimes.

One of the techniques of reaching this goal is selection, marginalization, and exclusion of persons, groups, and organizations that deviate from the nationalist master narrative. This is for instance the case with Copts in Egyptian textbooks,[6] or the Berbers and Jews in Moroccan history who challenge the unity of the nation.[7] It refers also to oppositional political currents. From the current textbooks one would almost forget that the Middle East and North Africa has known strong communist, Islamist, and trade union movements, as well as independent liberal thinkers. The homogeneity of the national identity is overemphasized,[8] while historical determinism has the purpose to show the inexorable march of history leading to the present regimes that serve the needs of the people.[9]

Critics have argued that the way to counter this authoritarian, hegemonic, exclusive, nonpluralistic history is to (1) stimulate multiple and multicultural interpretations of history, including different viewpoints of historical, cultural, and religious actors; (2) give back agency to historical actors and challenge master narratives; (3) include and critically discuss power relations and the dynamics of politics in history in the Arab world; and (4) make history interesting for pupils by demonstrating that it is part of their identity formation and plays an important role in achieving political awareness.[10]

In this chapter I will try to demonstrate that the introduction of a citizenship-centered interpretation of Arab history can help to overcome these shortcomings. Recently attempts have been made to introduce citizenship studies to the Middle East as a means of drawing attention to agency, contention, social movements, political actors, and notions of civility.[11] In contrast to prevailing scholarship that focuses on nationalism, Islam, the state, civil society, and the roots of authoritarianism, this interpretation argues that since the nineteenth century there have always been contentious movements that have promoted a rights discourse and developed strong notions of citizenship.[12] Specific citizenship regimes are produced in a struggle between the state and movements that claim (equal) rights.

I will give a brief overview of what such an interpretation would look like for the period dealt with in Arab textbooks, which mostly cover the period from the early nineteenth-century encounter with Europa until full independence in the 1950s. The modern history of citizenship in the Middle East and North Africa starts when the premodern political order of Islamic empires is transformed and a modern bureaucratic state arises. A crucial development is the Tanzimat reforms (1839–1876), when the Ottoman state started to intervene more deeply into the lives of its subjects, attempting to turn them into what can be considered citizens. Prominent among those reform measures was the introduction of a conscription army and the proclamation of juridical equality of Christians and Jews and Muslims and the development of public schooling.[13] Equal and shared citizenship was represented by "Ottomanism," a new ideology that portended to present a more abstract loyalty to the Ottoman state rather than loyalty to the sultan. Growing nationalism would ultimately undermine the loyalty to empire, and new entities of loyalties and belonging would emerge that would end the multi-religious and multi-ethnic diversity of the Ottoman Empire. In the Arab East (Mashriq), Arab nationalism gradually emerged after World War I. Earlier, in the Arab West (Maghreb), French colonialism had replaced Ottoman rule, by incorporating Algeria into the French republic after the invasion of 1830 and turning Tunisia and Morocco into protectorates in 1881 and 1912, while Italy occupied Libya in 1912. Egypt would develop its own citizenship regime under Mehmed Ali (1805–1849) and his successors. After the British occupation in 1882 and the "veiled protectorate" it became a monarchy in 1923 until the military coup of 1952 of the Free Officers, in nationalist historiography called the July Revolution.

Although historical research has always focused on European impe-rialism and the response in the form of nationalism and Islamic move-ments as identity movements in the struggle for independence, recent historical research has demonstrated that the concept of citizenship and equal rights played an equally important role in these movements. "Imagined communities" were in fact imagined communities of citizens who were politicized and demanded political, economic, cultural, and social rights. This was already expressed in the constitutions of the nine-teenth century and especially in the Young Turk Revolution of 1908.[14] Despite the prevalent image of ethnic minorities struggling for inde-pendence, several groups tried to integrate into the Ottoman Empire and become loyal citizens.[15] Criteria for inclusion and exclusion into newly constructed political communities was heavily debated at the time.[16] This is not surprising, as during the struggle for independence both the Islamic and the secular nationalist movements began to hold (colonial) governments responsible for providing necessary services and demanded equal rights for all citizens.[17] They demanded constitutions, which restricted the power of the ruler (colonial power), secured freedom of expression and organization, as well as, later, claims to the rights to edu-cation, equal pay, equal job access, and political representation. The emergence of these demands has been related to the development of the public sphere, the rise of an Arabic press, and a new reading public. Egypt, for instance, which had a rich cotton export economy, developed a public sphere already before the Urabi Revolution of 1881–1882, when for the first time terms such as *ahali, 'amma,* and *sha'b* in the modern meaning as the "people" claiming rights were used.[18] In Syria these terms were introduced during the Young Turk Revolution of 1908, and in Iraq they appeared somewhat later during the first rebellion against the British in 1920, the same period when they became more widespread in Tunisia. Throughout the interbellum these terms associated with the modern term for citizenship (*muwatana*) were further developed and pushed by major nationalist movements, which derived their legitimacy from petitions and campaigns to speak in the name of the people. Impor-tant examples are the *tawkilat* (representation) of the Wafd in 1919 and petitions of the Tunisian Destour Party in 1920. The colonial state countered these movements by on the one hand developing a policy of divide and rule and social, ethnic, and religious differentiation, and on the other hand building alliances with local notables (*'ayan, dhawat*) willing to work with colonial rulers.[19]

Likewise, the phase of radicalization of the nationalist movement in the 1930s can be analyzed in the light of evolving notions of citizenship.[20] A crucial development in this period is the development of the concept of the social contract between citizens and between citizens and the state. While the rights discourse of the previous period had focused on the elite and sovereignty,[21] after the 1930s political rights deepened and social and economic rights were added. Radicalization was also reflected both in a stronger tendency toward "foreign" exclusion, as well as a broadening of indigenous citizenship by the inclusion of the middle and lower classes and its deepening in the adoption of social and economic rights, promoted by labor unions and activist intellectuals.[22] These new rights were pioneered by the Egyptian trade union movement and the Tunisian General Labor Union (UGTT) in Tunisia, founded in 1946 by Farhat Hached, while the new middle classes looked to the state to provide jobs, expand education, and attain independence and national sovereignty. The intellectual groundwork for these new, more inclusive notions of citizenship was developed by organizations such as the al-Ahali group in Iraq,[23] which later developed into the National Democratic Party, and the Wafdist Vanguard in Egypt.[24] One of the most successful inclusive organizations of the 1940s and 1950s, that succeeded in mobilizing broad segments of the population, bridging the gap between Islamic modernists and secular trends and incorporating the labor movement, was the Neo-Destour in Tunisia.[25] The next phase would occur in the run-up to independence and in the years afterward, when the different wings of the nationalist movement fought for power, determining the citizenship regime for the next decades. The victory of King Muhammad V over the Istiqlal, Bourguiba over Salah ben Youssef, the army in Egypt over the Muslim Brotherhood, determined not just who held power but also which citizenship regime would prevail over the next decades until the social pact of independence collapsed with the introduction of neoliberalism in the 1990s. Although in all cases authoritarian regimes won out, many of these more inclusive, cross-sectarian, cross-cultural, and democratic trends remained active underground and would reemerge at a later date.

Aside from a tool of historical analysis, citizenship is as a concept also important for other reasons. Citizenship not only impinges on political rights and inclusion or exclusion of the political community, but also relates to daily conduct, or what can be called civility and related norms and values of tolerance, acceptance of pluralism, and rejection of discrimination. These forms of "everyday citizenship" not only infuse a political culture but also are embedded in an overall culture of a country.[26] In Islamic reformist terms it is reflected in more liberal interpretations of *akhlaq* (ethics), *wasatiyya* (the middle way), or the "common good" (*maslaha al-'amma*) and *jihad al-nafs* (self-discipline and attainment of moral excellence).[27] In its more secular liberal form it is represented by the idea of enlightenment (*tanwir*) and stands opposed to dominant vertical relations of dependency, patronage, paternalism, and clientelism.

This relationship between citizenship (*muwatana*) and its values is represented in civic courses and citizenship education.[28] The Carnegie Endowment in one of its reports stated that "democracy will thrive only in a culture that accepts diversity, respects different points of view, regards truth as relative rather than absolute, and tolerates—and even encourages—dissent."[29] Education and the acquisition of specific skills ("citizenship skills") to learn to inquire, question, participate, and communicate should empower students, and encourage "critical thinking, creativity, and exercising one's duties and rights as citizens."[30]

To be sure, citizenship is not a linear development toward greater liberal emancipation. In fact, citizenship has had a hard time in the Middle East and North Africa, and modern history in the region can be regarded as a long sequence of suppression of notions of equal citizenship. In the monarchies citizenship is a gift (*makrama*), not a right. It can be rescinded at will; in the republics the well-known, so-called authoritarian populist social contract entails an exchange of political for economic and social rights.[31] And yet, neglecting citizenship both as a historical concept and as a practice of everyday citizenship is a grave mistake, as many of the popular movements of the past decade in the Arab world are citizen movements that feed upon past experiences and examples.[32]

Methodology

Here I analyze a series of modern history textbooks used in high schools in three Arab countries—Egypt, Tunisia, and Morocco—covering the first grade until the last class of high school.

For Tunisia I concentrate on two books of the middle school (ages thirteen to fifteen).[33] I concentrate on these books because they give a more complete picture of Tunisian history. For Morocco, I analyze two history textbooks for the last two classes of high school.[34] For Egyptian history, I use two books for the first and third grade of preparatory school (ages twelve and fourteen).[35] For modern history, I compare an older book, in use in 2015–2016 and written by at least one well-respected Egyptian historian, 'Asim al-Disuqi,[36] and compare it with a revised, later book.[37] This comparison is illustrative of the way al-Sisi tries to suppress any notion of citizenship. For the same reason, I include a first-grade book on pharaonic history.

An indication of state control is that the more recent Egyptian books are written by anonymous authors and, therefore, by the state, while the previous ones were obviously written by a group of named professors and teachers. The top-down approach is also apparent in the Tunisian textbooks, which are written by "inspectors" (*mutafaqqid*) of the Ministry of Education, although, in contrast to Egypt, they are named, while the Moroccan textbooks are written by a combination of named inspectors (*mufattish*) and teachers.

I analyze these books in the following manner: (1) against the background of citizenship and notions of citizenship as they appear in recent Middle Eastern and North African historical writing; (2) the way they encourage or discourage a civic spirit of critical thinking, creativity, and exercising duties and rights as citizens; (3) the narrative and structure of the text, as well as the kind of terminology the textbooks use, especially surrounding the meaning of the Arabic term for citizenship (*muwatana*); and (4) their inconsistencies, for the term "citizenship" does appear in the texts but in haphazard ways. It is mostly in the ambiguities, contradictions, and inconsistencies of the use of the term *muwatana* that one can trace the manner in which the authoritarian state tries to appropriate historical notions of citizenship and rights but at the same time adapts and remolds them to produce obedient, model citizens who fit its repressive citizenship regime.

It is noteworthy that aside from these historical books there is also "civil education" (*tarbiya al-madaniyya*)[38] in the upper classes. The Tunisian books integrate history, geography, economics, and sociology, but history is mostly ancient history and civil education is completely separate from history and deals with topics such as rights of children, rights of women, duties in the family, and rule of law.[39]

Egypt

Much has been made of the rewriting of Egyptian history under President al-Sisi and the way it claims to secure the legacy of the January 25

Revolution and the preservation of Egypt's revolutionary heritage.[40] The technique it uses is to absorb claims of participation, and civil and social demands of citizens in an authoritarian state. A good example is the textbook on pharaonic history. The pharaonic period in Egyptian history is, of course, not associated with modern citizenship, or with the modern authoritarian state. Nevertheless, what strikes the reader is the (anachronistic) interweaving of terms associated with citizenship with those of authoritarianism. The obvious goal is to instill in pupils the existence and merits of a strong Egyptian state since the earliest pharaonic times. For instance, the transition of the seventh dynasty to the tenth dynasty is described as a period of "weakness," because "security (*aman*) was threatened, instability (*'adam istiqrar*) and chaos (*fawda*) reigned supreme, and laws were neglected."[41] After Akhnaton, again "new laws and measures were taken to establish internal stability (*istiqrar*) and end chaos (*fawda*)."[42] It is here that rights and an authoritarian state are combined, for "pharaohs were proud to give workers (*'ummal*) their rights (*huquq*) and end the *corvée*."[43] In the chapter on politics and administration, the emphasis is on the natural order and the benevolence of the ruler, which is based on hierarchy, the centralization of power, and the struggle against forces that threaten central power (*al-sulta al-markaziyya*).

One of the few cases where there is mention of resistance is at the end of the sixth dynasty, when the people rise up against injustice (*zulm*) and oppression (*idhtihad*). This revolution (*thawra*) was anachronistically based on the "value of the individual" (*qima al-fard*) and the "idea of equality" (*fikra al-musawat*). However, also here the pharaoh is portrayed as a benevolent ruler who "should look after his [people's] interests (*masalih*) and their aspirations (*tumuhat*)." When stability was reestablished, the power of the pharaoh was restricted and "kings (*muluk*), their ministers and local governors were proud to base their relations with their subjects (*ra'aya*) on justice (*'adala*)."[44] The existence of a just regime is underlined by information that the police (*shurta*) "had a special place among the people (*sha'b*)." Moreover, "the civil system was at the service of the people and had the task to maintain peace and security for the citizens (*muwatinun*) and to uphold the existing order (*al-nizam al-'amm*)." The relations between pharaoh and citizens were "regulated by a constitution (*dustur*) and laws and duties that respected human rights and basic liberties."[45] The result was that in society "social justice" reigned supreme. The system allowed "sons of society" (*abna' al-mujtama'*) to participate in mutual help, or "what is called today civil society," to tackle social problems and give advice (*nasa'ih*) to the rulers.[46]

A more obvious case of using history under Sisi to support the authoritarian state is to compare two books on modern Egyptian history published in 2015 and 2018. *Modern History of Egypt and the Arabs,* last published in 2015, was written well before that date for the highest grade of secondary school, by five authors, among them the well-known and highly respected historian 'Asim al-Disuqi.[47] It covers the same material as the simplified *Modern History of Egypt and the Arabs* in the Silsila series, published in 2018,[48] but is a much more sophisticated textbook. In the introduction the authors seem to be aware of the general critique of Egyptian textbooks. They claim to give special attention to developing the critical skills of pupils in order to promote their "capacity of understanding, analysis and creativity, instead of memorization and rote learning." Each chapter starts with a statement of its objectives and what the pupil is supposed to know after having finished it. The chapters end with questions about the meaning of the text.

To be sure, both books are the products of the Egyptian historical school under Nasser, with its heavy emphasis on economic substructure, politics, and the adverse effects of imperialism and its modernization paradigm and political expediency.[49] In the end, both books have the same teleology of nation-building and modernization as the other textbooks.

However, the first part of the 2015 modern history of Egypt is remarkably open-minded and even contains some idea of agency and citizenship. In the section on the French occupation (1798–1801), the authors even discuss the principles of the French Revolution. And despite the revolts against the French in Cairo, the authors describe some of the French reforms as beneficial. Among them are the introduction of political participation (*musharaka fi-l-hukm*) of the ulama and notables in the Cairo council (*diwan*) as representatives of the people.[50] Likewise the authors do not just eulogize Muhammad Ali (1805–1848), who in cruder nationalist historiography is often regarded as the first Egyptian nationalist hero (although he was from Albania and did not speak Arabic). Instead, they point out how he violated the agreement with the Cairene population—somewhat anachronistically called "the will of the people" (*irada al-sha'b*)—by dismissing its leader, Umar Makram.[51] These sections of the book are the most interesting, because they are lively and give insight into the workings of politics. For instance, in analyzing the power struggle between Muhammad Ali and Umar Makram, the authors introduce a number of political terms that are crucial for understanding citizenship and the idea of rights. Pact (*mithaq/'ahd*), trust (*thiqa*) between ruler and ruled, representative (*mumathil*) of the people, delegated power (*wilaya*), and political oversight (*wisaya*) are posed against absolute power (*hukm mutlaq*) of the ruler in such a way that the pupil understands these early Egyptian democratic/political participatory experiments.[52] In analyzing the difference between executive and legislative power, a topic that reoccurs throughout the first part of the book, the authors analyze how the first dominates the latter. They show that the first Egyptian parliament, of 1866, was not a democratic organ, and that despotic rule (*istibdadiyya*) of khedive Tawfiq, supported by British and French dual control, prevailed. The authors demonstrate, correctly, how the struggle for a constitution and broader representation of Egyptians and their demand for increased powers of national oversight (*muraqaba wataniyya*) is connected to the struggle for independence and was in the interests of Egyptians.[53] Here again, new political terms are introduced such as "representative life" (*haya niyabiyya*), elections (*intikhabat*), the rise of political parties, contestation, and the publication of the first political pamphlet (*bayan*). In this light the authors praise one of its leaders, Sharif Pasha, as the "man of the civil constitution" (*rajul dusturi madani*).[54] They also make clear how political grievances are connected to social and economic issues such as discrimination of the Egyptian military and the exorbitant taxes imposed on the population to repay the national debt to foreign bondholders. The political analysis remains interesting in the next chapter as well, where the authors analyze the constitution of 1923 and Egypt enters its "liberal stage" (*marhala libraliyya*). The authors wax in praise of constitutional rights such as freedom of the press and freedom of belief (based on the nationalist slogan of the 1919 Revolution, "religion for God and the nation for all"); Article 23, which considers the "people the source of power"; equality before the law; civil and political rights; and finally the division between executive, legislative, and judicial powers. The fall in 1924 of the first government of the Wafd Party, which led the nationalist uprising against the British in 1919, is lamented.[55]

However, after this encouraging first part of the book in which pupils are introduced to key liberal political concepts and the dynamics of a (somewhat biased and outdated) secular liberal interpretation of Egyptian history,[56] the narrative abruptly changes tack, leading to the next stage inaugurated by the military coup d'état of July 23, 1952, the so-called July Revolution, which is regarded as the fulfillment of Egypt's history. How is this abrupt change in content reconciled with the previous part of the textbook? First by drawing a bleak picture of the end of the liberal era under a monarchy that succumbs to terrorism of the Muslim Brotherhood, political "chaos" (*fawda*), "corruption" (*fasad*), "dissolution" (*inhilal*) of political parties, "instability," military defeat in Palestine, "feudalism" (*iqta'*), and poverty of workers. Second, by providing democratic legitimacy of the Free Officers through the electoral victory of the Free Officers and Muhammad Naguib to the Officers Club in December 1951, a prelude to the 1952 coup d'état and a nonevent compared to the role of the constitution of 1923. Third, through the six "principles of the revolution," which supposedly sum up all the complex trends that emerged in the run-up to the revolution: ending imperialism and its henchmen; ending monopoly and the dominance of capital; ending feudalism; establishing social justice; creating a strong national army; and establishing "sound" (*salima*) democratic life. The authors seem to suggest that, as democracy and political participation never were regarded as part of Egypt's destiny, but social justice was, the latter trumps the former.[57]

The rest of the book, the fifth and sixth chapters, on the Arab countries, prepares the ground for the victorious Nasserist state on the regional pan-Arab stage.[58] The last regular very long chapter covers the rise of Egypt's Arab leadership and the wars with Israel.[59] This chapter, of course, is a legitimation of the central role of the army in Egyptian history. But the most astonishing chapters are the last two, which deal with the January 25 Revolution of 2011 (the Arab Spring in Egypt) and the June 30 Revolution in 2013 (Sisi's military coup), in which the authors accomplish the trick of connecting mass uprisings in favor of political, social, and economic rights of citizens with the reestablishment of the authoritarian Egyptian state under Sisi. This is done by "demonstrating" that the military coup of July 2013 was the fulfillment of the January Revolution. Three reasons are given for the first uprising. The first is the betrayal of the goals of the July Revolution (1952) to achieve social justice. This is not entirely far-fetched, because although the Nasser regime was authoritarian it did provide for a social contract in which Egyptians hand in their political rights in return for economic and social rights. In that sense the argument that the sale of the public sector to capitalism undermined the state's control over the economy and its ability to achieve a "social balance" between Egyptians, threatening "social peace" between its different classes, is valid. The second reason, the failure to establish political participation and real democracy under Sadat and Mubarak by preventing political parties to organize themselves, is interesting as it should be read as an introduction of Sisi's attempt to absorb democratic demands into the new authoritarian state. The third reason is the liberation of the Islamist movement under

Sadat. This argument is immediately used to show why the January Revolution failed: the Islamist taking over of the revolution. As for the June 30 Revolution, it is legitimized because Brotherhood president Mohamed Morsi "failed to solve any of the issues the masses of the people suffered from, especially social justice," and because his rule became a "dictatorship."[60] The mass protests against Morsi in June 2013 are regarded as a people's plebiscite that legitimized a new revolution made by the military, who "brought Egypt back on the right track to implement democracy and support the interests of the people and achieve progress, development and prosperity."[61]

It is obvious that the 2018 version of the history textbook has the purpose to prevent any possibility of misreading Egyptian history. As in the pharaonic history textbook, the new modern history textbook unabashedly is meant to legitimize the present authoritarian regime. This is achieved by erasing any critical analysis that might lead the pupil to discover the history of rights, political struggle, as well as "civil education"—development of critical faculties—that can be found in the first part of the 2015 book. The theme of the textbook is to find the real representatives of the people who can bring about "stability" (*istiqrar*). History is divided into winners, those who have "success" (*najah*), and the losers, those who "fail" (*fashal*), in achieving these goals. The message is that only a strong state can guarantee stable and independent economic, political, social, and cultural development. And only a strong state can protect the identity of Egypt and its "cultural personality" (*shakhsiyya*). The Free Officers, who took power in 1952, are the most successful, while their predecessors, if successful at all, were only so in a limited way and during a restricted period. They failed because their rule was marred by "absolute personal power," or it was undermined by a "divided cultural movement" (*haraka thaqafiyya mutanawaʿa*),[62] internal divisions (*inqisam*) in their ranks, and succumbing to confusion (*ikhtilat*), as during the Urabi Revolution in 1881–1882,[63] or, as was the case with the political parties that emerged at the beginning of the twentieth century, the Watani Party and Umma Party, they "were divided in their views with regard to expressing interests and political forces."[64] If, for instance, the nationalist Wafd Party was the result of "expressions of the unity of the nation" (*mazahir wahda al-wataniyya*) between Muslims and Copts, it failed to "complete [the] people's revolution"[65] and achieve independence. The message is that Sisi's rule is a direct continuation of this master narrative of the march of history under the custody of the authoritarian state.

Tunisia

On the whole, Tunisian textbooks are much more sophisticated and are not as blatantly ideological as the Egyptian ones, at least not in an authoritarian sense. Here I analyze two textbooks for the third (highest) grade of secondary school. These textbooks have a much more open, less self-centered view than the Egyptian ones, situating Tunisia in a much broader Mediterranean, regional, and even global historical context (*zuruf*). The introduction of the first book explicitly states that its aim is to instruct pupils to "think critically" and to "develop an academic attitude."[66] To emphasize its liberal content, the first page consists of an image of the original Declaration of Human Rights and the Citizen.[67] Instead of a dominant, unidimensional historical narrative of succeeding phases, like in the Egyptian textbooks, this approach integrates philosophy, economics, and politics into a complex narrative that provides room to develop critical thinking. This is done by centralizing "documents" (*wathiqa/watha'iq*) with quotations from famous thinkers, treaties, or paragraphs of history books. Questions at the end of the chapter stimulate debates of the documents. The summations (*istikhlas*) at the end of each chapter are usually objective and are not meant to impose a point of view.

The two books differ in focus. The first book is more oriented to culture, economy, and administration (*tasarruf*),[68] the second to science (*sha'b 'ilmi*) but in fact focuses on modern history of Tunisia.[69] Both books start with European history and then move on to Tunisian history. Here I concentrate especially on the second book, as it has a much larger section on modern Tunisian history. The problem with these books is that they follow a highly Eurocentric view of history, in line with Tunisia's francophile founder Habib Bourguiba (1903–2000), who regarded Tunisia as much a part of Europe as of the Arab world.[70] This view also informs pupils' view of citizenship, agency, and ideology. For instance, the first document is a sentence from Kant's "What Is Enlightenment?" in which people are called upon to use their "rationality" (*'aql*) instead of basing their conduct on tradition (*irshad*); the sixth document contains a quote of Voltaire's on absolutism; the seventh document is about Diderot's critique of "religious fanaticism" (*ta'assub al-dini*); and the eleventh document is about Rousseau's theory of the "common will" (*irada al-'amma*).[71] The summation at the end of the chapter focuses on rationalism, emancipation, equality (*masawat*), freedom, tolerance (*tasamuh*), and progress (*taqaddum*) versus privilege (*imtiyazat*) and despotism (*istibdad*). It also points out that these things developed in a free public sphere, salons, and coffeehouses.[72] All these elements are purported to have returned during the French Revolution, when the Third Estate rose up and demanded its rights and universal "new principles" (*mabadi' jadida*) by French "citizens" (*muwatinun*).[73]

The main theme of Tunisia's modern history is that despite its brutal subjugation, exploitation, and repression by the French, Tunisia upheld the ideals of French enlightenment throughout its struggle for national liberation. It is, therefore, not surprising that the first chapter on Tunisia opens with the reproduction of the Security Covenant of 1857, which granted Christians, Jews, and Muslims equal rights and is regarded as a logical sequence to the declaration of the rights of man, much like the Tanzimat in the Ottoman Empire.[74] The second and third chapters are basically attempts to apply the principles of the French Revolution of equal political, economic, and social rights by the Islamic reformist movement of the nineteenth century and the nationalist movement of the twentieth. This means that, on the one hand, the narrative focuses on the negative side of France's imperialism during the Regency: its indebtedness and foreign economic control, leading to French occupation as laid down in the Bardo Treaty (1881) and La Marsa Convention (1883)—all of which are extensively analyzed.[75] On the other hand, reform (*islah*) of the army, administration, expansion of education, the greater influence of the population on the ruler, the security treaty, and the constitution of 1861 (proudly mentioned as the first of the Arab world) are also seen as part of that influence.[76] These reforms are purported to have failed largely because French colonial rule did not uphold the republic's democratic and egalitarian principles. The two political parties, the Destour Party, founded in 1920, and its split-off, the Neo-Destour, established in 1934, through their names (constitution) are portrayed as the very embodiment of French enlightenment. The book goes on to analyze Tunisian history in the broader context of global economic developments, the competition between colonial powers, the rise of fascism, World War II, the decline of France's power after World War II, the foundation of the United Nations, and the struggle for independence.[77]

To be sure, despite the focus on citizenship and emancipation, this is not a liberal textbook. How then is citizenship defined and how is agency formulated? The language is activist and the emphasis is on agency: nationalist forces "raise their voice . . . for freedom," defend "legal rights," and reject rule by the "minority" (*qilla*) of *colons* (French settlers); "citizens" (*muwatinun*) send their representative (*munathil*) to the Paris Peace Conference in 1919;[78] political participation (*tashrik/ musharaka*) takes form in the famous boycott of the French tramway in

1912 and demand of equal pay of Tunisian workers.[79] To underline these activities, the program of the Destour Party, with its demands for equal pay, free and fair elections, freedom of press and organization, and mandatory education, is fully reproduced.[80] The first major Tunisian political publication (*La Tunisie Martyre/Tunis al-Shahida*) by ʿAbd al-ʿAziz al-Thaʿalbi is praised for its demand for a constitution, responsible government, and national sovereignty (*al-siyada al-wataniyya*),[81] while the foundation of the Tunisian trade union UGTT and its bylaws guaranteeing equal pay for workers "regardless of their nationality (*jinsiyya*) and religion" is praised.[82] But, like all nationalist narratives, the focus is on the collective and the success of the nationalist movement in achieving independence. Moreover, only the trend that won is given space. This is the trend in the Neo-Destour represented by the new generation of political leaders, Habib Bourguiba, al-Tahir Safr, and Mahmud al-Matari, who realize that "moderation" (*tahdiʾa*) does not work and that "mass mobilization" (*tabiʾa al-jamahir al-shaʿbiyya*) is the only means to become politically effective.[83] Collective action is in the end successful because the UGTT, led by Farhat Hashad, made a crucial contribution to national liberation.[84] Other factors are the expansion of education and the press and the growth of the reading public.[85]

Given the heavy emphasis on rights, emancipation, and citizenship, and the fact that Tunisia is one of the countries that was successful in toppling the dictatorship in power in 2010–2011 during the Arab Spring, one would expect that the same critical analysis of history would be continued after independence. History is the best means to review Tunisia's authoritarianism. This, however, is not the case. In the end, the nationalist narrative trumps the inclusive narrative of citizenship, which should include analysis of conflicting trends, internal debates, and dissidence, and do justice to the losers in the struggle for power. In fact, the split within the Destour in 1934 is the last instance of dissension that is analyzed; all later internal struggles are ignored, and unification of the different trends within the nationalist movement is portrayed as the reaching of "maturity" (*nadj*) of the nationalist movement under the Neo-Destour.[86] In the rest of the chapter, after independence the successes of the new regime are summed up: expansion of universal education, equality of women, nationalization of French property, the new "fully democratic" constitution of 1959, and the introduction of five-year plans.[87] Ignored is the bitter struggle between Salah bin Youssef and his followers—the "Youssefistes"—and Bourguiba, which represents not only a struggle for power after the return of Bourguiba from his exile in 1950, but also a fundamental struggle between a more

Islamist, pan-Arab wing supported by Zaituna mosque-university, the ulama, and its students, and the more secular, pro-French orientation of Bourguiba.[88] In this sense, the emphasis on citizenship, human rights, and equality reflects Bourguiba's own pro-French, secular attitudes and excludes all those forces that have been critical of his policy.[89]

Morocco

Comparing Moroccan history textbooks to those of Egypt and Tunisia is worthwhile because of the different history of Morocco. First, it is centered around the Alaoui dynasty, founded in 1660, which during the struggle for independence succeeded in outflanking the nationalist movement and, in contrast to the Bey in Tunis and King Faruk in Egypt, continued its rule into the post-independence era. Second, as the dynasty legitimated itself in religious terms such as *sharif* (family of the Prophet Muhammad), it could not base itself on the march of history toward enlightenment (*tanwir*) as in Tunisia, or the state as the embodiment of sovereignty, security, and stability as in Egypt. On the other hand, in an age of mass politics, it had to justify itself toward its citizens as its representative. The strategy had to locate citizenship (*muwatana*) in a more traditional, religious setting, allowing it to develop as an "authentic" relationship between the ruler and his "subjects" (*ra'aya*). The trick is to downplay the weaker moments of rule when the representative of the population demanded larger say in political affairs. The most famous instance is the *bay'a* in 1908, when Moulay Abdelhafid had to accept his ascension to the throne on the condition of getting rid of pervasive French economic and political influence.[90] The other technique is to appropriate and absorb the nationalist demands for rights and equality in the person of the sultan/monarch as the embodiment of benevolence and justice.

For Morocco I analyze two history textbooks. The first is for the first grade of upper secondary school,[91] and covers the nineteenth century and beginning of the twentieth century; the second is for the second grade and covers the twentieth century and beginning of the twenty-first century.[92] Like in the Tunisian textbooks, Moroccan history is situated in global history and especially European history. Only the last chapter of the first book, covering four subchapters and one folder, or 60 of the 221 pages, focuses on Morocco in the nineteenth century leading up to the French protectorate of 1912. The second book takes the narrative where the first book leaves off. It is divided into two sections, the first covering global history in the interbellum, the economic crisis of the 1930s, the second the transformations from World War II to the beginning of the twenty-first century. As in the Tunisian textbooks, each subchapter of the books consists of numbered documents of quotes and parts of books. The source of each document is given and accompanied by three questions on the content of the material. In contrast to the Tunisian textbooks, however, the Moroccan textbooks do not end with a synopsis, and neither are there connecting narratives, which leaves the pupil with only the "documents." This must encourage debate but is probably also confusing.

As in the Tunisian textbooks, much space is given to European history and Europe's economic and political transition in the nineteenth and twentieth centuries. But in contrast to Tunisian textbooks, reform is regarded as a threat as well as a beneficial development. The first book starts out with the 1848 bourgeois revolutions in Europe, the extension of enfranchisement (*haqq al-taswit*), the introduction of universal suffrage in France, and the end of slavery. Citizenship (*muwatana*) is related to greater integration of the nation through means of communications, education, and the rise of a press.[93] The emphasis is, however, on the adverse effects of capitalism, the expansion of European markets, concentration of capital, and the creation of monopolies. In the chapters describing the social history of Europe, the focus is on the emergence of class differences and class struggle. Surprisingly for a state-sponsored book, considerable room is given to explaining the different forms of socialism and anarchism in France and England, as espoused by Saint Simon, Charles Fourier, Robert Owen, and Pierre-Joseph Proudhon. Their goals for a "change of society" (*taghyir al-mujtama'*) and "to achieve a more just social system for society as a whole" are extensively analyzed and praised.[94] The whole of the second section is devoted to European expansion, imperialism, and colonial exploitation, especially of Africa. This is regarded in the text as integral to the European economic system, and all the anti-imperialist thinkers from Hobson to Lenin are extensively quoted.[95]

It is in the last section of the book, with the title "The Islamic World Faces European Expansion," that the modern history of the Alaoui sultanate begins. Again the ambivalence of reform is prominent. A full-page image of Ottoman sultan Abdulhamid II (1876–1909), who led the reaction against the Tanzimat reforms and dissolved parliament in 1878, paves the way for the defense of a conservative response to the Western challenge. A quote from Abdelhamid's memoirs exemplifies the conservative protest against Western reform: "Innovation (*tajdid*) demanded by them [liberals and Western powers] in the name of reform (*islah*) has been the source of our decline (*idmihlal*). . . . Reform is the disease (*da'*) rather than the remedy (*dawa'*) and is the reason for the end of the empire."[96] In a later quote on the failed reforms of Khayr al-Din al-Tunisi in Tunisia, the same critique of reform is expressed.[97] But this is not consistently so. In other sections of the textbook, not only are Muhammad Ali's reforms praised, but also is the Nahda (cultural renaissance). Napoleon's invasion and spread of new ideas (*afkar jadida*) as well as translations in Arabic of Western thought are praised and the importance "public opinion" (*ra'y 'amm*) is stressed. Even Catholic and Protestant missionaries are applauded for their role in the "revival of Arabic language, renewal and publication of Islamic ideological heritage (*turath*) . . . which in the end was transmitted from culture (*adab*) to politics (*siyasa*)." Surprisingly, it is argued that their reformist ideas challenged the "backwardness" (*ta'akhkhur*) of Islamic society.[98] Even more surprising is that in the dispute between the traditional thinkers (*al-mufakkirun al-taqlidiyyun*) and moderate reformers, in the end the textbook supports the "liberal reformist thinkers" (*al-mufakkirun al-islahiyyun al-libraliyyun*).[99] This ambivalence returns in the chapters on reform in Morocco, from Moulay Muhammad bin 'Abd al-Rahman (1822–1859) to Moulay Abdelhafid (1908–1912). The presentation of numerous documents is supposed to demonstrate the weakness of reform because either it was supported only by the sultan, lacked attention, or was misunderstood by the ulama. In conclusion a critical quote states that reforms were "intended to open the markets of the country to capitalist markets . . . which means that they were series of imperialist manipulations."[100] The implication is that reform directly led to the French protectorate of 1912.

The last and by far most interesting part of the second book is a "work file" of assignments for pupils, titled "Constitutional Foundations in the Maghreb at the Beginning of the Twentieth Century." Five constitutional proposals drawn up by Moroccans between 1900 and 1908 call for a completely new relation between the sultan and members of society. In contrast to the earlier critique of reform, the largely democratic proposals suggest that only on the basis of democratic reform would the state have been able to resist French imperialism. The first proposal, the project (*mashru'*) of Bensa'id, calls upon the ruler to install in every town a council (*majlis*), consisting of the "people of knowledge and opinion," who will "look into matters concerning the interests of the country (*masalih al-balad*)." The second proposal seeks the solution in the appointment of a council of notables (*majlis al-'ayan*), consisting of tribal and urban leaders to "discuss (*mushawara*)

. . . matters of common interest (*al-amr al-'amm*)." The third project, called the "Memo of Ali Zunaybar," launched in 1906, entails the election (*intikhab*) of "a council of enlightened notables led by the best of them" to "adopt reforms and apply them to all governmental interests (*masalih al-hukuma*)." Another project for a constitution of the same year (*mashru' dustur*), calls upon all tribes and towns to elect a representative (*na'ib*) for a parliament (*majlis al-umma*) for the duration of five years. In 1908 two other events occurred demonstrating the change in relations between ruler and ruled, although they are more traditional. The first is the famous conditional pledge of allegiance (*ba'ya*) to Moulay Abdelhafid of 1908 that only after he revokes concessions made to France can he count on the support of the ulama, and the other is a constitutional proposal that goes much further and demands equal treatment of all citizens (called *wataniyyun*) in taxes, the introduction of education for girls, and majority vote (*bi-hukm akthariyya*). Although these proposals are aimed "to spread justice to citizens/persons of the subjects" (*nashr al-'adala fi afrad al-ra'iya*) and call for greater political participation, and, therefore, certainly imply a growing awareness of citizenship and rights, they are described as curtailing despotism but are seen as means of empowering the nation against foreign intervention.[101]

How does the theme of reform in the service of the country return in the next textbook? Again, by far most of the book is devoted to international developments (the fall of the Ottoman Empire, the Wall Street crash, the Russian Revolution, World War II, decolonization in Asia, and the Mashriq). Morocco is analyzed in these larger contexts.[102] Naturally, much attention is given to the background of the establishment of the protectorate in 1912, the installment of Governor-General Lyautey, and his role in "pacifying" Morocco from 1912 to 1936.[103] Revolts are mentioned, especially the Rif revolt of 'Abd al-Karim al-Khattabi (1920–1925). However, in the transition to independence, the role of sultan Muhammad V is stressed and pictures of him giving speeches and press conferences make his image familiar.[104] Competing nationalist parties, such as the Istiqlal Party, are mentioned only in a graph representing the nationalist opposition and its newspapers and are for the rest ignored. Although citizenship is mentioned in Muhammad V's speeches, it is clearly formulated in a passive manner using the term "subjects" (*ra'iya/ra'aya*) rather than the modern term "citizens" (*muwatinun*), which connotes rights. In a 1952 speech he regards citizens as "my subjects" (*ra'ayatuna*) and his benevolent role: "since my ascension to the throne I have exerted myself to improve the conditions of my subjects" (*tahsin ahwal al-ra'iya*). His appropriation of nationalism and the discourse of rights is skillfully made in his critique of the

French for neglecting the "just treatment of rights of my subjects," lack of "respect for the sovereignty of the country," and the "unity of its soil" (*wahdat al-turab*), thus preventing the country from "enjoying its full rights."[105] The absorption is finally legitimized in the last file on the "specificity" (*khususiyya*) of Morocco.

Conclusion

This chapter has demonstrated that the concept of citizenship (*muwatana*) as a bundle of political, economic, social, and political rights does appear in textbooks in Egypt, Tunisia, and Morocco. This is not really surprising as the citizen emerged with the modern state, which derives its legitimacy from representing its citizens. The state has to show that its citizens actively support its policies and that its existence is a historical necessity. Rather the question is in which form citizenship appears and which political interests it serves. As critics have pointed out, citizenship is part of a master narrative of nationalist/religious emancipation and development of the nation. Egyptian history has developed inexorably to the 1952 July Revolution and the development of an all-powerful state from Nasser to Sisi that has absorbed the interests of its citizens by guaranteeing stability, security, and independence. Tunisian history is a master narrative of enlightenment, rationalization, secularization, and nationalist emancipation from the French under the leadership of Bourguiba, while Moroccan history is the narrative of the monarchy as the representative of the people who put their trust in the wisdom of the sultan/monarch, who is also divinely guided.

If there is room for agency of historical actors, creativity, the emergence of alternative movements, subversive ideas, individual intellectuals, or competing political leaders, notions of citizenship and rights, which provide insight into political processes, in textbooks these are always presented as distant in history as possible. In Egypt these occur in the analysis of the power struggle between Mehmed Ali and Umar Makram at the beginning of the nineteenth century, the Urabi Revolution in 1880–1882, and to a lesser extent the 1919 Revolution. In Tunisia, they are found in Europe and especially French history with its human rights, development of a parliamentary system, socialism, and even anarchism. First the Destour Party and later the Neo-Destour represented the demands of the nation in Tunisia. In Morocco, the best examples for the demand of rights go back to the early twentieth century. Only in these specific sections are new terms introduced and pupils given the conceptual instruments to analyze political developments. Concepts of rights, representative government, elections, division of power, pacts, and trust between government and people are analyzed and praised and associated with the rise of a new relationship between citizen and state. At the same time the emergence of these potentially disruptive trends is mostly associated with weaknesses of the political system, increasing foreign economic and political intrusion, and deep divisions within society rather than early attempts at democratization and developing alternative concepts of citizenship and political communities.

In all three cases, the analysis of conflicts and internal debates, leading to alternative historical directions, is ignored. Even if the textbooks are structurally more open, as in Morocco and Tunisia, because they are based on documents rather than closed narratives, the information given on independent movements, internal conflicts, and alternative social movements, except for the few cases mentioned earlier, are insufficient to stimulate debate on historical developments that might challenge the dominant narrative. Socialist, communist, and Islamist movements; liberal intellectuals; and internal dissenters are expunged from history. Social movements such as trade unions and feminist movements, unless they supported the winning party, are silenced. The role of minorities is repressed. In Tunisia, especially an oppositional trend such as the Youssefistes, the followers of Salah ben Youssef, the main opponent of Bourguiba, assassinated by the Tunisian regime in Frankfort in 1961, is not mentioned. Likewise, the Moroccan nationalist Istiqlal Party and its leader, Allal al-Fasi, the main challenger of Mohammed V, is ignored. Remarkable is also that political Islam and Islamic reformist movements hardly figure in these textbooks. The Muslim Brotherhood, founded in 1928 and the largest movement before 1952 in Egypt, is first mentioned when it is part of the political turmoil leading to the July Revolution in 1952. The second time it is mentioned is when it is suppressed under Sisi. Neither is the use of Islamic themes for mobilization of the Tunisian population against the French addressed.

That even Tunisia, often considered as the country to have made a successful transition to democracy, has not been able to write an inclusive, revisionist history since 2011, is surprising.[106] How threatening historical revisionism is for the identity of Tunisia, state legitimacy, and vested political interests is made clear from the sensitivity of the subject.[107] Especially attempts to rehabilitate Salah Ben Youssef have led to violent debates.[108] A reconciliation committee of transitional justice (L'Instance de la Vérité et Dignité) that investigated crimes against humanity, torture, and victims of repression of the regimes of Bourguiba and Ben Ali from 1955 to 2013 was vehemently opposed[109] and failed to rehabilitate the opponents of the regime.[110] Neither have there been attempts to come to terms with the Ben Ali period. As a result, eight years after the revolution, textbooks do not include the history of Ben Ali,[111] and the Ministry of Education actively resists addressing the violation of human rights during the Bourguiba period in school curricula that it controls through its inspectors.[112]

In Egypt it looked as if just after the January 25 Revolution in 2011 the master narrative in textbooks would end. But a report on the effect that this revolution had on history textbooks written between the revolution of 2011 and the military coup d'état in 2013 shows that the revolution was ascribed to the military and not the people. Most of the thirty textbooks analyzed by Patricja Sasnal were left unaltered and written by the same authors. The latest are even anonymous. Their purpose remained the same: to instill a national feeling of pride in Egyptian history, despite its authoritarian past.[113] At some point it seemed that the January 25 Revolution would be completely erased from history,[114] but as we have seen, the Sisi regime managed to incorporate the uprisings into its historical duty to protect the population against chaos.

In Morocco, despite the reevaluation of the repression under King Hassan II, the "Years of Lead," little has changed in the textbooks. No history textbook touches upon these years.[115] Neither has the unified Arabic character of the country been contested, despite the powerful Amazigh (Berber) movements that have demanded equal cultural rights.

This does not mean that history is not contested. Lively internet debates are held on the nature of national history. Since immediately after Ben Ali's fall, Bourguiba's authoritarian, nondemocratic legacy has been heavily challenged in Tunisia,[116] and different groups have demanded rehabilitation of political leaders and the end to the expunging of movements from history.[117] Especially since the emergence of the Islamist movement, attention has been asked for the prominent role of Islam in the formation of Tunisia's history and identity. The same applies to Morocco,[118] where, for instance, Jews demand their inclusion into Moroccan history.[119] The result is that official textbooks are becoming increasingly separated from the reality of society.

Notes

1. Hassani-Idrissi, "Pour une autre réforme de l'enseignement de l'histoire au Maroc."
2. Attalah and Makar, *Nationalism and Homogeneity in Contemporary Curricula.*

3. Hassani-Idrissi, "Manuels d'histoire et identité au Maroc"; Ennaji, "Multiculturalism, Citizenship, and Education in Morocco."

4. Abdou, "'Confused Multiple Deities, Ancient Egyptians Embraced Monotheism.'"

5. Abdou, "Construction(s) of the Nation in Egyptian Textbooks." See also the interview with Mostafa Hassani-Idrissi and Mohammaed El Ayadi in La Rédaction, "Comment est l'histoire enseignée," *Zamane,* January 29, 2019, https://zamane .ma/fr/comment-lhistoire-est-elle-enseignee.

6. Abdou, "Copts in Egyptian History Textbooks."

7. Sebat, "Mon Souhait: l'enseignement du Judaïsme Marocaine."

8. Attalah and Makar, *Nationalism and Homogeneity in Contemporary Curricula,"* p. 14; Abdou, "Construction(s) of the Nation in Egyptian Textbooks," p. 81.

9. Faour and Muasher, *Education for Citizenship in the Arab World,* p. 15.

10. Hassani-Idrissi, "Pour une autre réforme de l'enseignement de l'histoire au Maroc"; Faour and Muasher, *Education for Citizenship in the Arab World;* Ennaji, "Multiculturalism, Citizenship, and Education in Morocco."

11. There is no history of citizenship for the Middle East and North Africa. For attempts to collect contemporary research on the topic in all its diverse forms, see Meijer and Butenschøn, *The Crisis of Citizenship in the Arab World;* Butenschøn and Meijer, *The Middle East in Transition;* and Meijer, Sater, and Babar, *The Routledge Handbook of Citizenship in the Middle East and North Africa.*

12. The history textbooks almost all end with the attaining of independence; only the Egyptian ones continue to the present.

13. For a recent nuanced work on this topic, see Sharkey, *A History of Muslims, Christians and Jews in the Middle East.*

14. Campos, *Ottoman Brothers.*

15. See, for instance, Julia Phillips Cohen, *Becoming Ottomans.*

16. See, for instance, the article on Boutros Boustani (1819–1883) by Makdisi, "After 1860."

17. Thompson, *Colonial Citizens.*

18. Fahmy, *Ordinary Egyptians.*

19. Robson, *States of Separation.*

20. See Meijer, "From Colonial to Authoritarian Pact."

21. Maghraoui, *Liberalism Without Democracy.*

22. See Beinin and Lockman, *Workers on the Nile.*

23. Dawisha, *Iraq,* pp. 47, 59.

24. Meijer, *The Quest for Modernity.*

25. Perkins, *A History of Modern Tunisia,* pp. 95–129.

26. Ismail, *Political Life in Cairo's New Quarters.*

27. Baker, *Islam Without Fear.*

28. The report in Faour and Muasher, *Education for Citizenship in the Arab World* (p. 8) makes a distinction between "civic education" and "citizenship education"; the first is minimal while the latter is broader and based on critical thinking.

29. Ibid., p. 1.

30. Ibid.

31. Hinnebusch, "Liberalization Without Democratization in 'Post-Populist' Authoritarian States."

32. For an analysis of recent citizen movements in the Rif in Morocco and in Iraq, see Meijer, "Economic Deprivation, Political Corruption and the Rise of New Citizen Movements in the MENA Region."

33. *Kitab al-tarikh li-tilamidh al-sana al-thalitha min ta'lim al-thanawi: al-Adab wa-l-iqtisad wa tasarruf,* No. 3 (Wizara al-Tarbiyya, no date); *Kitab al-tarikh li-tilamidh al-sana al-thalitha min ta'lim al-thani: Sha'b 'ilmiyya,* No. 3 (Wizarat al-Tarbiyya, no date).

34. Although they have no date, they are still in use because they have been chosen from the list of 2018–2019 schoolbooks: *Fi Rihab al-Tarikh, Al-Sana al-awla min silk al-bakaluriya: maslik al-adab wa-l-'ulum al-insaniyya: maslik al-lugha al-'arabiyya bi-l-ta'lim al-asil* (Kitab al-Tilmidh wa-l-Tilmidha, Wizarat al-Tarbiya wa-l-Takwin al-Mahani, no date); *Fi rihab al-tarikh* (Kitab al-Tilmith wa-l-Tilmitha, Wizarat al-Tarbiya al-Wataniyya wal-Takwin al-Mahani, 2016) for second year of the baccalaureate.

35. *Silsila al-imtihan fi al-tarikh Misr al-hadara li-l-saff awwal al-thanawi 2018: Kitab al-Sharh* (Cairo: Dawliyya li-l-Tiba' wa-l-Nashr, 2017); *Silsila al-imtihan 2018 fi-l-tarikh Misr wal-'Arab al-hadith li-l-saff thalith al-thanawi,* Part 1 *khass bi-l-sharh* (Cairo: Dawliyya li-l-Tiba' wa-l-Nashr, 2017).

36. 'Asim al-Disuqi et al., *Tarikh Misr wa-l-'Arab al-hadith li-l-saff al-thalith al-thanawi* (no publisher, no date). It is for school year 2015–2016 and probably published in 2015.

37. *Silsila al-imtihan 2018 fi-l-tarikh Misr wa al-'Arab al-hadith li-l-saff thalith al-thanawi,* Part 1, *khass bi-l-sharh* (Cairo: Dawliyya li-l-Tiba' wa-l-Nashr, 2017).

38. *Kitab al-muwad al-ijtima'iyya li-tilamidh al-sana al-sabi'a al-ta'lim al-asasi: al-tarikh, al-jiughrafiya al-tarbiya al-madaniyya* (Wizarat al-Tarbiya, no date), No. 7; *Kitab al-muwad al-ijtima'iyya li-tilamith al-sana al-thamina mij ta'lim al-asasi,* No. 8; *Tarikh, al-jiughrafiya al-tarbiya al-madaniyya* (Wizarat al-Tarbiya, no date); *Kitab al-muwad al-ijtima'iyya li-tilamith al-sana al-tasi'a min ta'lim al-asasi* (Wizarat al-Tarbiya, no date), No. 9.

39. See, for instance, *Kitab al-muwad al-ijtima'iyya li-tilamidh al-sana al-sabi'a al-ta'lim al-asasi: al-tarikh, al-jiughrafiya al-tarbiya al-madaniyya* (Wizarat al-Tarbiya, no date), No. 7, pp. 211–280.

40. Raghavan, "In New Egyptian Textbooks, 'It's Like the Revolution Didn't Happen.'"

41. *Silsila al-Imtiham fi al-tarikh Misr al-hadara,* p. 43.

42. Ibid., p. 47.

43. Ibid., p. 62.

44. Ibid., p. 76.

45. Ibid., p. 79.

46. Ibid., p. 89.

47. 'Asim al-Disuqi et al., introduction to *Tarikh Misr wa-l-'Arab al-hadith li-l-saff al-thalith al-thanawi* (probably 2015).

48. *Silsila al-imtihan fi al-tarikh: tarikh Misr, wa-l-'Arab al-hadith,* 2018.

49. Di-Capua, *Gatekeepers of the Arab Past;* Gorman, *Historians, State and Politics in Twentieth Century Egypt.*

50. *Tarikh Misr, wa-l-'Arab al-hadith,* pp. 9, 12.

51. Ibid., p. 18.

52. Ibid., pp. 18–19.

53. Ibid., p. 49. For more on the Urabi revolution, see Juan Cole, *Colonialism and Revolution in the Middle East.*

54. *Tarikh Misr, wa-l-'Arab al-hadith,* p. 52.

55. Ibid., pp. 74–77. For the version in the preparatory textbook, see *Silsila al-imtihan 2018 fi al-tarikh Misr, wa-l-'Arab al-hadith,* p. 112.

56. The liberal history of Egypt has been heavily contested as paternalistic and Orientalist. See Maghraoui, *Liberalism Without Democracy.*

57. *Tarikh Misr, wa-l-ʿArab al-hadith,* pp. 81–89.

58. Ibid. See chapter 5 on the expansion of imperialism in Arab countries before World War I until independence and chapter 6 on the expansion of imperialism in Arab countries in the Ottoman Empire after World War I.

59. *Tarikh Misr, wa-l-ʿArab al-hadith,* chapter 8.

60. Ibid., p. 162.

61. Ibid., p. 165.

62. *Silsila al-imtihan 2018 fi-l-tarikh Misr wa al-ʿArab al-hadith li-l-saff thalith al-thanawi,* Part 1, *khass bi-l-sharh* (Cairo: Dawliyya li-l-Tibaʿ wa-l-Nashr, 2017), p. 60.

63. Ibid., pp. 86–87.

64. Ibid., p. 102. A caption enumerates the diversity of the political parties, giving the impression of chaos.

65. Ibid., p. 108.

66. *Kitab al-tarikh li-tilamith al-sana al-thalitha min al-taʿlim al-thanawi: shaʿb ʿilmiyya,* "Introduction," p. 4.

67. Ibid.

68. *Kitab al-tarikh li-tilamidh al-sana al-thalitha min al-taʿlim al-thanawi: al-adab, wa-l-iqtisad wa-l-tasarruf.*

69. *Kitab al-tarikh li-tilamidh al-sana al-thalitha min al-taʿlim al-thanawi: shaʿb ʿIlmi* (Tunis: al-Jumhuriyya al-Tunisiyya Wizara al-Tarbiya, al-Markaz al-Watani al-Baidaghuji, 2017).

70. For more on Bourguiba's relations with France, see Camau and Geisser, *Habib Bourguiba.*

71. *Kitab al-Tarikh li-Tilamidh al-Sana al-Thalitha min al-Taʿlim al-Thanawi: Shaʿb ʿIlmi,* pp. 8–9.

72. Ibid., pp. 14–17.

73. Ibid., pp. 18–32.

74. For the reproduction of the Security Covenant, see *Kitab al-Tarikh li-Tilamidh al-Sana al-Thalitha min al-Taʿlim al-Thanawi: Shaʿb ʿIlmi,* p. 77, and for its analysis, pp. 86 and 91.

75. For the full text of the Bardo Treaty, see *Kitab al-Tarikh li-Tilamidh al-Sana al-Thalitha min al-Taʿlim al-Thanawi: Shaʿb ʿIlmi,* pp. 97–98. For the full text of the La Marsa Convention, see pp. 99 and 105.

76. *Kitab al-Tarikh li-Tilamidh al-Sana al-Thalitha min al-Taʿlim al-Thanawi: Shaʿb ʿIlmi,* pp. 90–92.

77. European and international developments are given ample attention on pages 108–158.

78. See Document 2, concerning the joint Algerian-Tunisian letter sent to President Wilson, p. 178.

79. See "Explanation," p. 180.

80. See Document 7, on the program of the Destour Party, p. 182.

81. Document 9, on the unity of the Destour Party, p. 183.

82. Document 15, on the bylaws of the Tunisian Trade Union of 1924, p. 186.

83. *Kitab al-tarikh li-tilamidh al-sana al-thalitha min al-taʿlim al-thanawi: shaʿb ʿilmi,* p. 206.

84. Ibid., p. 230.

85. Ibid., p. 232.

86. Ibid., pp. 232–235.

87. Ibid., pp. 237–256.

88. Perkins, *A History of Modern Tunisia,* pp. 115–121, 126–129.

89. See, for instance, Bessis and Belhassan, *Bourguiba.*

90. For more on the event, see Pennell, *Morocco Since 1830,* pp. 137–141.

91. *Fi rihab al-tarikh: al-Sana al-awla min silk al-bakaluriya* (Dar al-'Alamiyya li-l-Kitab, 2016), intended for fifteen-year-olds.

92. *Fi rihab al-tarikh: al-Sana al-al-thaniyya min silk al-bakaluriya* (Dar al-'Alamiyya li-l-Kitab, 2016); this book is meant for children of sixteen.

93. *Fi rihab al-tarikh: al-Sana al-awla min silk al-bakaluriya,* pp. 17–26.

94. Ibid., pp. 46–47.

95. Ibid., pp. 66–67.

96. Ibid., p. 122.

97. Ibid., p. 148.

98. Ibid., pp. 125–140. On "certain factors leading to the backwardness of Islamic society," see p. 140.

99. Ibid., p. 156.

100. Ibid., p. 188.

101. Ibid., pp. 197–200.

102. *Fi rihab al-tarikh: al-Sana al-al-thaniyya min silk al-bakaluriya* (Dar al-'Alamiyya li-l-Kitab, 2016), pp. 53–58.

103. Ibid., pp. 63–83.

104. Ibid., pp. 98–103.

105. Ibid.; see Documents 17, 18, and 19 on p. 160.

106. Lucenti, "La nouvelle réforme scolaire en Tunisie."

107. Lakhal, "Interview avec Sghaier Salhi."

108. Ben Hédi, "Tunisie."

109. Ben Hamadi, "Au cœur de l'IVD: 60 ans d'histoire à reconstituer."

110. Verdier, "Il faudrait un audit pour sauver la justice transitionnelle en Tunisie."

111. Vidano, "Dans les manuels scolaires, l'Histoire de la Tunisie s'arrête en 1964.

112. "Pour l'Instance Vérité et Dignité, le ministre de l'Éducation Hatem Ben Salem empêche ses directeurs généraux de participer aux activités de l'IVD," *Huffpost,* November 29, 2017, https://www.huffpostmaghreb.com/2017/11/29/ministere -de-leducation-i_n_18680488.html.

113. Sasnal, *Myths and Legends.*

114. Raghavan, "In New Egyptian Textbooks."

115. La Rédaction, "Comment est l'histoire enseignée," *Zamane,* January 29, 2019.

116. An early example of this debate on "authoritarian democracy" is represented in Borsali, *Bourguiba à l'épreuve de la démocratie, 1956–1963,* and Ghorbal, *Orphelins de Bourguiba et héritier du prophète.*

117. Dahmani, "Tahar Ben Ammar."

118. Hassani-Idrissi, "Pour une autre réforme," p. 74.

119. Sebat, "Mon Souhait."

4

University Reforms in Egypt and Morocco

Florian Kohstall

In the 1980s, Jamil Salmi, the coordinator of the World Bank's tertiary education program from 2006 to 2012 and a leading figure in university reform, emphasized an interesting paradox of education reform in Morocco: for the political elite, debating higher-education reform packages figures very prominently on the agenda. In a country with high rates of illiteracy and low educational enrollment, however, this reform rhetoric concerns only a relatively small part of the population. Reforming higher education, he argues, would be primarily a distraction from other pressing issues in the field of social policy.[1] From being a critic of the focus of debate on educational policy, a decade later Jamil Salmi had become an important advocate for university reform. As a lead author of the World Bank's "Building Knowledge Societies" report, he was one of the main promoters of building world-class universities in developing countries as a means to overcome the knowledge gap and reach international competitive standards, such as in university rankings and publication indicators.[2]

Jamil's career trajectory reflects the change of paradigm in higher-education policy in the Middle East and North Africa (MENA), though more in rhetoric than in realities on the ground. While access issues, such as student enrollment and the expansion of university infrastructure, have long dominated reform efforts, recently the discourse on creating knowledge societies has become the omnipresent jargon of reform. Despite this shift in focus, the gap between reform rhetoric and practices persists. As Grindle observes in this volume (Chapter 9), the commitment to education, especially access to it, is a popular platform, regardless of regime type, but relatively few steps are undertaken to engage in comprehensive reform processes. Each time a comprehensive process is initiated, its implementation remains piecemeal and discontinuous.

The possibility of comprehensive reform is an optimistic vision promoted by governments and development agencies. Especially in the higher-education sector, fundamental changes are rare, and if they occur, they typically are the product of a complex mix of tools and practices introduced by different actors on different levels, from international agencies to domestic policymakers to the different lower-level stakeholders, such as university administrators, professors, and professional associations. For example, the so-called Bologna process in Europe acted as a magic wand for reform in many European countries after decades of within-country debates without tangible intermediate results. The Bologna process reminds us how a rather spontaneous meeting of educational leaders in an appropriate setting can trigger unexpected results. This process initiated on a transnational level by a statement of intent has affected universities more than any other national reform plan in the two decades that preceded it, primarily through the introduction of European-wide harmonization of study programs and a joint credit system.[3]

In order to understand inadequacies of university reforms in the countries of the Middle East and North Africa, we have to set aside the vision of comprehensive reform. Higher-education policy is not a linear process from problem-identification through agenda-setting to implementation and evaluation. Given population growth in the Arab region, the challenge of reforming universities is enormous. The sheer magnitude of the challenge is further enhanced by the reluctance of ruling elites to risk real reforms, and by the resistance of those crucial for their success, including professors and students. As reflected in the case studies of Egypt and Morocco in this chapter, comprehensive plans typically fail because they ignore the embeddedness of the system and the path dependency of actors highly resistant to change. Between rapid population growth, financial restrictions, and the priority of security over autonomy, and the fact that most reform models are necessarily imported, there remains little room in which comprehensive reforms can be conceived and implemented.

This chapter approaches the political economy of education reform in the MENA region by comparing how two countries that differ widely in their higher-education systems and their structures of governance have been influenced by international norms to reform their university systems. Reform processes initiated in the early 1990s in Egypt and Morocco aimed at moving from concern only with continuous expansion of higher education to upgrading the quality of education, mainly by setting incentives for faculty members to undertake pedagogical reforms, most especially those focused on curricula. In both countries, the World Bank had a crucial impact in putting reform on the agenda and then in preparing action plans. The policies that were adopted then determine the debate until today. By and large, declared reform goals have not been met in either case. The comparison of Egypt, which has the largest university system in the Arab world, to Morocco, a middle-size country in terms of higher education, provides insights into how different countries in the region cope with the imperative of reform stimulated by internationalization and why achievements remain limited. Ultimately, the chapter questions internationalization as the appropriate framework for university reform in the Arab world and highlights several specific problems, many of which result from the authoritarian governance of Arab universities. This problem is typically neglected by international organizations and their best-practice models deemed universally appropriate by them. Framed in terms of state capacity this raises a twofold question: the ability of the state to cope with internationally induced reform pressure on the one hand, and the ability of specific reform actors within the state to introduce change in highly centralized and state-controlled systems. The interplay of international actors with domestic constituencies is the crucial nexus in order to explain reform results and to illustrate more broadly how regimes interact with international actors when their primary concern is to maintain power. The main evidence upon which the chapter draws is provided by reform commissions and committees in Morocco and Egypt in the 1990s and 2000s and the impacts of international donor organizations on them. While there have been some important changes in policymaking since the 2010–2011 uprisings, recent developments show how the networks previously established still play a prominent role in the reform process. Before addressing the reforms of the past two decades, I will consider how internationalization as the dominant paradigm of university reform is reconciled with legacies of higher-education development in Egypt and Morocco.

Internationalization and University Autonomy

Today the internationalization of higher education appears in numerous forms. It concerns student and faculty exchanges, binational study programs, and the establishment of offshore campuses. One cannot imagine any reform without the participation of bilateral and international donor agencies and reference to what happens elsewhere. In addition, the worldwide comparison of universities through international rankings preoccupies university administrators and faculty members, to say nothing of political leaders.

Internationalization is broadly defined as the policies and practices undertaken by academic systems and institutions—and even individuals—to cope with the global academic environment. The motivations for internationalization include commercial advantage, knowledge and language acquisition, enhancing the curriculum with international content, and many others. Specific initiatives such as branch campuses, cross-border collaborative arrangements, programs for international students, establishing English-medium programs and degrees, and others, have been put in place as part of internationalization. Efforts to monitor international initiatives and ensure quality are integral to the international higher-education environment.[4]

The definition illustrates already that internationalization encompasses a wide range of measures introduced by different actors on different levels. Egypt now hosts branch campuses and foreign universities. Together with Morocco it is the country most open to joint programs with the European Union (EU). Both countries are the champions in the MENA region in participating in Erasmus+ and Horizon 2020 projects, the EU's main programs to stimulate mobility and transnational cooperation in teaching and research.[5] Egypt, with its large department supervising overseas study, has been sending PhD students with scholarships abroad for decades. It was the main provider of professors for the emerging higher-education systems in the Gulf Cooperation Council (GCC) countries, Iraq, and the Maghreb. Until today, its universities attract students from African countries and Asia, although in declining proportionate numbers. Morocco relies until now on France as its main donor of development aid, especially in the field of culture and education. From an importer of reform, it has become an exporter of reform for the Bologna process–inspired LMD (license, master, doctorate) system toward sub-Saharan francophone Africa. However, despite their openness, the university ecosystems in both countries remain highly centralized, university governance structures resist attempts to adapt to international norms, and, due to financial limits and visa restrictions, most students remain untouched by the international programs that have been introduced over the decades.

While internationalization could be perceived as the main driver for university reform worldwide, the lack of university autonomy and academic freedom, together with rapid population growth, inhibits many reform initiatives in the population-rich countries of the Middle East and North Africa. The lack of university autonomy, a strong characteristic of university governance in all Arab countries except Lebanon, where all universities except one are private, is the principal obstacle to internationalization.[6] As stated in the preceding definition, internationalization is driven by many different actors, including universities themselves. By restricting their autonomy, states prevent universities and their members from choosing their own reform paths.

A History of Fragmentation and Parallel Systems

The history of higher education in Egypt and the Middle East thus remains a history of fragmentation and concurring legacies. Since the establishment of professional schools by Muhammed Ali Pasha in the nineteenth century, Egyptian rulers in most cases preferred to bypass existing universities (e.g., Al-Azhar) in order to introduce change into higher education. Instead of reforming existing institutions, reformers established new ones to realize their reform ambitions. In the beginning of the twentieth century, Cairo University was established in the midst of the anticolonial struggle by nationalist leaders to serve as a paradigm for modern secular universities. The model spread over large parts of the Middle East, but the university's autonomy lasted for only two decades before it came under state control and became subservient to the political and economic goals of the postcolonial order.[7] Only the American University in Cairo managed to preserve its special autonomous status, due to a state treaty between the United States and Egypt.

Different legacies have shaped the rapid expansion of post-independence higher education, key of which were Gamal Adbul Nasser's policies of universal access and government job guarantees for graduates. Financial constraints and security concerns began to overtake these policies. In the 1980s the job guarantee was modified and then finally abandoned in practice. The remuneration system for professors became linked to their teaching load, transforming the university into an institution of recitation and repetition. Security concerns were forced high onto the agenda in the 1970s, when leftist and Islamist groups struggled for control of student bodies on university campuses. Under the tutelage of President Abd al-Fattah al-Sisi, security concerns have been ratcheted up yet more.

Egyptian public universities, some of them enrolling more than 250,000 students, must now compete with newly created private universities such as the German University of Cairo or the British University in Egypt, not only for funding and faculty, but also for political and public attention. While reforms of the public higher-education system largely failed under Mubarak, there is a strong move of entrepreneurs and philanthropists to build up a parallel system. Still contested, this parallel private system that caters largely to reasonably well-off students is also a product of internationally inspired reforms. While such universities are mostly established for profit, with little time or money spent on research, international donors typically praise them as lighthouses in an ocean that might one day become the new centers of educational excellence in the region.[8]

Egypt: The World Bank and Its Engineers

The new enthusiasm for higher-education reform expressed by international donor organizations such as the World Bank after the end of the Cold War and first implemented in Eastern Europe and former member states of the collapsed Soviet Union, swept after a certain delay into North Africa. By the end of the 1990s Egypt and Morocco were involved in loan negotiations to reform their higher-education systems. Both countries not only adopted the rhetoric of reform, from establishing excellency universities to systems of quality assurance, but also emulated practices of so-called good governance by appearing to include a wide range of stakeholders into the policymaking process.

Egypt's higher-education reform process over the past three decades can be roughly divided into three phases. In the first phase, which commenced in the 1990s, successive governments under president Hosni Mubarak initiated a process of widening the scope of participation in university reform. Through the law on private universities, promulgated in 1994, they allowed philanthropists and entrepreneurs to establish private universities in a so-far state-dominated system. This added a new component to a higher-education landscape made up only of public universities, Al-Azhar, the American University in Cairo, and the widely neglected and low-performing technical colleges. After the establishment of the first private universities, domestic policymakers also attempted to change public universities in order to improve their quality, through a grant-based approach sponsored mainly by the World Bank, but also by other donors. The second, very short phase, was triggered by the 2011 popular uprisings. Political protests quickly spilled over onto campuses and opened a window of opportunity for university reform through the election of university presidents and deans, accompanied by a vibrant debate on student participation and curricula reform.[9] This window was shut down when the political transition phase came to an end with the military coup of 2013, initiating the third phase, during which steps toward more university autonomy and academic freedom were halted as university campuses were increasingly securitized. Previous reform plans initiated under Mubarak became dead letters. Under the rule of Sisi, new mega-projects have been put forward in part to distract public attention from the deficiencies of public institutions, including higher-education ones.[10]

The Shift from Access Orientation to Quality Reforms

Addressing now the first phase in greater detail, the reform process of public universities under Mubarak officially started in 1998 with the establishment of the National Committee for Higher Education Reform. Formed by the minister for higher education and scientific research, Moufid Shehab, this committee included a relatively wide range of stakeholders, among them university presidents, deans, educational experts, and representatives from different formal opposition parties. The committee was in charge of elaborating a national reform plan, which it presented to the 1999 National Conference organized by the Supreme Council of Universities, Egypt's governing body for universities. The committee's work and the conference received financial support from the World Bank, and the latter was held in the presence of numerous international education experts who presented best-practice examples for university reform.[11] The process was unprecedented in that it included a wide range of actors charged with devising a national action plan that would facilitate the shift from quantity to quality in higher education. While some of those involved still advocated quantity over quality of reforms, including free and unlimited access to higher education and building of new universities, a new coalition emerged that aimed at focusing on curricular reform, teacher training, and making the university attain international standards. The World Bank made good governance a precondition to grant a loan for the so-called Higher Education Enhancement Program (HEEP). However, only six out of the twenty proposals of the national action plan received funding. The World Bank decided not to include politically controversial and financially costly projects such as a raise in professorial salaries and a reform of the central admission system, led by the Maktab al-Tansiq (Office of "Coordination," meaning University Placement), that allocates study places according to student scores on the high school secondary certification examination. Instead it preferred to widen the scope of participation through a grant-based approach that would include faculty members in the implementation phase of the program by encouraging the development of new teaching programs, the establishment of a national system for quality assurance and accreditation, and the reform of the departments of education to train primary and secondary school teachers. A national university information system and the reform of technical colleges also received seed funding. HEEP was a novel, cautious attempt by the World Bank and other donors to introduce a set of measures aimed at improving quality of rather than access to education.

The Limits of Pluralization

The coalition network that emerged from this process included those who defended quality-centered reforms. This coalition was dominated by a group of professors from the faculty of engineering of Cairo University. Those professors had previously been involved in the reform of the faculties of engineering in Egypt's public universities through a pilot project financed by the World Bank in the early 1990s. Through this project they were well connected to international organizations and familiar with examples of best practices, benchmarking, and standards set by the World Bank. After implementing the reform of the engineering faculties, the World Bank aimed at generalizing the reform for all public universities with the support of professors from the pilot project. These professors prepared several reports and studies, which later served as guidelines for the national reform plan. Though not a homogeneous group, they were all trained at foreign universities in France, Germany, and the United States and brought with them the ideas of implementing certain foreign models in order to reform Egyptian public universities. When the World Bank adopted the HEEP loan and the project started, these professors occupied key positions in the Ministry of Higher Education and in a specially created reform unit within it. One of them, Hani Mahfouz Helal, became minister of higher education in 2006.

The Egyptian reform process initiated at the end of the 1990s displays several features that can be directly linked to the configuration and reconfiguration of the political regime. From its beginning, inclusion was limited in the Egyptian reform process. No Islamists, no leftists, no students, and no critical professors were formally consulted. The minister of higher education and research, who formed the committee, was careful not to expand participation beyond the realm of the ruling

National Democratic Party (NDP) and officially sanctioned opposition parties. The composition of the committee thus illustrated the limits of pluralization in Egypt. Once the reform plan was initiated, with the loan provided by the World Bank, the NDP tried to capture, hence to jeopardize, the program. Gamal Mubarak, the president's son, created in 2003 a policy secretariat with several subcommittees within the NDP. He made education reform a top priority and brought in Hossam Badrawi—the owner of several hospitals and an acclaimed expert in education policies—as head of the committee in order to revive the debate on education reform also within the parliament. Badrawi drew up his own reform plan that included again the expansion of higher-education access through the establishment of new universities. Thus, the consensus reached with the World Bank was again subject to debate, a step that the Bank considered as an unnecessary politization of the reform.[12] While the engineers were energetic in touring Egyptian universities with their PowerPoint presentations of the newly designed grant schemes, they received but tepid support from the NDP, and hence little support within Egypt's public universities. With their workshops and training sessions, they reached only a small proportion of faculty members, mostly in those departments that do not suffer from the structural problems of overcrowding, namely the sciences. Many measures remained what World Bank projects often are: an isolated pilot that never reaches the stage of comprehensive reform. It is symptomatic that the different reform units established to implement the World Bank–sponsored reform were placed in a newly equipped building far from the universities and the Ministry of Higher Education. In the ministry, a strategic planning unit for the World Bank's project was placed on a separate, well-renovated floor to impress donor organizations, while the rest of the ministry's bureaucracy and structure remained untouched by these modernization efforts. A greater focus was meanwhile placed on such highly visible projects as the establishment of a National Agency for Accreditation and Evaluation, into which Hossam Badrawi successfully placed his sister Nadia as head of the project.

Egypt's higher-education reform was also affected by the intrafactional struggle within the National Democratic Party, which reached its heights during the 2005 parliamentary elections.[13] It became part of the contentious politics that surrounded those elections and could be perceived as a harbinger of the Arab uprisings.[14] In opposition to the plan to establish the National Agency for Accreditation and Evaluation, a group of professors opposed this national system in the absence of clear guidelines and consultation with faculty members. The March 9 movement in 2004 asked for the reinstatement of the autonomy of the university. The group formed parallel to the at least symbolically powerful movement Kifaya (Enough), which protested the president's attempt to position his son as a possible successor. Several persons were linked to both movements. Thus, the reform initiated with the World Bank was also a victim of Egypt's ongoing political crisis, in which several policy reforms were used by Gamal Mubarak and his group in order to present himself as successor to his father.

After the Uprising

The 2011 uprising introduced a short but significant change for the direction of the reform process. The agenda was now dominated by the protests, which quickly spilled over to campuses. Students and professors demanded removal of the old guard from campuses and protection of academic freedom. During 2011 and 2012, elections for deans and university presidents were held, initially spontaneously and then uniformly at all public universities, although in the absence of an established legal framework. The reform of the university law and student by-laws remained under debate, and these laws have not yet been officially adopted. The elections frequently brought the old guard back into power again and were criticized for polarizing, even corrupting, the faculty. Despite such setbacks, stakeholders in universities appreciated the new spirit of debate and openness that had been stimulated by innumerable campus events and by the reestablished Egyptian National Student Union, an organization that had been banned since the end of the 1970s.

This spirit came to a halt immediately after the 2013 coup, when new restrictions were imposed on universities. In October 2014, universities were among public institutions placed under military control, thereby allowing the military to enter campuses while rendering crimes on campus subject to military prosecution. University presidents were given the right to expel students for a broad range of offenses, including "subverting the educational process, endangering university facilities, targeting members of the academic and administrative staff or inciting violence on campuses."[15] In subsequent steps university presidents were also given the right to refer teaching staff to disciplinary boards "for participating in partisan activities," among other vague offenses. Sisi thus turned back the clock of the 2011 uprising, which had introduced a vibrant debate on campus on the self-governance of the university. An unprecedented wave of arrests on campuses followed.[16] This brought a climate of fear on all levels to universities, making any reform from within a university extremely difficult. Parallel to the crackdown on university professors and students, a commitment was formed with the adoption of a new constitution aimed at increasing annual spending on university teaching and research. It was, however, not clear how this spending could be efficiently allocated, given the huge constraints posed on the governance of universities. This funding has not been forthcoming. Instead money has been spent in association with new mega-projects, such as a sprawling international campus in the newly established administrative capital for joint study programs with foreign universities. Sisi's policy seems in line with further "diversifying" higher education and pushing the privatization of the early 1990s toward a new level. In these new efforts, the president relies on the old networks.

When al-Sisi seized power in 2013, he did not place Mubarak's network of supporters in the first row. His nomination of ministers suggested the consolidation of the security forces and the military in the government. Still, the reform entrepreneurs from the faculty of engineering retain a certain influence on university reform until now. In 2011, when the consequences of the 2011 uprising reached universities, namely with the election of university presidents and faculty deans, and when the universities affirmed their autonomy and became the main actors of reform, the engineers disappeared from the scene. But this remained a short intermezzo. Already during the rule of Mohamed Morsi they appeared again at meetings and conferences, organized by international and bilateral donor organizations. For many donors, the "youth revolution" was a good reason to invest in higher education in order to respond to the discontent of students that had indeed played an important role in the uprising.[17] In the name of Egypt's new, yet uncertain "transition," they organized numerous conferences with domestic stakeholders. If they aimed at attracting the new actors of the revolution, they had only limited access to these new intermediaries and lacked trust in the still widely unknown "youth without leaders." Thus, they relied to a great extent on the engineers for issuing invitations to these conferences. Through their expertise and their close links to donors, the engineers remain an indispensable resource for the Ministry of Higher Education. They are, for example, in charge of identifying international partners for the implementation of Sisi's new projects, namely the university projects for the new capital, promoted by the law on the establishment and organization of international branch campuses. The yet difficult-to-identify policy networks under Sisi illustrate that there are several circles, between which new and old actors circulate relatively freely. Donors do play a major role in keeping these circles and networks alive, not only through training but also through renewing the actors' social and political capital through participation in projects and international and national conferences.

Thus, Egypt's university reform, initially prepared with the World Bank, illustrates not just how the regime under Mubarak crafted the World Bank's quest for good governance according to the configuration of its political regime. It also illustrates how a group of reform entrepreneurs may survive the ruptures of Egypt's uprising and transition. If such ruptures contribute to the emergence of new actors, these new actors do not necessarily replace the old ones. In this regard, donors and their reference to internationalization not only contribute to the reproduction of established policy networks, but also are a major obstacle to change, stabilizing the limited-access order in reform networks.[18]

Morocco: University Managers Versus Ministers

Comparing Egypt with Morocco reveals a different scenario of implementing the politics of internationalization in the university sector. The roots of the still-ongoing process also date back to the 1990s. The World Bank as in Egypt had a crucial impact on framing the crisis of higher education and putting its reform on the agenda. However, in the implementation phase, the adaptation of international norms was mainly shaped by Morocco's former colonial power, France. The comparison of Egypt's and Morocco's reform process not only illustrates the crucial interplay of different multilateral and bilateral donors, but also underlines how regime configurations determine the reform process and how this process is driven by different change teams. Compared to Egypt's presidential regime, Morocco's "globalizing monarchy"[19] is characterized by party pluralism and relatively vibrant professional associations and civil society actors, all acting beneath the supremacy of the palace. These actors also buffer reform demands and are used by the palace to diffuse reform pressure.

In contrast to Egypt, Morocco survived the Arab uprisings without having to replace the head of state. To tame the February 20 protest in 2011, King Mohammed VI established the Consultative Commission for the Reform of the Constitution, which prepared constitutional changes adopted via referendum in June 2011. Moreover, he accelerated the establishment of the Economic and Social Council, reactivated the National Initiative for Human Development, and granted more independence to the National Council on Human Rights. In combination with anticipated parliamentary elections and the subsequent change in government—entrusted for the first time to Islamist Justice and Development Party leader Abdelilah Benkirane—this strategy effectively weakened the 2011 protests.[20] In reacting to the 2011 protests, Mohammed VI deployed a "governance toolkit" that had already proved successful under the rule of his father and had been improved during the past decade. The highly controversial issue of education reform was at the center of this toolkit.

The King's Consensus-Building

The origins of Morocco's current higher-education reform can be traced back to the mid-1990s when King Hassan II tried to integrate the socialist opposition party into the government, shortly before his son Mohammed VI succeeded him in 1999. In 1995, the king made use of a World Bank report on the crisis of Morocco's education system in order to reject a parliamentary report spearheaded by the opposition. After assigning the leader of the Socialist Union of Popular Forces (USFP) party, Abderrahmane Youssoufi, to government responsibilities, he announced the establishment of the Special Commission for Education and Training (COSEF). This commission was composed of senior officials from all political parties and professional syndicates as well as representatives of nongovernmental organizations (NGOs) active in the education sector. The commission was meant to establish a national consensus on education policy, in particular on the most controversial issues, such as on the use of the Arabic language and tuition-free education.[21] After only four months of debate, the parties presented the Charter on Education and Training. The charter was intended to serve as a "moral compass" for education policy regardless of which party would be in government.[22]

The decisionmaking process in Morocco differed significantly from that in Egypt as far as pluralism and representation were concerned. By integrating the country's most important political parties and syndicates, the palace could pretend to represent the diversity of Morocco's political landscape and, above all, integrate different political currents from leftist to Islamist into the political process. While the king's adviser Meziane Belfkih and his experts closely monitored the commission proceedings, most political parties, syndicates, and experts accepted the palace's tutelage. Through this type of inclusion into the policy process, the palace built a buffer against contentious politics. Powerful syndicates like the National Syndicate for Higher Education (SNEsup) entered the realm of politics through participation in COSEF and, in exchange, they had to refrain from protest, at least temporarily. The socialist USFP, at the time in government, had to accept that education reform, one of its key interests, would have to be negotiated with the palace. Thus, COSEF was also a mechanism to concentrate decision-making in the palace's hands while providing the donor community with the image of a participatory process.

Selecting University Leaders

In Morocco, the implementation phase of the reform appeared thorough and comprehensive. Unlike Egypt, where reform was introduced through financial incentives for existing faculty, Morocco's university reform started from the top through a change in universities' leadership. After all political parties approved a university law in 2000, a new system for selecting university presidents and faculty deans was implemented. Faculty members suggested three candidates through elections, but the final selection of the candidate was left to the palace. According to the Charter on Education and Training and the new university law this selection process should grant more autonomy to the university. But through carefully using the power of having the final say, the palace affirmed its direct control over universities. In case the selection of the faculty did not meet the expectations of the palace, the list was sent back to the university. Instead of strengthening the autonomy of the university, the new nomination procedure was a tool to strengthen ties with powerful stakeholders and to clientelize them. The new university presidents became the main actors in the reform. In line with what happens in many universities in the world, university presidents became real managers of their institutions. This new responsibility in the hands of university presidents localized protest and thus made it easier to diffuse.[23]

A good example of the new power of university presidents was the introduction of the so-called license, master, doctorate system in 2003. As discussed earlier for the Bologna process, this French adaptation of the process acted also in Morocco like a magic wand for a reform that had long been debated. Since the approval of the new university law in 2000, the Ministry of Higher Education had set up several commissions and committees to discuss the establishment of a new pedagogical framework for universities. Different foreign models were considered, but no consensus was reached on how they could be implemented and translated into new courses and curricula. When the minister had to step down in 2002, a committee composed of university presidents and professors seized this opportunity to finalize the pedagogical reform draft, endorsing the LMD system as the best solution. The new minister had no choice but to adopt it, if he wanted to move forward with reform.[24] The reform was presented as a necessity, with no alternative, to associating Morocco with the European Higher Education Area (EHEA).[25]

Transnational Reform Networks and the Limits of Internationalization

The introduction of LMD illustrates that sector elites, namely university presidents called into these commissions, were able to considerably shape the policy reform, as long as the authority of the king remained untouched. Moreover, it illustrates the continuous French impact on university reform in Morocco, namely through transnational networks. When the aforementioned committee endorsed LMD, it was inspired by a joint meeting between the Conference of French University Presidents (CPU France) and the newly created Conference of Moroccan University Presidents (CPU Morocco). France had just adopted the introduction of the LMD system, and the first new license courses were to be initiated in the university year 2003–2004, when Morocco decided to apply this model in order to associate itself with the EHEA. France acted in fact as a translator of the European Bologna process and supported the Moroccan education reform with a budget of 10 million euros per year. The joint meetings between CPU France and CPU Morocco became a strong tool to debate and conduct the Moroccan reform process. Thus, France jumped on the bandwagon of Morocco's university reform, which had been instigated by the World Bank. Through the backdoor of its university presidents, it presented itself again as the main sponsor of policy orientations in Morocco. For France, Morocco remains by and large the main destination of foreign aid, and most of this aid is channeled into the education system.[26] France still considers Morocco as a bridgehead into francophone Africa.

The strong links established between the two CPUs illustrate a new form of transnational exchange, with ideas floating mainly from north to south globally. While the narrative of introducing the LMD system is mainly based on the benefits for student mobility through harmonizing diplomas, this barely reflects the reality. Student mobility between France and Morocco de facto decreased, while the joint reform framework allows French and European universities to more easily introduce their own programs on the Moroccan market, often with high tuition fees.[27] But in terms of governance, this exchange strengthened the role of university presidents in Morocco and made them the main reform entrepreneurs. While French university presidents are elected, the Moroccan presidents gain all their power and legitimacy through their nomination by the king. Thus, they are more powerful than the government in the reform process. Consequently, Morocco's higher-education reform, initiated by a new selection system for university presidents and followed by a pedagogical reform brokered between Moroccan and French university presidents, is mainly in the hands of the palace and its "governors" within the universities. The subsequent ministers in charge of higher education, if they are part of a USFP or an Islamist Justice and Development Party government, can only moderate the reform process. They do, however, directly face the continuous discourse on the crisis of universities in Morocco.

Morocco's higher-education reform remains very controversial. Many professors saw the LMD reform as a top-down decision they were forced to accept. They felt disregarded by a reform that would not improve teaching conditions or student mobility between universities.[28] Lacking substantial investments in infrastructure and payments, the new degrees only served faculties suffering less from overcrowding and already benefiting from cooperation with European universities, a phenomenon also observable in Egypt. However, protests against the reform remained sporadic and isolated in Morocco. Before 2011, student protests took place in specific faculties and centered on corporatist demands such as tuition fees and the material conditions of students. After 2011, several initiatives emerged advocating reform of the education system. But the National Union of Moroccan Students (UNEM), which once represented the large majority of Moroccan students, remained in a deadlock due to the conflict between Islamist and leftist factions. While students and graduates played an important role in the 2011 protests, UNEM could not gain ground through them. Students indeed participated in protests through channels not directly linked to the university. In sharp contrast with Egypt, the 2011 protests in Morocco remained more localized and more strongly grounded in political affiliations. While the February 20 movement successfully galvanized protest in Morocco after the uprisings in Tunisia and Egypt, it depended on the support of existing political parties and the NGOs. This factor inhibited the spillover into a more lasting multisectorial uprising and made the movement more vulnerable to the palace's reform responses.[29] Many former student activists and professors critical of the regime had been co-opted through "commission politics," the regime's discourse on social policy reform and democratic transition in the decade preceding the Arab uprisings. Various royal initiatives such as education reform and subsequent initiatives such as the reform of the law on personal status and the vast operation of the National Initiative for Human Development integrated many professors and university leaders as experts into the realm of power.[30]

Conclusion

Morocco's higher-education reform stimulated pockets of resistance. But the palace carefully established ties with sector elites during this process. Before confronting the university with change, the palace created a consensus on the future directions of reform. It efficiently promoted a new university law and reorganized universities from the top through the selection of new presidents. In Egypt, the change team, made up of engineers, put new initiatives on the agenda but had a limited impact on the implementation of the reform. In Morocco, newly selected university presidents became a change team in the implementation phase. This contrast notwithstanding, results of reform in both countries are limited when evaluated as improvements of the educational fabric. They illustrate how one regime, in this case the Moroccan monarchy, is more successful in building a buffer against protest. In particular, the wide stakeholder participation in the reform process was important to spread responsibility for reform on multiple shoulders. In Morocco, reform kept university leaders, professors, and students busy, while in Egypt it deepened the gap between reform-oriented faculty members and those resisting it.

Comparing Egypt's and Morocco's higher-education reform shows that both countries have undertaken several steps to adjust universities to a global education market. But the comparison also reveals important contrasts in how the two regimes have prepared and implemented reforms. While Morocco chose a more inclusive decisionmaking process, Egypt's reform process is characterized by the regime's limited capacity to integrate different stakeholders, by its nepotism, and by not addressing the controversial issues of reform. Those contrasts are not unique to university reform: they illustrate the distinct types of governance the two regimes established prior to the uprisings. In Morocco, the palace's flexibility in responding to popular demands with apparent reforms remains the most important silencer of protest. And the politics of commissions became the palace's favorite instrument for monitoring reforms. Other types of reform, such as the law on personal status, were prepared under similar conditions.[31] The palace has repeatedly relied on this system, whereby representatives from political parties and the civil society are handpicked by the king in order to administer change and expand the dense fabric of political intermediaries.

This type of governance builds on a unique form of pluralism, one of political parties and civil society organizations beneath the supremacy of the king. It enables the palace to present itself as the agenda-setter of reform and to constantly reestablish ties with political and sector elites. As Gregory Gause has argued, it is not necessarily a unique legitimacy or functional superiority that makes monarchies better at adjusting to international norms and new actors in the political arena.[32] Rather, the Moroccan monarchy draws on an extraordinary ability to build new coalitions, integrate new actors, and extend its pluralism when necessary. This makes it much more difficult for opposition to emerge and then organize. Political parties' desires to shape policies provide impressions of change, which in turn neutralizes popular resistance. In addition, political parties and associations channel popular demands and diffuse protest.

Morocco's reform appears more comprehensive by changing the rules of nomination for university presidents and replacing successive presidents and deans before engaging in a relatively wide-ranging pedagogical reform that eventually ended in an adapted version of the European Bologna process. Through a more inclusionary process, Morocco managed to build a wider ownership of reform, an inclusion that could happen only in a system that allows for a variety of political mediators beneath the supreme authority of the palace.

Therefore, the result of this reform should be measured not just in terms of policy output, such as how it improved the system under reform. And the reference to internationalization as the main driver for reform should not be interpreted as a dismissal of the importance of national political actors. In Egypt we have observed how reform prepared with the World Bank contributed to the emergence of reform entrepreneurs, namely the professors of the faculty of engineering. In Morocco, higher-education reforms have reinforced the role of university presidents as the managers of the university and the main interlocutors of reform. The formation of these reform entrepreneurs appears as a crucial feature for reforms that are closely prepared and implemented with multilateral and bilateral donors: they act as the intermediaries of the international actors and the entry point for the acclimatization to international norms within a certain policy area, in Egypt more during the policy-formulation phase and in Morocco during the implementation phase.

The extent to which these reform entrepreneurs can internationalize educational systems in North Africa is open to question. Strongly embedded in specific national configurations, they are easily co-opted by political regimes seeking to extend their control over sectors such as education. In Morocco the palace reestablished control over university leaders in a period when it had to cede control over the formation of governments and its policies, thus stabilizing its transactions with sector elites. Egypt's engineers display the features of a largely apolitical group that defends the imperative of internationalization without engaging in partisan struggles. Their career during Egypt's uncertain transition period illustrates that they act as important intermediaries between donors and the regime, independent of who is ruling.

Internationalization in the reform process of Egyptian and Moroccan universities has taken different forms. In Egypt its tools, namely the grant-based reform approach and attempts to introduce the benchmarking of quality education through accreditation and evaluation, have provided a script for university reform. In Morocco, the French adaptation of the Bologna process became the framework for reform. The proximity of certain donors (France in the case of Morocco, the World Bank in the case of Egypt) seems to be an important explanation for varieties of internationalization in university reform in the Middle East and North Africa. But in strongly state-controlled university systems, neither accreditation nor the European process to foster student mobility will provide per se the script for the solution of the crisis of higher education. Universities must acquire the necessary autonomy to emancipate from political games in the transnational configuration that surrounds them.

Notes

1. Salmi, *Crise de l'enseignement et reproduction sociale au Maroc.*
2. Salmi, *The Challenge of Establishing World Class Universities.*
3. The decision to harmonize study programs throughout Europe, initiated at a conference of only four education ministers at the Sorbonne University in 1998, was followed by a meeting of 388 European university presidents in Bologna in the same year. They signed a Magna Carta that emphasized the values of university autonomy and the mobility of students. In 1999, European education ministers signed the Bologna Declaration, which became the funding document to harmonize study programs and introduce a credit system by 2010. See, e.g., Maassen and Musselin, "European Integration and the Europeanisation of Higher Education," pp. 3–14.
4. Altbach and Knight, "Internationalization in Higher Education: Motivations and Realities."

5. European Commission, "Erasmus + for Higher Education in Morocco," November 2018, https://ec.europa.eu/programmes/erasmus-plus/sites/erasmus plus2/files/erasmusplus_morocco_2018.pdf.

6. Mazawi, "Contrasting Perspectives on Higher Education in Arab States."

7. Reid, *Cairo University and the Making of Modern Egypt.*

8. See, for example, the presentation of the German Academic Exchange Service (DAAD) of the German University in Cairo in Kanine, "GUC: Studieren in Ägypten." On how private universities enhance inequality in access, see Buckner, "Access to Higher Education in Egypt."

9. Kohstall, "Die ägyptische Revolution als Generationenkonflikt."

10. See Springborg, Chapter 5, in this volume.

11. Supreme Council of Universities (Egypt), ed., *Higher Education Enhancement Program—International Symposium,* 2 volumes (Cairo: Ministry of Higher Education and Scientific Research, 1999).

12. Interview with a World Bank senior representative in Cairo, 2014.

13. Blaydes, *Elections and Distributive Politics in Mubarak's Egypt.*

14. Kohstall, "From Reform to Resistance."

15. Scholars at Risk and Association for Freedom of Thought and Expression, "Joint Submission to the Universal Periodic Review of Egypt by Scholars at Risk and the Association for Freedom of Thought and Expression in Egypt," https://www.scholarsatrisk.org/wp-content/uploads/2019/04/Scholars-at-Risk-AFTE -Egypt-UPR-Submission-1.pdf.

16. Ibid.

17. Kohstall, "From Reform to Resistance."

18. North, Wallis, Webb, and Weingast, "Limited Access Orders in the Developing World."

19. Henry and Springborg, *Globalization and the Politics of Development in the Middle East.*

20. Boukhars, "The Lesson from Morocco and Jordan."

21. "Lettre Royale de Feu Sa Majesté Hassan II du 8 mars 1999," in COSEF, *Messages et extraits des discours royaux (Mars 1999–Septembre 2000),* edited by Commission spéciale éducation/formation (COSEF), Rabat, Morocco, 2000, pp. 14–15.

22. Author interview with the president of COSEF, Rabat, 2006.

23. For the importance of decentralized governance, see Hess, "From the Arab Spring to the Chinese Winter."

24. Kohstall, "From Reform to Resistance."

25. Benchenna, "L'appui de la France à la Réforme de l'Enseignement supérieur au Maroc."

26. Ibid.

27. Ibid.

28. Ghouati, "Réforme LMD au Maghreb: éléments pour un premier bilan politique et pédagogique."

29. Benchemsi, "Feb20's Rise and Fall"; also Vairel, "'Qu'avez-vous fait de vos vingt ans?'"

30. Vairel, "'Qu'avez-vous fait de vos vingt ans?'"

31. Maddy-Weitzman, "Women, Islam, and the Moroccan State."

32. Gause, "Kings for All Seasons."

5

Educational Policy
in Sisi's Egypt

Robert Springborg

Having the largest educational system in the Arab world and one wrestling with many challenges—ranging from coping with an annual student intake that now exceeds 2 million children; to balancing public, private, and mixed educational providers; to shifting the purpose of education from preparing civil servants to creating the skills and mentalities required to accelerate sluggish economic growth—Egypt provides a useful case study of how educational policy is driven by and reflects interests in a limited-access order and the cross-pressures to which those in control of it are subjected. While Egyptian educational policy is more akin to that in other authoritarian Arab republics, it is not profoundly dissimilar to that in the monarchies in both content and its reflection of the underlying political economy.

Need for Educational Reform in Egypt

Region-wide and global drivers of educational reform are abundantly apparent in Egypt. Public education is abysmal, paradoxically expensive for families, especially poor ones, and a significant cause of political discontent. The system is ranked by the World Economic Forum as 130th out of 137 in the world, with primary education ranking 133rd, Egypt's lowest ranking on the almost 100 indicators from which the Global Competitiveness Index is constructed.[1] Its fourth-grade students were ranked second to last in the Progress in International Reading Literacy Study.[2] Although almost 90 percent of the Ministry of Education's budget is allocated to personnel salaries, teachers are poorly paid and so typically moonlight or extract fees for private tutorials from their students, the latter of which have resulted in household expenditure on education exceeding that of the government's. About one-third of teachers are "not educationally qualified" and professional development programs are "seriously deficient."[3] Egyptian teachers spend the least amount of time actually teaching (39 percent) of teachers in all countries for which the 2019 World Bank study reports data.[4]

The Egyptian educational system is analogous to a supertanker, its sheer bulk impeding rapid, dramatic course changes. Primary, preparatory, and secondary education has over 20 million students enrolled in about 60,000 public schools. The 2014 constitution's requirement that public education be equivalent to 4 percent of gross domestic product (GDP) has yet to be realized. The maximum proportion allocated to education in republican Egypt was 5.7 percent of GDP in 1983. Overall government expenditure as a proportion of GDP has fallen steadily since the 1960s, at 10 percent now, less than half of what it was then. Of this shrinking pie, education's share diminished from some 15 percent in the early 2000s to some 11 percent in 2008, since which time it has slid further to some 9 percent.[5] The average class size in Egypt is about double global benchmarks.[6] Of public funds spent on education, some 30 percent go to tertiary institutions, whose enrollments, which were 2.7 million in 2017, constitute only about 12 percent of all students.[7] In the Middle East and North Africa (MENA) as a whole, 24 percent of public expenditure on education is for the tertiary sector, the second highest rate in the world, led only by North America. But whereas North America has more universities in the world's top 500 than any other region, only one of Egypt's twenty-four public universities is in the top 500—in the 300–400 range—with the next four highest-ranking Egyptian universities in the 700–1,000 range.[8]

The hurdles to be overcome, in short, are high and require budgetary outlays beyond those currently or in the foreseeable future likely to be made. Concerned by the dilapidated state of Egyptian education, in 2018 the World Bank extended a $500 million loan to finance its upgrading by expanding kindergarten education by 500,000 children, creating 50,000 new teaching jobs, and by providing up to 1.5 million digital-learning devices to high school students and teachers. As part of the reform package the government announced it was in 2019 replacing the existing, generally unpopular general secondary school examination taken at the end of three years of high school with a dozen exams spread over the three years. That decision, however, had not been implemented by the end of the 2020 academic year.

Whether the finances will be available to support the reforms within a reasonable period is questionable. Tariq Shawki, minister of education, estimates they will cost $1.5 billion in addition to the $500 million World Bank loan, noting that his projections indicate it will take fourteen years for that amount to be allocated.[9] In May 2019, Minister Shawki complained to the parliamentary budget committee that the Ministry of Finance's allocation to education for 2019–2020 of 99 billion Egyptian pounds was "insufficient to cover basic needs," for which he claimed at least 138 billion pounds was required. Of that requested 138 billion, 110 billion was for teachers' salaries alone, which the minister had hoped to increase. He ended his lament by saying that his ministry in the previous year had to cut its spending by 50 percent and to forgo plans to repair schools and build new ones.[10] In sum, the government seems unprepared to put its money where its mouth is regarding public education.

Policy Objectives and Implementation

This ambitious if underfunded reform program is not the only change envisioned. The military government, in power since July 2013, has turned on the civil service, one of the major props of all previous republican regimes. Intent on shrinking its role and size, it has sought to accelerate the shift in the focus of education away from training potential civil servants. In this effort it is trying to kill three birds with one stone—one administrative, one political, and another developmental. It wants to produce technocratic-managerial cadres subordinate and loyal to the military to assume administrative functions traditionally performed by the more autonomous civil service. It also wants those cadres to assume political intermediary functions between the population and the military, enforcing and legitimating its rule. And third, it is hoping that these newly graduated cadres will contribute to the promised emergence of a knowledge economy. Pursuant to these intertwined objectives the regime in 2017 created the National Training Academy, "a scientific institution to train youth for public service, as well as to improve their abilities and skills and produce cadres capable of holding leading posts in state sectors." It is modeled on the French Ecole Nationale d'Administration, with which it conducts joint programs. It reports directly to the president and is staffed by "Egyptian experts with international expertise." Its programs are designed to "build human beings culturally, artistically, literarily and politically."[11] According to an article in the state-owned press, "Many of the academy's graduates are now assisting ministers and governors and occupying leading posts."[12]

The objective of creating loyal technocratic cadres shapes policy while exemplifying the regime's intent to respond to public pressure. President Abd al-Fattah al-Sisi has personally identified himself with educational reform. In a December 2018 meeting with his minister of education, for example, Sisi was reported to have "expressed his support for developing the educational system within the framework of the state's strategy to build the Egyptian character and invest in human beings." He emphasized the importance of the "latest technologies and scientific developments . . . and giving attention to sports and physical activity."[13] Possibly reflecting the president's personal interest in bodybuilding and his oft-stated desire to toughen up his fellow Egyptians, his and his close associates' pronouncements and proposals frequently contain reference to the need for sticks as well as carrots to drive educational policy forward. In 2018, for example, Minister Shawki floated the trial balloon of limiting or even terminating free education, implying among other things that each family should be allowed free education for only two children.[14] His deputy announced the intent to criminalize "private education centers," which are group tutorials offered by teachers after hours, possibly attempting to balance this threat to teachers' incomes with proposed legislation to imprison students who physically or verbally abuse teachers.[15]

Privatization

Driven by financial imperatives as well as the desire to improve overall educational quality and the even stronger desire to train a new technocratic administrative elite, the government is seeking to privatize education at all levels. About 10 percent, or some 2 million, of the country's 18–20 million (the figures vary) primary and secondary students are presently in private schools, a proportion considerably below the global average and even further below that for middle-income countries.[16] The most expensive of existing private schools are the international ones, in which total tuition for twelve years costs up to 3 million Egyptian pounds ($176,500). In December 2018, EFG Hermes, the country's leading investment bank, announced that its Egypt Education Fund had attracted investment from "high-net worth individuals and institutional investors from Egypt, the GCC [Gulf Cooperation Council], and Southeast Asia" of $119 million for its "education platform built in exclusive partnership with Dubai-based GEMS Education, one of the world's oldest and largest K–12 private education providers." EFG Hermes predicted the fund would return 25 percent annually and within three years would have thirty schools educating 40,000 students.[17] No statement was made about anticipated tuition and fees.

Of the country's fifty universities, twenty-six are private.[18] Ninety-four percent of university students attend public universities, indicating that the average size of public universities is much larger than that of private ones.[19] In August 2018, President Sisi signed a new law making it easier for foreign universities to open branches in Egypt, at which time the minister of higher education announced that six new international universities would be established in 2019. Less than a year later, in the presence of the head of the Engineering Authority of the Armed Forces—essentially the largest construction firm in Egypt, which both lets contracts and implements them—the minister of higher education announced that eight new international universities would be established by 2020 in the authority's lavishly funded prestige project of the New Administrative Capital. All of them, he declared, would be modeled on the University of Canada in Egypt, the first scheduled to open its doors in the new capital.[20] Sisi had stated a year previously that no new university could be established without being in partnership with one of the world's top 50 universities and that "we are not ranked in the top 500 universities in the world. I will return Egyptian universities to the top 50."[21] This may be a difficult goal to achieve since many universities, including the University of Liverpool, have refused to enter into agreements with Egyptian universities or to establish branch campuses because of fear of "reputational damage."[22] Another impediment to the effective functioning of all private universities is their lack of autonomy from the presidency, from which they must have approval before establishing a new department or program, abolishing an existing one, or raising fees.[23] Sisi seemed to violate his own edict against the creation of new all-Egyptian universities when he announced in July 2019 the founding of the private Heliopolis University. He declared that "making a profit is not the main purpose of establishing the university," but did not specify what its main purpose is or who owns it.[24]

The possibility that Egyptian universities might again become attractive to foreign students, especially those from the Middle East and Africa, as they had been for previous generations, seems remote, given "the loss of competitiveness of its higher education institutions . . . which no longer provide high quality higher education and hence no longer attract foreign students." The analyst who offered this interpretation concluded that "the flow of foreign students into the country is likely to continue to decrease."[25] As for Western students, the appeal of education in Egypt is, according to Amy Austin Holmes, a professor at the American University in Cairo, much diminished by the absence of academic freedom. Since 2013 more than 1,100 students have been arrested, another 1,000 expelled on political grounds, and 21 extrajudicially killed. The killing of Cambridge PhD student Giulio Regeni, the incarceration of University of Washington PhD student Walid al-Shobaky, and the use of universities by the regime as agents of surveillance facilitated by university presidents and deans, all of whom since 2014 have been appointed by the president, are notable deterrents. Since 2015 tenured faculty can be dismissed for political activism or "vague ethics violations." The intelligence services must approve participation by faculty members in international conferences, as well as the hiring of foreign faculty. In November 2018 the University of Alexandria required of all PhD and MA theses that they "conform to Egypt's Vision 2030."[26] The attractiveness of domestic universities even to Egyptians is further reduced by the generally poor financial returns from tertiary education. Of Egypt's unemployed, more than one-third have undergraduate or graduate degrees.[27]

So as not to be left out in the rush to privatize, Egyptian public universities were authorized by legislation passed in March 2019 to establish "nonprofit," fee-charging universities in partnership with international universities. Speaking in favor of the draft legislation, a member of the education committee of parliament noted that the state provides free university education to 3 million students, which costs more than the government can afford, and so it needs to "reduce the deficit of the university education budget." His estimate was that 750,000 students would prefer "private or nonprofit education"—fully a quarter of all students. Mohamed Khalil, a former undersecretary of the Ministry of Higher Education, commented that "the principle of free education is not wrong but has been misused in Egypt since 1952. . . . [F]ree education, and in particular university education, is a type of support offered by the state to those who cannot afford it."[28]

Privatization of education from kindergarten through university, in other words, is driven primarily by the government's desire to reduce its substantial fiscal deficit. The consequence will be the institutionalization of a trinary system at all levels: free public institutions at the bottom catering to the least well-off; middle-ranking institutions involving some type of public-private partnership and attracting those in the middle class who can afford to pay moderate fees; and top-end international private schools and universities catering overwhelmingly to wealthy Egyptians.

Governmental Control and Mobilization

While encouraging privatization, the government is simultaneously bringing private schools and universities under more direct, obtrusive control. Sisi's remarks just quoted are indicative of new constraints placed on private universities, including the requirement they partner with international institutions. As for pre-tertiary private schools, the big change is Arabization of the first six years of teaching, including mathematics and science, with English being taught only as a second language during that period, including in the so-called language schools, which have typically taught in English and whose share of age cohorts has been steadily increasing since the Mubarak era. This move has been strongly criticized by parents and teachers, but to no avail.[29] What seems a related change is a new requirement "agreed" between the Ministry of Education and the chairman of the International Schools Association that international schools "teach school subjects that are related to the national identity in line with the international curricula."[30]

These changes, reminiscent of those in the Nasser era, are intended to facilitate governmental oversight and to promote discipline, Egyptian nationalism, and loyalty to the military. An anecdotal example of initiatives to oversee private education was provided by a visit by the governor of Qalyubiya province to a kindergarten, where he spied images of Disney characters, including Mickey Mouse, on the walls. He immediately decreed that they be replaced by drawings of "military martyrs, so that children will look up to them as role models. These characters are U.S. made, whereas we have our own noble figures who can deepen children's patriotism and love of country." The Ministry of Education echoed the theme, announcing the formation of a committee to implement the order.[31]

A more systematic initiative was the intended launching in 2018 of what was then said to be 79 of a planned 200 "Japanese schools," which more than 30,000 students would attend. In the event, the launch was postponed for a year to "better prepare and ensure a sufficient level of quality and selection criteria," according to the Ministry of Education.[32] The schools are supported by the Japanese International Cooperation Agency, and their declared purpose, according to the Japanese ambassador to Egypt, is to "teach students the main principles of discipline, commitment, and respect for time."[33] The special curriculum and teaching method is referred to as *Tokkatsu,* which is intended to produce a "balanced development of intellect, virtue and body by ensuring academic competence, rich emotions and healthy physical development." Minister of Education Shawki declared at the opening of one of the schools that "the goal of the new educational system is to build a new, different Egyptian generation."[34] The schools will teach the Egyptian curriculum but include "distinctive features of Japanese education," including "cleanliness and self-reliance."[35] The minister noted that "the idea for these schools comes from El-Sisi's admiration of the Japanese character."[36] A year later it was reported that in 2018–2019 only 35 Japanese schools had in fact been opened, that 5 more were added in 2019–2020, and that the ultimate goal of 200 schools had been halved.[37] Possibly the relatively high fees of 10,800 Egyptian pounds ($630) annually deterred potential students, for those with sufficient means might well prefer other types of international schools.[38]

Emphasis on discipline in the new, so-called cumulative secondary school system was underscored by the distribution of Samsung tablet computers to what is intended ultimately to be to all students entering high school. They have the capacity to monitor the location of students, and hence their school attendance, a minimum number of days of which are required for eligibility to sit for compulsory examinations. The Ministry of Education's criminalizing "unauthorized education centers" and threatened imprisonment of offenders as well as of students who physically or verbally abuse their teachers are further examples of tightened discipline.[39] Minister Shawki noted that objection against the computers and centralized examination marking made possible by them was "incited by teachers involved in private tutoring so they promoted among students that the tests would be difficult and they themselves have failed to answer the practice modules."[40] When the minister announced the results of the 2019 secondary school certificate examinations, on which the pass rate was the highest in three years and 4 percent above the previous year's results, he claimed "they did not adequately reflect the students' real abilities but are a result of their becoming expert in sitting exams as a result of private lessons."[41]

The overall emphasis on order and strict discipline was underscored by President Sisi himself, who at the outset of the new school year in 2018 publicly informed the minister of education that "I am going to visit lots of schools and I am going to sit with my grandchildren in order to follow up on the quality of the education."[42] The emphasis on education's role in instilling discipline and ethics in addition to loyalty was underscored just prior to the commencement of the 2019 academic year when the Ministry of Social Solidarity announced that all university students would be required to take lessons in a new "anti-divorce program" called *mawadda* (affection), intended to "qualify university students for marriage and educate them on how to choose their partners and handle marital conflicts." The ministry noted that it inaugurated the program in response to Sisi's call for action to combat Egypt's high divorce rate, which he said alarmed him.[43]

The government has also sought to use education as a screening device, both for sensitive governmental and media positions as well as to weed out Islamists wherever they might be found. Recruitment of public prosecutors was delayed for four years as the 800 graduates from the 2015 class of law schools who had applied for vacant posts were subjected to rounds of examinations by nonjudicial authorities never previously involved. Key among these exams were those administered by the General Intelligence Service intended to test "for religious, political, sexual and social tendencies, and loyalty to the country," as one successful candidate reported.[44] Fewer than 200 of the 800 applicants passed the intelligence service's test despite the fact that most were honor students. Those who passed were then subject to additional tests by the highly politicized Administrative Prosecution Agency. As one lawyer commented, "the new procedures undermine the entire process because security standards cannot be the basis for appointment to the judiciary."[45] An outcry from judges about the involvement of security services in the recruitment process caused President Sisi to deny that "he or other parties were interfering in the appointment process." The fact that "hundreds of candidates for positions in other judicial bodies are still waiting" implied that they too were being screened by intelligence services.[46]

The abrupt removal in August 2019 of Osama Kamal, a popular television presenter, revealed the behind-the-scenes role of graduates of the eight-month Presidential Leadership Program, founded by presidential decree in 2015 and supervised by the Ministry of Defense and the cabinet. Open to university graduates between twenty and thirty years of age, it "targets young future leaders and enables them to acquire the skills they need to learn about governance, administrative and political fields."[47] A group of these graduates were employed by the General Intelligence Service to supervise editorial commentary on all stations under the holding company Egyptian Media Service, owned by the service. When Kamal ignored an order from the group to make a minor editorial change in a program on August 2, they removed him. This censorship role was presumably among the functions Sisi had in mind for these graduates when he announced in April 2017 that they would fill "crucial roles in the presidency, ministries, and governorates."[48]

The government has also been seeking to bring established Islam in the form of Al-Azhar University under its more direct control so as to remove any residual presence of Muslim Brothers there and to deploy the institution in its wider campaign to counter antigovernment Islamism. The Ministry of Military Production signed a protocol in January 2017 with Al-Azhar to establish fourteen secondary technical institutes in 2017–2018 and another fifty in 2018–2019. In discussions between the Grand Imam of Al-Azhar, Ahmad al-Tayyib—a longtime if careful opponent of President Sisi—and General Muhammad al-Assar, the minister of military production, agreement was reached on transfer of various types of electronic and other equipment to the newly created secondary institutes, presumably in exchange for Al-Azhar submitting to the military's oversight.[49] Al-Tayyib's ambitious efforts to internationalize Al-Azhar, including through the creation in 2018 of the Al-Azhar International Academy, which enrolled trainee imams from twenty foreign countries, as well as through the global reach of its Observatory for Combating Extremism and its eighteen international alumni associations, intensified his conflict with President Sisi over control of the institution and its activities. In January 2019 al-Tayyib was banned by Sisi from traveling abroad without official permission from the presidency.[50]

The political uses of education by the government include deployment of schools and universities to mobilize students in its support. An example was provided during the constitutional referendum of April 2019 on amendments that would extend President Sisi's current term by two years, grant him the right to run for a third, six-year term, and further entrench the dominant political power of the military by granting it the right to intervene in politics to "protect the civil state." Four days prior to the referendum, students at Mansoura University, accompanied by those from the military academy, were assembled in an auditorium where they were addressed by administrators and faculty, who led them in singing a pro-regime, patriotic song associated with the July 2013 coup and urged them to vote in favor of the amendments. The university's student union held a photo competition in which students were invited to submit photos of themselves and their families displaying their fingers stained with the purple ink applied at voting booths. Winners were awarded free trips to Alexandria, Cairo, or Port Said. The president of Cairo University promised students in a speech just prior to the referendum that their support of it would be rewarded with partial exemptions from tuition fees and a grade-point bonus of 5 percent. At Fayoum University the president and his assistants led students clad in T-shirts bearing the phrases "Egypt's Future" and "Students for Egypt" on a march to the polls. Some professors were reported to have threatened students with reductions in their grades if they did not participate. At the South of the Valley University, faculty members accompanied students on buses to polling stations. No objections appear to have been raised in parliament or the government-controlled media to what on the face of it appeared to be regime-supported violations of the regime's own prohibition of political activities on campuses.[51]

Just as the military-dominated government employs carrots and sticks to induce loyalty in university students, so it also does with university faculty members and administrators. In July 2019 it announced that junior faculty and administrators would be trained "in leadership and organizational skills at Nasser Higher Military Academy, under the supervision of sociology professors and military generals." A government source noted that the sociology professors to be involved in the training "are known for their loyalty to the ruling political system, their close ties with army generals and their support for the military ideology and its leadership methods." The title of the training program is "Strategic Studies and National Security." Its declared intent is to "unify the vision of staff members and employees regarding national security concepts." The curriculum is focused "on the role of the armed forces on the political, economic and social levels." In comments to a reporter on the new training program, a faculty member at the American University in Cairo observed that in addition to this further military encroachment into tertiary education, the military had also taken over all food services at Cairo University.[52]

The Military as Educator

As with the civil service and the private business sector, whose functions the military has largely usurped, so has the military become an education service provider in competition with both public and private schools. Mention has just been made of collaboration between the military and Al-Azhar in operating secondary technical institutes. As part of its counter-terror campaign the military opened four new primary schools in north and central Sinai under the control of the commander of the East of Suez Canal Counter-Terrorism Forces. An opening ceremony for one, held on the forty-fifth anniversary of the October War "victory," was attended by the commander of the Third Field Army.[53]

The jewel in the crown of the military pre-tertiary educational system is the Badr International School, opened in a military zone on the outskirts of Cairo in 2015, two years after the then defense minister, Abd al-Fattah al-Sisi, issued the order for its creation. A reporter who visited the school observed that its "managers and staff see their role not only in educational terms, but as a patriotic duty, holding themselves responsible for enhancing the image of the military and introducing activities that develop the nationalistic sentiments of the students."[54] The commander of the Third Field Army attends the school's monthly board meetings. Among its facilities are a swimming pool and numerous playing fields and courts. The school's website declares that the school is the product of the armed forces and "is being implemented successfully by the primary decision maker and supervisor himself, Egyptian President Abdel Fattah al Sisi." The site further notes that "we proudly follow the code of conduct of Egypt's Armed Forces." This third educational initiative focused on patriotism, discipline, and loyalty to the military and the president begs the question of its origins. What were the sources that inspired the military to directly sponsor and operate schools?

The Badr School is remarkably reminiscent of the so-called Napola, the acronym for Nationalpolitische Lehranstadt (National Political Institution of Teaching), the secondary schools established by the German National Socialists after they took power in 1933. The main task of what ultimately became forty-three such schools, educating at least 6,000 pupils at any one time by 1945, was "education of national socialists, efficient in body and soul for the service to the people and the state."[55] They were elite preparatory schools initially directly under the authority of the national minister of education and then, from 1940, under their own national Obergruppenfuhrer (inspector). The curriculum included heavy doses of National Socialist ideology and physical fitness training. All students wore the uniform of the Hitler Youth.

It is an open question as to whether President Sisi or any of his advisers were aware of this precedent when he decreed the Badr School be created. It is too soon to determine if it will serve as a recruitment channel into the military or possibly elite units within it or some part of the state apparatus controlled by it. In the case of the Napola schools, a plurality of their graduates joined the Schutzstaffel (SS), with others being recruited by the government. But whether it was a conscious model for the Egyptian leadership or not, its similarity attests to ambitions for youth quite like those of Germany's National Socialists, who were to recruit carefully selected, dedicated, even fanatical loyalists to serve the regime.

Another possible and contemporary source of inspiration for the Badr School, and also for some of the new curricular and language impositions on both public and private schools, is East Asia. The new Japanese schools are explicit copies of that East Asian model, whereas elite schools under the Chinese Communist Party, intended to educate party cadres and prepare them to rule, may have also informed Egyptian leaders when making their recent choices about changes to the educational system. Of possible relevance is the fact that since 2014 President Sisi has visited China six times. Still another example that might have inspired creation of the Badr School and military intervention into the educational system more generally is that provided by Russia's military intelligence agency, the Organization of the Main Intelligence Administration (GRU), and by the successor to the Committee for State Security (KGB), the Federal Security Service (FSB), through which President Putin rose to power. Both are involved in designing and implementing curricula in Russian schools, curricula that include cryptography, military training, and overall discipline. Graduates are typically recruited into either the GRU or the FSB.[56]

Conclusion

Educational reforms currently under way in Egypt are driven in part from the bottom up by popular discontent with the country's educational system. But the military government is choosing to respond to that pressure in ways that suit its interests far more than those of most members of the public, especially those of the middle and lower classes. It wants simultaneously to reduce governmental expenditures on education, train obedient implementers of regime policies, and reinforce loyalty of youths to the Egyptian nation and those controlling it. These top-down reforms, decreed in the absence of meaningful stakeholder participation, are justified as responses to bottom-up pressures and as the government standing up to the selfish interests of entrenched interests, especially teachers.

These new policies, however, depart profoundly from best practice in educational reform, which emphasizes the need for stakeholder participation by parents, teachers, students, administrators, and employers, coupled with enhanced autonomy within a decentralized framework. The primary source of external funding for the new policies for public education, the World Bank, has not imposed conditionality requiring such participation on its $500 million loan. The content of the various new educational policies, the absence of adequate funding in their support, their emphasis on control, the fact that they have been decreed in the absence of stakeholder input, and their obtrusive restrictions on private schools and universities are bound to perpetuate, even intensify, present inadequacies.

Educational reform in other Arab countries may be more open to stakeholder participation, less financially constrained, and not driven so completely by regime preoccupation with instilling loyalty, creating dutiful administrative cadres, and deterring dissent or even expression of dissatisfaction with government services. If that were the case, such reform would adhere more closely to international best practice and presumably, therefore, have better prospects for success. In Egypt's case, however, common global drivers of educational reform are acted upon in pursuit of and so reflect regime interests, with scant regard for abstract best-practice norms or more concrete preferences of stakeholders. Egyptian "educational reform" is thus a misnomer. Policy changes illustrate the increasingly widespread displacement of liberal by authoritarian educational models, the primary purposes of which are more political than educational. By supporting such alleged "reforms," the World Bank signals the acceptability of authoritarianism in general and authoritarian educational policies in particular. Those in the Bank responsible for offering financing of Egypt's educational system should have read the relevant studies their very own institution has produced. They should have imposed conditionality that the principles espoused by their organization be incorporated into Egypt's educational policies. Ultimately, however, the World Bank's financial support may be more wasted than pernicious. Recent changes to the Egyptian educational system, some made possible by that financial support, are so closely identified with the character, preferences, and political interests of the president that they are unlikely to long outlive his presidency.

Notes

1. Schwab, "The Global Competitive Report 2017–2018."
2. Abdel-Razek, "Investing in Education," p. 1441.
3. Sobhy et al., "Civil Society and Public Policy Formation."
4. El-Kogali and Krafft, *Expectations and Aspirations,* p. 23.
5. Abdel-Razek, "Investing in Education," p. 1441.
6. Ibid.
7. Sobhy et al., "Civil Society and Public Policy Formation."
8. "Academic Ranking of World Universities," *Shanghai Ranking,* 2019, http://www.shanghairanking.com/ARWU2019.html. See also Ghamrawy, "Egypt Looks to Foreign University Campuses to Boost Education"; and "Cairo University Achieves Huge Leap in 2019 Global Rankings," *Egypt Today,* September 8, 2019, https://www.egypttoday.com/Article/1/74583/Cairo-University-achieves-huge-leap -in-2019-global-rankings.
9. Al-Ashkar, "Rebuilding Education in Egypt."
10. Essam El-Din, "Budgetary Woes," p. 1443.
11. Zalata, "Interview."

12. Thabet, "Journey to the Future on Board the NTA."

13. Barsoum, "Sisi Discusses Developing Education in Egypt with Minister."

14. "Free Education Needs Reconsidering: Egypt's Education Minister," *Egypt Independent,* November 11, 2018, https://ww.egyptindependent.com/free-education -needs-reconsidering-egypts-education-minister.

15. "Draft Law to Criminalize Egypt's Unauthorized Private Education Centers: Minister," *Egypt Independent,* October 28, 2018, https://ww.egyptindependent.com /draft-law-to-criminalize-egypts-unauthorized-private-education-centers-minister.

16. Reda, "New Cumulative Secondary System to Be Applied 2018/19."

17. "Egypt Education Fund Oversubscribed with Commitments of $119M: Hermes," *Egypt Today,* December 23, 2018, https://www.egypttoday.com/Article/3 /62457/Egypt-Education-Fund-oversubscribed-with-commitments-of-119M-Hermes.

18. Ghamrawy, "Egypt Looks to Foreign University Campuses."

19. Abdel-Razek, "Investing in Education."

20. "Egypt to Construct 8 International Universities in New Administrative Capital by 2020," *Egypt Independent,* February 24, 2019, https://ww.egyptindependent .com/egypt-to-construct-8-international-universities-in-new-administrative-capital -by-2020.

21. Ghamrawy, "Egypt Looks to Foreign University Campuses."

22. Holmes, "Egypt's Lost Academic Freedom."

23. Sisi, for example, issued decrees in September 2019 permitting the Nile, British, and Ahram Canadian universities to establish various faculties and the Nahda University to raise fees by 5 percent. "Egypt's Sisi Issues Four Decrees for Private Universities," *Ahramonline,* September 11, 2019, http://english.ahram.org .eg/News/346566.aspx.

24. "Sisi Issues Decree to Build a New Private University Near Cairo," *Egypt Today,* July 18, 2019, http://www.egypttoday.com/Article/1/72925/Sisi-issues-decree -to-build-new-private-university-near-Cairo.

25. Romani, "The Politics of Higher Education in the Middle East," p. 6. The minister of higher education and scientific research, Khalid Abd al Ghaffar, claimed in September 2019 that Egypt ranked among the twenty most attractive countries for international students and that 70,000 were at that time studying in Egyptian universities. He provided no sources for either claim. See "Egypt Among 20 Most Attractive Countries for International Students: Minister," *Egypt Independent,* September 8, 2019, https://www.egyptindependent.com/egypt-among-20-most-attractive-countries-for -international-students-minister.

26. Holmes, "Egypt's Lost Academic Freedom."

27. Abdel-Razek, "Investing in Education."

28. Mostafa, "Egyptian Public Universities Seeking to Make Profits."

29. Reda, "New Cumulative Secondary School System."

30. "Egypt Education Ministry, Int'l Schools Association Sign Cooperation Protocol," *Ahramonline,* September 13, 2018, http://english.ahram.org.eg/NewsContent/1/64 /311508/Egypt/Politics-/Egypt-education-ministry,-intl-schools-association.aspx.

31. Taha and Morgan, "Mickey Mouse Expelled from Egypt Schools."

32. "Egypt's Sisi Approves Loan to Support Japanese Schools Programme," *Ahramonline,* October 18, 2018, http://english.ahram.org.eg/NewsContent/1/64 /313605/Egypt/Politics-/Egypts-Sisi-approves-loan-to-support-Japanese-scho.aspx.

33. "Egypt's Japanese Schools Are Unique and Successful," *Egypt Independent,* September 23, 2018, https://www.egyptindependent.com/egypts-japanese-schools -are-unique-and-successful-japanese-ambassador.

34. "I Will Personally Monitor the Progress of the New Education System, Says Egypt's Sisi," *Ahramonline,* September 19, 2018, http://english.ahram.org.eg/News

Content/1/64/311851/Egypt/Politics-/I-will-personally-monitor-the-progress-of-the-new-.aspx.

35. Reda, "New Cumulative Secondary School System."

36. Barsoum, "Sisi Discusses Developing Education."

37. "Egypt to Open Five New Japanese-Style Schools as Registration Starts for Coming School Year," *Ahramonline,* May 2, 2019, http://english.ahram.org.eg/NewsContent/1/64/330907/Egypt/Politics-/Egypt-to-open-five-new-Japanesestyle-schools-as-re.aspx.

38. Ibid.

39. "Draft Law to Criminalize Egypt's Unauthorized Private Education Centers: Minister," *Egypt Independent,* October 28, 2018, https://ww.egyptindependent.com/draft-law-to-criminalize-egypts-unauthorized-private-education-centers-minister.

40. "Exclusive Interview: Education Minister Details New System," *Egypt Today,* December 3, 2018, https://www.egypttoday.com/Article/2/61368/Exclusive-Interview-Education-minister-details-new-system.

41. "High School Results Dilemma in Egypt," *Ahramonline,* July 19, 2019, http://english.ahram.org.eg/NewsContentP/1/338104/Egypt/High-school-results-dilemma-in-Egypt-.aspx.

42. "I Will Personally Monitor the Progress of the New Education System, Says Egypt's Sisi," *Ahramonline,* September 19, 2018, http://english.ahram.org.eg/NewsContent/1/64/311851/Egypt/Politics-/I-will-personally-monitor-the-progress-of-the-new-.aspx.

43. "Egypt to Make Anti-divorce Program Mandatory for Graduation Starting Next Academic Year," *Ahramonline,* July 17, 2019, http://english.ahram.org.eg/NewsContent/1/64/338156/Egypt/Politics-/Egypt-to-make-antidivorce-program-mandatory-for-gr.aspx.

44. Mostafa, "Judicial Candidates Forced to Undergo Unprecedented Evaluations as Presidency Exerts Further Control."

45. Ibid.

46. Ibid.

47. As cited in Hakim, "Sacking TV Presenter Osama Kamal."

48. Ibid.

49. "Azhar Grand Imam, Military Production Min. Discuss Bilateral Cooperation," *Egypt Today,* April 3, 2019, https://www.egypttoday.com/Article/1/67845/Azhar-Grand-Imam-military-production-min-discuss-bilateral-cooperation.

50. Eltohamy, "Sisi Keeps Watchful Eye on Al-Azhar's Growing Role Abroad."

51. Abu Emiara, "Carrots and Sticks."

52. Youness, "University Staff in Egypt Receive Military Training."

53. "Armed Forces Open 4 Schools in North Central Sinai in Tandem with CSOs," *Egypt Today,* October 18, 2018, http://www.egypttoday.com/Article/1/59143/Armed-Forces-open-4-schools-in-North-Central-Sinai-in.

54. Afify, "The International School of Egypt's Military."

55. "National Political Institutes of Education," Wikipedia, https://en.wikipedia.org/wiki/National_Political_Institutes_of_Education. See also Helen Roche, "Surviving 'Stunde Null': Narrating the Fate of Nazi Elite-School Pupils During the Collapse of the Third Reich," *German History* 33, no. 4 (December 2015): 570–587.

56. Troianovski and Nakashima, "How Russia's Military Intelligence Agency Became the Covert Muscle in Putin's Duels with the West."

6

The Impact of Poverty and Corruption on Educational Quality in Tunisia

Lindsay J. Benstead

Unlike in many other Arab countries, Tunisia came into its independence with a strong, centralized education system.[1] As early as the 1880s, the French colonial administration expanded higher education to produce students who possessed more vocational and technical skills. While this system was initially intended to educate the children of French residents, Tunisians were able to enroll their children in these schools. French colonial authorities did not destroy local economic, political, and social institutions to the degree that they did in neighboring countries.[2] Instead, they safeguarded infrastructure and created educational institutions that the young state could continue to build upon in future decades.

Throughout the first half of the twentieth century, primary and secondary school enrollment in Tunisia and worldwide grew dramatically.[3] Bourguiba and later Ben Ali renewed the state's commitment to education to promote economic development—which they saw as crucial to fostering regime legitimacy—making education free and compulsory in 1958. Between 1975 and 2004, Tunisia saw a dramatic increase in enrollments largely driven by an expansion in girls' and women's education.[4] By 2002, the Education Act expanded compulsory education for children ages six to sixteen. In the years that followed, Tunisia obtained a literacy rate of 80 percent for adults and 97 percent for youth (fifteen to twenty-four years).[5] Over time, girls' enrollment outpaced that of boys', resulting in a gross enrollment-ratio gender parity index in secondary school of 1.1 percent (2006).[6] In the years since Tunisia first took part in the Trends in International Mathematics and Science Study (TIMSS) in 1999, it has consistently been one of the top-performing countries in the Arab region, ranking second in mathematics and third in science in all of the Arab countries in 2007.[7]

Yet Tunisia still falls short of its goal of enrolling all young people in school and preparing a work force with the skills needed in the job market. In the country as a whole, 10.4 percent of youth aged eight to seventeen years (about 178,000 Tunisian young people) were not enrolled in school,[8] according to a report produced by the Program on Governance and Local Development.[9] Also, its educational outcomes are less robust than what would be expected based on its monetary investment.

Tunisia has a centrally organized and funded education system and thus, in principle, students might encounter an equitable school system across areas, regardless of the development level of the area or the socio-economic resources of the family. Yet it is highly unequal, in terms of both infrastructure and management of human and material resources. At the same time, too little is known about why some students encounter lower-quality education and more corruption than others.

To fill this gap, I draw on the Local Governance Performance Index (LGPI), a survey of nearly 3,600 Tunisians conducted in February 2015 by the Program on Governance and Local Development with the support of the Hicham Alaoui Foundation, to explore why the quality of schools and the need to make informal payments vary across students from different social backgrounds and municipalities. The results reveal important insights about crucial reforms that are needed. Poorer households and those in less affluent regions suffer lower-quality schools with more teacher favoritism and absenteeism. They are also more likely to encounter less efficient school systems and have problems such as the need to repeat a grade. Moreover, transparency is a significant problem; 7 percent of families—disproportionately those in rural areas—made informal payments in the previous year to solve a problem (e.g., being expelled or failing a class or grade, to enroll the child in school, or to obtain government assistance to pay for school). Yet there is important variation across municipalities that is unexplained by family and regional economic income. On the whole, coastal areas have higher-quality schools than those in the interior.[10] But there are examples of both better-managed schools on the coast as well as poorly run schools in popular areas of the capital, Tunis. More research is needed to understand how and why management of schools at the local level shapes the educational outcomes of students.

Clientelism and Corruption in
Tunisia's Centralized Education System

Tunisia has several features that have been useful in developing its education sector and expanding enrollment. Its colonial educational institutions, while they were open only to Tunisian elites, provided a foundation upon which the Tunisian government could build. But Bourguiba also regarded socioeconomic development, which included seeking full enrollment and literacy, as a power-consolidation strategy. Other government policies through the Ben Ali era also proved crucial. Due to family-planning policy, Tunisia has a small, relatively more mature population—which has reduced the size of its youth bulge—23 percent of the population is aged fourteen years and younger (2014)—and helped it keep pace with the growing need for education spending. Tunisia is a developing country with limits on what it can spend. Yet with a gross domestic product (GDP) of $4,391 per capita, ranked 140th worldwide (2017), Tunisia also spends a robust level of public investment in education infrastructure: 20 percent of the state budget (7 percent of GDP).[11]

Yet improvements in education quality did not keep pace with expansion in enrollment, due in part to the development of a robust authoritarian regime with weak rule of law.[12] The limited-access order that emerged ossified regional disparities, increased income inequality, and, critically, offered few avenues for citizens to demand government accountability in schools and other public sectors. Even though Tunisia has a centralized education system that could distribute resources fairly, it has consistently invested more in coastal areas, resulting in higher enrollment rates and quality in these areas.[13] As in other places, the regional disparities created structural barriers to upward economic mobility for children from the rural interior and western regions of the country. Moreover, the legacy of authoritarianism has not yet been replaced by robust democratic accountability, at either the central or the local level. This means that corruption can persist, and ineffective personnel may not always be held accountable, even in the case of absenteeism or acceptance of informal payments.

Despite having transitioned to a minimalist democracy since the fall of the Ben Ali era, Tunisia has not yet witnessed the decentralization of power over education from the central to the local governments. Education policy continues to be the purview of the Ministry of Education, which sets curriculum and distributes funding through the governorates to the local school systems. Under a law passed in the 1980s designed to consolidate power under the central government, local councils had limited revenue and policymaking prerogatives, making them largely dependent on Tunisia's central government.[14] According to Clark, Dalmasso, and Lust, "tutelle and oversight reduced the municipality's role during the Ben Ali period largely to the management of buildings and services, primarily trash collection."[15] Municipalities managed urban planning but had little influence over health, education, and other vital services.[16] Local councils and authorities had no budgetary power over schools and limited ability to oversee schools. Moreover, the Democratic Constitutional Rally (RCD) controlled political life through its national headquarters and local branches. The education sector in Tunisia was susceptible to the same clientelistic and corrupt practices that permeated other parts of the authoritarian regime under Bourguiba and Ben Ali.[17]

A local government law was passed before the 2018 municipal elections, but its implications for the education sector are not yet fully developed. Moreover, weak rule of law under the previous authoritarian regime has not yet been transformed by the nascent democratic political order that has emerged in Tunisia since 2011. The potential for the mismanagement of local schools by the centralized education system and weak rule of law, which make it difficult for education professionals to be held accountable, is exacerbated by the centralized nature of the national baccalaureate exam. This system places a great deal of pressure on students and their families to obtain high test scores as the only means to progress from high school to university studies and thus to access opportunities important for social mobility. This high-stakes system along with quality deficiencies and lack of transparency leads families to invest heavily in tutoring and extra classes, leading to a de facto form of privatization of the system.[18] Families spend more on tutoring and other services than the entire state budget, and this leads wealthier families to have advantages. It also expands the supply and demand for bribes to help students succeed in the high-stakes game.

Tunisia's Education System

Tunisia's education system is a centralized, test-based system modeled on the French tradition of primary, secondary, and post-secondary education. While optional for students, preschool education is supervised by the Ministry of Education and provided by public, private, and quasi private-public options. As of 2003, 22 percent of children from three to six years of age were enrolled in preschool programs in Tunisia.[19] The compulsory primary education consists of six years of primary and three years of preparatory education (i.e., lower-secondary). Upon completion of their lower-secondary studies, students take the national final exam of elementary studies. Those who receive a score of at least 50 percent pass and receive the diplomacy of elementary studies completion and are permitted to continue to high school. Otherwise, they must repeat the final grade and retake the exam. Failure at this stage leads some students to drop out of school.

Thus, students take two key exams—one at the end of elementary school and one at the end of high school—that determine whether they will be able to continue their education, what they can study, and thus what their life opportunities will be. The culmination of students' studies for those wishing to pursue further academic training is the national baccalaureate exam. Only students who pass the baccalaureate are permitted to enter post-secondary school. Those who do not pass are given a high school diploma and can then work or go on to private schooling. In 1995, 42.5 percent of baccalaureate entrants passed the test, making test preparation a high-stakes endeavor for students and their families.[20] As a result, families invest substantial resources in private tutoring to avoid their children losing the ability to advance in their studies.

Tunisia's centralized, bureaucratic system—when coupled with weak rule of law—weakens corruption control and accountability for teachers, administrators, and bureaucrats at all levels of the system. But it is not just overt corruption that is a concern; use of *wasta,* or connections, also greatly shapes access to and ability to resolve problems within schools. Teachers may offer extra tutoring, which leads to favoritism and creates a perverse incentive to provide low-quality teaching during the regular school day. They may also subtly or directly refuse to solve students' "problems" without receiving payments, or simply respond more quickly to families that provide such "gifts" or exchanges of interest.

Accordingly, I expect that students living in regions that have experienced less public investment (e.g., rural areas and interior regions) and from families with less income, regardless of their region of residence, will experience lower-quality education across a range of measures, including educational problems and the need to make informal payments.

Hypotheses

1: Students from the interior and western regions of Tunisia will suffer lower school quality and be more likely to make informal payments than those from coastal and eastern regions.

2: Students from less affluent families will suffer lower school quality and make more informal payments (i.e., bribes) than those from wealthier families.

Data and Methodology

The data used to test these hypotheses are from the Local Governance Performance Index, a large survey of Tunisians conducted in February 2015 by the Program on Governance and Local Development. The survey includes approximately 200 interviews in each of the eighteen municipalities and is weighted for national representativeness (see Table 6.1). The LGPI's national sample size ($N = 3,600$) permits fine-grained analysis of a relatively uncommon experience of paying bribes in the education context nationally. Yet by drawing large samples at the local level (200 interviews per municipality), municipal-level comparisons are also possible (e.g., a comparison of school quality in the Tunis municipalities of Cité el Khadra and Jebel Jelloud).

Table 6.1   Characteristics of Municipalities in Tunisia, 2015

Governorate	Municipality	Region	Percentage Rural	Rate of Potable Water Hookup (%)	Distance (km) to Regional Hub (Tunis, Sousse, or Sfax)
Sfax	Sfax Ville	Center east	0.0	98.0	1
Tunis	Cité el Khadra	Northeast	0.0	97.7	6
Tunis	Jebel Jelloud	Northeast	0.0	97.6	5
Tunis	La Marsa	Northeast	0.5	96.1	19
Bizerte	Bizerte Nord	Northeast	12.9	95.4	65
Monastir	Monastir	Center east	2.1	94.9	22
Bizerte	Mensel Jemil	Northeast	37.1	94.3	59
Mahdia	Mahdia	Center east	10.2	93.7	60
Monastir	Tebolba	Center east	100.0	93.1	42
Sfax	Sekiet Eddayer	Center east	0.9	92.9	5
Monastir	Moknine	Center east	17.3	92.1	36
Sfax	Sfax Sud	Center east	0.0	88.7	2
Mahdia	Ksour Essaf	Center east	97.9	84.1	70
Bizerte	Bizerte Sud	Northeast	20.4	74.3	65
Siliana	Gaafour	Northwest	97.1	72.5	110
Siliana	Siliana Ville	Northwest	16.7	70.1	127
Siliana	Bouarada	Northwest	54.5	69.5	93
Mahdia	Souassi	Center east	50.7	58.6	81

Sources: For percentage rural, Local Governance Performance Index. For rate of potable water hookup and distance to regional hub, National Institute of Statistics; data file provided directly to author.

The municipalities represent a wide range of urban and rural districts located in the north and center of the country and have varying economic profiles, allowing scholars to understand the impact of poverty at not only the individual but also the municipality level on education access and quality. The rate of water hookup in homes is lowest in Siliana-Nord/Ville (70.1 percent) and highest in Sfax-Ville (98.0 percent). Sfax is a regional hub, while Siliana is located 127 kilometers from the closest major city (see Table 6.1).

Education Questions

The survey was conducted at the household level. Households were selected using a probabilistic sample and one adult was randomly selected within each household. The survey respondent selected could be a mother or father of the child or in some cases another adult such as an aunt, uncle, or grandparent. The questionnaire asked a battery of questions about each child individually so that the unit of analysis is the child. The respondent was first asked to list the gender and age of all the children seventeen years or younger who normally sleep at the home. Then one child was selected at random by the tablet computer, and a battery of questions was asked about his or her school experience. Then the same battery of questions was repeated for up to six randomly selected children.

Since the average family size is small in Tunisia, most respondents answered the education battery no more than two times. Sixty-three percent of respondents skipped the education battery because they had no children seventeen years of age or younger living at their home; 1,344 respondents (37.2 percent) had one or more children at home. While this is surprising, Tunisia's population of 10.8 million (2013) is among the least-youthful of societies in the Arab region. Tunisia has a population growth rate of just over 1 percent per year.[21]

Education Quality and Transparency

Respondents were asked to rate various dimensions of school quality. Figure 6.1 shows assessments of infrastructure and quality in Tunisia's schools in the sample as a whole. Nearly 40 percent indicated that the toilets were clean and a similar proportion (41 percent) stated that their child's school had a parents' association. About half (52 percent) indicated that their school had only one shift and 66 percent stated that the school was well-built. About 69 percent of boys and girls were perceived as being safe going to school. Nearly 80 percent (79 percent) stated that it was untrue that teachers were frequently absent, and most (90 percent) believed that teachers did not show favoritism to students who took special classes with them, and 93 percent studied in classes of fewer than forty students.

Four of these indicators (i.e., small class size, teachers not absent, lack of shifts, and teachers not showing favoritism) are highly correlated and combined into a school-quality scale ranging from a low of –3.0206 to a high of 1.5746,[22] the first of three dependent variables examined in this chapter. Table 6.2 gives the mean school-quality score for the first randomly selected child in the survey. The municipalities with the worst-quality schools were in Bizerte, a large northwestern coastal governorate, and Tebolba in the Sahelian region of Monastir, while the best was Jebel Jelloud, an industrial area in the governorate of Tunis. Other top-performing municipalities were in the eastern coastal region of Sfax.

Figure 6.1   Components of Social-Quality Index, Tunisia, 2015

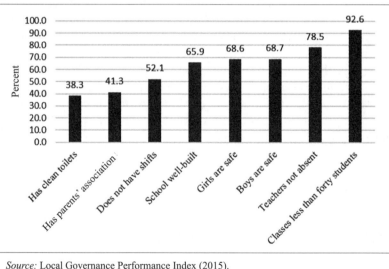

Source: Local Governance Performance Index (2015).

Note: Question wording: "Thinking about your nth' child; I'm going to read to you a series of statements about the school that he or she attends. Please tell me if it is true or not. 1. School is well-built. 2. There are clean toilets. 3. Classrooms have more than 40 students. 4. The school has two or more shifts. 5. Teachers are frequently absent. 6. Girls are safe going to/from school. 7. Boys are safe going to/from school. 8. The school has a parents' association. 9. Teachers favor in performance evaluations students who attend after-school study sessions. 1 = True, 2 = Not true."

Table 6.2 Mean School-Quality Index in Tunisia by Municipality, 2015

Bizerte Sud (Bizerte)	–0.87
Tebolba (Monastir)	–0.41
Bizerte Nord (Bizerte)	–0.38
Bouarada (Siliana)	–0.23
Sekiet Eddayer (Sfax)	–0.19
Mensel Jemil (Bizerte)	–0.17
Moknine (Monastir)	–0.09
La Marsa (Tunis)	–0.06
Monastir (Monastir)	–0.02
Souassi (Mahdia)	0.08
Gaafour (Siliana)	0.09
Mahdia (Mahdia)	0.13
Cité el Khadra (Tunis)	0.16
Ksour Essaf (Mahdia)	0.17
Siliana Ville (Siliana)	0.21
Sfax Ville (Sfax)	0.34
Sfax Sud (Sfax)	0.43
Jebel Jelloud (Tunis)	0.55

Source: Local Governance Performance Index (2015).
Note: School quality ranges from a low of –3.0206 to a high of 1.5746.

Respondents were also asked whether the student experienced a problem at school such as failing or being expelled during the previous year and, if so, how they addressed the problem. One common problem is grade repetition; grade repetition is associated in the education literature as a form of inefficiency that is usually the result of a poor system rather than of the individual. For example, in Egypt, repetition rates are high—among youths aged eighteen to twenty-two years, 21 percent had repeated a grade in Egypt—and rates are higher among boys and poorer families.[23] In Tunisia, rates are lower; among six- to sixteen-year-olds, 6.2 percent had repeated at least one grade. While this is lower than in Egypt, it still indicates the need to address the root causes of inefficient schooling.[24]

One cause of children repeating grades is encountering problems such as failing a class due to not having money for extra classes or experiencing teacher absenteeism. In the sample as a whole, 13 percent of the respondents stated for at least one of the children in the survey that there had been a problem in the previous year such as failing a class or being expelled.[25] The extent to which this was the case ranged from high in Bouarada (Siliana) of 38 percent to none in Jebel Jelloud (see Figure 6.2). Very few students (3 percent) encountered a problem in Bizerte Sud, a relatively poor area in the west of the country, while a quarter of households with children in the Tunis municipality of La Marsa did.

Figure 6.2   Percentage Reporting a Problem at School, Tunisia, 2015

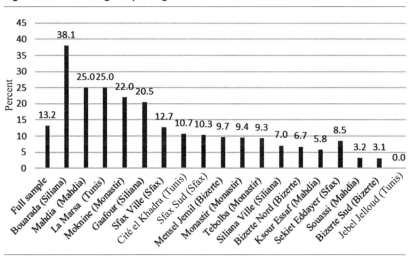

Source: Local Governance Performance Index (2015).
Note: Question wording: "In the last year, have you experienced a problem with this child's education at this school (such as s/he was failing a class, being expelled, etc.)?"

The survey also asked several questions about instances in which an informal payment (i.e., bribe) had been paid to address problems at school (see Figure 6.3). The third dependent variable, having paid a bribe, was coded as 1 if the respondent answered for any of the children living with them that they had paid a bribe in the past year.[26] Possible reasons for paying the bribe included (1) to address a problem with this child's education such as she or he was failing a class or being expelled, (2) to enroll a child in school, (3) to pass courses, (4) to obtain government assistance to pay for this child's education in the past year, or (5) to address an unspecified issue with teachers or principals at a child's school. Seven percent of respondents indicated that they had paid a bribe for one or more of these reasons in the past year. The proportion of respondents who had done so ranged from 32 percent in Tebolba to none in Bizerte Sud, Bouarada (Siliana), Monastir, Souassi (Mahdia), and Jebel Jelloud (Tunis).

Results and Discussion

I use multivariate regression to assess the factors that explain lower perceived school quality and a higher likelihood of experiencing problems.

Figure 6.3   Percentage Reporting Having Made an Informal Payment at School, 2015

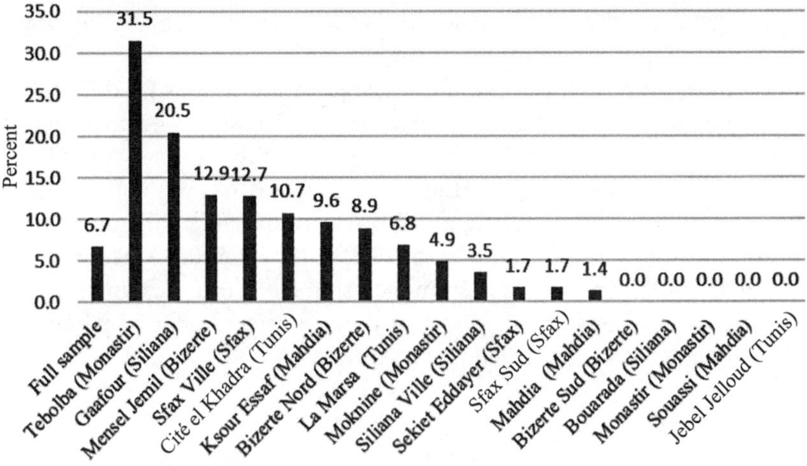

Source: Local Governance Performance Index (2015).

Note: Question wording: LGPI 513.1—"In the last year, have you experienced a problem with this child's education at this school (such as s/he was failing a class, being expelled, etc.)?" (if yes) LGPI 513.4—"Did you have to make an informal payment to solve a problem at this school?" LGPI 514.1—"Did you have difficulty enrolling your child in this school?" LGPI 514.4—"Did you have to make an informal payment to enroll this child?" LGPI 523 LONG—"Last academic year, how much was paid in informal payments (e.g., bribes) for things like your child to attend this school or to pass courses?" LGPI 527 LONG—"Did you get government assistance to pay for this child's education in the last year?" (if yes) LGPI 528 LONG—"Did you have to make an informal payment to get this assistance? Do you do any of the following for a child living here: Giving informal payments to teachers or principals at a child's school?"

I use three outcome variables: (1) higher school quality, an index ranging from a low of –3.0206 to a high of 1.5746, as shown in Table 6.2 and analyzed using ordinary least squares (OLS) regression; (2) a binary outcome measured as 1 if the respondent reported that at least one child in the home had experienced a problem in the past year, as shown in Figure 6.2 and analyzed using logistic regression; and (3) a binary outcome indicating whether the respondent reported that the household had paid at least one informal payment (i.e., bribe) in the preceding year, shown in Figure 6.3 and analyzed using logistic regression.

Measurement of Independent and Control Variables

I include several independent and control variables in the models, as well as post-stratification weights.[27] The models are robust to multiple specifications. I include respondent gender to control for the possibility that a parent or guardian of one gender may be more or less knowledgeable about the child's schooling or answer in an agreeable way. I also include higher education in four categories: no schooling (= 1), primary (= 2), secondary (= 3), and college or above (= 4). Higher religiosity is measured on a scale of 1 to 10 (i.e., 1 if she or he never prays, goes to mosque, or reads/listens to religious literature, and 10 if he or she often does these things). Higher social status is a scale of the number of items owned, including a car, refrigerator, and computer.[28] Rural residence is measured according to whether the interview was located in an urban (= 0) or rural (= 1) commune using the census designation, and district fixed effects are included for the localities. About 28 percent of the respondents were located in rural areas.

Higher Perceived School Quality

School quality varies systematically across the eighteen municipalities in the sample, controlling for other factors. As shown in Table 6.3, the best-quality schools are located in Tunis and Sfax. Relative to the comparison group, Bizerte Nord, eight districts have significantly higher school quality. The highest-performing schools are in Jebel Jelloud (Tunis), which also drops out of the second and third models because no respondent reported that their child experienced a problem or that they made an informal payment in Jebel Jelloud. Most of the highest-performing municipalities are located on the coast, but two are in Siliana, which is located in the northwest region of the country. Approximately 70 percent of families in these areas have water hookup.

Other municipalities in Tunis, Cité el Khadra, and La Marsa have lower school quality and are not significantly better than the base case, Bizerte Nord (see Figure 6.4). All else being equal, Bizerte Sud performs significantly less well than Bizerte Nord ($p < 0.05$). These results show that while school quality is generally better in the coastal, eastern areas of the country than in the west and south, some municipalities perform better or worse than might be expected based on their location and socioeconomic development as measured by indoor water plumbing.

Yet the family's socioeconomic status and the education level of the adult family member consistently shape education quality across the country, in support of my second hypothesis. As shown in the first model, more educated respondents and those with higher socioeconomic status have access to higher-quality schools for their children, all else being equal (see Table 6.3, first model). Students from families with

Table 6.3 Determinants of Higher-Quality Education in Tunisia, 2015

Independent Variables	Model 1 Quality Higher Education Quality Ordinary Least Squares Coefficients	Model 2 Quality Experienced a Problem Logistic Coefficients	Marginal Effects[a] (predicted probabilities)[b]	Model 3 Transparency Made an Informal Payment Logistic Coefficients	Marginal Effects[a] (predicted probabilities)[c]
Individual-level					
Female respondent	0.07 (0.07)	−0.04 (0.22)	−0.01 (0.04)	−0.17 (0.28)	−0.01 (0.01)
Higher education	0.10 (0.05)*	−0.33 (0.15)*	−0.05 (0.03)†	0.17 (0.20)	0.01 (0.01)
Higher religiosity	0.00 (0.01)	0.06 (0.04)	0.01 (0.01)	0.03 (0.05)	0.00 (0.00)
Higher social status	0.16 (0.08)*	−1.13 (0.27)***	−0.18 (0.10)†	0.20 (0.32)	0.01 (0.01)
Female child	0.00 (0.07)				
Rural				1.95 (0.38)***	0.16 (0.09)†
Municipality[d]					
Bizerte Sud	−0.46 (0.22)*	−1.01 (1.19)	−0.11 (0.13)		
Bouarada	0.20 (0.21)	1.95 (0.70)**	0.44 (0.13)***		
Cité el Khadra	0.37 (0.24)	1.51 (0.89)†	0.33 (0.20)†		
Gaafour	0.50 (0.21)*	1.06 (0.72)	0.22 (0.14)		
Jebel Jelloud	0.80 (0.23)***				
Ksour Essaf	0.50 (0.20)*	0.11 (0.86)	0.02 (0.14)		
La Marsa	0.31 (0.22)	2.22 (0.74)**	0.50 (0.14)***		
Mahdia	0.49 (0.18)**	1.56 (0.67)*	0.34 (0.12)**		
Mensel Jemil	0.20 (0.22)	0.41 (0.87)	0.07 (0.16)		
Moknine	0.29 (0.18)	1.40 (0.67)*	0.30 (0.12)*		
Monastir	0.20 (0.20)	1.19 (0.79)	0.25 (0.16)		
Sekiet Eddayer	0.13 (0.19)	0.58 (0.77)	0.11 (0.14)		
Sfax Sud	0.72 (0.19)***	0.97 (0.75)	0.20 (0.15)		
Sfax Ville	0.65 (0.19)***	1.11 (0.74)	0.23 (0.15)		
Siliana Ville	0.61 (0.19)***	−0.29 (0.81)	−0.04 (0.12)		
Souassi	0.46 (0.19)*	−0.92 (0.95)	−0.11 (0.12)		
Tebolba	−0.05 (0.19)	0.27 (0.78)	0.05 (0.13)		
Weight	−0.01 (0.03)	−0.07 (0.07)	−0.01 (0.01)	0.08 (0.09)	0.00 (0.00)
Constant	−0.72 (0.22)***	−0.203 (0.79)*			−3.68 (0.09)
N	900	865		900	
F	(23) = 4.59***	(21) = 98.75***		(11) = 43.55***	
R^2/Pseudo R^2	0.1076	0.1433		0.0988	

Source: Local Governance Performance Index (2015).

Notes: †$p < 0.10$, *$p < 0.05$, **$p < 0.01$, ***$p < 0.001$. Two-tailed test. Standard errors in parentheses.

a. $\partial y/\partial x$ for variable means, change of dummy variables from 0 to 1.

b. Reference group is female respondent with a high school degree (= 3), median religiosity (= 5), low socioeconomic status (= −1.33), in Bizerte Nord.

c. Reference group is female respondent with a high school degree (= 3), median religiosity (= 5), low socioeconomic status (= −1.33), in Bizerte Governorate.

d. Reference group: Bizerte Nord is the reference group for Models 1 and 2. Bizerte governorate is the reference group for Model 3.

Figure 6.4   Predicted School Quality Score, by Municipality, 2015

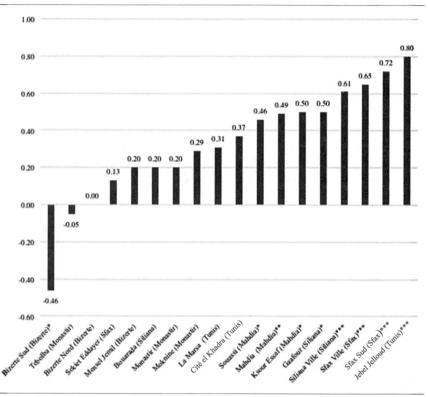

Source: Local Governance Performance Index (2015).
Note: * $p < 0.05$, ** $p < 0.01$, *** $p < 0.001$.

fewer resources encounter more difficulties, even if they live in coastal governorates. Those in the interior who have more income receive better education than the poor, even if they live in the interior. This only partially supports expectations of my first hypothesis.

It is somewhat surprising that socioeconomic class is as strong a predictor of school quality. This suggests that school quality, which in the first model is a school- or classroom-level perception, is driven not only by the economic situation of the municipality, but also by the family's socioeconomic status. This may be because private tutoring and other sources of private funds for schools have a substantial impact on the overall quality of the classroom and school environment in Tunisia, as they do in Egypt.[29] As a result, school quality in Tunisia departs somewhat from the notion of neighborhood effects resulting from disparities in public funding. While these disparities exist, private sources of funds also have an outsized impact on school quality.

Perceived school quality does not vary systematically for girls and boys. What appears to explain school quality is the socioeconomic and educational level of the parent and features of the funding and management of the school system itself at the local level.

Higher Incidence of Problems in School

Socioeconomic status is also a driver of problems that students encounter at school such as failing a class or being expelled. Children from less affluent families with less educated parents are more likely to have problems in school (see Table 6.3, second model). For a female respondent with median religiosity (= 5), low socioeconomic status (= −1.33), who lives in Bizerte Nord, being illiterate is associated with a 5 percent increase in the probability of experiencing a problem over a respondent with a graduate education ($p < 0.10$). For this same respondent, having the lowest level of socioeconomic status is associated with an 18 percent increase in the likelihood of experiencing a problem at school compared to a respondent with the highest level of income ($p < 0.10$). However, there is no impact of the respondent's religiosity on either indicator of school quality.

Figure 6.5 shows the predicted probability of having at least one child in the household who experienced a problem depending on whether the child is at the lowest or highest level of socioeconomic status. The probability is very high (over 60 percent) for children from low-income families in Cité el Khadra (Tunis), La Marsa (Tunis), and Bouarada (Siliana). Among high-income families, the predicted probability that at least one child in their house has experienced a problem in school is never more than 7.9 percent, the probability for La Marsa. The gender of the child is not included in this regression because the dependent variable corresponds to whether one or more children in the household of any gender experienced a problem in school (to increase the number of reported problems needed to estimate the regression). However, the LGPI reports low gender differences in the prevalence of those experiencing problems; 15 percent of boys and 13 percent of girls had experienced a problem.

Making Informal Payments

Residing in a rural area was the only factor that significantly predicted having made an informal payment to enroll a child or resolve a problem

Figure 6.5   Predicted Probability of Child Encountering a Problem in School, by Municipality, 2015

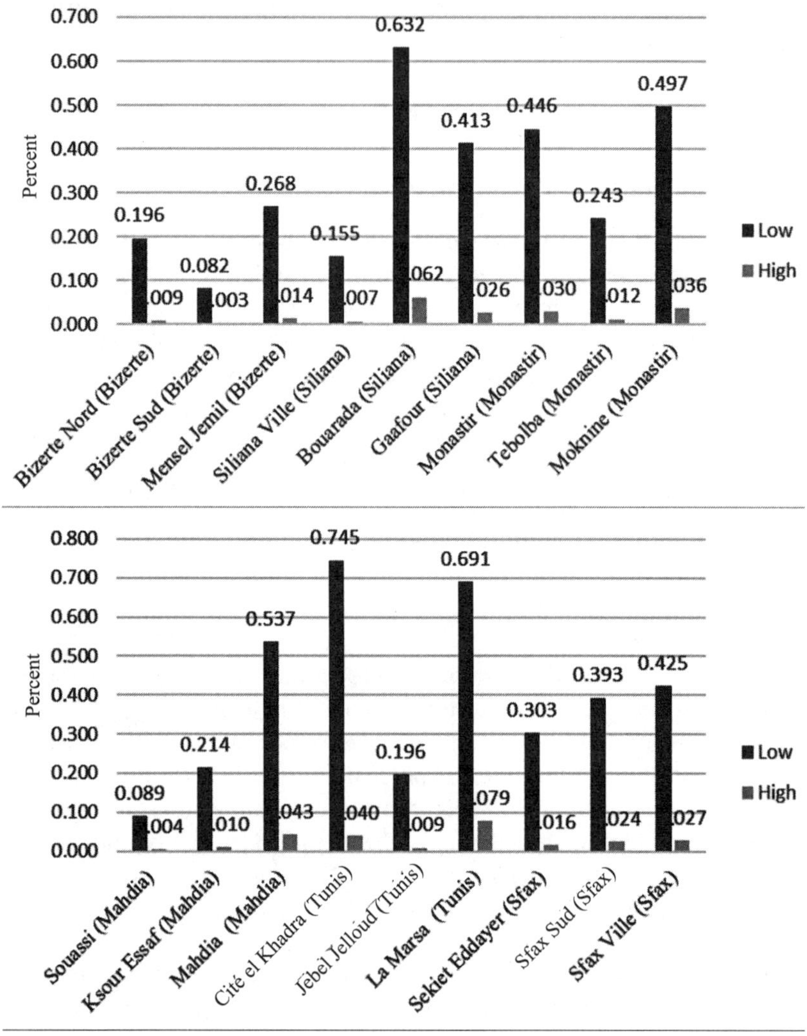

Source: Local Governance Performance Index (2015).

at school (see Table 6.3, third model). Those in rural areas were 16 percent more likely to have made a payment than those in urban areas, but the effect does not reach conventional significance levels ($p < 0.10$). Because informal payments, uncommon or common, are underreported, the governorate-level fixed effects are used instead of municipal-level fixed effects. There were no statistically significant differences across the governorates in the likelihood of paying a bribe, contrary to my first hypothesis. Moreover, parental education or income was unrelated to the likelihood of making an informal payment, contrary to my second hypothesis. This may be because families with different income levels may make informal payments and that it is the overall prevalence of such payments that is most crucial.

Conclusion and Implications

Due to Tunisia's centralized education system, it is theoretically possible to distribute resources in an equitable way that helps ensure that the education system is a means of social mobility for all families. Yet centralized policies are seldom uniformly implemented across localities or institutions.[30] Despite Tunisia's centralized system, students encounter unequal education opportunities based on their economic resources and region of residence. This is due in large part to the need for and prevalence of private tutoring, which is a subtle form of privatization common in Arab countries, including Egypt.[31] All else being equal, poor households in Tunisia and those with less educated parents face lower-quality education systems with higher teacher absenteeism, larger class sizes, and poorer facilities. Tunisians in rural areas, where state capacity is weak, are more likely than those in urban areas to need to pay bribes to improve the educational experience of their children. This situation is particularly troubling in a system in which two national tests determine whether students advance to higher education and enjoy improved employment opportunities.

In addition to the role that economic inequality plays in undermining education quality, the high prevalence with which families report paying bribes to obtain or improve educational outcomes is alarming. Given the small number of observations and the sensitivity of the issue, more in-depth research involving focus groups, and indirect methods such as experiments to assess the degree to which informal payments are being made, are needed. Actual levels of corruption in the education sector may be higher. The Arab Barometer found that many citizens believe that *rahswa* (bribes) are needed to obtain a better education. The proportion who stated that this was the case was 64 percent in Egypt, 62 percent in Lebanon, 55 percent in Sudan, 54 percent in Morocco, 53 percent in Algeria, 53 percent in Yemen, 52 percent in Iraq, 50 percent in Tunisia, 33 percent in Palestine, 32 percent in Libya, and 29 percent in Jordan.[32]

The results presented in this chapter challenge existing literature that sees the Tunisian education system either in monolithic terms, hailing its quality vis-à-vis other countries in the region,[33] or in a stylized way in which the well-resourced coastal region is juxtaposed against the underprivileged interior. The best-quality schooling is in the coastal areas of Tunis and Sfax. The results presented here complicate this picture and show that economic resources shape the quality of education received, regardless of region. Families with fewer resources encounter more difficulties and have lower-quality schooling options in economically neglected areas of Tunis than in some districts in the interior.

This subnational variation in educational opportunities merits additional investigation. Qualitative research is needed to understand why municipalities that are otherwise similarly placed—for instance, those within the same municipality—are marked by vastly differing levels of school quality. For instance, the Program on Governance and Local Development report found that La Marsa, a municipality in the governorate of Tunis, has a dropout rate of 14 percent, which is twice that of Cité el Khadra, another area in the same governorate. In the governorate of Monastir, the rates in Tebolba and Moknine are 23 percent and 16 percent, respectively, compared to just 9 percent in the governorate's seat of Monastir.

While such an investigation is outside the scope of this chapter, the analyses presented here should serve as a basis for case selection for researchers seeking to conduct a qualitative research project in two municipalities using either a similar or different system design. Funding levels are one potential source of inequalities, but management and professionalism may also play a strong role in shaping the differences observed across municipalities in Tunisia. For instance, in a study of Pakistan, Naviwala finds that increases in the education budget might be misspent on building projects with huge kickbacks to companies or salary increases to teachers without appropriate monitoring of their performance and attendance at work.[34]

It is also important that gender differences across students did not appear in perceived school quality in the first model, the only model in which it was possible to include a measure for the gender of the child. This is consistent with what we know about girls' access to education in Tunisia. The Program on Governance and Local Development report shows that Tunisian girls are more likely than boys to be enrolled in school, with 11.9 percent (107,674) of the males and 8.9 percent (70,667) of the females not attending. Moreover, the report found that there is no significant difference in the use of private tutors, suggesting that Tunisian parents, on the whole, do not privilege boys' education over girls'. Tunisia's success in reducing gender inequality in educational attainment is due to the sustained effort by Bourguiba and Ben Ali to promote women in politics and the labor force, which included gender quotas for management positions in state-run enterprises and elected assemblies and resulted in higher returns from educating girls.[35]

However, it is important to consider that gender gaps have not been eliminated in Tunisia. Girls in poor, rural areas often do not experience a return to education because there is less employment for them.[36] This is problematic. Moreover, while this reverse gender gap is inconsistent with stereotypes about the Arab world, women are also enrolled in school in greater numbers in many other Arab countries as well, especially at the tertiary level. But this may not be the case in all countries. For instance, Benaabdelaali Wail, Said Hanchane, and Abdelhak Kamal find regional and gender gaps in the GINI index of inequality in Morocco, which may be more typical of many Arab contexts.[37] Gender and other forms of inequality in educational attainment hamper human development,[38] reinforce economic cleavages, and make conflict and political instability more likely.[39] And they are concerns in all Arab countries to one degree or another.

To address regional inequality in school quality, increases to the state budget for preschool, tutoring, and safety (e.g., school buses, better toilets) are important. But neither increased state funding nor decentralization alone will redress problems of mismanagement and corruption. Rather, reforms to the transparency of elections and the overall system of government accountability are critical to ensuring that the poor and those in rural areas can hold their elected officials and bureaucrats accountable. Changes must provide ways for parents and community groups to participate directly in institutions that decide how educational resources are spent and strengthen mechanisms, including electoral and judicial transparency, that ensure rule of law, reduce corruption, and create a rational-legal framework between citizens and the state.

Such reform will not come easily, but its potential rewards for economic growth and a stronger democracy are compelling. There is a robust relationship between higher levels of mass, primary, and tertiary education and democratization.[40] Yet as other authors in this volume illustrate, greater spending on education does not automatically produce citizens who will reject authoritarianism. Despite the many deep socioeconomic challenges that are gripping the country, a democratic Tunisia is in a unique position to create an equitable and transparent education sector and reap the rewards of greater prosperity and a more open society in the years ahead.

Notes

1. Perkins, *A History of Modern Tunisia.*
2. For example, in Algeria, where educational institutions were undermined by colonial powers, see Benstead and Reif, "Polarization or Pluralism?"
3. Degorge, "The Modernization of Education."
4. Trabelsi, "Regional Inequality of Education in Tunisia."
5. Benstead, "Tunisia," in *The Government and Politics of the Middle East and North Africa.*
6. *The Development of Education National Report of Education, Republic of Tunisia (2004–2008),* as cited in "Education in Tunisia," https://en.wikipedia.org /wiki/Education_in_Tunisia#cite_note-13.
7. Ibid.
8. The official Ministry of Education statistic (2012–2013) is 107,000 (under 16).
9. Program on Governance and Local Development (GLD), "The Tunisian Local Governance Performance Index: Selected Findings on Education," Report prepared by Lindsay Benstead, Kristen Kao, Adam Harris, Pierre Landry, Ellen Lust, and Natalia Stepanova, http://gld.gu.se/media/1108/report-education_eng.pdf.
10. Marie Thourson Jones, "Regional Disparities and Public Policy in Tunisian Education."
11. *The Development of Education National Report of Education, Republic of Tunisia (2004–2008),* as cited in "Education in Tunisia," https://en.wikipedia.org /wiki/Education_in_Tunisia#cite_note-13.
12. Bellin, "The Robustness of Authoritarianism in the Middle East: Exceptionalism in Comparative Perspective."
13. Trabelsi, "Regional Inequality of Education in Tunisia."
14. The central government set the parameters of the taxation system. Municipalities collected tax on land, industrial establishments, and hotels. See Clark, Dalmasso, and Lust, "Not the Only Game in Town."
15. Interview with Mokhtar Hammami, the general director of the General Direction of Public Local Collectivities (GDPLC), in Clark, Dalmasso, and Lust, "Not the Only Game in Town," p. 10.
16. Yerkes and Marwan, "Decentralization in Tunisia."
17. Milovanovitch, "Trust and Institutional Corruption."
18. Lust, Landry, Benstead, and Malouche, "The Tunisian Local Governance Performance Index."
19. *The Development of Education National Report of Education, Republic of Tunisia (2004–2008),* as cited in "Education in Tunisia," https://en.wikipedia.org /wiki/Education_in_Tunisia#cite_note-13.
20. Ibid.
21. US Department of State, "Tunisia," March 9, 2012, https://web.archive.org /web/20121013143542/http://www.state.gov/outofdate/bgn/tunisia/196390.htm. The nature of the questionnaire may also have incentivized respondents and interviewers to not report every child living in the household in order to reduce the survey length.
22. Lust, Landry, Benstead, and Malouche, "The Tunisian Local Governance Performance Index."
23. Elbadawy, "Education in Egypt."
24. Soussi and Bouhlila, "Child Labor and Schooling."
25. This variable is computed as 1 if, for any of the questions in the survey, a problem was reported. This is to increase the number of observations for the dependent variable. The same approach is used for informal payments.

26. Figures 6.1 and 6.2 (Models 1 and 2) show answers for the first randomly selected child per respondent. Figure 6.3 (Model 3) shows the answers for any child living in the household in order to increase the number of reports of corruption, which are relatively rare due to the sensitivity of the topic.

27. I included weights and fixed effects for the municipality (Models 1 and 2) or governorate (Model 3).

28. For more information on coding, see Program on Governance and Local Development (GLD), "The Tunisian Local Governance Performance Index: Selected Findings on Education," report prepared by Lindsay Benstead, Kristen Kao, Adam Harris, Pierre Landry, Ellen Lust, and Natalia Stepanova, http://gld .gu.se/media/1108/report-education_eng.pdf.

29. Elbadawy, "Education in Egypt."

30. Lin, *Reform in the Making.*

31. Elbadawy, "Education in Egypt."

32. Arab Barometer, "Fact Sheet: Are Arab Citizens Satisfied with the Education System?" January 13, 2020, https://www.arabbarometer.org/2020/01/we-asked-over -25000-arab-citizens-to-evaluate-the-educational-services-in-their-country-here-is -what-we-found-out/.

33. Masri, *Tunisia.*

34. Naviwala, "Why Can't Pakistani Children Read?"

35. Benstead, "Tunisia," in *Palgrave Handbook of Women's Rights.*

36. Trabelsi, "Regional Inequality of Education in Tunisia."

37. Wail, Hanchane, and Kamal, "A New Data Set of Educational Inequality in the World."

38. Klasan, "Low Schooling for Girls"; also Siddhanta and Nandy, "Gender Gap in Education."

39. Ferranti, Perry, Ferreira, and Walton, *Inequality in Latin America.*

40. Sanborn and Thyne, "Learning Democracy." Moreover, education is typically underfunded in authoritarian regimes; see Feng and Zak, "The Determinants of Democratic Transitions."

7

US University Campuses in the Gulf Monarchies

Christopher M. Davidson

The Gulf monarchies, and especially the two wealthiest per capita—the United Arab Emirates (UAE) and Qatar[1]—are now home to several branch campuses of some of the premier US research universities, including New York University (NYU), Georgetown, Northwestern, Texas A&M, Carnegie Mellon, and Virginia Commonwealth. Likewise, leading French and British universities are well represented, with La Sorbonne,[2] University College London,[3] Aberdeen,[4] and several others having also established a presence. Though this phenomenon is by no means unique to the Gulf states, with similar sorts of arrangements having also emerged in China, Singapore, and elsewhere, nothing seems comparable to the scale and intensity of the branch campus-building in the UAE and Qatar.[5] Besides, unlike the highly populated East Asian states, all of which have sizable domestic student markets, the UAE and Qatar are home to only a few million residents, of whom only 10 and 12 percent, respectively, are actual citizens, with the vast majority being low-wage migrant laborers.[6]

How then are we to explain this remarkable situation, much of which has arisen in only the past ten to fifteen years? Specifically, what have been the intended objectives—official and unofficial—of establishing all these outposts, from the perspectives of both the host governments and the educational institutions themselves? Moreover, have any of these objectives actually been met, and is there evidence that such an apparently high-capacity macro-level educational strategy has helped or hindered vital micro-level development processes in these countries? Finally, and most broadly, do the results thus far indicate that these wealthy authoritarian states retain "limited-access orders" in which only privileged residents can access certain benefits and freedoms (as understood by a seminal World Bank policy research working paper),[7] or do they instead suggest a willingness to engage in the sort of reforms that may eventually support the kind of open-access orders most often found in the developed world?

Beyond compiling and assessing the available hard data relating to these institutions and the indigenous higher-education environment in these two states, this chapter seeks to furnish answers to these questions by content-analyzing relevant US university and Emirati/Qatari government press releases; by interpreting applicable US government data; and by compiling the findings of the now significant number of nongovernmental organization (NGO), think tank, and broadsheet investigative reports on the topic. In an effort to provide further layers of understanding, the chapter also draws on those existing statements in the public domain made by individual administrators, faculty, or others involved in the establishment or functioning of these institutions, alongside an author-conducted (and necessarily anonymized) survey of seventeen practitioners either currently or formerly affiliated with five of these branch campuses.[8]

Official Explanations

Most of the official explanations put forward by the US universities opening branch campuses in the UAE and Qatar have tended to focus on intended contributions to their hosts' long-term economic development. In particular, as both the UAE and Qatar are committed to reducing their reliance on oil and gas export revenues and boosting their non-hydrocarbon gross domestic product (GDP), much of their governmental planning documentation refers to the need to build up "knowledge economies" to serve as umbrellas for higher-education institutions and advanced technology businesses along with other public and private sector research and development facilities. For example, the UAE's "Vision 2021 National Agenda" calls for a "first rate education system" as part of a "competitive knowledge economy,"[9] while Qatar's "National Vision 2030" aims to "lay the foundations for a diversified and competitive knowledge-based economy."[10]

Led by citizens, these emerging knowledge economies are also intended to increase the proportion of citizens working in the private sector, which in the UAE and Qatar (and indeed all the Gulf states) remains heavily dominated by expatriates. The UAE government, for example, has set itself the target of "increasing Emiratization ten times in the private sector,"[11] while the Qatari government has established a "Qatarization" initiative, having sought advice from the World Bank.[12] Although rarely pointed out directly in official planning documents, but nonetheless widely referred to in academic circles and by members of the business elite, such knowledge economies are seen as one of the few politically viable ways of diversifying the economic base and nationalizing the labor force. This perception is largely explained on the grounds that the sort of employment created will be more palatable to the new generation of Emirati and Qatari citizens (most of whose parents enjoyed generous "rentier state" public sector employment)[13] than the sort of work—often more clerical or menial—usually associated with expatriates.

Launched in 2010, for example, New York University's liberal arts–focused UAE campus in Abu Dhabi has specified it is there to "advance NYU as a model university for the 21st century and contribute in multiple ways to the development of a sustainable, knowledge-based economy in Abu Dhabi."[14] Launched a year earlier, Georgetown's international studies–focused Qatar campus has similarly stated that its mission is to "work with our partner, Qatar Foundation, in its endeavours to achieve the Qatar National Vision 2030 and help develop Qatar's knowledge economy."[15] Moreover, Georgetown's numerous other US neighbors in Qatar have been making much the same claim, with the journalism-focused Northwestern even explicitly describing itself as "part of a wider investment agenda by the Qatar Foundation to bring world-class higher education to the country and to enable its transition to a knowledge-based economy."[16]

In this context, the inviting and funding of leading US research universities to set up branch campuses has almost certainly been seen as a means of "fast-forwarding" the emergence of knowledge economies on the basis that these more established institutions can quickly train up an indigenous cadre of new research professionals and—via a demonstration effect—help diffuse their research culture to the local economy. After all, despite "national" government-run universities having existed for decades (UAE University was founded in 1976 and Qatar University was founded in 1973), their contributions to fostering a research culture appear to have been limited, despite the significant resources allocated to their development.[17]

Meanwhile, from the perspective of the US universities, most of the explanations publicly put forward by senior academic administrators have also tended to concentrate on two further aspects: their institutions' global missions, of which opening branch campuses in several different parts of the world is seen as an essential and inevitable component of their expansionary plans; and (more ideologically) the golden opportunity for their institutions to play some sort of nongovernmental, education-led, missionary or bridging role to help bring different cultures and civilizations closer together. In this second sense at least, there is perhaps some common ground with the "original" US universities in the Arab world—the Syrian Protestant College (renamed the American University of Beirut) and the American University of Cairo.[18] Indeed, respectively established in 1866 and 1919 by Christian missionary organizations, the former's guiding principle was that its students would leave after "believing in one God, in many gods, or in no God . . . [but that it would] be impossible for anyone to continue with us long without knowing what we believe to be the truth and our reasons for that belief"; while the American University in Cairo was more generally expected to promote "good moral and ethical behaviour."[19]

NYU, for example, has stated that its UAE campus represents "a diverse and vital center of distinctive education and scholarship, actively embedded in NYU's global network, [that] will be recognized as the model for a new paradigm in higher education: the university as an engine of a more peaceful, cooperative, and productive world." It has also claimed that its Abu Dhabi branch "will be an essential institution in and of Abu Dhabi, a leading global city that is open and dynamic, economically and culturally vibrant, and a magnet for diverse and creative people from across the UAE and around the world."[20] Similarly, Georgetown has stated that its Qatar campus is "dedicated to fulfilling Georgetown University's mission of promoting intellectual, ethical, and spiritual understanding through serious and sustained discourse among people of different faiths, cultures, and beliefs." It has also claimed that the campus will "undertake education, research, and service in order to advance knowledge and provide students and the community with a holistic educational experience that produces global citizens committed to the service of humankind."[21]

Unofficial Explanations

Beyond the Emirati and Qatari governments' official, political economy–driven explanations, several scholars have suggested that the hosting of such US university branch campuses is also (and perhaps even more importantly) an element of what have become increasingly dynamic and multifaceted foreign policies.[22] Viewed through this lens, the inviting and funding of internationally respected institutions (and their constituent high-profile academics and research networks) to the UAE and Qatar represents a new component of the preexisting, long-standing strategy of Gulf sovereign wealth funds or ruling-family members investing in a range of cultural, sporting, and leisure institutions in the United States, Britain, and other Western powers. Over the years such investments have been perceived as helping to build up attractive "soft power" ties (as per Joseph Nye's definition)[23] in the countries that the Gulf states continue to regard as their most steadfast security guarantors. In this sense, the UAE and Qatar's burgeoning relations with prestigious US universities, as with their state-linked purchases of the famous Manchester City and Paris St. Germain football clubs,[24] or their associations with the most renowned French and British museums,[25] provide an additional "soft" means of complementing established "hard power" arrangements with the Western powers (most of which have involved the continuous purchasing of Western armaments, or the semi-permanent hosting of Western military facilities).

For the universities involved, on top of any putative globalizing or ideological agendas, the opportunity to attract very generous external funding also seems to have been a significant factor, even if not explicitly stated. After all, for many years a number of leading Western universities (and research-focused think tanks) have already been soliciting and accepting Gulf government or ruling-family donations—mostly to help build new facilities or endow new programs or professorships—and so in this sense the branch-campus strategy represents something of a logical development. According to a 2018 dataset published by the US Department for Education's *Foreign Gifts and Contracts Report,* over the preceding six years the Gulf states accounted for nearly a quarter of all foreign donations to US universities, with Qatar providing $1.3 billion and the UAE $213 million (and Saudi Arabia $581 million).[26] Correspondingly, it has been widely reported that in recent years the Gulf states have also been among the biggest donors to leading US think tanks, with a 2014 *New York Times* investigation revealing that millions of dollars of Emirati and Qatari funding has recently been gifted to organizations including the World Resource Institute, the Stimson Center, the Middle East Institute, the Center for Strategic and International Studies, the Brookings Institution, and the Atlantic Council.[27] While no up-to-date figures exist for British universities or research institutions, data assembled for the period up to 2008 indicate that at least $90.8 million (and possibly as much as $188.4 million)[28] had been donated by the Gulf states, including substantial sums from Qatar and at least $22.9 million from the UAE (and at least $53.3 million from Saudi Arabia).[29]

In this context it would seem important to differentiate between the presence of the elite research institutions in the Gulf that are the focus of this study—all of which have had the financing of their branch campuses underwritten by their hosts (and in some cases appear to have also enjoyed financial support for their home US campuses or overall budgets)—and the various other, arguably less prestigious, Western universities that have also tried to establish a presence in the Gulf. In the first category, for example, it was described in 2011 how "the financing of NYU Abu Dhabi is noteworthy. . . . [T]he college is being entirely paid for by Abu Dhabi, the largest and richest of the United Arab Emirates, which has so far provided generously, including financial aid for many students and a promise to build a sprawling campus."[30] Moreover, in 2011 it was also reported that La Sorbonne Abu Dhabi's "developer, owner, and operator" was the Abu Dhabi government-linked Manhal Development Company.[31] Since then (or at least for the period 2012 to 2018), the US Department for Education's *Foreign Gifts and Contracts Report*'s dataset reveals that NYU has received thirty-four further payments totaling $80.7 million from a range of Emirati government entities, Emirati conglomerates, and anonymous UAE-based donors. Even more generously for those with Qatar campuses, during this six-year period alone Georgetown received $350.9 million from Qatar-based sources; Northwestern $340.2 million; Texas A&M $274.7 million; Carnegie Mellon $266.2 million; and Virginia Commonwealth $40.7 million.[32]

Although it is difficult to determine exactly how these funds have been disbursed by the recipient universities (their memorandums of understanding with the UAE and Qatar have mostly remained secret),[33] they are often listed as "contractual payments" rather than as gifts; seem to have focused on faculty salaries and other campus-running costs; and appear to have come with few explicit strings attached. As NYU's president Andrew Hamilton recently clarified, "The relationship with the [UAE] government is a partnership. . . . [T]he partnership and the generosity of the UAE government helped build the campus, it helps run the campus on a day-to-day basis." He also claimed that "all academic matters, all appointments, all research emphasis, classroom materials, topics, curriculum all are determined by NYU and that is a very clear part of the understanding in the interaction that NYU has with the UAE."[34] For those institutions with Qatar campuses, the situation seems to have been more or less the same, with the primary funding vehicle being the Qatar Foundation for Education, Science, and Community Development—a state-financed umbrella entity that describes itself as a nonprofit organization and was cofounded by the former ruler, Hamad bin Khalifa al-Thani, and his influential wife, Moza bint Nasser al-Misnad (the latter still serving as its chairperson).[35]

According to the author-surveyed practitioners either currently or formerly affiliated with five of the branch campuses, almost all highlighted the extraordinarily generous financial support provided by the host governments, with many describing a culture of high salaries, generous (and in some cases exorbitant) travel expenses, good-quality living accommodation, and a range of other perks and benefits they might not have been able to enjoy as a faculty member in the United States.[36] They also pointed to very substantial student scholarships, and in some cases almost unlimited resources available for students, including well-stocked libraries and a plethora of high-end information technology equipment.[37] With regard to the exact disbursement processes, none were able to illustrate the exact mechanisms; however, several stated that senior Emirati and Qatari officials were certainly involved alongside the university administrators, even if behind the scenes.[38]

Although the second category (of less prestigious and lower-ranked Western universities) currently includes some solid higher-education providers and good potential contributors to Gulf knowledge economies (including the University of Connecticut in the United States; Britain's Middlesex, Heriot Watt, Bolton, and Strathclyde; and Australia's Wollongong, Murdoch, Curtin, and Western Sydney), they do not appear to have been able to offer their hosts the same sort of big brand "soft power" opportunities as have the elite institutions. As such they have tended to receive little or no state funding for their operations and have mostly been treated as strictly private sector business ventures. Rather than locating themselves in Qatar or the UAE's wealthiest constituent emirate of Abu Dhabi, these foreign branch campuses have tended to base themselves in Dubai's educational "free zones" (as discussed by Jason Lane in his comparative study of branch campuses)[39] or in the UAE's less resource-rich "northern emirates," to keep their costs low. Nevertheless (and in something of a parallel to the wave of US universities that attempted to established branches in Japan in the 1980s and early 1990s),[40] many have still struggled to be profitable and in some cases have had to close down and withdraw, having apparently been offered no support from their hosts. In 2009, for example, George Mason University had to terminate its Ra's al-Khaimah campus before graduating a single student, while in 2010 Michigan State University opted to close its Dubai campus, having intended to recruit as many as 1,000 students but having only ever had 85 undergraduate students.[41]

Objectives Met?

Measuring the overall "success" of these US university branch campuses (or at least those of the elite institutions that are the primary focus of this study) is not easy due to the lack of quantifiable indicators and the fairly short length of their presence in the Gulf. Regarding the political economy objectives, however, it seems clear that the expected contributions to building a knowledge economy have not yet materialized. Now several years and in some cases more than a decade after their founding, only very small numbers of actual citizens have been educated by these institutions with an even smaller number having then gone on to be employed in the UAE or Qatar. Instead, the vast majority of their graduates have been expatriates or international students who then appear to go on to seek work elsewhere.

In New York University's case, for example, only 74 of the 389 students (19 percent) composing its class of 2022 on its UAE branch campus are Emirati citizens, while 45 are US citizens and—as per official statements—"students from South Korea, Egypt, India, Pakistan, United Kingdom, China, Jordan, and Poland make up the next largest cohorts with eight or more students from each country in the class."[42] According to the branch campus's publicly accessible employment data, 62 percent of its graduates from the recent class of 2018 are employed (with 25 percent in postgraduate education), but only 49 percent of these employed graduates are working in the UAE, with the NYU not providing data on how many of these are actually Emirati citizens employed in the UAE, and in particular in the UAE's private sector.[43]

Meanwhile, for Georgetown's Qatar campus, only 42 percent of its class of 2018 graduates are listed as being Qatari citizens and only 111 of its total current number of 249 students (45 percent) are listed as being Qatari, with the remaining students comprising forty-four different nationalities. Its new class of 2022—made up of forty-two different nationalities and hailing from twenty-nine different countries—seems to have an even lower proportion of citizens (32 percent). Regarding employment, only 64–73 percent of its total of 389 to 439 graduates since the campus was founded in 2009 (there are conflicting statistics) are recorded as being employed, with no data available on how many of these are Qatari citizens. Although there is very limited publicly accessible data on how many graduates (of all nationalities) have been employed in Qatar, it is stated that a total of thirty-five former students now work for the Qatari government or public sector, and that there are six graduates working for PriceWaterhouseCoopers.[44]

The other US branch campuses seem to tell a similar story, even if data are a little less clear (or sometimes absent), especially regarding eventual employment destinations. The latest annual report, published by Northwestern's Qatar campus, states that after ten years of operating, the overall student body now comprises 53 percent Qatari citizens with the others hailing from twenty-five countries.[45] Similarly, Texas A&M's engineering-focused Qatar campus states in its most recent report that 56 of the 110 bachelor degrees awarded in 2017 (51 percent) were to Qatari citizens, and that its new class of 2020 included sixty Qatari students (55 percent), which was described as "the largest intake of Qatari freshmen ever."[46] Carnegie Mellon's business, science, and information technology–focused Qatar campus states that it has 388 current students and a total of 679 to 769 alumni (there are conflicting statistics), of which 44 percent are Qatari citizens. Its most recent annual report, however, states that its graduating class of 2018 comprised ninety students, of whom only thirty-five were Qatari citizens (39 percent). A number of Qatari public sector entities and international multinationals are listed as graduate employment destinations, and a claim is made that "more than 80 percent live and work in Qatar," although a breakdown as to how many of those working in Qatar (as opposed to simply "living" in Qatar) are actually Qatari citizens is not provided.[47] Virginia Commonwealth's Qatar campus states that it has 339 current students and 624 alumni, and that 62 percent of its current student body are Qatari citizens. Although this is the highest proportion of citizens studying in any of the US branch campuses, the most recent alumni split seems to have been exactly fifty-fifty.[48]

According to the author-surveyed practitioners either currently or formerly affiliated with five of the branch campuses, all have confirmed that the bulk of students they have educated have been foreigners and that there were never internal institutional objectives that the majority of students would eventually be citizens.[49] Going further, some admitted that when they arrived, they were surprised as to how few citizens there actually were in their classes and expressed incredulity that such significant Emirati and Qatari state resources were essentially being lavished on foreign students.[50] With regard to employment destinations, about three-quarters of those surveyed revealed that of those citizens they had taught and remained in contact with, the majority of those who had gone on to work had found traditional government or other public sector jobs, with very few entering the private sector.[51] Some also expressed concern that the private sector was still "looked down upon" by the citizens they had taught, regardless of any high-level knowledge economy–building or labor-nationalization initiatives.[52]

As for any demonstration effect, the presence of the US universities does not yet seem to have made a particularly strong impression, with the indigenous higher-education institutions all remaining very low in world rankings and apparently still lacking in research capacity, research impact, and graduate employability. According to the 2019 QS Top Universities rankings, for example, UAE University is only 350th in the world, while Qatar University is only joint 332nd (and by comparison they are both well below comparable institutions in Kazakhstan and Malaysia).[53] Similarly, according to the *Times Higher Education* rankings, UAE University is only between 351st and 400th in the world, while Qatar University is even lower at between 401st and 500th in the world (and by comparison they are both well below comparable institutions in Cyprus and Estonia).[54]

Regarding the unofficial "soft power" objectives, early indications are that these arrangements have also not quite worked out as hoped. In many cases the branch-campus strategy has generated negative international headlines for the UAE and Qatar (and the universities involved), with a significant range of commentators—including current and former faculty at these institutions (and even former students)—having put forward a number of serious complaints. Among other things, these have included concerns over the lack of protection of freedom of speech, the apparent existence of a culture of censorship or self-censorship, and the perceived human rights violations of many of the migrant workers involved in building and maintaining the campuses.

NYU's branch campus, for example, has been accused of shying away from researching potentially sensitive topics (with it being described by the *Chronicle of Higher Education* as a "careful guest in a foreign land"),[55] and it has suffered a number of visa denial issues for incoming faculty. In 2015 Andrew Ross, a professor of social and cultural analysis at NYU's home campus who has written critically on migrant labor issues, was blocked from boarding an aircraft bound for Abu Dhabi. A year later an Egyptian doctoral student who had been awarded a research fellowship had her visa denied, and in 2017 more NYU home-campus faculty members (Mohamad Bazzi and Arang Keshavarazian) were also denied visas. Bazzi and Keshavarazian both later claimed to the *New York Times* that they were blocked on the basis that they were Shiite Muslims.[56] In more bad press, in 2014 the *New York Times* launched an investigation into what it claimed were abuses suffered by the laborers who had built NYU's Abu Dhabi facilities, and in 2018 the newspaper reported that the university had dragged its heels before publishing a promised compliance report and that many laborers were still owed wages.[57] Beyond NYU, other Western branch campuses in the UAE have faced similar issues, with *Le Monde* voicing "suspicions of censorship" with regard to La Sorbonne's branch campus,[58] and with the unexplained cancellation of the appointment of Leila al-Omrani (a French academic of Algerian origin) as the head of its department of philosophy and sociology.[59]

The Qatar campuses have also suffered public criticism, with a former Georgetown branch-campus faculty member publishing a book in 2017 that described a culture of book-banning, "not-so-soft censorship," and "implicit boundaries." The author also noted how other faculty members were careful not to criticize the ruler, that a faculty member had repeatedly had his visa revoked after writing critically about a country allied to Qatar, and that in one case a faculty member had chosen to publish an article on Islamic sectarianism under a pseudonym.[60] The same year it was also reported that an MA student at Georgetown's home campus who had earlier written critically about labor rights in the Gulf was denied a student visa to spend a semester at the Qatar campus. Although she did eventually travel to Qatar on a tourist visa, she was reportedly detained on arrival and questioned for several hours.[61]

Meanwhile, a former Northwestern faculty senate president raised academic freedom concerns with regard to the branch campus in an interview with the *Washington Post,* and on a separate occasion a current branch-campus faculty member told the newspaper that professors do indeed have to exercise caution.[62] Controversially, in 2015 a survey led by the campus's dean that asked questions such as "Is your country heading in the right direction?" reportedly had its Qatar-related answers removed, whereas answers relating to other Arab countries were still included.[63] In February 2020, Northwestern hit the headlines again following an announcement that a planned performance at the Qatar campus by the gay-friendly Lebanese band Mashrou' Leila had to be canceled (and moved to the Chicago campus). Though Northwestern's administration claimed the cancellation was due to security concerns, the Qatar Foundation stated that it was due to "a conflict with Qatari laws and customs."[64] Given the predominantly business, technology, and arts focus of the other campuses, there seem to have been fewer such episodes. However, in 2014, *Love Comes Later,* a novel self-published by Virginia Commonwealth branch-campus faculty member Mohanalakshmi Rajakumar, was reportedly banned without explanation, and the following year certain artwork displayed on the campus was understood to have been removed following objections from Qatari students.[65]

According to the author-surveyed practitioners either currently or formerly affiliated with five of the branch campuses, almost all agreed that there does exist a culture of self-censorship and confirmed that—in some cases—there have been sporadic episodes of direct censorship.[66] Most pointed to criticism of Islam and the UAE or Qatari states (and especially their ruling families) as the key red lines.[67] Other sensitive topics that they felt they needed to shy away from included laborers' rights and certain international issues such as Israeli relations, the Muslim Brotherhood, and the rise of extremist organizations such as al-Qaeda and Islamic State.[68] Although only just over half of those surveyed explicitly stated that there was less academic freedom on the branch campuses than on the home campuses of their institutions,[69] it was noted that very few junior branch-campus faculty members had any experience of teaching on the home campuses.[70] Meanwhile almost all reported that they felt restricted in their ability to teach in a fully objective manner,[71] and that there were widespread concerns over the lack of a true tenure system (with most appointments being made through renewable three- or five-year contracts).[72]

In this regard, despite any protections enshrined in the branch campuses' memorandums of understanding with their host governments, and despite their clearly privileged "soft power" status, they still seem to be vulnerable to some of the same problems as the indigenous universities, which have often been described as suffering from a culture of censorship. As a recent visiting scholar to the UAE's national university put it, "censorship is regularly applied to academics and scholarly events";[73] and as a widely read *Foreign Policy* essay has noted, there exists a "depressing pattern that has seen the UAE authorities take closer control of domestic academic institutions. . . . [T]he UAE currently is a deeply inimical place for the values that universities are supposed to uphold."[74] Meanwhile in Qatar, as well as banning "fad hairstyles" and "inappropriately coloured hair," its flagship state university has responded to anonymous student criticism over "inappropriate titles" in its library by establishing a "censoring policy on books where we were able to delete the books which are against our culture according to clear standards before they reach the library's index."[75]

Still-Limited Access Orders?

Despite some undoubtedly excellent individual student experiences and numerous world-class research outputs from branch-campus faculty members, the data thus far with regard to institutional objectives may eventually expose the strategy (and the institutions involved) to accusations—even within the host countries—of forming expensive "bubbles." In particular, there may emerge a feeling that the branch campuses are only really of benefit to "insiders" (including a small number of citizens, wealthy expatriates, and international students); that they are unlikely to benefit any "outsiders" (the remainder of the citizenry and the less affluent bulk of the expatriate population); and that they do not even contribute meaningfully to long-term economic or political development in the UAE and Qatar. In this context, the current results do not suggest the branch campuses have represented part of an "open-access order"—as per the World Bank's terminology—and, if anything, they seem to indicate a further reinforcement of the existing "limited-access order" in these states. Indeed, to borrow from Pierre Bourdieu's concept, the apparently limited freedoms experienced by the branch campuses seem to confirm a continuation (or perhaps a diluted version) of the same sort of "structure of the field of power" long experienced by the Gulf's indigenous universities.[76]

To some extent this may have been an inevitable, path-dependent outcome, as beyond the higher-education sector both Qatar and the UAE remain deeply authoritarian political societies with almost no real freedoms or civil liberties, and with decisionmaking still heavily dominated by ruling-family members and their closest allies. In fact, according to what headline data are available on the comparative state of democracy in the region, it appears that the UAE may have actually become more authoritarian since the branch campuses were first established. A decade ago, for instance, Freedom House (a US government–funded organization)[77] had awarded both the UAE and Qatar the scores of 5.5, 5.0, and 6.0 for "freedom," "political rights," and "civil liberties" (on a scale of 1–7, with 7 being the worst).[78] These were poor sets of scores, but nonetheless placed the two states almost on a par with the likes of Kazakhstan and the Democratic Republic of the Congo; were modest improvements on the past; and perhaps indicated that things were moving in the right direction, albeit very slowly.[79] By 2018, however, the UAE had slipped substantially to 6.5, 7.0, and 6.0, while Qatar scored 5.5, 6.0, and 5.0 (with deteriorating political rights).[80] In fact, according to Freedom House's metadata, the UAE had become the twenty-ninth least-free state in the world (worse than Chad and Iran), while Qatar was forty-seventh (worse than Brunei and Myanmar).[81]

Correspondingly, the Economist Intelligence Unit's democracy index paints a very similar picture, with the UAE now ranked 147th in the world (the twenty-first lowest, and below states such as Djibouti and

Russia), while Qatar is ranked 133rd (below Egypt and China).[82] Data from the Varieties of Democracy or "V-Dem" project (based at the University of Gothenburg)[83] have demonstrated much the same sort of situation, with Qatar currently receiving even lower scores than the UAE on its "liberal democracy," "deliberative democracy," and other democracy-related indexes. In fact, the UAE's "deliberative democracy" has worsened over the past decade, while both Qatar's "liberal democracy" and "deliberative democracy" scores have worsened.[84]

Beyond such comparative data, it is also notable that in the era since the branch campuses were first established, even government officials themselves have made sure to lower international expectations as much as possible. Writing in a state-owned newspaper, for example, the UAE's minister of state for foreign affairs has made it clear that political parties and a multiparty system (which are often regarded as requirements for successful democracy)[85] are never going to be part of his government's "end goal." As he put it, "this model does not correspond with our culture or historical development. . . . [A]n important component of this model is the organised political party. We have a natural aversion to political parties because in the Arab world these parties have disintegrated into tribes, clans and sectarian groups."[86] Meanwhile in Qatar, despite the existence of a constitutional mandate (as per the country's 2004 constitution), elections for the government's forty-five-member advisory council have been repeatedly delayed (most recently in 2016, when a decree was issued to delay the elections for a further three years),[87] while election turnouts for municipal elections have now begun to decline.[88]

Future Prospects

Looking forward, it seems likely that the branch-campus strategy is going to face strong headwinds, not only due to the discomforting headlines and the lack of robust political economy success indicators, but perhaps also due to the recent belt-tightening in the oil and gas export–dependent Gulf states. After all, even the UAE and Qatar have had to lower their "breakeven" fiscal oil prices substantially,[89] and both have now begun to tap into international sovereign debt markets.[90] In part, this more challenging economic environment has been a function of external, macro-level factors outside the UAE and Qatar's control, most notably in the wake of the "shale revolution" in the United States;[91] the consequent international oil glut;[92] and oil prices plunging by more than $70 per barrel from June 2014 to January 2016 (and then falling even further in early 2020).[93] Given the data available, and especially given that most of the US and other Western branch campuses appear to be funded on an ongoing rather than an up-front lump-sum basis, in more indigent scenarios it seems possible that future contract renewals may either not take place or lead to significant reductions in funding.

In early 2019, for example, it was announced that the programs offered by University College London's Qatar branch campus were to be slimmed down and that the operation would shortly be terminated due to lack of market demand. Although further official information on the decision is not yet available, it has been confirmed that college's contract with the Qatar Foundation was due to expire in 2020 and that following a mutual decision there would be no renewal.[94] Worryingly, according to an investigation by the college's student magazine, it has been claimed that the Qatar campus had become a "running sore for college management," that it had suffered "at least two major public scandals," and that in 2014 a senior college official had already requested that University College London's "relationships in Qatar need to be reviewed in light of a changed political context there."[95]

Nevertheless (and notwithstanding the college's pending departure), both the UAE and Qatar appear to have recently entered into a particularly turbulent period in their history, and in this context any international relations benefits the branch campuses are seen as providing (especially as links to the United States and other Western powers) may be seen as having increased in value. After all, in the past few years both the UAE and Qatar have become enmeshed in numerous conflicts (both directly and by proxy);[96] cyber warfare campaigns;[97] and—against each other—what seems to have become an intractable dispute over the role of Islam in politics (which has already resulted in a three-year economic blockade led by the UAE and its allies against Qatar).[98]

In the absence of "hard power" solutions, and with the need to keep competing to maintain their mutual superpower protectors aboard, such "soft power" assets may still be seen to have a role to play, at least for the time being. For example, in Georgetown's case (which is perhaps the most directly "useful" to Qatari policymakers given its focus on international affairs), several pages of its branch campus's 2017–2018 annual report were dedicated to displaying the pro-Qatari role it felt it had been playing since the beginning of the blockade. Notably, under the banner of "Qatar Blockade: GU-Q on the Frontlines," the report detailed several visits by high-ranking Qatari officials who hosted Georgetown-branded discussion panels and delivered (what seem to have been one-sided) addresses on subjects such as "Leadership and

Resilience in Emergency Management"; "The Resilience of Qatar's Growth: Economic Blockade Is a Blessing in Disguise"; and "The Ingredients of Qatar's Success Under the Blockade."[99]

Conclusion

Though the evidence presented in this chapter indicates that the publicly stated objectives of the branch-campus strategy have not yet been met (especially with regard to the building of knowledge economies or the providing of some sort of demonstration effect), there is little to suggest that the strategy's original, official goals were never intrinsically genuine. Certainly, there seems little doubt that the UAE and Qatar were (and remain) theoretically committed to diversifying their economies, boosting their private sectors, and weaning their citizens from public sector employment. There is also little to suggest that the authorities have privately viewed the strategy as merely a means of producing another layer of loyal citizen-technocrats to serve in their rentier states (as perhaps has been the case in other Arab authoritarian states).[100] Equally, it would be hard to make the case that the US universities involved were purely financially motivated from the very beginning and did not at some stage see branch campuses as real opportunities to further both their expansionary global missions and their more ideological, civilizational aims.

Instead, rather than some sort of calculated rationalist autocratic strategy to manipulate well-established but cash-hungry institutions, a more credible explanation is that the branch campuses were likely subsumed by much bigger and more powerful dynamics beyond the control of the US university administrators (and perhaps even the Emirati and Qatari officials) initially involved. In this context, the big-brand US universities soon found themselves incorporated as expensive but potentially extremely useful "soft power" assets into the UAE and Qatar's increasingly assertive foreign policies, especially as regional and international tensions began to rise. Meanwhile, with the institutions having clearly found themselves having to slot into existing "fields of power" (much like the UAE and Qatar's indigenous universities), it was soon apparent that their capacity to survive and prosper in such deeply authoritarian political societies would eventually rest on their willingness to effect a number of significant academic compromises.

As such, beyond a broader inability to help shift their hosts from limited- to more open-access orders, the branch campuses seem to have evolved as partly co-opted/transplanted higher-educational institutions, while at the same time emerging as products of some sort of endogenous political experimentation. Certainly, in many respects they seem particularly good examples of what Calvert Jones has described as the "stylized, plug-and-play idea of the West that might, like an 'app,' be used to install a depoliticized liberal culture [in the Gulf states]."[101] Thus, for Western institutions (or liberal institutions more generally) looking at the region from outside-in, the branch campuses in the UAE and Qatar may soon be seen as predictable, powerful, and very visible reminders of the sort of inconsistencies one might reasonably expect to encounter when partnering or collaborating with wealthy authoritarian regimes.

Notes

1. In 2017 the UAE's gross domestic product (GDP) per capita was $40,699 and Qatar's was $63,506. By comparison, Kuwait's was $29,040; Bahrain's $23,655; Saudi Arabia's $20,761; and Oman's $15,668. The World Bank, "Development Indicators: GDP Per Capita," 2020, https://databank.worldbank.org/indicator /NY.GDP.PCAP.CD/1ff4a498/Popular-Indicators.

2. The Sorbonne established a campus in the UAE in 2006. See "About Us," Sorbonne University Abu Dhabi, https://www.sorbonne.ae/about-us.

3. University College London established a campus in Qatar in 2012. See Strzyżyńska, "Sheikh It Off."

4. In January 2019, Aberdeen University announced a $127 million expansion in Qatar: "Aberdeen University Announces £100m Expansion in Qatar," BBC, January 25, 2019, https://www.bbc.com/news/uk-scotland-north-east-orkney-shetland -47002388.

5. These include New York University in Shanghai, Duke University in Kunshan, and (on a more autonomous level) Yale University in collaboration with the National University of Singapore. See Guo, "Top U.S. Colleges with Branches Overseas."

6. In 2017 the UAE's total population was 9.4 million and Qatar's was 2.6 million. According to official UAE census data, in 2010 there were only 947,997 citizens, i.e., about 10 percent of the total. With regard to Qatar, data are less reliable; however, according to one third-party investigation, only about 313,000, or 12 percent, of Qatar's population are actually citizens. "UAE Fact Sheet," 2019, http://u.ae/en /about-the-uae/fact-sheet; and Dsouza Communications, "Population of Qatar by Nationality," 2017, https://priyadsouza.com/population-of-qatar-by-nationality-in -2017.

7. North, Wallis, Webb, and Weingast, "Limited Access Orders in the Developing World."

8. The author-conducted survey was carried out between October 25, 2018, and June 1, 2019.

9. Ministry of Cabinet Affairs, "National Agenda," United Arab Emirates: The Cabinet, 2019, https://uaecabinet.ae/en/national-agenda.

10. "Economic Policy," State of Qatar Government Communications Office, 2019, https://www.gco.gov.qa/en/focus/economic-policy.

11. Ministry of Cabinet Affairs, "National Agenda," United Arab Emirates: The Cabinet, 2019, https://uaecabinet.ae/en/national-agenda.

12. Al-Subaiey, "Qatarization Policy."

13. Michael Herb, for example, has classed the UAE and Qatar as examples of "extreme rentier states," a category he defines as one in which citizens have a "privileged claim on rent revenues" and in which "a large majority of citizens depend for their pay checks on oil revenues, not on taxes levied on the private sector." Herb, *The Wages of Oil,* pp. 14–15.

14. "Vision and Mission," New York University Abu Dhabi, 2019, https://nyuad.nyu.edu/en/about/nyuad-at-a-glance/vision-and-mission.html.

15. "Mission, Vision, and Strategy," Georgetown University in Qatar, 2019, https://www.qatar.georgetown.edu/about/mission-vision.

16. "About Northwestern Qatar," Northwestern University in Qatar, 2019, https://www.qatar.northwestern.edu/about/index.html.

17. For a further discussion of the national universities, see "Objectives Met?" on pages 132–136 of this chapter.

18. The Syrian Protestant College was renamed the American University of Beirut in 1920. See "A Brief History," American University of Beirut, https://www.aub.edu.lb/doctorates/Pages/history.aspx; and Murphy, *The American University in Cairo,* p. 1.

19. "A Brief History," American University of Beirut, https://www.aub.edu.lb/doctorates/Pages/history.aspx; also Sharkey, *American Evangelicals in Egypt,* pp. 154–167.

20. "Vision and Mission," New York University Abu Dhabi, 2019, https://nyuad.nyu.edu/en/about/nyuad-at-a-glance/vision-and-mission.html.

21. "Mission, Vision, and Strategy," Georgetown University in Qatar, 2019, https://www.qatar.georgetown.edu/about/mission-vision.

22. See, for example, Antwi-Boateng, "The Rise of Qatar as a Soft Power and the Challenges," pp. 41–42; Ulrichsen, *Gulf States in International Political Economy,* p. 79; Davidson, *After the Sheikhs,* pp. 103–104.

23. According to Joseph Nye, countries can develop attractive "soft power" assets to help co-opt rather than coerce others into offering them support. For a full discussion see Nye, *Soft Power.*

24. In 2008 the Abu Dhabi United Group for Development and Investment (owned by the UAE's minister for presidential affairs, Sheikh Mansour bin Zayed Al-Nahyan) bought Manchester City. In 2011 the Qatar Investment Authority (and now Qatar Sports Investment) bought Paris St. Germain. See "Hughes to Hold City Owner Talks"; Jackson, "Qatar Wins 2022 World Cup Bid"; and "Le Qatar sans limite," *Le Parisien,* March 7, 2012, https://www.leparisien.fr/sports/football/psg/le-qatar-sans-limite-07-03-2012-1893594.php.

25. Long in the pipeline, in 2017 Le Louvre Abu Dhabi finally opened, while in 2018 the British Museum renewed an earlier ten-year agreement to help establish the Zayed National Museum, also in Abu Dhabi. Dennehy, "British Museum Renames Gallery After Sheikh Zayed"; Langton, "Emmanuel Macron and UAE Leaders Formally Open Louvre Abu Dhabi."

26. *Foreign Gifts and Contracts Report,* Data.gov, https://catalog.data.gov/dataset/foreign-gifts-and-contracts-report-2011.

27. Qatar has funded the Atlantic Council, the Brookings Institution, and the Middle East Institute. The UAE has funded all the above, in addition to the Center for Strategic and International Studies, the Stimson Center, and the World Resource Institute. See Lipton, Williams, and Confessore, "Foreign Powers Buy Influence at

Think Tanks"; and Williams, Lipton, and Parlapiano, "Foreign Government Contributions to Nine Think Tanks."

28. It is unclear what proportion of the $75 million in donations from Islamic countries to the Oxford Centre for Islamic Studies originated from the Gulf states.

29. Draege and Lestra, "Gulf-Funding of British Universities and the Focus on Human Development," pp. 40–42.

30. Daley, "N.Y.U. in the U.A.E."

31. "Mubadala Moves 49% Stake in Paris-Sorbonne University, Abu Dhabi," *Gulf News,* April 20, 2011, https://gulfnews.com/business/mubadala-moves-49-stake-in-paris-sorbonne-university-abu-dhabi-1.796657.

32. "Foreign Gifts and Contracts Report," Data.gov, https://catalog.data.gov/dataset/foreign-gifts-and-contracts-report-2011.

33. An exception being Texas A&M, which—following a *Washington Post* request and a subsequent ruling by the Texas attorney general's office—was eventually forced to disclose its $76 million a year agreement with the Qatar Foundation. See Anderson, "Texas University Gets $76 Million Each Year to Operate in Qatar, Contract Says."

34. "Excerpts from Andrew Hamilton's Interview with Washington Square News," *Washington Square News,* May 14, 2019, https://nyunews.com/news/2019/05/14/nyu-president-andrew-hamilton-interview-with-washington-square-news.

35. "About Qatar Foundation," Qatar Foundation, https://www.qf.org.qa/about.

36. Of the 17 surveyed, 14 provided similar such comments.

37. Of the 17 surveyed, 13 provided similar such comments.

38. Of the 17 surveyed, 5 provided similar such comments.

39. See, for example, Jason Lane's case study on international branch campuses in Dubai: Lane, "Importing Private Higher Education," pp. 371–372. For an earlier discussion on these Dubai campuses see Davidson, *Dubai,* p. 118.

40. In the 1980s and early 1990s, 32 US institutions attempted to establish branch campuses in Japan. Today only the branches of Temple University (founded in 1982) and Lakeland University (founded in 1991) survive. See Fukurai and Yusuke, "American Universities in Japan," p. 86; also "About Us," Temple University of Japan, tuj.ac.jp/about/japan-campus/index.html, and "About Us," Lakeland University Japan, https://luj.lakeland.edu/About-Us.

41. Lewin, "University Branches in Dubai Are Struggling"; Abramson, "Michigan State to Close Dubai Campus."

42. "Class of 2022: 389 Students and 84 Nationalities," New York University Abu Dhabi, October 2, 2018, https://nyuad.nyu.edu/en/news/latest-news/community-life/2018/october/class-of-2022-announcement.html.

43. "Life Beyond Saadiyat: Class of 2018," New York University Abu Dhabi, 2018, https://nyuad.nyu.edu/content/dam/nyuad/academics/undergraduate/career-development/life-beyond-saadiyat/report/20180220-life-beyond-saadiyat-report.pdf.

44. "Annual Report: 2017–18," Georgetown University Qatar, pp. 7–12, 21, 24, 31, 33, https://issuu.com/sfsqcomm/docs/ar_2017-18-final-112618.

45. "NU-Q: Year in Review 2018," Northwestern University Qatar, p. 2, https://www.qatar.northwestern.edu/about/annual-report/2018.html.

46. "Annual Report 2016/2017," Texas A&M at Qatar, *issuu,* March 24, 2018, pp. 6–7, https://issuu.com/tamuq/docs/annual_report_2016-2017_aw.

47. "CMU Q at a Glance," Carnegie Mellon University Qatar, December 11, 2017, https://www.qatar.cmu.edu/about-us/media-resources/press-kit/attachment/cmu_q-at-a-glance; and "Carnegie Mellon University in Qatar's Annual Report: 2017–2018," *issuu,* December 4, 2018, pp. 12–16, https://issuu.com/carnegiemellonqatar/docs/cmu-q_ar2018_lowres.

48. "Context: 2016–2018," Virginia Commonwealth Qatar, pp. 68–69, Qatar.vcu /publications.

49. Of the 17 surveyed, 17 made similar such comments.

50. Of the 17 surveyed, 4 made similar such comments.

51. Of the 17 surveyed, 13 made similar such comments.

52. Of the 17 surveyed, 8 made similar such comments.

53. Referring to Al-Farabi Kazakh National University (ranked 220th) and Universiti Teknologi Malaysia (ranked 228th). "QS World University Rankings 2019," QS Top Universities, https://www.topuniversities.com/university-rankings/world -university-rankings/2019.

54. The Cyprus University of Technology and the University of Tartu are both ranked between 301st and 350th in the world. "World University Rankings 2019," *Times Higher Education,* https://www.timeshighereducation.com/world-university -rankings/2019/world-ranking.

55. Lindsey, "NYU–Abu Dhabi Behaves Like Careful Guest in Foreign Land."

56. Nir, "N.Y.U. Journalism Faculty Boycotts Abu Dhabi Campus."

57. Chen, "N.Y.U. Promised Reforms in Abu Dhabi."

58. Miller and Stromboni, "Sorbonne Abou Dhabi."

59. Redden, "Persona Non Grata"; Nir, "N.Y.U. Journalism Faculty Boycotts Abu Dhabi Campus"; and Miller and Stromboni, "Sorbonne Abou Dhabi."

60. Referring to Wasserman, *The Doha Experiment;* also see Redden, "The Doha Experiment."

61. Referring to Kristina Bogos; see Redden, "Visa Denied."

62. Anderson, "Northwestern Professor Raises Questions About Its Branch in Qatar"; also Anderson, "Can U.S. Universities Thrive in the Persian Gulf?"

63. Anderson, "In Qatar's Education City, US Colleges Are Building an Academic Oasis."

64. Younes, "Northwestern University's Precarious Role Under Qatar's Repressive Laws."

65. Anderson, "In Qatar's Education City, US Colleges Are Building an Academic Oasis."

66. Of the 17 surveyed, 15 made similar such comments.

67. Of the 17 surveyed, 15 made similar such comments.

68. Of the 17 surveyed, 7 made similar such comments.

69. Of the 17 surveyed, 9 made similar such comments.

70. Of the 17 surveyed, 11 made similar such comments.

71. Of the 17 surveyed, 15 made similar such comments.

72. Of the 17 surveyed, 16 made similar such comments.

73. Nagle, "Academic Freedom."

74. Ulrichsen, "Academic Freedom and UAE Funding."

75. "QU Library Row Sparks Debate over Academic Freedom, Cultural Values," *Doha News,* September 10, 2013; "Students Sweat, Celebrate New QU Dress Code Banning Tight Clothing, 'Fad' Hairstyles, Tattoos," *Doha News,* September 14, 2012.

76. To use Pierre Bourdieu's terminology. Bourdieu, *Homo Academicus,* pp. 40–41.

77. The major grantor for Freedom House is listed as the US government. See "Financial Statements Year Ended June 30, 2016, and Independent Auditors' Report," Freedom House, January 31, 2017, p. 21, https://freedomhouse.org/sites /default/files/2020-02/FINAL_Freedom_House_Audited_Financial_Statements _2017.pdf.

78. Freedom House, "Freedom in the World 2008: United Arab Emirates," *refworld,* https://www.refworld.org/topic,50ffbce524d,50ffbce5268,487ca26ac,0,FREEHOU

„ARE.html; Freedom House, "Freedom in the World 2008: Qatar," *refworld,* https://www.refworld.org/docid/487ca2402.html.

79. Kazakhstan was awarded 5.5, 5, and 6, while the Democratic Republic of Congo was awarded 5.5, 6, and 5. Freedom House, "Freedom in the World 2008: Freedom in the World Countries," https://freedomhouse.org/sites/default/files/2020-02/Freedom_in_the_World_2008_complete_book.pdf.

80. Freedom House, "Freedom in the World 2019: United Arab Emirates," *ECOI,* https://www.ecoi.net/en/document/2006464.html; and Freedom House, "Freedom in the World 2019: Qatar," *ECOI,* https://www.ecoi.net/en/document/2016035.html.

81. Ranked by aggregate scores. Freedom House, "Freedom in the World 2019," https://freedomhouse.org/sites/default/files/Feb2019_FH_FITW_2019_Report_For Web-compressed.pdf.

82. The Economist Intelligence Unit, "Democracy Index 2018: Me Too? Political Participation, Protest and Democracy," pp. 39–40, https://275rzy1ul4252pt 1hv2dqyuf-wpengine.netdna-ssl.com/wp-content/uploads/2019/01/Democracy _Index_2018.pdf.

83. The Varieties of Democracy project has multiple funders, including the European Research Council and the Swedish Research Council. V-Dem Institute, "Funders," https://www.v-dem.net/en/about/funders.

84. In 2008 the UAE's liberal democracy score was .08 (on a scale of 0 to 1) and its deliberative democracy score was 0.15; in 2018 its liberal democracy score was 0.11 and its deliberative democracy score was 0.12. In 2008 Qatar's liberal democracy score was 0.1 and its deliberate democracy score was 0.09; in 2018 its liberal democracy score was 0.09 and its deliberative democracy score was 0.06. The Varieties of Democracy project understands liberal democracy as "emphasising the importance of protecting individual and minority rights against the tyranny of the state and the tyranny of the majority," and understands deliberative democracy as "the process by which decisions are reached in a polity. . . . [A] deliberative process is one in which public reasoning focused on the common good motivates political decisions—as contrasted with emotional appeals, solidary attachments, parochial interests, or coercion." V-Dem Institute, "2019 Data," https://www.v-dem-net/en /data/archive/previoius-reference-materials/reference-materials-v9.

85. See, for example Dahl, "What Political Institutions Does Large-Scale Democracy Require?," pp. 196–197; and Cohen, "Deliberation and Democratic Legitimacy," p. 356.

86. Citing the minister of state for foreign affairs in Gargash, "Amid Challenges, UAE Policies Engage Gradual Reforms."

87. The Economist Intelligence Unit, "Emir Postpones Legislative Election Until 2019," July 20, 2016, http://country.eiu.com/article.aspx?articleid=1604426344.

88. Gengler and Al Ansari, "Qatar's First Elections Since 2017 Reveal Unexpected Impact of GCC Crisis."

89. In the UAE's case, its breakeven fiscal oil price fell from $91 a barrel in 2014 to $66 in 2020. In Qatar's case its breakeven fiscal oil price fell from $58 in 2014 to $38 in 2020. See Federal Reserve Bank of St. Louis, "Breakeven Fiscal Oil Price for United Arab Emirates," October 19, 2020, https://fred.stlouisfed.org/series /AREPZPIOILBEGUSD; and Federal Reserve Bank of St. Louis, "Breakeven Fiscal Oil Price: Qatar," October 19, 2020, https://fred.stlouisfed.org/series/QATPZPIOIL BEGUSD.

90. In February 2019, it was reported that a recent UAE debt law had opened the path for government-backed entities to begin issuing sovereign bonds. In 2018 and

then again in March 2019, Qatar sold bonds worth $12 billion each for a total of $24 billion. See Fattah and El-Din, "U.A.E. Federal Bank to Sell Bond Following Passage of Debt Law"; and Barbuscia, "Qatar Sells Triple-Tranche Jumbo Bond to Raise $12 billion."

91. US oil production rose from about 7.5 million barrels per day in 2010 to about 12.7 million barrels per day in 2015, largely due to advanced hydraulic fracturing and computer-aided drilling techniques used to extract oil from existing shale formations. See BP, "Statistical Review of World Energy," 2019, p. 16, https://www .bp.com/content/dam/bp/business-sites/en/global/corporate/pdfs/energy-economics /statistical-review/bp-stats-review-2019-full-report.pdf; Crooks, "The US Shale Revolution"; and Manning, "The Shale Revolution and the New Geopolitics of Energy."

92. From 2010 to 2015, total world oil production rose from 83.2 million barrels per day to 91.5 million barrels per day, mostly due to the increase in US production. See BP, "Statistical Review of World Energy."

93. In June 2014, Brent crude oil was $111.80 per barrel, and in January 2016 it was $30.70. Since then the highest oil price was $81.03, in October 2018. In March 2020 it began to fall further, reaching just $19.07 at the beginning of April 2020. US Energy Information Administration, "Europe Brent Spot Price FOB (Dollars per Barrel)," https://www.eia.gov/dnav/pet/hist/rbrteD.htm.

94. Redden, "University College London to Close Qatar Campus."

95. Strzyżyńska, "Sheikh It Off."

96. Examples of direct conflicts include the UAE's involvement in Yemen and to some extent its involvement in Libya. Examples of proxy conflicts include groups backed by the UAE and Qatar in Libya, Syria, Somalia, and elsewhere.

97. There are now numerous accounts of cyber warfare operations involving the UAE and Qatar, some of which have been directed against each other. See, for example, Schectman and Bing, "Exclusive"; Voreacos and Riley, "Trump Fundraiser Claims Qatar Used U.S. Firm in Hacking"; and Gambrell, "U.A.E. Cyber Firm DarkMatter Slowly Steps Out of the Shadows."

98. Three years into the "Qatar crisis" dispute between Qatar and the "Anti-Terror Quartet" (the UAE, Saudi Arabia, Bahrain, and Egypt), which began in June 2017, the consensus is that there is no immediate end in sight. For representative discussions, see Davidson, "Up for Debate"; Kinninmont, "The Gulf Divided"; Dickinson, "Exporting the Gulf Crisis"; and Knipp and Mellouk, "Qatar Boycott Three Years On."

99. "Annual Report: 2017–18," Georgetown University in Qatar, pp. 7–12, https://issuu.com/sfsqcomm/docs/ar_2017-18-final-112618.

100. Calvert Jones describes the sort of loyal technocrats one might expect to find in rentier states as "a collectivist, unreflective, unquestioningly obedient citizenry." Jones, "Seeing Like an Autocrat," p. 25.

101. Ibid., p. 35.

8

Foreign Scholarship Programs in Algeria and Saudi Arabia

Adel Hamaizia and Andrew Leber

The idea of funding university students to venture abroad for studies, to obtain high-quality education and technical know-how not available at home, is not a new one. Education officials the world over have placed considerable hope in the "'plausible' impact of scholarships on social change and development," despite the limited range of studies that have gauged returns on investment through cost-benefit analyses.[1] This is true for the Middle East and North Africa (MENA) as well—Muhammad Ali Pasha of Egypt, who sent several military cadets on the first of several student missions to Europe in 1826, would no doubt have recognized similar efforts by rulers such as Shah Mohammad Reza Pahlavi of Iran, Saddam Hussein, and Muammar Qaddafi to send students abroad for higher education and technical training.[2]

Given the numerous organizational and financial hurdles facing root-and-branch reform of MENA-region institutions of higher education, exchange programs seem to offer a way forward by "jump-starting" economies and state bureaucracies with a select vanguard of graduates—costly on a per capita basis, but less expensive overall than a complete overhaul of sprawling domestic higher-education systems.[3] Furthermore, they offer authoritarian regimes the advanced training offered by the "liberal" universities abroad without the need for relaxed controls on university spaces at home.[4]

Sidestepping these immediate challenges raises new concerns, however. Even if discussions of "liberal education" can elide aspects of illiberalism within the Western academy, considerable evidence suggests that higher education acquired abroad within liberal democracies can encourage democratization in home countries.[5] As opposed to domestic educational institutions, officials in sending countries have minimal control over the curricula that students are exposed to abroad. Steering positions only to clients and cronies of political insiders may keep students in line yet is unlikely to maximize economic returns by selecting students primarily on merit.[6] Furthermore, even talented graduates may grow frustrated if they return home to limited economic opportunities, either challenging insiders' hold on rent streams through domestic opposition or undermining the economy by venturing abroad in search of gainful employment ("brain drain").[7]

When are state institutions plagued by considerable corruption able to prevent exchange programs from becoming yet another stream of rents for well-connected insiders? What are the prospects for states in the Middle East and North Africa seeing any clear return on their investments in expensive foreign educations for select citizens?

Elite Consensus and Islands of Excellence

Existing work suggests several possible explanations for where and when we should expect these study-abroad exchanges to succeed as bureaucratic "islands of excellence," isolated from becoming yet another source of rents for patronage.[8] International scholarships represent an ideal candidate for such bureaucratic isolation. They promise outsized developmental gains as returning students become job-makers rather than job-takers, they can be administered by a relatively small number of highly skilled education officials, and they operate on a budget small enough (compared to broader education budgets) to avoid being an obvious target for patronage. We, therefore, seek an explanation for when privileged insiders are most likely to agree to support such programs, and to isolate them from struggles of "competitive clientelism" among different political factions.[9]

First, access to economic resources may afford regimes leeway to expand scholarship programs while distributing other forms of political perks instead—the well-connected can directly fund patronage networks (or elite education of clients) with other rent streams.[10] Such regimes are able to fund both "guns" and "butter"—social welfare programs as well as repressive apparatus—and hence are less concerned about the mobilizing potential of well-educated political entrepreneurs.[11]

Second, state ideology may play a role in encouraging elite cohesion around critical developmentalist projects, particularly ideologies born of sustained, violent conflict aimed at national liberation or social revolution.[12] This may encourage an elite consensus around isolating scholarship programs from patronage networks, given the importance of rapidly increasing state capacity and generating economic growth. Additionally, the legitimacy and authority of political insiders—acquired in the course of the struggle—is harder for educated outsiders to challenge.

Third, political institutions may encourage more cooperative relations among elite factions. Menaldo suggests that the MENA region's monarchies govern via a more consensual style of rule that might facilitate agreement over preserving scholarship-program positions as a meritocratic public good rather than dividing them up as a private stream of rent.[13] Alternatively, the crosscutting coalitions underpinning the monarchies of the Arab world might insulate them from concerns over isolated political challenges stemming from these programs.[14]

Finally, higher levels of elite conflict should have a negative impact on the quality of scholarship programs. When elite factions are locked in a struggle for the upper hand, policies that serve society writ large are more likely to be used as a means to undercut rivals and construct personalized networks centered around patronage.[15]

To be sure, many of these factors may be interdependent. Greater access to resource rents might ward off factional conflicts, or political institutions may shape the ability of regimes to generate financial flows.[16] To explore which of these factors can help explain the success of scholarship programs, and provide guidance as to their political and technical feasibility within the MENA region, we compare the historical trajectories of Saudi and Algerian scholarship programs. In doing so, we select for states with considerable hydrocarbon resources—limiting our insight into the region's resource-poor countries but ensuring we focus on scholarship programs large enough to leave a considerable evidentiary trail.

Process-tracing these programs from the mid-twentieth century to the present day allows us to test their historical trajectory against theoretical expectations.[17] The boom-and-bust cycles of international oil markets permit us to observe whether crashing oil prices in the 1980s undercut scholarship programs, or whether the 2003–2014 commodities boom served to reestablish academic exchanges. Furthermore, the differing origins of the Algerian republic and the Saudi monarchy in anticolonial struggle and conservative consolidation, respectively, offer insight into the role of ideology and political institutions in safeguarding these programs. Finally, the Algerian civil war (1991–2002) and the elite infighting that followed in its wake contrast with stable elite relations in Saudi Arabia up until quite recent times.

In all, we find little concern from either Algerian or Saudi officials over the potential for foreign educations to reshape students' attitudes; both regimes were able to monitor students while abroad, while would-be dissidents were more likely to remain abroad rather than returning home. Still, while both Algeria and Saudi Arabia were able to maintain somewhat meritocratic scholarship programs when each was governed by a relatively unified elite, factional conflict in Algeria transformed the country's study-abroad opportunities into yet another reward for competing patronage networks. We also note that these programs appear far more successful at staffing state bureaucracies than jump-starting economic development and diversification, raising questions about their cost-effectiveness and sustainability even in the most successful cases.

Scholarships and Statebuilding Through 1980

At the outset of statebuilding projects in Algeria and Saudi Arabia, developmental imperatives spurred the creation of relatively meritocratic scholarship programs to supplement domestic education institutions. The conservative, counter-revolutionary consolidation of the Saudi state proved the equal of Algeria's anticolonial ideology in motivating rapid drives to convert resource wealth into capable states and economic growth. Still, the returns on scholarship programs during the first oil boom demonstrate the importance of a dynamic economy at home in encouraging students to return from their time abroad. At the same time, growing bureaucratic infighting in Algeria started to undermine the meritocratic nature of selection processes.

Algeria at Independence: Scholarships by Any Means

Following the 1954–1962 bloody war of national liberation after more than a century of French settler-colonial rule, the newly independent state of Algeria emerged from the colonial era lacking in educated and trained human resources. With settlers in control of over 60 percent of the colony's income (approximately $1.2 billion out of $1.8 billion), around 70 percent of the Algerian population lost employment as settler-owned farms and factories shut down in 1962.[18] Ninety percent of Algeria's Muslim population was illiterate at independence, albeit with significant regional disparities.[19] The country's million settlers made up almost all of the professional trades despite representing only 10 percent of the country's population; approximately 90 percent of them fled the country that summer—including almost all of Algeria's teachers.[20] In terms of higher education, the new state inherited one single university, in Algiers—its library and numerous medical laboratories burned to the ground by French paramilitaries—and two annexes, in Constantine and Oran.

The first president of Algeria, Ahmed Ben Bella, was keen on pursuing a socialism centered around domestic development above all else, with state investments in education as a driving force of economic growth.[21] In addition to the goal of increasing literacy rates and primary and secondary school enrollment, higher education was identified as a critical tool for statebuilding, economic development, and training an adequate number of "cadres" who would fill administrative, technical, and managerial positions within the new and fast-growing bureaucracy.[22]

Although many Algerians were invited abroad for educational purposes at the expense of "supporting" countries, from Egypt and the Soviet Union to the United States, Algeria had also started its own foreign scholarship program. The foreign scholarship program was characterized throughout the 1960s by the absence of a centralized structure for the management of scholarships—several ministries and government entities maintained their own programs. For example, the national oil company Sonatrach, the principal actor in the country's mainstay industry since the organization's founding in 1963, was heavily involved in the scholarship system. Sonatrach aimed to support the national drive for skills acquisition writ large while fostering a new generation of managers for its own purposes.[23] The period up until 1970 saw international scholarships expand rapidly, to over 800 a year for much of the decade.[24]

Path dependency from the precolonial period (in terms of language, logistics, and family ties) would continue to steer Algerian migration—including student flows—to France. Under the terms of the Evian Accords, which granted independence to Algeria, a fairly liberal freedom of movement continued between former colony and colonizer. By 1965 there were an estimated half a million Algerians in France, many of whom were students who remained in France after completing their higher education, although many French-taught students did return to Algeria.[25] According to a former Algerian minister who completed his studies in France in the 1960s, the period was the start of an "ironic situation in which we [Algerians] were disproportionately going to study in the country of those that made us [Muslim Algerians] illiterate. . . . [L]anguage and familiarity are powerful tools."[26] The decades that followed continued to see a pattern of Algerian students going to study at institutes of higher education in France.

State Centralization of Scholarships: 1970–1980

Increased hydrocarbon revenues resulting from the 1971 nationalization of the oil and gas industry, and subsequent Arab oil embargo of 1973–1974, provided ample funds to spend on Algeria's developmental drive—with higher education ostensibly playing a central role. In 1971, a reform of higher education was followed by myriad scientific programs and projects aimed at supporting the country's developmental goals. While the number of scholarships exploded along with government spending writ large, infighting among Algerian ministries began to transform the program from a channel for "open-access" knowledge transfer to yet another form of patronage.

Initially, the scholarships-abroad program was more firmly embedded within the country's wider development project and education commitments. An eightfold budget increase between 1970 and 1977 was reflected in expenditures of 280 million dinars on domestic scholarships—covering a full 65 percent of Algeria-based students by 1978, making higher education an attainable goal for the masses. The Arabization drive continued as well, with 32 percent of students studying at Arabic-language universities by 1978—up from just 8 percent in 1971. Despite the exponential growth in graduates, the ideologically driven Arabization project led to continued manpower shortages in key areas—particularly the hard sciences, given the dearth of scientific output in the Arabic language.[27] Reflecting broader problems in economic planning, university graduates often obtained the credentials but not the skills required for the job market.

Curricular concerns were less of a concern for students sent abroad. In addition to the communist Soviet Union, Eastern bloc countries including Bulgaria, Poland, East Germany, Romania, Czechoslovakia, and Hungary also supported training of Algerian students, particularly in areas such as medicine (Bulgaria) and energy studies (Romania).[28] While France continued to be a primary destination for Algerian students, diplomatic friction between Algeria and France and growing trade ties with an energy-hungry United States led to more students being sent there as well. According to a memo from the then-secretary of state, Cyrus Vance, some 1,600 Algerian students were in the United States in 1977, funded through Algerian government scholarships.[29]

With quality control out of Algerian planners' hands, officials at the Ministry of Higher Education focused on gradually insulating the initiative from bureaucratic infighting. Two decrees in 1971 and 1972 specified eligibility criteria, stipend levels, and the rights and duties of students and interns abroad.[30] The decrees were accompanied by the new state institutions that centralized control of scholarship programs under the Ministry of Higher Education (for general administration of scholarship programs) and the Ministry of Interior (specifically focused on internships).[31] By the end of the 1970s, it appeared that the centralized, unified approach headed by the Ministry of Higher Education was a clear improvement on arbitrary decisions by individual ministries or state-owned enterprises, with more transparent selection criteria accompanying an expanding number of positions.

Yet even during the early years of the boom, this restrained factional conflict was putting strain on meritocratic criteria—and returns on the program might be less than anticipated. A former official who worked at the Algerian Ministry of Higher Education in the middle to late 1970s described the selection process as "meritocratic for the most part, though the *ma'arifa* [form of nepotism] had started to rear its ugly head . . . especially in non-scientific subjects." Officials also began to realize that not all students could be enticed to return home. "For some it was a case of better salaries in the US, France and so on. . . . [F]or some it was a case of living in capitalist democracies. . . . For others it was as simple as finding a spouse during their studies . . . [even for] those that studied in Eastern bloc countries."[32]

Scholarships in Saudi Arabia: Physical Capital into Human Capital

Saudi scholarship programs pre-dated the country's formal independence, going back as early as 1927; as in Algeria, they aimed at rapid acquisition of human capital for a severely underdeveloped country.[33] Yet only after World War II did the Saudi state begin to regularly finance students to study abroad, initially through enrollments at regional universities such as Cairo University and at universities in the United States as early as 1947.[34] The Saudi Arabian Educational Mission opened in New York City in 1956, a year before the kingdom's first domestic university (now known as King Saud University) opened.[35]

In Saudi Arabia, along with other oil-rich monarchies of the Gulf Cooperation Council (GCC), rulers burnished their claims to power with developmental projects centered around technocratic modernization rather than revolutionary populism.[36] Scholarship programs were seen as critical to staffing a rapidly expanding state bureaucracy, one that faced ever-growing developmental responsibilities.[37] An attempt to force the recall of all Saudi students in 1955 by conservative clerics (a crucial source of support for the Saudi regime) fearful that "subversive ideas" were undermining religious devotion in the country, faltered in the face of the kingdom's need for skilled professionals.[38] Advisers from the Ford Foundation tasked with overseeing bureaucratic reform in the 1960s noted that "a shortage of trained personnel is the most critical hindrance to more effective government performance."[39] While scholarship programs alone could not resolve these challenges, they could at least provide the core of management for key state agencies. ARAMCO offered its own scholarships to the United States and the American University of Beirut for similar reasons, often benefiting Shiite Saudis from the country's Eastern Province who otherwise struggled to access government programs.[40]

The oil boom of the 1970s supercharged these efforts as rising demand, Organization of Petroleum Exporting Countries (OPEC) oil cuts, and the 1973–1974 Arab oil embargo sent prices skyrocketing. By 1980, students from OPEC countries made up more than a third of foreign students in the United States, including nearly 10,000 Saudi exchange students.[41] For Saudi students, these numbers could belie turbulent study-abroad experiences. Even acquiring a scholarship to begin with could be a confusing process: "It took me two months just to gather from the various government ministries and complete the required documents for my scholarship," reported one student in 1980.[42] A common complaint was inadequate preparation in English, coupled with challenges negotiating financial transactions and university bureaucracies in the United States.[43] More concerning, field reports by Saudi bureaucrats and original research by Saudi students abroad noted considerable challenges of substance abuse, financial troubles, and even sexual misconduct among students abroad.[44] Prince Faisal bin Musaid would provide a notorious example of these challenges of adjustment; reportedly banned from travel in 1973 due to a drug-related conviction while in the United States, he assassinated King Faisal bin Abdulaziz in 1975.[45]

Still, most students seemed to benefit from their experiences abroad, with meritocratic selection processes exposing a limited yet diverse selection of students to life abroad. Alyahya's survey responses turned up accounts of students abroad taking advantage of newly available physical or mental health services for the first time,[46] discovering and finding fulfillment in student groups,[47] and finding a greater sense of self-fulfillment.[48] Various studies of the Saudi exchange-student population likewise provided evidence of more liberal social attitudes resulting from contact with American citizens and media,[49] particularly when compared with peers in the Saudi university system.[50] Nor did Saudi scholarship programs result in a noticeable brain drain, with most students returning home to the kingdom at the end of their period of study to reconnect with family and take up well-paid jobs in the bureaucracy.[51]

Boom into Bust: 1980–2000

The initial boom in scholarships proved politically and economically unsustainable in the face of challenges brought on by falling oil revenues and major conflicts that marked the 1980s. While the falling price of oil initially encouraged some efforts at greater efficiency and transparency in Algerian exchange programs, factional infighting followed by outright civil war would see scholarship programs increasingly used as a reward for political clients rather than as a tool of political development. Saudi scholarship programs likewise greatly diminished in scale, partly as a concession to religious conservatives who railed against the cultural influence of Western mores. However, individual Saudi scholarships were never parceled out as political spoils to the same degree as in Algeria.

Algerian Brain Drain at the Height of the Boom

For Algeria, the early 1980s remained a period of unprecedented oil prices and subsequent largesse for higher education, given its importance to President Chadli Bendjedid and his pursuit of liberalizing economic reforms.[52] Bendjedid's government framed the scholarships as an emblem of the regime's commitment to the broad distribution of oil rents and to economic modernization, legitimizing the rule of a regime that framed its commitments to society in developmental and nationalist terms. The foreign scholarship program frequently featured in state-led propaganda, including in large media spectacles broadcast via state media. President Bendjedid regularly addressed students in long speeches, emphasizing the students' avant-garde role as "the men of tomorrow and the cadres of the future, of the near future."[53] Seminars on studying abroad were organized before students left for their academic pursuits, which served as a final opportunity for ideological indoctrination as well.

Scholarship programs were still seen as a means to broader policy goals rather than a form of direct patronage, with Bendjedid redirecting scholarship destinations to help break away from the socialist model of his predecessor, Houari Boumediene. Starting in the 1980s, fewer students were being sent to Yugoslavia, the Soviet Union, and other Eastern bloc countries, as most technology-oriented training was redirected toward Western countries. Far from fearing the return of dissident students, officials at times allocated positions to isolate students and academics who contested the Arabization reforms or who espoused growing conservative ideologies. "The scholarships were often used as a convenient instrument to export anti-Arabists and, quite frankly, anybody who was deemed a 'troublemaker.'"[54]

The Bendjedid government nearly tripled the number of students abroad within five years, funding them more generously as well.[55] Financial resources for scholarship beneficiaries included more generous stipends, an allowance covering the cost of moving fees, a family stipend (30 percent extra for a spouse, and 20 percent extra for each child), and an annual return flight (for student and any family). By 1983, scholarship stipends were between approximately $1,000 and $1,400 per month—more than five times Algerian gross domestic product (GDP) per capita at the time.[56] In addition to scholarship stipends, university staff and state bureaucrats could keep their salaries during their studies abroad, and were permitted to transfer up to 50 percent of their wages abroad.[57]

During the early 1980s, legislation was promulgated to further unify and centralize the structures responsible for administering and managing international scholarships. A decree of February 1981 established the National Commission for Education Abroad (CNFE). The decree also defined selection criteria for scholarships and emphasized that scholarship opportunities would be tied to academic performance (at least on paper). Yet despite efforts to reform the selection process for the growing number of students, the rate of student returns continued to fall. Upward of 70 percent of students (and some years over 90 percent) failed to return home as expected.[58]

The reasons for this low return rate—part of a broader Algerian brain drain—were several and wide-ranging. However, one central issue was the lack of any reintegration plan for returnees, coupled with additional bureaucratic hurdles for those who did not study in France. Yahia Zoubir, an Algerian academic who studied on a scholarship in the United States in the late 1970s, was told "that I 'might' [obtain] a job in a remote area, with no promise of housing," and was made to explain how his US degree matched the French system, leaving him with "a degree that the government had funded but would not recognise before redefending my PhD thesis."[59] In the words of an Algerian student who had gone to the United States on a government scholarship in the 1980s, "You could have gone to MIT or Harvard, but your degree would not be recognised in Algeria, while if you had studied in a low-ranking university that nobody had heard of in France, you were good to go."[60] An additional barrier for some who had studied abroad was Algerian policies of compulsory conscription, which meant that returning students faced demands for military service regardless of their education or career plans.

Saudi Scholarships and Threats to "Intellectual Security"

While most Saudi scholarship students returned home to find well-paid jobs in the country's burgeoning bureaucracy, concerns of cost and ideological contamination led to a prolonged lull in exchange programs. Saudi oil income tapered off dramatically in the early 1980s as the country scaled back production, even as concerns about cultural "corruption" stemming from the program made it a prime candidate for cutbacks. The changes brought about by life abroad were not always to the liking of Saudi officials—from the 1950s onward, students had a tendency to return with "problematic" commitments to social reform and political change.[61] Concerns about Saudi students' political activities in the United States had already led to another pause in new scholarships by the early 1970s, only to resume as petro-dollars poured in following the oil boom.[62]

More dramatically, the start of the 1980s saw severe cutbacks in scholarships awarded, preceding crashing oil markets but perhaps reflective of major cutbacks in Saudi production levels (see Figure 8.1). Religious conservatives had likewise long harbored suspicions of the potential "corrupting influences" of study abroad in the West.[63] These views gained the upper hand in 1979, when the seizure of the Grand Mosque of Mecca by religious extremists and the overthrow of the Shah in Iran prompted the Saudi royal family to recommit to deeply conservative social policies as a means of shoring up their religious legitimacy. Decisions by the Council of Ministers and Council of Senior Scholars (composed of top religious officials in the kingdom) in 1980–1981 sought to place strict limits on the number scholarships awarded while limiting them to older, married, conservative Saudi men.[64] As numbers tapered off, comparatively few students were sent abroad during the 1980s and 1990s, mainly to undertake training for specific government roles.

Crashing-Out in Algeria: 1986–1999

The oil price collapse of 1986 put severe pressure on the Algerian budget, in turn prompting a review of the scholarship program that reduced the number of scholarships awarded and (in theory) refined the

Figure 8.1   GCC Students in the United States, 1950–2000

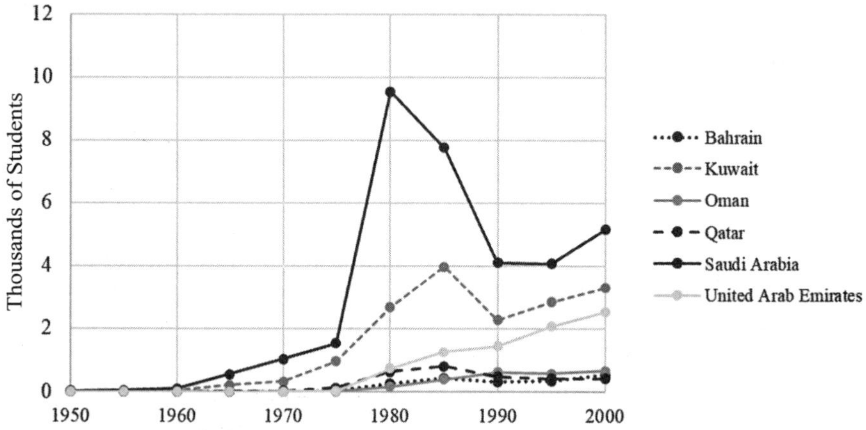

Source: Compiled by authors using data from Institute of International Education, "Open Doors."

selection process even further.[65] Algeria's commission on international scholarships was reconfigured and tasked with administering a smaller number of sector-specific scholarship programs in cooperation with technical ministries. This reform led to a quota system allocating a certain number of scholarships to each ministry, in line with the importance of each ministry.[66] The education ministry remained in control of selection processes, but not the scientific and research committees. In the decades that followed, the number of state-funded international scholarships would never again reach pre-1986 levels.

The government also reduced costs by opting to fund shorter study programs, including distance-learning programs coupled with short-term internships.[67] Furthermore, foreign scholarships were rearranged to fund mainly postgraduate degrees. During the 1987–1988 academic year, just 6.7 percent of all students abroad were enrolled in bachelor degree programs. Even PhD scholarship numbers fell dramatically, from 4,600 students in the 1986–1987 academic year to 2,723 students in 1987–1988 (see Figure 8.2). Those students sent on PhD scholarships were expected to return and serve as supervisory and managerial staff at universities.

As government austerity measures provoked mass riots in 1988 and an abortive political opening through 1992, the increasingly violent conflict in the country's streets and among elite factions only encour-

Figure 8.2   Algerian Scholarships, 1963–1992

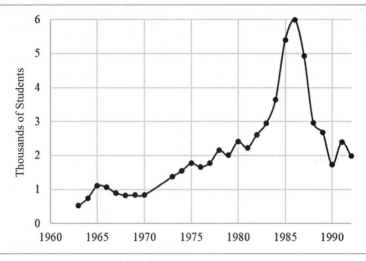

Source: Compiled by authors using data from Kadri, "La formation à l'étranger des étudiants Algériens," p. 121.

aged further brain drain among students sent abroad. This was true even for marquee employers such as Sonatrach. "The number of students we expected to return from scholarships abroad and to work with us at SONATRACH, especially engineers and managers . . . continued to fall throughout the 1980s," noted one former executive with the company. "After the '86 price collapse and then [nationwide riots in] 1988, very few were returning. . . . [T]hose in oil/gas were going to the US or to work at ARAMCO, ADNOC etc [oil companies in the Gulf]."[68]

Structural adjustment programs aimed at rebuilding Algeria's shattered economy resulted in considerable fiscal consolidation and subsequently fewer resources for higher education, including scholarships abroad, by mid-decade. Allocations to the education sector fell to 17 percent of the state budget in 1997, down from 25 percent of a much larger budget a decade earlier.[69] For those scholarships still awarded, the country's continued reorientation toward a market economy meant a further reorientation toward Western countries (see Figure 8.3 for change in destination countries). In 1982, socialist countries received the largest number of government-funded students sent abroad for studies. That year, the Soviet Union hosted 1,072 Algerian students, while France counted 721, the Federal Republic of Germany counted 422, and the United Kingdom registered 321. By 1994, a year prior to Algeria's enrollment in an International Monetary Fund (IMF) program, the former Soviet Union received just 209 Algerian students, compared to 1,270 hosted by France, which represented 64 percent of all government-funded international scholarships that year. Between the middle and late 1990s the scholarship system experienced a continued decline in the number of students being sent abroad, as the program became increasingly associated with opacity, favoritism, and patronage.

Scholarships and the New Oil Boom: Consolidating Old Trends

The course of the two countries' scholarship programs during the 2000s commodities boom points to the significant political barriers in the way of utilizing scholarships as a work-around to the contradictions of limited-access orders. While King Abdullah inaugurated an eponymous scholarships program (the King Abdullah Scholarship Program [KASP]) to send hundreds of thousands of Saudi students abroad, Algerian scholarships have remained few in number and plagued by corruption and favoritism. Factions among the Algerian elite have preferred to invest in more direct forms of patronage, whatever the opportunity cost for the

Figure 8.3   Algerian Foreign Scholarships Awarded by Destination Region, 1989–1994

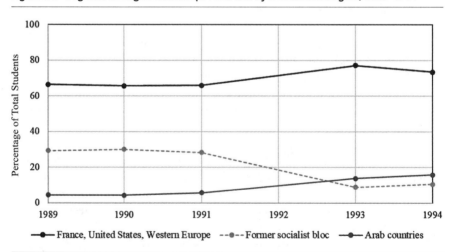

Source: Data compiled by authors from Labdelaoui, "La migration des étudiants Algériens vers l'étranger," p. 121.

country writ large, while steering many remaining scholarship slots toward trusted political clients or their families. Even the successes of the Saudi programs, whether providing state agencies with educated technocrats or encouraging social liberalization through time spent abroad, have come at an enormous cost, calling into question the utility of the entire approach.

Rent Distribution and Brain Drain 2.0 in the Bouteflika Era: 1999–2009

Unmoored from any developmental schemes or industrialization strategies, and viewed as only accelerating the country's brain drain, what remained of the Algerian scholarship program was widely used to reward the clients of privileged factions and their children. Following a bleak decade for the country, Abdelaziz Bouteflika ascended to the presidency in April 1999, succeeding Liamine Zeroual as head of state for the next twenty years. In his first two terms he sought to end the conflict and deliver a measure of political stability, ultimately via the amnesty framework of the 2006 Charter for Peace and National Reconciliation (approved via referendum in 2005). Economic development plans, however, lacked any clear ideological or technocratic framework other than piecemeal rent distribution and the construction of clientelist networks. Following the austere 1990s, this approach was sustained during Bouteflika's initial decade in office by ever-higher oil prices, peaking at $147 per barrel in July 2008.

The scholarship programs largely fell by the wayside as selection processes became increasingly vague and disconnected from merit-based criteria. In 2004, the president halted all funding for study abroad at the bachelor's level, and significantly decreased the overall number of students—a tacit admission that financing young Algerians to study abroad was largely paying for them to emigrate. Until then, students who achieved the best grades in the national exams for the baccalaureate had been rewarded with scholarships to study abroad. As Bouteflika commented, "the people will not sow for others to harvest; this is my message to new graduates."[70]

Reductions to the scholarship program were criticized by academics and more development-minded policymakers outside the Ministry of Higher Education. They argued for the reform of scholarship programs rather than outright closure. Professor Omar Aktouf, an Algerian academic at HEC Montreal, argued on an Algerian independent radio station that the decision challenged all conventional wisdom pertaining to strategies adopted by emerging and developing economies.[71] "What are our means to train engineers at the level of Chinese, and Japanese engineers? How, and with what?"[72] Some sociological research does suggest that poor incentives within the Algerian academic system, rather than the Algerian economy or the political climate as a whole, led to poor return rates. Many interviewees in a study of the international scholarships program complained about the lack of dynamism in the Algerian research system, and the general feeling of stagnation among those scholars who did return.[73] Demands for displays of political allegiance within the university system provided further incentives for academics to leave, and constrained those who stayed.[74]

Despite these arguments, changes to the scholarship program prioritized immediate political returns as well as guarantees (through family or material incentives) that students would return. Where at least some of the returns from the first oil boom were invested in coherent development schemes, the high-oil-price 2000s "laid [the foundations] for the institutionalisation of corruption and bribery . . . which touched all segments of society including the distribution and allocation of international scholarships."[75] It had long been beneficial to be a member of the National Liberation Front (FLN) (the ruling party) in order to benefit from certain rents and to gain protection; this was now increasingly true even for academics and students. One academic in Oran explained: "I was assaulted by a student affiliated to FLN, however, he continued at the university with total impunity."[76] Furthermore, according to several academics, some students joined the FLN with the belief that applications for scholarships abroad would be stronger if they came from card-carrying members of the ruling party. Interestingly, return rates improved dramatically as administrators ensured that only those with a demonstrated vested interest in the Algerian regime's continuation (material or otherwise) were funded to go abroad. Patronage has at least ensured the physical return of graduates (see Figure 8.4), even if the economic returns remain unclear.

9/11 and the King Abdullah Scholarship Program

The 2000s saw a major boon to Saudi scholarship programs in the form of the King Abdullah Scholarship Program, leading Saudi Arabia to become one of the largest sources of foreign students in the world. In a dramatic expansion of past programs, the stated goals of KASP were to go beyond staffing ministry offices, to equip young Saudis with the skills, drive, and even (implicitly) social attitudes to support a diversified economy. While the Saudi government was hardly free of corruption

Figure 8.4   Returns of Algerian Scholarship Beneficiaries, 1980–2005

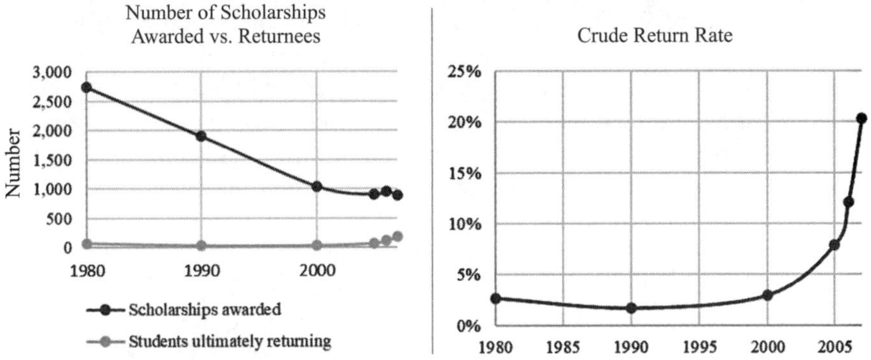

Number of Scholarships
Awarded vs. Returnees

Crude Return Rate

—●— Scholarships awarded

—●— Students ultimately returning

Source: Data compiled by authors from Khaled, "Politique de formation à l'étranger et l'émigration intellectuelle Algérienne," p. 137.

during this time, relatively meritocratic selection processes permitted a diverse array of students to venture abroad. Additionally, King Abdullah (2005–2015) expended significant political capital to ensure that KASP and other foreign-education programs were largely shielded from conservative criticism.

Several factors contributed to the Saudi government making such an enormous investment in scholarship programs (first announced in 2005). First, the program came after considerable scrutiny of the US-Saudi relationship in the wake of the 9/11 terrorist attacks, with American public opinion of Saudi Arabia dropping from about a 50 percent favorability rating in February 2001 to just 30 percent a year later.[77] New visa regulations created immense backlogs for Saudis seeking to travel to the United States, including students.[78] Any international scholarship program for Saudis would invariably lead many to study in the United States, with expanded people-to-people interactions (as well as considerable tuition dollars) serving to shore up this important relationship. US diplomats speculated that the initiative had been sparked by suggestions of a much more modest US-Saudi scholarship program during then–crown prince Abdullah's meeting with President George W. Bush in April 2005, while American media frequently interpreted the program to be a sign of US-Saudi reconciliation.[79]

KASP would also fulfill similar human-capital goals to previous scholarship programs, only on a much grander scale. One Saudi scholarship administrator described it as an "enlightenment project" aimed at bringing a wide range of knowledge back to the kingdom rather than a more "tailored" program aimed at the specific needs of ministries or universities.[80] The program was ostensibly merit-based, although a secondary "track" allowed initially self-funded students to apply for government funding later.[81] The sheer number of students sent abroad was impressive not only in comparison to the kingdom's recent past, but even compared with peer monarchies in the GCC and elsewhere in the MENA region (see Figure 8.5). A conservative estimate of expenses for US-based students alone amounts to over $2 billion in recent years (not including support staff or dependents of students), with the Saudi government funding over $20,000 in tuition and fees for the median public-university student and nearly $50,000 for the median private-university student. This has amounted to multiple times the cost of the entire US Fulbright program in recent years (see Figure 8.6)— and as much as 10 percent of all Saudi Arabia's domestic spending on higher education.[82]

While more Saudi exchange students than ever before have come to study a range of subjects, a small number of specializations has tended to dominate. In 2015, for example, engineering and related disciplines accounted for nearly half of all male Saudi students abroad (up from

Figure 8.5   MENA Students in the United States as a Percentage of 2005 Levels, 2000–2015

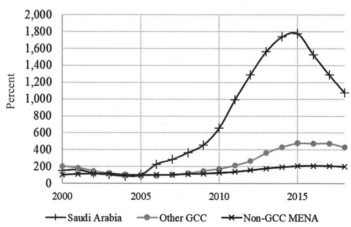

Source: Data compiled by authors from Institute of International Education, "Open Doors."

Figure 8.6   Annual Cost of Fulbright and King Abdullah Scholarship Program, Students in the United States, 2005–2017

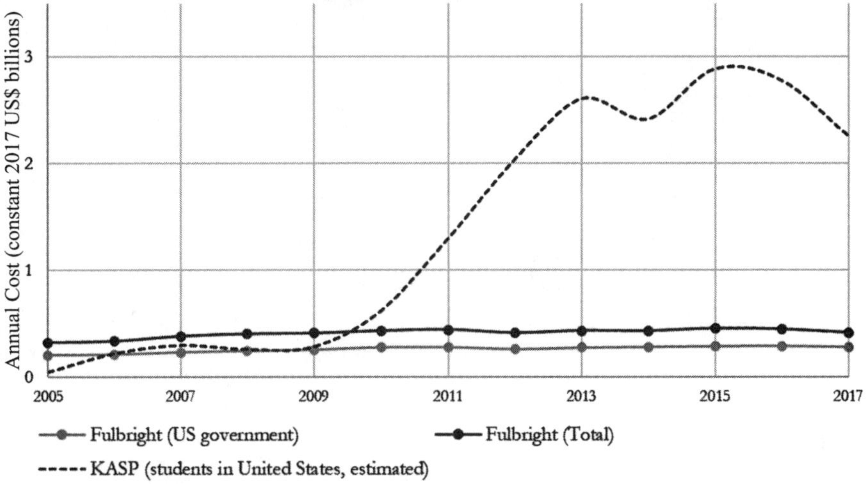

Fulbright (US government)   Fulbright (Total)

- - - - - KASP (students in United States, estimated)

Sources: US tuition data from College Board; income data from the Federal Reserve Bank of St. Louis. KASP estimates based on Ministry of Education data on students in the United States, and an assumption that 95 percent of students attend the average public university while 5 percent attend the average private university. Fulbright data from Fulbright Foreign Scholarship Board (FFSB) annual reports, Bureau of Educational and Cultural Affairs, US Department of State.

Notes: Data compiled by authors. Estimated costs include tuition and board, as well as an estimated stipend amount of 50 percent of the median individual US income.

just 15 percent in 1995), while Saudi women were largely concentrated in medicine and healthcare (24 percent), engineering (16 percent), and various commercial and business degrees (23 percent).[83] Saudi men tend to predominate in the scholarship program overall (over 75 percent of students abroad in recent years), albeit mainly at the undergraduate level, where family concerns about young women living abroad might be more relevant. Saudi women studying abroad are more likely to be pursuing advanced degrees, in relatively equal numbers to Saudi men (see Figure 8.7).

While KASP sidestepped clerical oversight of the university system, the program was never free of scrutiny from conservative commentators who feared that returning students would import Western cultural values.[84] Barely five years into the program, religious scholar Abdulmuhsin al-'Abbad wrote an open letter to the royal court warning that the program would only increase the number of "Westernizers" whose minds were "polluted by what they have encountered in the

Figure 8.7   Saudi Students on Study-Abroad Scholarships, 2017

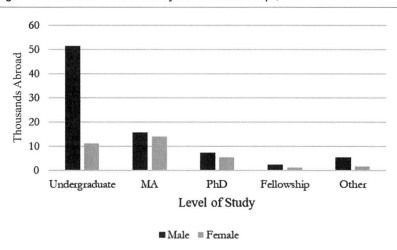

Source: Data compiled by authors from *Annual Reports on Higher Education,* Saudi Arabian Ministry of Education, previously the Ministry of Higher Education.

West."[85] This letter would in turn be included in a book-length treatment of the issue by 'Abd al-'Aziz bin Ahmed al-Baddah, who connected scholarship programs in general to civilizational decline in Muslim countries and subversion from within by foreign powers.[86] These commentators' fears would seem to be borne out by descriptive and anecdotal evidence that exchange students have acquired more "liberal" social values while abroad (particularly in the United States, Canada, and the United Kingdom).[87]

Still, Saudi policymakers retained royal backing to defend programs against conservative criticisms.[88] In the early 2000s, the mounting toll of extremist ideologies within the kingdom (through several high-profile terrorist attacks) tilted policymakers toward embracing exchange programs rather than international branch campuses in order to facilitate widescale cultural exchange.[89] King Abdullah demonstrated a willingness to push back against clerical discontent whenever it interfered with plans to expand access to foreign education.[90] Supportive commentators stridently defended the program as a key tool for economic development and modernization in the kingdom, while others pointed to the hypocrisy of some in criticizing the program even as they sent their own children to study abroad.[91] As the scholarship program brought in more and more students from across the kingdom—"from remote villages in the South, North, East and West [of the Kingdom], and people who had never had a passport"[92]—the idea of venturing abroad for education became harder to portray as exotic and threatening.

Scholarships and a Low-Oil Future: Sustainable in the Extreme?

While recent low oil prices have impacted both Saudi and Algerian budgets, scholarship policies now appear locked into separate trajectories—as a source of patronage in Algeria, as a tool of social engineering and economic development in Saudi Arabia. In Algeria, scholarships have largely ceased to boost the country's reserves of human capital, although a few short-term programs provide a handful of meritocratic opportunities. Saudi officials have imposed stricter requirements on scholarship recipients, moving away from past policies of foreign education en masse but sustaining the program overall. Even in the face of declining oil prices, the job prospects of returning students are far better than for domestic Saudi graduates—yet it is unclear if even returning students can do much to diversify the kingdom's economy.

Continued Clientelism and Limited Access in Algeria: 2009–2019

The Bouteflika era entered its second decade with little disruption, sustained by high oil prices, associated rent distribution (whether through subsidies, housing schemes, cheap loans, or social services), and continued clientelism. As the government continued to grapple with a university system designed to provide higher education en masse with little concern for quality or the demands of the job market, a five-year development plan (2009–2014) incorporated plans to reform the sector, excluding the study-abroad program. Although these plans were made possible by higher rents—budgets called for a meaningful increase in government spending on research and development, for example—there was no attempt to restore previous cuts to government-funded scholarships for studies abroad.

Toward the end of Bouteflika's third term, however, the allocation of scholarships was reorganized in an attempt to rationalize and enforce criteria for awarding positions. To be sure, the change in policy held out hope for some qualified researchers or high-performing students (ranked in the top three of undergraduate or postgraduate programs) to obtain funding, with some evidence that this actually happened.[93] An allowance of slots awarded to degree-holding "permanent staff" in public institutions or government agencies, however, continued to permit allocation of funding as patronage. Even where students made it abroad, preparing them to make the most of their education was not a priority. Students might be sent to countries where they lacked necessary language training or were funded so poorly they could barely survive on the basis of government funding alone. As a result, as one Algerian education policy expert noted, "students abroad are [often] forced to work long hours in order to top up their income for the month and cover costs. Of course, this has implications for the time that is lost for studying."[94]

In addition to the limited-access foreign scholarship programs, there was an alternative, more democratic program created for short-term study abroad, namely Le Programme National Exceptionnel (PNE). Established in the early 2000s, but propelled into popularity by the late 2000s, the program is an opportunity for doctoral students enrolled at an Algerian university to benefit from grants to study abroad for six to twelve months (sometimes up to eighteen). Researchers are tasked with finding a supervisor/host at suitable universities abroad, and they are expected to be in good standing, as well as having reached the latter stages of their doctorates. Some of the aims of the Ministry of Higher Education, through the PNE, which it administers, are to support research collaboration with foreign partners, and to help develop capacities for researchers who will become the future academicians at Algerian universities.[95] There are additional incentives for science-enrolled students who may find equipment and facilities abroad that are lacking at home. According to an Algerian education policy specialist, "the PNE is for the most part meritocratic, and represents a less risky option for the government in losing more Algerian brains to western countries, as doctoral students are often older, often married with children, and much more likely to return. . . . [I]n fact to my knowledge, the return rate has been very high with only some cases of abscondment and the like."[96] While researchers do not gain foreign credentials per se, the program does represent a limited opportunity to develop state capacity in the academic sector.

Beyond government-funded scholarships, there are two other main routes for Algerians to study abroad. The first is to self-fund, which has grown increasingly popular in line with a rising middle class in Algeria. France remains by the far the most popular country for Algerians to travel to, presumably as a result of language, family ties, and relatively lower costs (compared to the United Kingdom or the United States). In the latest available statistics, Algeria was among the top three countries sending students to France, behind Morocco but ahead of China, with around 30,000 students in-country in 2018 compared with a little over 1,000 student visas granted to Algerians in the United Kingdom and barely 200 in the United States during the same year.[97]

Algerian students might also apply to foreign scholarship programs. These opportunities are almost always based on academic merit and tend to offer a clear and transparent selection process. Some programs are Algeria-specific, serving a soft-power objective for international partners (whether countries, companies, or foundations), while some are open to all regardless of students' country of origin. French companies and universities have funded some of Algeria's most talented students to study or train in France. The US Fulbright program (thirty-three scholarships awarded to Algerians between 2014 and 2018) and the United Kingdom's Chevening scholarship (twenty-five awarded in the same period) are also popular, albeit in a limited way. Other European and Asian countries also have various funding schemes for students that Algerian students have benefited from. Most of these programs fund tuition fees, cover living expenses, provide health insurance, and pay for an annual return flight. While there have been attempts by the Algerian Ministry of Higher Education to regulate the selection processes for these scholarships, these have largely proved unsuccessful. There are some exceptions, however, particularly with Indian- and Chinese-funded scholarship programs.[98]

Although some deserving Algerian students benefit from scholarships, the program is a microcosm of the rent-seeking and cronyism within the Algerian regime more broadly, in which a well-connected few benefit at the expense of the broader public.[99] Beyond the exemptions for permanent staff, for example, the 2014 decree also provided a special exemption for the children of Algerian diplomats—one devoid of any meritocratic requirements. Conversations with researchers and journalists revealed that the "children of diplomats" category has become a means for the family of well-connected individuals to access scholarships legally, regardless of abilities or qualifications. According to one staffer working at an Algerian mission in a European capital, "Many of the [diplomatic] scholarships holders in the past have not been relatives of diplomats. . . . [T]here have [also] been instances where scholarship holders . . . used both their maiden name and family name to benefit twice."[100] The official who oversees scholarships and international cooperation at the Ministry of Higher Education has maintained his position for decades.[101] Under Bouteflika, numerous other bureaucrats retained offices through successive governments, enabling the institutionalization of secrecy, opacity, and corruption.

While connected children and relatives are sent abroad, the Algerian university system has continued to deteriorate in the face of growing numbers of students and dwindling resources following the 2014 fall in oil prices—despite the fact that each student costs the Algerian state the equivalent of $6,000 per year, or more than the country's per capita GDP.[102] The declining conditions in the higher-education sector have had knock-on effects in Algerian research and development more broadly, further undermining the country's prospects for future development. Algeria, like the other countries of North Africa, continues to lose thousands of qualified doctors, scientists, and even petroleum engineers to France, other European countries, and the Gulf.[103]

In contrast to the praise lavished on students as a "vanguard of the future" in decades past, present-day Algerian officials have tended to downplay any need for intellectual achievements that rank on a global scale. In 2018, then–minister of higher education Al Tahar Hajjar sparked anger in intellectual and academic circles when he criticized the meaning and value of Nobel Prize winners, suggesting that Algeria did not need any: "What will it benefit me when an Algerian student gets the Nobel Prize, even if we get ten of them?"[104] The government-funded scholarship program has gone from being a marquee policy for Algerian developmentalists to something approaching a state secret; the unavailability of data and lack of transparency around the government-funded scholarships abroad program is infamous among academics in Algeria.[105]

Retrenchment Without Restriction in Saudi Arabia

Since the 2014 decline in oil prices, threats to the continuation of KASP have been more fiscal than ideological. Dwindling oil revenues have encouraged program administrators to "right-size" KASP (now the Guardian of the Two Holy Mosques Scholarship Program) by focusing scholarships on more-qualified candidates and more-selective schools, yet overall numbers of scholarship students remain considerably above pre-2005 levels. In terms of managing political challenges to the Saudi regime, in-person and online surveillance programs have largely helped ward off the potential for student political activism abroad. By contrast, trying to use tuition dollars as a tool of coercive diplomacy, such as in the case of retaliation against Canada, to be discussed later, has proven largely ineffective.

The Saudi state's efforts to scale back spending have led policymakers to reorient and streamline the program while still making study abroad a real possibility for thousands of Saudis. By 2017 (the latest year for which data are available), 116,000 scholarship students were abroad—still a sizable number, but down from the 143,000 abroad in 2012.[106] Admissions to various scholarship programs have undoubtedly fallen, from an average of around 15,000 students at all levels of study in 2011–2013 to fewer than 8,000 students in recent years.[107] In addition to tighter entry requirements overall, new restrictions limited eligibility for self-funded students to those studying medicine or STEM subjects (science, technology, engineering, and mathematics) as well as those at exceptionally high-ranked programs and institutions.[108] "You've taken care of [this cultural opening]," noted one former official from the Saudi Arabian Cultural Mission (SACM) in the United States. "Now we need to think about investing in particular minds and capabilities . . . to build the human-resources infrastructure for the future."[109]

The "Vision 2030" reforms championed publicly by Muhammad bin Salman (first deputy and then full crown prince of the kingdom) have leaned into the kind of social engineering envisaged by at least some of KASP's early advocates—promoting "modern" values of toleration and acceptance in pursuit of a more socially liberal society.[110] One official involved in developing KASP even believed that "without the returns of the program our conservative communities would not easily accept . . . [the current] cultural and social reform process" of Vision 2030.[111] Even as the various new agencies and initiatives associated with Vision 2030 employed numerous talented graduates of the scholarship program, reforms to the scholarship program have restricted funding to top students and university programs. Amid a tighter job market at home, the Ministry of Education has particularly sought to tie scholarships more closely to future jobs in various government departments.[112]

While still an important source of Saudi soft power abroad (in terms of encouraging people-to-people contact), Saudi efforts to monitor students (and shield them from in-country laws) have attracted negative attention in recent years. The SACM, while primarily providing a range of support services to students, also works to monitor Saudi students abroad for any signs of political activity, whether online or off—often with the assistance of Saudi student groups established in part for this purpose.[113] Students have alleged that criticism of the Saudi government while abroad can result in repercussions for them or their families (starting with loss of scholarship support), even as other Saudi students credibly accused of criminal activity in the United States have allegedly relied on Saudi embassy officials to avoid penalties and prosecution.[114]

One potential threat to the program lies in the crown prince viewing scholarship dollars as a tool of coercive diplomacy in international disputes. The first noteworthy attempt came in reaction to Arabic-language tweets by the Canadian government regarding the arrest of several activists within the kingdom. Among other punitive measures, Saudi officials announced plans to relocate some 7,000 students on scholarship in Canada—something that Canadian officials feared might have a considerable economic impact on the country's higher-education system.[115] The Saudi government has thus far appeared to let existing scholarships play out rather than moving students immediately (for the most part), with the number of Saudi students in Canada continuing a slow decline from 2014.[116] While these measures have thus far failed to secure any concessions from the Trudeau government, they might deter other governments (or specific universities) from voicing criticisms of the Saudi government. Thus far, however, the short-term costs of this particular effort at "coercive diplomacy" have mainly been borne by Canadian universities and Saudi students.

The View from the Students

Beyond the political challenges of getting a scholarship program off the ground, a survey of Algerian and Saudi foreign-exchange students high-lights the challenge of ensuring that students return if they anticipate stagnant, unsatisfying careers at home.[117] Starkly divergent views on domestic opportunities are readily apparent in comparing students from the two countries. Among those currently studying abroad, for example, majorities from both countries saw a clear job-market advantage for those with overseas educations. Yet Saudi students were far more likely to anticipate returning home for work upon the completion of their time abroad—nearly 75 percent of Saudi students abroad anticipated heading home for work, compared with only 36 percent of Algerian students studying abroad (see Figure 8.8).

The hesitation of Algerian scholars to return home likely reflects concerns about limited job prospects and opaque bureaucracies that fil-ter back to the overseas student community. Large portions of both Saudi and Algerian students abroad (74 percent each) supported the idea of a jobs guarantee for scholarship holders—perhaps understandably, as they faced the prospects of returning home to find jobs themselves (see Figure 8.9).[118] While Algerians who had finished their time abroad felt similarly, only a minority of Saudi study-abroad graduates supported the guarantee (41 percent). One plausible interpretation is that Saudi students have returned home to a labor market (public or private) where

Figure 8.8 Students' Assessments of Scholarship Program, Algeria and Saudi Arabia, 2019

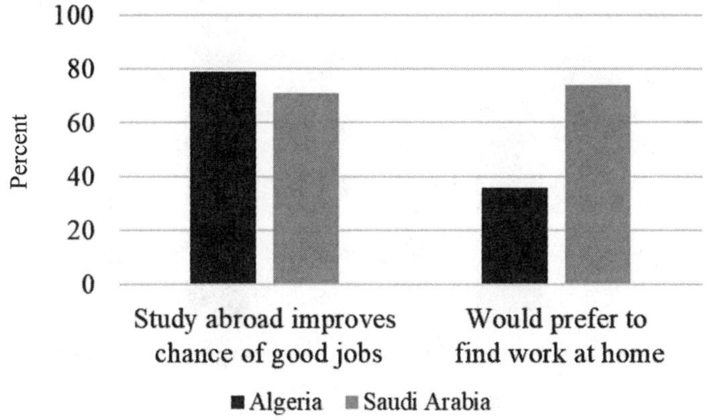

Source: Data compiled by authors via a snowball-sample survey of current or former study-abroad students from Saudi Arabia and Algeria fielded July–December 2019.
Note: Question wording: "Percentage of respondents currently abroad who agree, or believe, that . . ."

their experiences are more likely to be rewarded with promotion. This is further supported by the finding that Saudi overseas graduates are far more likely than Saudi peers currently abroad (or Algerians in general) to be "very interested" in the prospect of designing and implementing public policies—perhaps reflective of the frenzy of new positions opened up by the Saudi Vision 2030 reform project (see Figure 8.10).

Additionally, Algerian respondents appeared somewhat more comfortable in their surroundings while abroad, perhaps due to language proficiency and familial connections (in France, the primary destination for foreign students), although few valued spending time away from home for its own sake. They were more likely than Saudi respondents (37 percent vs. 19 percent) to view their host-country community as an important aspect of their experience abroad, even as Saudi respondents were more likely to value time away from home (47 percent vs. 28 percent).

Conclusion

A comparison of the Algerian and Saudi scholarship programs highlights the importance of an elite consensus behind developmental goals

Figure 8.9   Percentage of Students Who Agree That They Should Be Guaranteed a Government Job, Algeria and Saudi Arabia, 2019

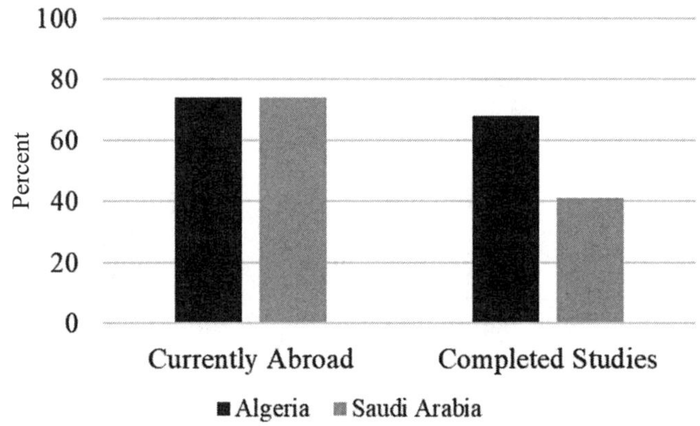

Source: Author survey.

in order to isolate even limited meritocratic education schemes from patronage networks. To be sure, both countries' access to considerable oil rents was critical to financing the costs of sending students on scholarship, monitoring their activities while abroad, and attracting them back home at the end of their studies. To the extent that monarchy or struggles of national liberation contribute to elite cohesion in general, they can be credited with helping to ensure relatively meritocratic scholarship programs benefited students—and state bureaucracies—in both countries through the 1980s. Yet where Saudi Arabia's "lost decades" of low oil prices never truly forced difficult choices about who might lose out amid austerity measures, Algeria's effective bankruptcy during the late 1980s sparked enduring elite conflicts that sapped developmental schemes of state investments and encouraged officials to steer scholarship positions to political clients and spare funds to their own pockets.[119] This raises doubts about the potential for scholarship programs to serve as public goods rather than private rewards in a region where numerous countries are beset by internal conflicts and governed by factious elites.

Several other observations emerge from our comparison. The first is that Algerian and Saudi policymakers were as likely to value exposure to foreign "ways of life" (whether the spirit of capitalism or cosmopolitan liberalism) as a way to socially engineer more liberal or productive

Figure 8.10   Percentage of Students Who Are "Very Interested" in "Designing and Implementing Public Policies" in Their Country, Algeria and Saudi Arabia, 2019

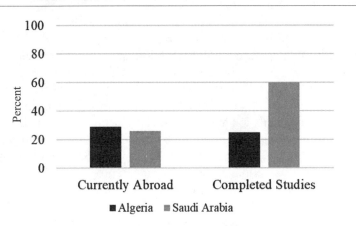

Source: Author survey.

Note: A similar pattern exists for "very" or "somewhat" interested, but not for "not very" or "not at all" interested.

populations, as they were to fear it as a threat to stability. Concerns posed by student dissidents can be monitored by informants and security officers or isolated by threats to cut off scholarship stipends.

The second is anecdotal evidence that these scholarship programs may only be furnishing sending countries with more qualified "job takers" than "job makers" who expand economic opportunities at home. Studies of domestic "social engineering" projects in the Arab Gulf monarchies suggest that students internalize a sense of entitlement rather than the value of self-reliance; more study is needed to see whether this holds among foreign-exchange students sent abroad at great expense.

Finally, there is a question of cost-effectiveness. There is little question that KASP has helped to engineer more socially liberal Saudi citizens through contact with the outside world.[120] Even as declining oil revenues have affected the scale of the kingdom's scholarship programs, rulers and bureaucrats still view them as a reliable policy tool for rapidly acquiring valuable expertise—at the close of 2019, the Ministry of Education announced a new round of scholarships to educate a new cadre of arts-and-culture teachers for revamped primary and secondary education curricula. Still, if the standard of cost-effectiveness remains Prince Bandar bin Sultan's quip—that "out of $400 billion, [say that] we misused or got corrupted with $50 billion"—then governments can justify such programs when they aim at economic growth rather than merely social change.[121]

Further research is needed, most pressingly on the economic impact of international scholarship programs. Are returning students more likely to encourage economic innovation and job creation upon return, even in inhospitable business environments? If so, how much do governments have to invest to obtain this benefit? Returnees from the King Abdullah Scholarship Program—and its successor exchange programs— seem an ideal population to study in order to begin answering these questions. Likewise, additional case studies of regional scholarship programs can further test and refine our initial conclusions about the role played by resource rents and elite conflict. Scholarship programs initiated by Saddam Hussein's Baathist regime (substantial oil revenues, limited factional conflict through the 1980s) and Bahrain's ruling monarchy (moderate oil revenues, heightened factional maneuvering post-2011) might be good grounds on which to start.

As it stands, study-abroad programs are not a panacea for the region's educational problems. Countries with deeply factionalized bureaucracies, such as Iraq, or with little money to spare, such as Egypt, are perhaps better off pursuing short-term programs like Algeria's PNE that can build up technical expertise without too great of an expenditure and without easily falling prey to political favoritism. Less wealthy countries such as Tunisia that can establish a degree of elite consensus through open political bargaining—as happened with landmark legislation to first outlaw violence against women (in 2017) and then ban racial discrimination (in 2018)— might be able to finance a more wide-ranging exchange program (perhaps with support from international donors). The wealthiest countries (per capita) in the region, such as Kuwait or the United Arab Emirates (UAE), will likely continue to pay a premium for large-scale skills acquisition or "cultural change" through study abroad.

Notes

1. Boeren, "Relationships Between Scholarship Program and Institutional Capacity Development Initiatives," pp. 59–60. Most existing cost-benefit studies have focused on programs financed by Western governments or multinational corporations. For a review of existing studies, see Martel, "Tracing the Spark That Lights a Flame," pp. 59–60.

2. Al-Tahtawi, *An Imam in Paris;* Shannon, *Losing Hearts and Minds;* Frosch, "Chaos at Home Stalls Tuition Aid for Libyan Students in U.S."; Schwartzstein, "How Saddam and ISIS Killed Iraqi Science."

3. Forster, "Why Are There So Few World-Class Universities in the Middle East and North Africa?"

4. On universities in the Middle East and North Africa as both a site of political contestation and a considerable burden on government finances, see Wickham, *Mobilizing Islam,* pp. 36–62; and Ketchley and Biggs, "The Educational Contexts of Islamist Activism: Elite Students and Religious Institutions in Egypt," pp. 58–61.

5. Spilimbergo, "Democracy and Foreign Education"; and Gift and Krcmaric, "Who Democratizes?"

6. Restricting programs to political "insiders" and their relatives is likely to pass over the most capable students. Additionally, students who obtain scholarships through political connections have limited incentives to invest in skills, rather than further connections, to gain future employment. This is analogous to the explanation for low firm productivity in the Arab world given in Hertog, "The Role of Cronyism in Arab Capitalism."

7. Huntington, *Political Order in Changing Societies,* pp. 48–49; Campante and Chor, "Why Was the Arab World Poised for Revolution?"; and Askari and Cummings, "The Middle East and the United States."

8. Geddes, *Politician's Dilemma,* pp. 61–67, 134. Also see review in Mehri, "Pockets of Efficiency and the Rise of Iran Auto."

9. The term is from Ellen Lust, albeit primarily in reference to elections, used to describe processes by which "elites and their supporters . . . compete over special access to a limited set of state resources that they can then distribute to their clients." Lust, "Democratization by Elections?," p. 122.

10. Hertog, *Princes, Brokers, and Bureaucrats,* pp. 267–268.

11. Eibl, *Social Dictatorships,* pp. 140–151.

12. Levitsky and Way, "Beyond Patronage," pp. 869–889; and Staniland, "Militias, Ideology, and the State," pp. 778–781.

13. Menaldo, "The Middle East and North Africa's Resilient Monarchs."

14. For coalitions, see Yom and Gause, "Resilient Royals." For the relative nonchalance of Gulf rulers in the face of social liberalization, see Calvert W. Jones, "Seeing Like an Autocrat," pp. 33–34.

15. This corresponds to the difference between North et al.'s idea of "fragile" LAOs, in which "violence potential is a principal determinant of the distribution of rents and resources," and "basic" LAOs, in which there are more institutionalized means of resolving disputes among competing elites. See also Waldner, *State Building and Late Development,* pp. 8–10.

16. See, for example, Wright, Frantz, and Geddes, "Oil and Autocratic Regime Survival"; and Gehlbach and Keefer, "Private Investment and the Institutionalization of Collective Action in Autocracies."

17. Thelen and Mahoney, "Comparative-Historical Analysis in Contemporary Political Science."

18. Bennoune, *The Making of Contemporary Algeria.* Dollar calculations made by the author at 1 US dollar = 353 old francs (1954—beginning of Algerian war for liberation); settlers who were a minority 10 percent of the Algerian population received roughly a total income of 414 billion old francs (approximately $1.17 billion), almost double the 223 billion old francs ($631 million) that the majority 90 percent received.

19. Merrouche, "The Long-Term Impact of French Settlement on Education in Algeria."

20. Bennoune, *The Making of Contemporary Algeria.*

21. Byrne, "Our Own Special Brand of Socialism." While Egypt had supported Algeria soon after independence by sending thousands of teachers as part of its

Arabization efforts, Ben Bella was especially keen on pursuing a domestically centered model of socialism modeled on Yugoslavia: "To me, Castro is a brother, Nasser is a teacher, but Tito is an example." See quote in Gregory, "Ahmed Ben Bella, Revolutionary Who Led Algeria After Independence, Dies at 93."

22. "Cadres" refer here to executives.

23. Kadri, "La formation à l'étranger des étudiants Algériens les limites d'une politique rentière."

24. Ibid., p. 121.

25. Viet, *La France immigrée.*

26. Interview with former Algerian minister, February 25, 2019, Algiers.

27. Bennoune, *The Making of Contemporary Algeria.*

28. Ghettas, *Algeria and the Cold War,* pp. 78–79.

29. Crandal, "U.S. and Algeria"; also Memorandum from Cyrus Vance, Secretary of State, to President Carter, 13 April 1977, NLC-128-12-7-11–7, NSC Declassification collection, Carter Library.

30. Decree numbers 71.78 and 72.160.

31. Kadri, "La formation à l'étranger des étudiants Algériens les limites d'une politique rentière."

32. Interview in Algiers, June 16, 2019, with a retired lecturer who had worked in Algeria's Ministry of Higher Education in mid-late 1970s.

33. Abdulgaddos al-Ansary, quoted in Al-Nassar, "Saudi Arabian Educational Mission to the United States," pp. 15–19.

34. Al-Nassar, "Saudi Arabian Educational Mission to the United States," pp. 43–44.

35. Ibid., pp. 45–46.

36. Bsheer, "A Counter-Revolutionary State," pp. 235–236; Toby Craig Jones, *Desert Kingdom,* pp. 54–79.

37. While substantial numbers of Saudi students have studied in the United Kingdom, France, and other countries, in this account I focus mainly on the United States—the kingdom's closest great-power security partner.

38. Vassiliev, *The History of Saudi Arabia,* p. 340.

39. Ford Foundation Archive, Series III, Box 5, Folder 1. FA 643, 1967 (April 1).

40. Matthiesen, *The Other Saudis,* pp. 68–69. Former Saudi minister of petroleum Ali al-Naimi, for example, studied on Aramco scholarships at nearly every level of his considerable education. "Saudi Arabia—'Ali Ibrahim Al-Na'imi," The Free Library, October 24, 2011, https://www.thefreelibrary.com/Saudi+Arabia+-+%27Ali+Ibrahim +Al-Na%27imi.-a0271064013.

41. "All Places of Origin: Previous Years: 1950–2000," Institute of International Education (IIE), Open Doors, https://www.iie.org/opendoors.

42. Alyahya, "Constructing a Comprehensive Orientation Program for Saudi Arabian Students in the United States," p. 63.

43. Al-Shedokhi, "An Investigation of the Problems Experienced by Saudi Students While Enrolled in Institutions of Higher Education in the United States," pp. 68–88.

44. Alawi, "The Effectiveness of Scholarship Education Abroad: Obstacles and Means of Development," p. 46. Also see Alyahya, "Constructing a Comprehensive Orientation Program for Saudi Arabian Students in the United States," pp. 74–88.

45. De Onis, "Faisal's Killer Is Put to Death," p. 7.

46. Alyahya, "Constructing a Comprehensive Orientation Program for Saudi Arabian Students in the United States," pp. 71, 89–90.

47. Ibid., p. 91.

48. Ibid., pp. 97–98.

49. See El-Banyan, "Cross-Cultural Education and Attitude Change"; Yousef, "Drug Problem and Social Change in Saudi Arabia"; and Alfauzan, "The Impact of American Culture on the Attitudes of Saudi Arabian Students in the United States Toward Women's Participation in the Labor Force in Saudi Arabia."

50. Akhtarkhavari, "The Perceptions of Education and Satisfaction of Saudi Graduates."

51. Alsalaam, "American Educated Saudi Technocrats: Agents of Change?," p. 20.

52. "Historical Crude Oil Prices (Table)," InflationData.com, ttps://inflationdata .com/articles/inflation-adjusted-prices/historical-crude-oil-prices-table.

53. Kadri, "La formation à l'étranger des étudiants Algériens les limites d'une politique rentière."

54. July 2019 interview with an Algerian policy analyst, based in the United States, who had benefited from a government scholarship in the 1980s.

55. See statistics in Kadri, "La formation à l'étranger des étudiants Algériens les limites d'une politique rentière."

56. Various interviews with Algerian scholarship beneficiaries, 2019; "Algeria GDP Per Capita," World Bank, 2018, https://data.worldbank.org/indicator/NY.GDP .PCAP.CD?locations=DZ.

57. Kadri, "La formation à l'étranger des étudiants Algériens les limites d'une politique rentière." Dollar calculation based on 9,000–12,000 francs at 8 francs = 1 US dollar exchange rate in 1983.

58. Lajal, "La migration des compétences Arabes, les causes et les propositions, le cas de l'Algérie." Also Labdelaoui, "La migration des étudiants Algériens vers l'étranger."

59. Telephone interview with Yahia Zoubir, Algerian academic, August 2019.

60. Interview with an Algerian professional who benefited from a state scholarship to the United States in the early 1980s, Algiers, June 2019.

61. Bsheer, "A Counter-Revolutionary State," pp. 233–277, especially p. 249.

62. Alfaleh, "The Impact of the Processes of Modernization and Social Mobilization on the Social and Political Structures of the Arab Countries with Special Reference to Saudi Arabia," p. 49.

63. Al-Sabbagh, *Al-ibti'ath wa makhatiruh.*

64. Al-Shaqawi, "Makhatir al-ibti'ath wa dhawabitihi"; and Alsalaam, "American Educated Saudi Technocrats," p. 41.

65. Decree 87-205.

66. Khaled, "Politique de formation à l'étranger et l'émigration intellectuelle Algérienne," pp. 109, 137.

67. Labdelaoui, "La migration des étudiants Algériens vers l'étranger," pp. 123–124.

68. July 2019 interview with a senior Algerian engineer working at ADNOC in Abu Dhabi, formerly a Sonatrach executive, who had studied on a state scholarship to the UK (undergraduate through doctorate).

69. Benziane, "Economic Reforms in Algeria and Their Impact on Higher Education and Student Benefits," p. 106.

70. Aktouf, "La décision de Bouteflika d'interrompre les bourses l'étranger a été une catastrophe."

71. Travers, "University Initiatives Melt Borders with Brazil."

72. Aktouf, "La décision de Bouteflika d'interrompre les bourses l'étranger a été une catastrophe."

73. Khaled, "Politique de formation à l'étranger et l'émigration intellectuelle Algérienne," p. 137.

74. Khelfaoui, "Le champ universitaire Algérien entre pouvoirs politiques et champ économique."

75. Interview with a lecturer at the University of Algiers, May 10, 2019. In interviews (May–July 2019) with former Algerian diplomats and academics, past examples of corruption pertaining to the scholarship system have included the alleged delayed disbursement of scholarship funds at an Algerian diplomatic mission in Europe, which allowed the ambassador to accrue the interest on the funds.

76. Interview with a lecturer at the University of Oran, June 2019.

77. "Country Ratings," Gallup, https://news.gallup.com/poll/1624/perceptions -foreign-countries.aspx.

78. Blanchard, "Saudi Arabia," pp. 39–41.

79. "Saudi Students Pour Into U.S. Colleges," CBS News, September 9, 2006, https://www.cbsnews.com/news/saudi-students-pour-into-us-colleges; Embassy Riyadh, "A Public Diplomacy Strategy for Saudi Arabia," Wikileaks cable: 05RIYADH9116_a, December 12, 2005, https://search.wikileaks.org/plusd/cables /05RIYADH9116_a.html.

80. Author communication with a former Ministry of Higher Education official, April 23, 2019.

81. Author interview with a former Saudi Arabian Cultural Mission (USA) official, October 18, 2018.

82. See Figure 8.6 for details on estimates of student living expenses and tuition fees. Also see "Saudi Government's Education Allocation Focuses on New Universities and Schools," Oxford Business Group, 2015, https://oxfordbusinessgroup.com /analysis/spend-away-government-spending-education-focuses-new-universities -and-schools.

83. Ministry of Education, Saudi Arabia, Annual Reports, https://hesc.moe.gov .sa/pages/default.aspx.

84. See Sudairi, "Fighting the Smokeless War."

85. User post on Multaqa Ahl Al-Hadeeth, June 30, 2010, http://www.ahlalhdeeth .com/vb/showthread.php?t=215854.

86. Al-Badah, *Al-'ibti'ath: tarikuh wa atharuh.*

87. Hall, "Saudi Male Perceptions of Study in the United States"; Alraddadi, "The Changing Socio-Political Attitudes of Saudi Students Studying Overseas"; and Sa'di and al-Harbi, "Al-taghayur al-qimi lada al-'aideen min al-ibti'ath al-khariji fi daw ba'th al-mutaghayirat al-nafsiyya wal dimographiyya," pp. 40–46.

88. Ottaway, "Saudi Arabia's Race Against Time," pp. 4–5. Also, author communication with a former Ministry of Higher Education official.

89. It is unclear which universities would have been interested at this point; author communication with a former Ministry of Higher Education official.

90. For example, King Abdullah fired Sheikh Saad al-Shethry from the Council of Senior Scholars after Shethry criticized the newly established King Abdullah University for Science and Technology (KAUST), which was to do away with the gender segregation that prevailed in much of the kingdom and which would be administered outside of the clerically controlled Ministry of Education. See "Saudi University Critic Loses Job," BBC, October 5, 2009, http://news.bbc.co.uk/2/hi /middle_east/8290260.stm.

91. Al-Manee'a, "Al-taghrib fi al-inghilaq." Also "Al-'aman al-fikri asas al-istiqrar," *Makkah,* June 2, 2014, https://makkahnewspaper.com/article/37597; and author communication with a former Ministry of Higher Education official.

92. Author interview with a former Saudi Arabian Cultural Mission (USA) official, October 18, 2018.

93. Author interview with an Algerian academic, July 2019.

94. Author interview with an Algerian education policy expert, February and May 2019, Algiers.

95. For the eastern region of the country, 350 PNE grants were approved for the academic year 2019–2020. This implies that at the national level the numbers are likely to be around one thousand. See "Résultats de evaluations scientifiques des doctorants proposées pour une formation a l'étranger dans le cadre du programme national exceptionannel P.N.E, dAnnée universitaire 2019–2020," pp. 7, 28, https:// www.univ-setif.dz/Relations-Exterieures/Resultats-PNE-2019.pdf.

96. Ibid.

97. For Campus France, "La France Attire de Plus en Plus D'etudiants Inter-nationaux," https://www.campusfrance.org/system/files/medias/documents/2018 -10/20181011%20Communique%20Attractivité.pdf. Also see Institute of International Education (IIE), "Open Doors," https://www.iie.org/opendoors.

98. Interview with an administrator at the Ministry of Higher Education in Algiers, July 2019.

99. Ibid.

100. Interview with an administrator at an Algerian diplomatic mission in Europe, June 2019.

101. Various interviews with Algerian academics in Algiers, May–July 2019.

102. Bensouiah, "HE System Under Pressure as Student Numbers Mount."

103. Toumi, "Is Algeria Facing a Brain Drain?" Also "No More Brain Drain: Sonatrach's New Leadership Team," By the East, August 14, 2018, https://www .bytheeast.com/2018/08/14/no-more-brain-drain-sonatrachs-new-leadership-team.

104. The minister was replaced earlier in 2019 as part of the last cabinet reshuf-fle that Bouteflika would preside over before being forced to resign on April 2 following mass protests; see Ghanmy, "Row over Algerian Education Minister's Nobel Prize Comments."

105. The authors conducted interviews in July 2019 with Ministry of Higher Education staff in Algiers. Although the interviewees had promised that they would provide data and figures on the scholarship program, nothing was sent over despite multiple follow-ups. The same has happened to other established academic colleagues based in Algeria.

106. Annual reports, Saudi Ministry of Education (formerly separate Ministries of Education and Higher Education).

107. Annual reports, Saudi Ministry of Education.

108. Paul, "Saudi Tightens Rules for Scholarships to Study Abroad."

109. Author interview with a former Saudi Arabian Cultural Mission (USA) official.

110. Calvert Jones, "Saudi Arabia's Crown Prince Wants to Reengineer His Country. Is That Even Possible?"

111. Author communication with a former Ministry of Higher Education official.

112. Concerns of graduates seeking jobs noted by Dr. Leila Al-Dakheil, former vice dean of scientific research at Princess Nora University, quoted in Taylor and Albasri, "The Impact of Saudi Arabia King Abdullah's Scholarship Program in the U.S.," pp. 109–118. Also see "Foreign Scholarship Tied to Employment," *Arab News,* June 9, 2015, http://www.arabnews.com/saudi-arabia/news/758566.

113. Royal Embassy of Saudi Arabia, Moscow, Wikileaks document 88149, Saudi Cables, July 23, 2009, https://wikileaks.org/saudi-cables/pics/c69bd1b2-b1c7-4f90 -a3e5-3f4221e5c94f.jpg; also al-'Abbas, "Amerika."

114. Quran, "Saudi Students in U.S. Say Their Government Watches Their Every Move"; and Kavanaugh, "He Was Accused of Killing a Portland Teen."

115. Al-Harbi, "Al-Harbish"; and Marcoux and Bargout, "How Events Unfolded After Foreign Affairs Minister Sent Tweet Rebuking Saudi Arabia."

116. Hounsell, "Thousands of Saudi Students Remain in Canada, Despite Riyadh's Pledge to Axe Scholarships."

117. The survey consists of 419 snowball-sample responses collected in May through November 2019, incorporating a series of questions about study-abroad programs.

118. Although not all students in the sample were on scholarships themselves, controlling for scholarship funding makes no difference to the analysis. Interestingly, respondents interested in language acquisition abroad (and perhaps less "cosmopolitan" prior to studying abroad) were more likely to seek a policymaking role upon returning.

119. Werenfels, *Managing Instability in Algeria: Elites and Political Change Since 1995,* pp. 55–61.

120. Jones, "Seeing Like an Autocrat."

121. Interview with Bandar bin Sultan, broadcast on "Looking for Answers," *Frontline* documentary, PBS, October 2001, https://www.pbs.org/wgbh/pages/frontline /shows/terrorism/interviews/bandar.html.

9

Lessons from Latin America

Merilee S. Grindle

All too frequently, children attend school but learn little. This situation is particularly prevalent in education systems in low- and moderate-income countries around the world.[1] Over the past two decades, most such countries have experienced considerable—and often exceptional—growth in the number of children who are attending school. In many, the level of enrollment through primary school is as high as it is in rich countries, and growth in access to secondary schooling is apparent worldwide. Improvements in the quality of education, however, have lagged far behind rates of enrollment, and in some countries levels of learning have actually declined. Indeed, while most children in poor and middle-income countries are attending school today, the education they receive is not preparing them to lead productive lives in the future.

This dynamic is clear in Arab countries. As indicated in Table 9.1, data show significant achievements in access to education, particularly in Algeria, Iran, Bahrain, Oman, Qatar, Egypt, the United Arab Emirates, Morocco, Palestine, and Kuwait—each of these countries ranking above the world average, with Lebanon, Comoros, and Yemen only slightly below it. At the same time, many of these same countries demonstrate extremely poor performance in the quality of education delivered, judged by scores on international examinations.[2]

As an example, Morocco's primary school enrollment rate, at almost 97 percent, is considerably above the world average. Nevertheless, on international tests of mathematics, science, and reading competency, only 35–41 percent of its fourth-graders pass beyond low international benchmarks for quality; sixth-grade reading scores are more than 140

Table 9.1 Access to and Quality of Education in Arab Countries

	Adjusted Net Enrollment Rate, Primary, 2016–2017	School Life Expectancy/ Learning, Adjusted for Years of Schooling	Fourth-Grade Mathematics, Percentage Reaching Low International Benchmarks, TIMMS 2015	Fourth-Grade Science, Percentage Reaching Low International Benchmarks, TIMMS 2015	Fourth-Grade Reading, Percentage Reaching Low International Benchmarks, PIRLS 2016	Sixth-Grade Mean Reading Score, PIRLS/PISA 2016	Expenditure on Education as Percentage of Total Government Expenditure
Algeria	99.4	5.7/—	—	—	—	350	—
Iran	99.3	6.4/—	—	—	—	428	3.8
Bahrain	98.9	6.1/6.0	72	72	—	446	2.3
Oman	98.8	6.3/—	60	61	59	418	6.7
Qatar	98.7	6.2/6.0	65	64	66	442	2.9
Egypt	98.6	6.3/6.0	—	—	—	330	—
United Arab Emirates	97.2	5.5/7.0	68	67	68	450	7.0
Morocco	96.9	6.8/4.0	41	35	36	358	—
Palestine	93.9	—	—	—	—	—	—
Kuwait	93.2	4.8/4.0	33	25	—	393	2.7
Lebanon	88.5	5.6/—	—	—	—	—	—
Comoros	84.2	6.1/—	—	—	—	—	8.3
Yemen	83.3	5.6/—	—	—	—	—	—
Mauritania	76.6	5.9/—	—	—	—	—	—
Sudan	62.1	4.7/—	—	—	—	—	5.2
Djibouti	55.1	3.3/—	—	—	—	—	5.1
Saudi Arabia	—	7.0/6.0	43	48	63	430	5.4
Jordan	—	5.9/—	—	—	—	—	—
World	91.1		median 93	median 95	median 96	median 500	—

Sources: World Bank, World Development Report 2018; EdStats.
Note: Data not available for Iraq, Libya, Somalia, Syria, and Tunisia.

points below the world median.[3] Moreover, although students in Morocco attend school for an average of six years, the amount of learning they acquire averages only four years. These indicators send a clear message: the most significant education challenge in the future for Morocco—and many other Arab counties—is to improve the quality of learning that occurs in its classrooms.

Why have countries in the Arab world advanced well in terms of access to schooling, but performed poorly on the quality of education delivered? The answer to this question is not obvious. Differences between access and quality cannot be explained by the amount of money spent on education, for countries vary considerably on this dimension, while showing significant access/quality gaps (see Table 9.1). Moreover, the answer cannot be failure to understand what is happening, for statistical data are widely available, and numerous national and international discussions are insistent in pointing out the gap and its implications for reform.[4] Nor can the answer be found in the lack of knowledge about what to do to tackle the difference, for there is ample research about how to address this problem, and education specialists have proposed a variety of models for enhancing learning. The 2019 World Bank report on education in Arab countries is a good example of a detailed and widely accessible assessment of what needs to be done.[5] Just as important, in a range of countries, governments have attempted to address the gap through new policy initiatives.

Nor can the access/quality gap be explained by state capacity to achieve one but not the other. The tasks involved in improving access and increasing quality are different, but equally daunting. Increasing access to education generally means that governments must build more schools; establish rules, standards, and hierarchies; hire and train more teachers and administrators; provide more textbooks, desks, chalkboards, and other inputs; and coordinate long chains of communications, logistics, and administration. Typically, reforms to improve the quality of education involve decentralization, increasing efficiency, improving teacher performance, and introducing greater accountability, better management, and student-centered learning and monitoring practices. Whether the effort is focused on improved access or quality, educational systems are vulnerable to resource constraints, bureaucratic delay and red tape, poorly motivated providers, logistical and communication failures, and faulty implementation efforts. Thus, from a financial and management capacity point of view, both are hard goals to achieve.

Distinct political dynamics in efforts to increase schooling and improve learning offer another explanation for the access/quality gap that is so common around the world. This chapter explores the nature of political interactions when efforts are made to design, approve, and implement education policies, applying a framework based on two assertions: (1) efforts to put new policies in place impose costs and benefits on various actors; and (2) those actors will use their political resources in efforts to increase the benefits they receive and minimize the costs they incur when policy changes are being discussed and put in place. More specifically, economic and political rewards are high for multiple actors in access-enhancing reforms; political and economic costs are high for these same actors in quality-enhancing reforms. Thus, in many education reform scenarios, they will support access-enhancing reforms but oppose those that seek to improve quality. Those committed to improving education—reformers—face significant opposition as they attempt to introduce quality-enhancing policies, and, as a consequence, schooling can surge at the same time that learning lags. This approach suggests that many efforts to improve the quality of education fail to be introduced or sustained because they are stymied by political opposition.

These political dynamics were useful in explaining outcomes in several Latin American cases, where almost all children have gained access to primary schools, but where the quality of what they learn remains disappointingly low.[6] Does the explanation also hold for countries in the Arab world?

This chapter suggests that while some political interactions in education reform initiatives seem to be similar, the Arab region features conflict over the content of what is to be studied and how it is to be taught, a debate that is much more muted in Latin America. Moreover, there is a wider range of actors engaged in contesting reform in Arab countries than is the case in Latin America. In several cases from Latin America, although the obstacles to change were considerable, reformers were able, at times, to maneuver around or negotiate with powerful opposition and succeed in introducing changed policies; in Arab countries, concerns about the content of learning and a wider range of actors opposed to change and the extensive power they wield may create even higher barriers to change. Improving the quality of education in such countries is not impossible, but may require even more strategic action on the part of reformers than was the case with their counterparts in Latin America.

A Political Lens on the Costs and Benefits of Education Reform

Policy advances and shortcomings in education can be understood in part by observing the distinction between the "easy" politics surrounding reforms focused on increasing access to schooling, and the "difficult" politics involved in improving the educational performance of children, their teachers, and their schools. From this perspective, "easy" and "difficult" politics reflect the range of political opposition that reformers face when attempting to introduce major policy changes in education systems.

Of course, to call some education reforms politically "easy" is not meant to trivialize the difficulty of the task—as indicated earlier, increasing access to schooling involves massive efforts by public organizations and officials, often at multiple levels of government. It requires bigger budgets for ministries of education; introduces a significant management challenge of transmitting policy goals into specific measures to be taken by numerous actors; occupies a large number of administrators overseeing specific initiatives; implies a Herculean effort to train a corps of teachers; entails building many new schools and classrooms as well as providing desks, textbooks, chalkboards, and pencils; and calls for extensive public information campaigns. Long chains of decisions and action extend from central policymakers and administrators all the way to schools, classrooms, teachers, students, and parents, and have to be coordinated, making implementation difficult. Moreover, the goalposts move over time, increasingly emphasizing the need to incorporate rural children and then other groups often marginalized in their societies, such as girls, cultural and ethnic minorities, and those with special needs.

Efforts to undertake these changes have been significant, not least for the political, bureaucratic, and other elites who are engaged in promoting such changes in their societies, and the way has often been studded with planning and logistical obstacles, mistakes, corruption, waste, and delay. Despite such challenges, access to schooling has grown significantly in a wide range of countries. These positive changes can be explained by considering them through a political lens.

From a political point of view, education advances tied to increasing access to schooling tend to be "easy," due to the nature of the policies themselves—they provide a range of benefits that can be distributed among important groups and broadly to communities who desire and appreciate them. Access initiatives increase budgets for ministries to employ more officials to undertake more programs, and to hire and train extensive numbers of teachers and ministry and school administrators—this kind of public sector job expansion has been an important building block of a foundational middle class in many countries and has often provided ready support for centrist political parties. Increased numbers of teachers and administrators contribute to union membership bases and finances as well as strengthening their sway with political parties and their impact on elections. The reforms pay for the construction of teacher training institutes and schools and the production of teaching materials, also creating jobs along the way. Efforts to get more children into school are visible and popular with parents and communities; politicians and parties are eager to claim credit at ribbon-cuttings for new infrastructure and the celebration of education campaigns.

A paradigmatic idea for national advancement—investment in schooling—and material incentives for multiple actors are aligned in encouraging access reforms, regardless of differences in how political systems function. Despite many challenges then, benefits of school expansion, in terms of payoffs to important political interests such as state bureaucracies, unions, parties, private sector elites, and individual politicians, support initiatives to increase access to schooling.

Using this same political lens, it is clear that quality-enhancing reforms are much more difficult to introduce and implement. In such cases, ministries and bureaucrats are called upon to be more efficient and accountable with the resources they have, and they often resist such efforts. In particular, they fear that their jobs may be at stake in efficiency and decentralization initiatives. Educators and administrators resent—and fear—being tested, measured, judged, and rewarded or punished based on their performance. They look to their unions to protect them from new standards, encouraging unions to reject such reforms. National bureaucracies and unions also generally resist efforts to empower local communities or parent organizations in schools, believing that decentralization initiatives diminish their own professional authority and power. Teacher training institutes, often allied with teachers' unions, challenge initiatives to alter their curricula and pedagogical theories. Improved learning may involve investment in new teaching materials but does not generally result in large benefits to construction firms and workers. Moreover, ribbon-cutting is not usually a feature of implementing efficiency or accountability measures—political parties and politicians find few reasons to champion quality reforms, which pit them against unions and a large electorate of bureaucrats and teachers.

At the same time, quality-enhancing reforms do not usually have rapid or highly visible payoffs, such as the construction of a new community school. Parents and voters are asked to trust that in a number of years, their children will be better prepared for the future; they may be skeptical about this eventuality, just as they are often skeptical about other promises made by politicians and political parties. Middle-class and business interests—important in the development of public education in many now-rich countries—are not usually major actors in promoting such reforms, either because they have already defected to private schooling or because they do not envision better public education as important to their economic futures. In some countries, even low-income families are deserting public education for fee-based schooling or that provided by the not-for-profit sector. Indeed, individual teachers may benefit from poor educational practices when they seek additional income through private tutoring after hours.

From a political perspective, commitment to quality-enhancing education reforms is vulnerable to resistance, often from the same organized groups—parties, politicians, unions, bureaucrats, local officials—that benefit from access-enhancing reforms. Thus, the political odds are stacked against the capacity to introduce and sustain this type of policy reforms, despite the frequency of high-level political rhetoric supporting them. Some groups are able to stymie efforts to design and introduce changes that promote learning; moreover, if reformers are successful in these phases of the policy process, there are many opportunities for opponents to ensure that new policies are not implemented effectively. Governors and mayors can resist "getting on board"; unions can go on strike; bureaucrats can delay action by claiming that capacity does not exist for effective implementation; and teachers and principals can remain passive in the face of new directives. In quality reforms, a paradigmatic idea for national advancement—improved education—is at odds with the incentives they offer to important political groups.

Often, of course, the purpose of education reform has been to improve both access and quality at the same time. Nevertheless, access-enhancing measures tend to move ahead, while quality-enhancing ones fail to be effectively undertaken or pursued, for the reasons outlined earlier. Equally troubling, over time, as access has increased, the groups who benefit from expanded schooling tend to become more organized, more vocal, and more politically important—that is, unions with larger memberships; bureaucracies with more administrators, units, and regulations; construction firms with politically important contacts and contracts; and groups with more effective organizations. Thus, over time, it can become increasingly difficult to withstand political opposition to quality-enhancing initiatives. To add to these poor odds, when quality does not improve in local schools, parents concerned about education often find other means to help their children than by organizing to demand systemic change—they pay for tutoring or enroll their children in nonpublic education programs. This further weakens the political incentives to improve learning.

The distinct politics of access and quality-enhancing reforms help explain relative success and failure in policy outcomes. Table 9.2 summarizes how such reforms affect different actors and characteristic political responses to them.

If political analysis is a useful way to understand why it is more difficult to introduce and sustain quality-enhancing reforms than it is for access-enhancing initiatives, then elaborating scenarios based on potential sources of support and opposition can provide insights to education reformers as they consider a variety of strategies for introducing, negotiating, communicating about, and implementing changes in national policies. Of course, any political analysis of reform scenarios is specific to time and place and focuses on a policy process that unfolds over time. For reformers concerned about finding room to maneuver to introduce change in contentious environments, analysis needs to be undertaken in real time and in full appreciation of historical and institutional contexts unique to each country. Reform is a process, and studies of it are most useful when they trace a process of reform that highlights the strategic action of proponents and opponents over time in particular contexts and then draws more general lessons from this process that can inform research, analysis, and action.

Table 9.2   The Politics of Educational Reforms: Access to vs. Quality of Education

	Access Reforms	Quality-Enhancing Reforms
Typical actions to carry out	• Build infrastructure • Expand bureaucracies • Increase budgets • Hire administrators • Hire service providers • Buy equipment	• Improve management • Increase efficiency • Alter rules/behavior of personnel • Improve accountability • Decentralize • Strengthen local control
Typical political implications	Creation of benefits: • Jobs • Construction and provisioning of contracts • Increased budgets • Increased power for ministries and managers	Imposition of costs: • Loss of jobs • Loss of decisionmaking power for some • New demands, expectations, responsibilities for others
Typical political responses	• Unions of providers welcome reforms and collaborate with them • Politicians welcome tangible benefits to distribute to constituencies • Communities are pleased to receive benefits • Voters support changes	• Unions of providers resist reforms • Administrators seek to ignore or sabotage change • Many politicians wish to avoid promoting reforms • Many voters unaware of changes (at least in short term)

Source: Grindle, *Despite the Odds*, p. 6.

A Political Lens on Latin American Reformism

In Bolivia, Ecuador, Mexico, Nicaragua, and the state of Minas Gerais in Brazil, national leaders and policymakers introduced quality-enhancing reforms in the 1990s.[7] These five cases were studied because they were unique in the region for being able to overcome resistance to new education policies. Thus, they provided an opportunity to explore the political dynamics of change initiatives that were put in place "despite the odds" favoring failure. "Success" was indicated by the ability of reformers to design, gain approval for, and implement new policies; the study did not seek to assess the extent to which the reforms had "worked" in improving quality. By tracing the process of reform and opposition to it, each case could be understood in terms of the political context in which the reform was attempted, while observing and assessing the strategic actions chosen by reform proponents and their opponents.[8] Thus, while these cases are two decades old, they remain useful in reflecting on the dynamics of how political actors challenged efforts to introduce reform initiatives in education and how reformers—in these cases, political, bureaucratic, and professional elites—acted strategically to overcome or maneuver around opposition to change.

Although most Latin American countries had emerged from a period of harsh authoritarian rule in the 1970s and 1980s, even in the more democratic settings of the 1990s policymaking remained a highly centralized process. Typically, education policy was formulated within national ministries of education, often with the engagement of academic specialists, union representatives and their party allies, and donor advisers.[9] Because most countries in the region had reached moderate economic development levels, the influence of international development agencies was felt more in the expertise they brought to the table than in the funding they provided. Parliaments were not active participants in policy planning and generally passively approved changes; when parliamentary support was not possible, policymakers used administrative rather than legislative means to advance new policies. Often, regional and local officials, teachers, and communities first learned of new policies when they were announced in national capitals. Although the regimes were largely structured as democracies with regular elections, checks and balances among institutions of government, and freedom of the press, only in Brazil was civil society widely organized for input into political and policy decisionmaking. Universities and think tanks were present in all countries, but few had much experience in discussing, debating, and planning policy with government officials.

The starting point for new reform initiatives in Bolivia, Ecuador, Mexico, Nicaragua, and Minas Gerais was a record of significant achievement in access to schooling. By the 1990s, very few children remained outside national primary education systems, and access to secondary schooling was growing impressively. Mexico's net primary enrollment rate was 100 percent, and in much poorer Bolivia and Nicaragua, the net rates were 91 and 72 percent, respectively, in 1990. In the five cases, education bureaucracies, teachers' unions, political parties, teacher training institutes, and a number of private sector enterprises had benefited from access initiatives in prior decades and had encouraged their development.

At the same time, data from national and international sources were available to indicate how poorly students were being educated. In each case, there were national and international discussions about the needs of the education sector; these discussions were well-provided with data and research about the importance of enhancing quality and about steps that could be taken toward it. In each of these cases, presidents or ministry leadership adopted the need for enhanced quality in education as a high personal priority for their tenure in office, often advancing their aims in the absence of strong party support.

Resources for education were of course limited, but reformers had come to believe that the constraints on "fixing" education had less to do with financial resources and more to do with structures and incentives within the sector. They planned changes that would increase efficiency, improve accountability, and decentralize control over schools and education decisionmaking. New curricula were included in the reforms, but only in Mexico did the issue of history textbooks—in an initiative to move away from highly critical views of capitalism and imperialism to an emphasis on globalization and integration—become contentious. The language of instruction was contested at modest levels in Bolivia, Mexico, and Ecuador, countries with significant indigenous populations. This debate was not about either/or language instruction, but rather focused on the appropriate age for introducing Spanish to indigenous children who did not speak Spanish at home.

Presidents and ministers worked to place quality education reform on the political agenda of their countries. Often, they were motivated by personal commitment to education, a belief that further development of the country in a context of globalization required reform, or a belief that educational advances would be helpful in dealing with social and economic cleavages. The political parties they represented were not programmatic ones and were not much engaged in shaping national leadership priorities. The reform initiatives were planned and coordinated by small teams of experts committed to change, usually appointed by political leaders to focus specifically on the design and implementation of change initiatives; their appointments were based on the targeted use of patronage rather than recruitment through a civil service system. Only Brazil had a structured and professional civil service at the time, and even its system was highly penetrated by patronage.

These teams usually reported to officials at relatively high levels in the education ministry; in Bolivia, where this institution was entrenched in its opposition to change, planning-ministry professionals took the lead. The teams were typically formed of specialists from universities and think tanks, advisers from the presidential offices, and donor-agency officials. Teams that proved most effective in planning and introducing new policies were characterized by a shared vision of what they wanted to accomplish, influential professional and friendship networks within government and international agencies, and stable composition over time. Universally, they limited participation in the discussion of change initiatives—usually at the expense of teachers' unions—and they relied on allies in leadership positions in the ministry or the president's office to be the public face of reform.

As they sought approval for new policies, the teams carefully considered how to deal with opposition and regularly consulted with their high-level allies in government. In particular, they considered whether the reforms should be promoted through legislative or administrative processes and they considered how the teachers' unions would be involved in policy discussions. To the extent that they entered into negotiation, they opted to discuss only the timing of new initiatives, whether the changes would initially be voluntary or mandatory, and the extent of incentives for individual teacher "buy-in" to the reforms. Whether to pursue the reforms or not was not on the table. In Bolivia, Ecuador, and Nicaragua, they refused to negotiate, seeking instead to maneuver around organized opposition.

Political leadership was critical to the work of the teams. In three cases, the lead reformer was a minister with a good relationship with the president. In Mexico and Bolivia, the president was the political voice of the reform, using his position to communicate about the changes envisioned and to build a coalition of allies in government and elsewhere. Importantly, these politically savvy individuals managed the timing of the introduction of reform—selecting moments to unveil them while public opinion was unfavorable to the teachers' unions (during strikes) or when their own popularity was high (in the "honeymoon" period after elections). They all used their powers of appointment to "seed" important positions in government with their policy and political supporters. In their communication strategies, they sought to frame the issues in positive terms, working to undermine the credibility of opposition from teachers' unions. In Minas Gerais, Bolivia, and Ecuador, presidents went far beyond token endorsement of the importance of education to national development; they repeatedly referred to the importance of quality in education for national development and kept high-level supporters "on message" during national political campaigns. Education reform was visibly high on their policy priority lists.[10]

In each case, the primary opposition to education policy reform came from strong teachers' unions. Because policymaking was highly centralized, teachers' unions were also centralized, enabling them to maximize their input into national decision- and demand-making. Unions were generally large and powerful; at the time, Mexico, for example, had only one union representing teachers and administrators, and this organization had over a million members. In many cases, a history of government-union negotiations had resulted in ministries or parts of ministries being colonized by unions, union-controlled hiring decisions for teachers and administrators, powerful linkages between union leaders and political-party leaders, and teacher training institutes serving as appendages of union organizations.[11] Union leaders were important national figures and none of the unions in the case studies was democratically controlled by its members. Clientelism and patronage networks often bound unions to government and political parties. Moreover, the unions represented a very high proportion of all teachers in each country, and in some cases had monopoly rights to represent them in salary and benefit negotiations. Thus, introducing changes that would impose significant costs on unions, party politicians, and bureaucrats was likely to be conflictual.

When the reforms were being discussed and introduced, union organizations in all five cases engaged in prolonged strikes. They snarled traffic in capital cities, they pitched tents in front of education ministries, they invaded ministry offices. They marched in capital cities and encouraged teachers to remain out of the classroom until their demands were met—they wanted better salaries and increased benefits before they would discuss other changes. They excoriated their governments for trying to destroy their legitimate rights, they protested against being excluded from deliberations, they mobilized votes against those who championed change, and they lobbied forcefully with political-party leadership. While their bureaucratic allies were not usually visible in the push-and-pull of support and opposition, they worked behind the scenes to slow or derail policy and implementation planning. Leadership at teacher training institutions provided intellectual challenges to the claims of the reformers. The opposition faced by the reform teams and their political leadership was fierce.

There was support for the changes among reformist elements at high levels in government, among academic experts, and among other educated elites. But in Latin America, as in other parts of the world, middle-class parents were not actively engaged because they had long ago abandoned public schooling by placing their children in private schools. Business leaders and their associations limited their activities to supporting alternative schools, especially at the tertiary level, or supporting voluntary sector alternatives for poor children. The Catholic Church and the burgeoning evangelical churches were not prominent actors in the reforms—in the nineteenth and early twentieth centuries, liberal reforms had entrenched secular political institutions and values and, in some cases, anticlerical politics. In more contemporary times, religious organizations were active in providing alternative education systems and, for the Catholic Church, higher-education options for citizens. At times, its leadership was brought to the table to mediate conflicts, but the Church was not otherwise an active or public participant in discussions of change. Parents—most of them poor—were not organized or vocal in the reform process.

The process of reform was best characterized as a moving scenario of strategies and counter-strategies, with actors assessing next moves as efforts to introduce change proceeded. Each reform initiative played out in a unique political environment, but at a more general level many pro-reform strategies paid off—seizing the initiative, using appointments to bring reformers to power, framing the issue in ways that disadvantaged the opposition, keeping the reform team united and on-message, and making decisions about when and what to negotiate. Nevertheless, a consequence of the top-down management of reform and the exclusion of lower-level officials, individual teachers, and parents was that while battles were won at national levels, states, local government, and schools ultimately became sites of contestation as the reforms were implemented. This did not fully derail the initiatives, but helps explain variation as governors, mayors, school principals, and teachers determined the fate of reform at more discreet levels of implementation.

In general, while reformers were smart strategic actors in gaining approval and implementing change, they were less effective in mobilizing sufficient regional, local, and parental support to ensure the sustainability of the changes they had successfully introduced. Reformist education initiatives in Bolivia, Ecuador, Mexico, Nicaragua, and Minas Gerais thus provide good lessons about what reformers can do to promote the changes they believe will enhance national development, but also some lessons about what they might do better next time around.

A more recent survey of the fate of quality-enhancing reforms in education, written by Barbara Bruns and Ben Ross Schneider, confirms the importance of political strategies if such changes are to be planned, approved, introduced, implemented, and sustained.[12] It points to the enduring power of teachers' unions and their centrality to any efforts to improve schooling. It also confirms the general reformist indifference of business and middle-class parents, as well as the relative powerlessness of individual teachers and poor parents in efforts to improve quality. In the two decades that followed the process-tracing research on reform initiatives in Bolivia, Ecuador, Mexico, Nicaragua, and Minas Gerais, many traditional political parties fractured and their replacements are often just emerging from popular movements, remaining weakly organized and without policy platforms. The survey also pointed to increased participation of the voluntary sector as part of reformist coalitions, but religious organizations remained marginal to the initiatives for change. In general, however, political conditions for introducing quality reforms have not eased or become less conflictual.

Nevertheless, in exploring a series of reforms from the 2000s in Mexico, Peru, Chile, Ecuador, Colombia, and the state of Rio de Janeiro in Brazil, the Bruns and Schneider survey indicates continued reliance on decisions to legislate change or rely on administrative actions to pursue it, the top-level management of communications, and decisions about how or when to negotiate or to confront unions. The issue of sustaining pro-reform coalitions to sustain reform initiatives was also of great importance. The review concludes with lessons for would-be reformers that expand on the earlier five-case study. It suggests that reformers need to review other efforts at reform to see what can be learned from them in terms of strategic actions and mistakes. It advocates careful mapping of potential sources of support and opposition to change, ensuring high-level backing for it, assessing the utility of compensatory policies or side-payments, undertaking efforts to weaken or divide opposition, paying particular attention to barriers to implementation, engaging public opinion, and making efforts to maneuver around teachers' unions to communicate with teachers.

The path toward education reform in Latin American countries continues to be fraught with obstacles, difficult to control, and peppered with opportunities for failure. An important lesson of the history of reformism from the 1990s through more recent experiences in the 2000s is that those who undertake to introduce and implement reform will no doubt experience multiple failures and need to remain committed to change, acting in politically smart ways over the long term. The fight for better educational quality in Latin American countries is far from won and the access/quality gap continues to haunt their futures.

A Political Lens on Arab Reformism

Can the analytic approach adopted in this chapter prove helpful in explaining the access/quality gap in Arab countries, as it did in Latin America? A definitive answer to this question awaits future research; data available on policy reform in these countries fall short of the detailed, country-level, process-tracing, and comparative case studies that were undertaken in Latin America and that are necessary for such analyses. Although there are many studies of the need for education reform in the region, those that trace the politics of designing, approving, and implementing policy changes are lacking. All too often, government rhetoric and plans for education reform are mistaken for reality and little is actually known about the politics or destinies of these initiatives; at times, studies point to the failure of reform initiatives to be introduced or implemented effectively.[13]

Moreover, political regimes and levels of stability vary considerably within the region, and wars and regime changes play havoc with the predictability of policy decisionmaking and implementation processes. While the Latin American cases of reform unfolded in new—and relatively stable—democracies, instability and authoritarian political systems are the norm in Arab countries; how policymaking and implementation occur in such settings is often opaque. Degrees and types of authoritarian governance may also be relevant; what, for example, explains the relatively better-quality measures of small Gulf states—Bahrain, Oman, Qatar, and the United Arab Emirates (UAE)—all, like Saudi Arabia, governed by closed monarchical regimes and oil rich, but more open to concerns about globalization?

Although process-tracing studies of policy initiatives are not available, some reform-relevant conditions can be inferred from the extensive literature on education in Arab countries. In particular, it is clear that education reform is widely discussed. Moreover, data indicate generally good performance in terms of access to primary schooling, often remarkable progress in encouraging female education, and increasing availability of secondary education.[14] Histories of education in the region suggest that nation-building and national identity were strong incentives for access-enhancing reform championed by postcolonial governments.[15] In the past two decades, policymakers, practitioners, and informed publics in the region have become increasingly aware of the importance of improving the quality of their education systems, giving students better and more relevant learning to equip them for the future.[16] Whether the goal is economic development, labor market modernization, gender equity, or poverty reduction, improved education is widely advocated as a critically important means for Arab countries to achieve it. And the failures of the education sector are well known; data are widely available for describing and analyzing gaps between schooling and learning. Many studies call attention, often urgently, to the need for policy change.

Country studies of conditions in the education sector and specific reform policies and programs are available for several countries and also offer insights into policy reform.[17] Egypt, Morocco, Jordan, Kuwait, Yemen, Tunisia, the United Arab Emirates, and Qatar are more often studied than other countries, indicating efforts to address the quality gap with new programs and policies, often with the assistance of donor agencies.[18] Thus, for example, Egypt has been the site of numerous initiatives to reorganize and improve the education sector since the 1940s.[19] The UAE has promoted education changes to make the country more "globalization-ready."[20] Qatar was the site of an ongoing effort to improve teacher accountability and quality.[21] Curriculum reform was attempted in Jordan, and such initiatives have a long history in Kuwait.[22]

Interestingly, in Egypt and the UAE, governments have recently renewed an emphasis on access-related reforms through efforts to expand secondary education and introduce preschool and kindergarten programs, necessitating the hiring of more teachers and administrators.[23] Expanding private or charter-type schools has also been on the reform agenda in Egypt and Morocco. Governments have not been passive in the face of intense discussion and data on the failures and promises of education. National plans for improvement are widespread— from "Education for the Knowledge Economy" in Jordan, to "Vision 2030" in Morocco, to "Vision 2021" in the UAE, to the "Education Reform Program" in Egypt, and more.

A review of literature about education policy in the Arab world indicates some similarities to discussions in Latin America.[24] For example, some of the themes that Arab reformers are concerned about are remarkably similar to those raised by their counterparts in Latin America. Thus, the imperative for decentralization, new models about how learning occurs, the importance of greater equity in access, teacher training linked to student-centered pedagogy, data and their implications for national development, and the challenges of technological innovation and globalization are all part of policy discussions in the region, just as they were in Latin America.[25] These issues feature prominently in the international dialogue about education and are replicated in domestic policy discussions.

In addition, just as in the Latin American cases, policy decision-making in Arab countries is highly centralized in national capitals and within the executive branch of government.[26] In the authoritarian context of many countries, policy is even more likely to be top-down and executive-centered, and the permeability of the decision process—the extent to which those not part of the executive are able to participate in such discussions—is even more limited. In another comparison, while formalized civil service systems are more widespread in Arab countries than they are in Latin America, patronage, clientelism, and politically sensitive appointments are intertwined with them. There is some indication that, despite the political nature of many public sector appointments, technocratic inputs into policymaking are common, just as they have been in Latin America.[27]

Teachers in Arab countries as well as in Latin America form a significant part of public sector employment, as do officials in large education ministries. As an example, in Egypt, some 8 million individuals work for government; 2 million of them are teachers, and education involves many additional employees in the education, culture, technology, higher-education, health and population, and local-development ministries. Teachers in Lebanon are also a very significant part of the public sector. Taken together, teachers and other civil servants are an important voice for public sector jobs, salaries, benefits, and the continuance of centralized ministry dominance over local government.[28] Where elections matter, public services are likely to be an important source of votes for parties and politicians that protect their often-privileged status—regular, if not generous, salaries, tenure in their positions, and access to a range of benefits.

Teachers' unions are ubiquitous in the two regions.[29] Among twenty-two Arab countries, at least seventeen have one or more unions; six have two or more; and Algeria has as many as nine. Among them, at least eight countries experienced teacher strikes or confrontations with government during an eighteen-month period in 2018 and 2019.[30] The organizations are large—Kuwait's teachers' union is the largest civil society organization in the country. The demands these unions make on Arab governments are similar to those heard in other regions of the world—better pay and benefits and protection of tenure. Additional research is needed about these organizations, particularly at the country and comparative levels, to understand their strengths relative to other political actors and their links to government. It is important to know, for example, that in Egypt, Bahrain, Kuwait, and Djibouti, unions have been met with repressive action by government; in some countries, on the other hand, unions have histories of close relationships with the state. In relation to the extensive power of teachers' unions in Latin America, do those in Arab countries pack the same political clout? This question remains unanswered.

In addition to these significant similarities between education policy and politics in Arab and Latin American countries, however, there are also some dramatic differences. In particular, a range of issues and the participation of additional actors in education initiatives are notable in Arab countries. In terms of issues central to concern about education, some are the same, as suggested earlier, but others are especially relevant to Arab countries. Thus, those concerned about education in the region worry about the role and impact of Islamist education; they are apprehensive about the language of instruction; they are uneasy about radical movements; and they debate how to educate refugees, what is being taught in madrassas, and the role of religion, authority, and loyalty to the state much more than is the case in Latin America.[31] Moreover, in discussions of education and its reform, issues of colonialism and state employment figure more in Arab countries than in Latin America.[32]

In addition, the role of international donors is more pronounced, as is concern about identity in discussions of curriculum reform; in Jordan, Qatar, and Kuwait, for example, the introduction of new curricula have sparked protests about the importation of foreign ideas.[33] Policymakers are also very aware of the way private tutoring of public-school students can undermine support for change, and the risks of decentralization for national security.[34] In Egypt in particular, tensions run high between those who argue for greater decentralization and those who are concerned about maintaining centralized control in a context in which national unity and stability have been fractured.[35] Policy and political elites in Jordan have resisted decentralization for similar reasons.[36] And in Yemen, the politically destabilizing impact of Islamist schools and madrassas has been a focus of considerable unease among policy and political elites.[37] More generally, policymaking discussions have indicated greater sensitivity to the threat of politically active young people than was the case in Latin America. The influx of Syrian refugees in Lebanon and Jordan has also become a source of concern about national identity and stability.[38] In addition, because the role of international donors was more prominent in Arab countries, they often had greater capacity to influence plans for reform initiatives, and were more often the target of nationalist backlash.[39]

Such issues were much less evident in education discussions in Latin America. In general, issues of national identity are more settled in that region, as are issues related to separatist movements and the legitimacy of the state. The role of religion and a secular or confessional state in education had been largely resolved in historical conflicts in the nineteenth and early twentieth centuries, and Catholic and evangelical school systems were not viewed as destabilizing to regimes in the region. Generally, choices about the language of instruction were discussed in countries with large indigenous populations but were not a central point of debates in national policy-reform initiatives. These are important distinctions in terms of understanding the politics of education reform in Arab countries, and suggest that in many ways, the substance of education reform—what should be taught, how it should be taught, and by whom—is more salient in these countries than was the case in the Latin American examples.

Equally important, a comparison of the actors involved in policy discussions and debates indicates the presence of participants in Arab countries who are less prominent or absent in the Latin American cases. In particular, because the military plays a large role in several Arab countries—Egypt is a prime example—military elites weigh in more often and have specific concerns about national security, loyalty to the regime in power, and the extent to which obedience and authority are being emphasized in curriculum changes. Military elites also favor centralized administrative control over schools and tend to be very skeptical about community participation in schools, fearing the intrusion of militant groups active in local areas.[40] Wars, regime changes, and threats to stability have heightened their concern about what is being taught in schools, how it is being taught, and how effectively the substance of education is being controlled.[41]

In addition, the central presence of clerical elites in education discussions in several countries is notable.[42] These actors are concerned with issues related to Islamic instruction in public schools, the structure of the curriculum, and the emphasis on authority and obedience to sacred texts. Dual education systems—one secular and one confessional—in Morocco and Egypt encourage competition for resources and students. And, because public services are more structured and controlled by civil service commissions and agencies, officials representing the public service are often actively engaged in education policy discussions, at least to the extent that public sector jobs and benefits are relevant. In some cases, militant groups and their alternative school systems also engage in contesting education reforms.[43] In several Arab countries, donor agencies are key actors because the resources they control are important; in Latin America, their resources tend to be less important, and they are more likely to have influence through the ideas they bring to the table.[44] Thus, a wider range of actors seem to be engaged in Arab countries compared to what is known about education reformism in Latin America.

Of course, each country is subject to unique historical, institutional, political, social, and economic conditions. Only detailed case studies at the country level can reveal what issues in education reform are most pressing and which actors are most likely to be "at the table" when important decisions about the future of education policy are being negotiated and determined in specific contexts. Such studies can also illuminate the relative power of various actors and how reform teams are poised to make strategic decisions about moving ahead with change initiatives. Politics is essential to understanding the fate of reform, but sources of conflict can differ from one context to another. Moreover, if the obstacles to reform are significantly different and more challenging in Arab countries compared to those in Latin America, reformers from the region will need to work even more strategically, build coalitions even more self-consciously, and perhaps weather even more defeats if quality-enhancing reforms are eventually to be introduced, implemented, and sustained.

Conclusion: Issues and Actors in the Future of Education Reform in the Arab World

While a better understanding of the political dynamics of Arab reformism awaits further research, this chapter suggests two possible areas in which quality-enhancing initiatives might differ from those in other regions. First, debates about the content of proposed reforms—what is to be taught, how it is to be taught, and who is in charge of teaching it—may have special resonance in the region. In addition, a wider set of powerful actors concerned about the introduction of change may be engaged in contention about reform. Legitimacy, authority, religious doctrine, national security, refugees, control over decisionmaking and administration, and threats from radical groups would seem to be prominent in reform discussions in the region, and military organizations, religious elites, militant groups, and alternative or parallel school systems add to the number of actors likely to be engaged in education policy politics.

Table 9.3 indicates how the issues and actors that appear to be important in education reformism in Arab countries might influence the politics of introducing and implementing quality-enhancing policies. It suggests several issues that appear to be of high salience in discussions of reform in the region, the contentious questions they raise, and the range of actors likely to be engaged in discussion, debate, and conflict over the nature of education reform in the region. Thus, while the framework summarized in Table 9.2 captures some of the dynamics of the distinction between access and quality reforms relevant to Arab countries, it may not reveal dynamics that are unique to the region. Table 9.3 suggests hypotheses about how the politics of reform might play out in the region.

Access to education is surprisingly high in many Arab countries. The more pressing issue of twenty-first-century education, then, is its quality and ability to ensure that children in the region are gaining the skills and competencies they will need in a complex and demanding future. But quality-enhancing reforms are challenging to plan, introduce, and implement because they are politically contentious. To be successful "despite the odds" against policy change, reformers in the region need to be able to address the contentious nature of reform initiatives and be skilled at devising strategies that enhance their influence and effectiveness while diminishing the influence of their opponents over the destinies of reform policies.

Table 9.3   Additional Political Issues and Actors in Quality-Enhancing Reform Initiatives in Arab Countries: Some Hypotheses

Relevant questions when the substance of education is at issue	• How effectively is state legitimacy conveyed? • How are authority and obedience taught/learned? • What frameworks for learning are most valuable? • What religious instruction is carried out? • What is the dominant language of instruction? • What is the role of alternative education providers?
Political implications of reforms that involve discussions about the substance of education	• Debate about the purpose of education • More actors mobilized to participate • National security and identity issues loom large in debates • Emphasis on centralization of control and homogeneity of instruction • Litmus tests for curricula, textbooks, training, hiring • Possible marginalizing/repression/co-optation of teachers' unions • Mobilization based on religious identity or claims
Potential political responses to reforms that raise issues related to the substance of education	• Military elites enter reform debates • Religious elites enter reform debates • Conservative political elites seek alliances with military and religious elites • Militant movements influence reform alternatives • Coalitions of reform prove particularly difficult to create/maintain • Alternative schools increase in popularity • International donors attacked for ideological bias, imperialism • Ideological divides deepen and mobilize public groups

Political mapping and the ongoing creation of strategic actions are thus useful tools that can be helpful to reform teams and their allies. Their utility, however, requires careful rethinking of some widespread assumptions about education and its reform. In particular, many current discussions of reform initiatives in countries around the world refer to "stakeholders" in education policy. Typically, stakeholders are children, parents, local communities, teachers, school principals, and local and regional officials; they are those who are expected to be directly affected by changed policies. In contrast, this chapter has consistently presented those engaged in discussions and debates about education as "actors," a term used intentionally to signal that in the political analysis of reform initiatives, those who need to be considered most carefully are those who have the greatest capacity to influence the content, timing, implementation, and sustainability of new policies.

Not all stakeholders have this capacity; children, for example, are usually considered unsuited for political action, parents are frequently unorganized for it, and individual teachers and administrators are often spoken for by their organizations. A distinction between stakeholders and actors emphasizes the reality that although a large number of children, parents, and teachers are expected to be affected by change, teachers' unions and government officials almost always have much more insistent voices in reform scenarios. Indeed, in large numbers of countries, political debate and action exclude many of those most likely to be directly affected by change.

Obviously, some actors—such as teachers' unions—are also stakeholders. And there is always the possibility that stakeholders such as parents can become organized or take to the streets to assert their voices as actors in education debates. Excluded groups and individuals might become actors through mobilization in various forms, suggesting that reformers could add to their coalitions for reform through such action. Moreover, some actors may be engaged in political contention over reform even though they are not so obviously affected by the policy—meaning, not obvious stakeholders—military elites, political parties, and religious organizations, for example. To reduce all of those affected by or interested in policy change to the common status of "stakeholder," as many current discussions do, ignores how power is distributed among them; some are powerful and able to make their voices heard in discussions, debates, and decisionmaking while others are marginalized, muted, or repressed.

Some current discussions of education policy also trivialize the work involved in making change happen by referencing the "political will" of a government to introduce reform. Although reformers tend to be optimists about the potential for change—even in the face of repeated failures—the likelihood of success in promoting reform is generally low. When failure occurs, governments are then excoriated for lacking political will to make change happen. And, in the unlikely event that reformers are able to introduce and implement new policies in contentious environments, governments are commended for having the political will to succeed.

Research into policy-change initiatives in any country, however, indicates that reformers are engaged in difficult and ongoing interactions with a variety of proponents and opponents of change. They do battle within political contexts that have enduring structures and behaviors but that are also subject to more immediate disruption and change. Factors such as the day's headlines and political or economic happenstance can open up or close off opportunities for strategic action, even in stable institutional and political contexts. Thus, if change occurs and is sustained in any given political context, it is the result of ongoing work by groups of committed reformers and their initiatives to build coalitions of support, to deal effectively with opposition, to manage their resources well, and to communicate their goals effectively—along with some luck brought into the bargain. Those who do not wish to see change happen are usually involved in the same kind of activities, but with very different goals in mind.

Power matters, as does its distribution among actors and would-be actors; reformers find themselves almost inevitably in the midst of contention. What they do and how they do it are subject to pressures, constraints, and moments of opportunity; when they act, they do so in very uncertain environments. The politics they practice and confront is serious and difficult. When reformers are successful, their commitment, ingenuity, and persistence should be studied and analyzed for what they can tell us about political interactions and the search for room for maneuver to introduce change. Political will cannot explain this ongoing and difficult process. Rather, it reduces their hard work to an unresearchable mystery.

Issues, actors, and strategic action are the stuff of the politics of education reform in Arab countries, just as they are in other environments. These factors are a worthy focus for research and discussion. As indicated in this chapter, efforts to undertake process-focused studies of reform initiatives would do much to illuminate the issues and actors engaged in efforts to introduce change, and the strategies that reformers and their opponents adopt. In turn, such research can do much to alert proponents of improved educational quality in the region to the nature of the challenges they face and opportunities to find room for maneuver in advancing their worthy goals.

Notes

1. This phenomenon is also prevalent in low-income urban neighborhoods and some rural areas in rich countries, although it is not considered in this chapter.

2. Data from 2015, 2016, and 2017 in the World Bank Education Statistics (EdStats) database, http://datatopics.worldbank.org/education.

3. Secondary school indicators are also low for learning. Primary schooling is used in the table to capture the largest number of students attending school. For secondary school performance measures, see the World Bank Education Statistics (EdStats) database, http://datatopics.worldbank.org/education.

4. In particular, international agencies such as the World Bank, UNESCO, UNICEF, the United Nations, and the European Union; bilateral agencies such as DfID, USAID; and others have encouraged extensive discussions of the importance of broad-based education for development. In the Arab world, governments such as those in Egypt, Kuwait, and Qatar have emphasized the importance of education to meet the challenges of globalization and the technology revolution.

5. See the World Bank Education Statistics (EdStats) database, http://datatopics .worldbank.org/education.

6. See Grindle, *Despite the Odds,* for detailed discussions of these reform initiatives. See also Bruns and Schneider, "Managing the Politics of Quality Reforms in Education"; and Kingdon et al., *A Rigorous Review of the Political Economy of Education Systems in Developing Countries.*

7. At the time of the research, Bolivia, Ecuador, Mexico, and Nicaragua had highly centralized education systems; in Brazil, states were principally in charge of education. Thus, the Brazilian state of Minas Gerais—with a larger population than most Latin American countries—was studied rather than the central government. Ultimately, the reform in Ecuador failed as it was being implemented because the president and team that were promoting reform were overthrown in a coup. The reasons behind the coup were not directly related to the education reform initiative.

8. Thus, the framework predicts that the political odds are stacked against quality-enhancing reforms; they should fail to be designed, approved, and implemented. In the five cases chosen, the study sought to explain why such reforms could sometimes be introduced and sustained, even when failure was predicted.

9. Teachers were generally hired at central levels of administration; teachers who wished to question their paychecks often had to travel to national capitals to make their cases effectively; textbooks were designed and distributed nationally; even school breakfasts and lunches were at times distributed from central warehouses (Grindle, *Despite the Odds*).

10. Typically, politicians offer rhetorical support to education in electoral campaigns. The extent to which they are ready to advance quality-enhancing reforms cannot be judged by such rhetoric alone—the extent to which it has priority and visibility among other policy promises is a more effective test of commitment.

11. Historically, when unions demanded pay increases from governments that were encountering significant economic problems, those governments often negotiated an increased presence of unions in government and increased benefits of other kinds rather than bowing to demand for salary increases.

12. See Bruns and Schneider, "Managing the Politics of Quality Reforms in Education."

13. See Chapter 4, pages 67–86, in this volume.

14. El-Kogali and Krafft, *Expectations and Aspirations,* provides a good summary of achievements and deficits in education in Arab countries.

15. See, for examples, Ennaji, *Multilingualism, Cultural Identity, and Education in Morocco;* Abi-Mershed, *Trajectories of Education in the Arab World;* and Kirdar, *Education in the Arab World.*

16. Rugh, "Arab Education"; El-Kogali and Krafft, *Expectations and Aspirations.*

17. See, for examples, Boutieri, *Learning in Morocco;* Cook and El Refaee, "Egypt"; Ennaji, *Multilingualism, Cultural Identity, and Education in Morocco;* Ginsburg, Megahed, Elmeski, and Tanaka, "Reforming Educational Governance and Management in Egypt"; Hovsepian, *Palestinian State Formation;* Kriener, *Lebanese, but How?;* Nasser, "Qatar's Educational Reform Past and Future"; Schaefer, *Political Revolt and Youth Unemployment in Tunisia;* Springborg, "An Egyptian Education"; and "Strengthening Education in the Muslim World: Country Profiles and Analysis," Washington, USAID, 2004.

18. See, for examples, Cook, "Egypt's National Education Debate"; Cook and El Refaee, "Egypt"; Ginsburg, Megahed, Elmeski, and Tanaka, "Reforming Educational Governance and Management in Egypt"; Mazawi, "Schooling and Curricular Reforms in Arab and Muslim Societies"; Nasser, "Qatar's Educational Reform Past and Future"; Tok, Alkhater, and Pal, *Policy-Making in a Transformative State;* and Gillies, *The Power of Persistence.*

19. Cook, "Egypt's National Education Debate"; Cook and El Refaee, "Egypt."

20. Calvert W. Jones, "New Approaches to Citizen-Building."

21. Tok, Alkhater, and Pal, *Policy-Making in a Transformative State.*

22. World Bank, *World Development Report 2018,* p. 12.

23. Springborg, "An Egyptian Education."

24. I consulted published books and articles in English only, surveying holdings in a major university library and several well-known journals that publish articles on the Middle East and education. I narrowed the review to publications from 2000 to 2019. While there is considerable literature on tertiary education in Arab countries, I also limited the review to materials relevant to primary and secondary schooling and learning. I sought information on twenty-two countries: Algeria, Bahrain, the Comoros Islands, Djibouti, Egypt, Iraq, Jordan, Kuwait, Lebanon, Libya, Mauritania, Morocco, Oman, Palestine, Qatar, Saudi Arabia, Somalia, Sudan, Syria, Tunisia, the United Arab Emirates, and Yemen.

25. Useful overviews of education statistics are found in World Bank, *World Development Report 2018;* El-Kogali and Krafft, *Expectations and Aspirations;* World Bank Education Statistics (EdStats) database, http://datatopics.worldbank .org/education; and UNESCO, *Global Education Monitoring Report—Accountability in Education: Meeting Our Commitments* (Paris, 2017). For helpful overviews of issues in Arab education, see Abi-Mershed, *Trajectories of Education in the Arab World;* Akkary, "Facing the Challenges of Educational Reform in the Arab World"; El Amine, *Reform of General Education in the Arab World;* Assaad, "Making Sense of Arab Labor Markets"; Brock and Levers, *Aspects of Education in the Middle East and North Africa;* Cochran, *Democracy in the Middle East;* Gross and Davies, *The Contested Role of Education in Conflict and Fragility;* Hefner and Zaman, *Schooling Islam;* Kirdar, *Education in the Arab World;* Lefevre, "The Coming of North Africa's 'Language Wars'"; Rugh, "Arab Education"; Salehi-Isfahani, "Education, Jobs, and Equity in the Middle East and North Africa"; and "Strengthening Education in the Muslim World: Country Profiles and Analysis," Washington, USAID, 2004.

26. See, for example, Tok, Alkhater, and Pal, *Policy-Making in a Transformative State;* Springborg, "An Egyptian Education."

27. See, for example, Tok, Alkhater, and Pal, *Policy-Making in a Transformative State.*

28. Rouag and Stejskal, "Assessing the Performance of the Public Sector in North African and Middle East Countries."

29. Education International publishes regular reports on union activity in a variety of countries. See also Ghosn, "Lebanese Teacher Unions in Turbulent Times."

30. From a review of Education International and English-language news items.

31. See, for examples, Abi-Mershed, *Trajectories of Education in the Arab World;* Boutieri, *Learning in Morocco;* Culbertson, *Education of Syrian Refugee Children;* Gross and Davies, *The Contested Role of Education in Conflict and Fragility;* Hovsepian, *Palestinian State Formation;* Kriener, *Lebanese, but How?;* Lefevre, "The Coming of North Africa's 'Language Wars'"; Maadad, *Schooling and Education in Lebanon;* and Springborg, "An Egyptian Education."

32. Lust, "Democratization by Elections?"; Springborg, "The Effects of Patronage Systems and Clientelism on Citizenship in the Middle East."

33. World Bank, *World Bank Development Report 2018,* p. 12; Nasser, "Qatar's Educational Reform Past and Future"; also MacKinzie-Smith, "Introduction."

34. See Jayachandran, "Incentives to Teach Badly."

35. Cook, "Egypt's National Education Debate."

36. Alayan, "History Curricula and Textbooks in Palestine."

37. "Strengthening Education in the Muslim World: Country Profiles and Analysis," Washington, USAID, 2004.

38. Culbertson, *Education of Syrian Refugee Children.*

39. World Bank, *World Development Report 2018;* Nasser, "Qatar's Educational Reform Past and Future"; Kohstall in Chapter 4 of this volume; Alayan, *Education in East Jerusalem.*

40. "Strengthening Education in the Muslim World: Country Profiles and Analysis," Washington, USAID, 2004.

41. See Springborg, "An Egyptian Education," and also in Chapter 5 of this volume; Cronin, *Armies and State-Building in the Modern Middle East;* Erdag, "Review of *Military Responses to the Arab Uprisings*"; Mohamed, Gerber, and Aboulkacem, *Education and the Arab Spring;* and "Strengthening Education in the Muslim World: Country Profiles and Analysis," Washington, USAID, 2004.

42. See Hefner and Zaman, *Schooling Islam;* Kriener, *Lebanese, but How?;* Schneider, *Mandatory Separation;* and "Strengthening Education in the Muslim World: Country Profiles and Analysis," Washington, USAID, 2004.

43. See, for example, "Strengthening Education in the Muslim World: Country Profiles and Analysis," Washington, USAID, 2004.

44. See Gillies, *The Power of Persistence;* and Ginsburg, Megahed, Elmeski, and Tanaka, "Reforming Educational Governance and Management in Egypt."

10

Lessons from East Asia

Alisa Jones

East Asia 5, Arab states 0. This is a common score-line for
the top-ten spots that East Asian and Arab states have taken in the international education assessments TIMSS (Trends in International Mathematics and Science) and PISA (Program for International Student Assessment), which have, respectively, been testing children aged approximately
nine and thirteen (in most education systems, fourth- and eighth-graders)
in science and mathematics every four years since 1995, and fifteen- to
sixteen-year-olds in reading, mathematics, and science every three years
since 2000.[1] In their mere two decades of existence, both assessments
have come to be seen by many policymakers as something of an educational attainment Olympics in which how high one's country places is a
badge of national pride, with a poor performance possibly triggering not
only a great deal of hand-wringing, but also even education reforms, a
phenomenon now widely labeled in education circles as "PISA-shock."[2]
In most TIMSS tests, East Asian states and territories have taken many of
the top spots, ahead of well-respected European competitors, such as Finland and the Netherlands, and high-performing Commonwealth countries,
such as New Zealand, Australia, and Canada, while Arab states languish
at the bottom of the rankings. Singapore has topped both lists more often
than not, with South Korea, Taiwan, Hong Kong, and Japan in rotation
for the remaining top slots. PISA results have similarly seen East Asian
states performing at the top level; indeed, China made an astonishing
debut in 2009 with a clean sweep of the "gold medals," repeating that in
2012, although since only Shanghai competed, other high-performing
Asian countries did not take it too much to heart.[3]

East Asia's generally outstanding education performance has led to an assumption that there is a "cultural" explanation for the region's success, a view bolstered by the above-average academic performances of East Asians immigrating from many of these countries to Europe and North America and of their second-generation offspring.[4] This has been reinforced by research that, though academically rigorous, has been conducted chiefly by educational economists with no reference to the historical, political, and economic contexts in which educational cultures and systems have developed.[5] The essentialist notions of Asian exceptionalism such claims perpetuate align with the broader "Asian values" thesis championed in the 1980s and 1990s by several regional political leaders, most notably the late prime minister of Singapore, Lee Kuan Yew, and former prime minister of Malaysia, Mahathir Mohamad. The central premise of Asian values was that "modernization" and "progress" need not follow "Western" models and could be achieved "the Asian way." Indeed, advocates argued that it was precisely "Asian" values of collectivism, cooperation, diligence, and thrift (juxtaposed explicitly or implicitly to "Western" individualism, competition, laziness, and profligacy) that had enabled the region's rapid development, a notion even the World Bank bought as a prime driver of the "East Asian miracle."[6] Although Asian values discourse lost much of its luster following the 1997 financial crisis, China's weathering of the storm and continued rise, the swift recovery of much of the region, and the growth of Vietnam (predicated on the *doi moi* reform program, not dissimilar to China's "reform and opening" policy) have allowed versions of this notion to persist, now under Xi Jinping increasingly trumpeted as a China model, not least by Xi himself and the Chinese press.[7]

What these models or values really are is, of course, much more complex than can be conveyed by the simplistic terms "Asian values" or "China model" (or any other model—there were Singapore and South Korea models before there was a China model, and a Japan model before that), and it is obvious from the terminology alone that the foundations on which the edifice of Asian values or models has been built are shaky at best. Over 2 billion people live in the East Asian states and territories discussed in this chapter, comprising hundreds of ethnic groups, speaking multiple languages, shaped by diverse religious and cultural traditions, with a vast range of historical and political experiences. It is impossible that they share a set of common values even within many countries, let alone across them all. This is not to suggest that "traditional" cultures are irrelevant, or that there are no persistent values or beliefs at all; it is simply to repudiate essentialist conceptions of "culture" as primordial, immutable, or singularly determinative. Indeed, Lee's and Mahathir's views, when more closely examined, are considerably more nuanced and historically rooted than would be suggested by the simplistic East-West binary that has lodged itself in the popular imagination and underpinned reductionist ideas about Eastern "collectivism" and Western "individualism" beloved both of intercultural management consultants and some East Asian leaders.[8]

This chapter seeks to move away from cultural explanations that lend themselves to assertions of fundamental incommensurability, and to explore instead more tangible drivers of education performance, asking what political, economic, and social conditions have prevailed in East Asia, affecting educational development. Given that many of these states were once governed by the same colonial masters as ruled much of the Arab world, and began their postcolonial development journeys mid–twentieth century with often comparably low literacy rates and high poverty levels, as well as being embroiled, in some cases for decades, in revolutions and hot or cold wars, it seems reasonable to ask what so many East Asian states have been doing "right" (and, by extension perhaps, Arab states "wrong"). These are, of course, difficult questions to answer. Aside from the fact that "success" and "failure" can only be partially represented by test scores, neither can be easily attributed to a single cause, be it financial resources, commitment to or misplaced priorities for education, religious or cultural prescriptions and proscriptions, or any other social, political, or economic conditions; rather, they are a product of an amalgam of factors that vary from state to state and that have evolved over time. Other chapters in this volume explore some of these relationships in the Arab world; this chapter attempts to identify some common features that have militated for educational success in East Asia, and to ask whether there are any lessons Arab states might learn from East Asian examples.

To facilitate fairer and, more important, useful comparisons with the Arab world, the chapter uses a broader definition of East Asia than is usual, including not only Northeast Asia (China, Japan, the Koreas, Taiwan, Hong Kong, and Macau) or historically "Confucian" states (Northeast Asia plus Singapore and Vietnam)—the two most widely used definitions[9]—but also Southeast Asia. This helps avoid unbalanced comparisons between mostly wealthy developed societies of Northeast Asia (the first definition) and much more economically diverse and mainly nondemocratic states in the Arab world on the one hand, as well as culturally essentialist comparisons between "Confucian" (the second definition) and "Islamic" societies on the other. Including Southeast

Asia, which has more middle-income and poor countries, as well as a mixed bag of political systems, greatly diversifies the East Asian picture, making it more comparable to the diversity of the Arab world. Significantly, Southeast Asia also includes two large Muslim-majority countries—Indonesia (population over 260 million) and Malaysia (over 30 million)—and one very small one, Brunei (less than 1 million). Comparisons with these countries may be helpful in assessing the ways in which Islamic traditions might have helped, hindered, or simply been irrelevant to the development of education.

The chapter begins by briefly outlining education performance gaps between East Asia and the Arab world before turning to an analysis of the historical, political, economic, and cultural contexts in which East Asia's education policies have been devised and implemented and intended results achieved or not. Given the large number of states and territories covered, the chapter provides only a general overview and some preliminary hypotheses, which further investigation is required to substantiate in order to ascertain more precisely what may or may not be useful or transferable to diverse political, economic, and cultural settings.

Education Performance

Development and "progress" were for many decades measured principally by gross domestic product (GDP), but by 1990 this had come to be understood as an indicator only of economic growth and not of the impact of said growth on the quality of human lives.[10] The Human Development Index (HDI) of the United Nations Development Programme (UNDP) was a response to this, endeavoring to capture wider and more people-centered measures of progress by adding to GDP health and education, measured, respectively, by life expectancy and mean years of schooling, a formula revised in 2010 to replace GDP with gross national income (GNI) per capita, adjusted by purchasing power parity (PPP). There is, unsurprisingly, a strong correlation between rich and poor countries and high and low levels of human development. The wealthiest Arab and East Asian states are thus found in the "very high levels of human development" category, and middle-income and poor countries from both regions generally quite close together in the lower categories (see Figure 10.1).

When GNI is excluded from the composite index, however, it becomes apparent that this is a major factor that accounts for parts of the Arab world, such as Qatar, the United Arab Emirates (UAE), and

Figure 10.1   HDI 2017, Global Rank by "Level of Development"

Very High	High	Medium	Low
7 Hong Kong	80 Lebanon	113 Philippines	155 Syria
9 Singapore	83 Thailand	115 Egypt	178 Yemen
17 Macau[a]	85 Algeria	116 Indonesia	
19 Japan	86 China	116 Vietnam	
21 Taiwan[a]	92 Mongolia	119 Palestine	
22 South Korea	95 Jordan	123 Morocco	
34 United Arab	95 Tunisia	132 Timor-Leste	
Emirates	108 Libya	139 Laos	
37 Qatar		146 Cambodia	
39 Brunei		148 Myanmar	
39 Saudi Arabia			
43 Bahrain			
48 Oman			
56 Kuwait			
57 Malaysia			

Note: a. The United Nations Development Programme (UNDP) and most other multilateral institutions do not collect data on Taiwan or Macau. Their HDI is calculated by their own government statistics bureau, following UNDP methodology.

Bahrain, placing highly on the HDI rankings, not too far behind the top East Asian performers, which, while also wealthy, typically have lower per capita GNI scores. Brunei, Singapore, Hong Kong, and Macau[11] are the only East Asian jurisdictions with incomes approaching or equal to those of the richest Arab states, and—aside from petro-state Brunei, which has long been wealthy—these incomes have caught up with Gulf states only in recent years.[12] High HDI scores across much of East Asia are thus largely attributable to better performances on the health and education indexes, and although most of the worst performers on the Education Index are in East Asia,[13] these are the poorest states, and overall East Asia performs better on the Education Index than Arab states with comparable HDIs (see Table 10.1).

Arab states have, nonetheless, been making great strides in increasing education access, improvements that are strikingly demonstrated when the Education Index is ranked by gains since 1990 (Table 10.2). Arab states take three out of the top four spots here, with Morocco the runaway winner by highest percentage improvement, more than doubling its 1990 score, although since it started almost on par with Myanmar and below even Laos and war-ravaged Cambodia, it still has a long way to go. Unsurprisingly, most of the high-performing East Asian states show far less progress, as their education systems were well

Table 10.1   Education Index, 1990–2017 (Ranked by 2017 Score)

Arab World	1990	2000	2010	2017	East Asia[a]	1990	2000	2010	2017
Saudi Arabia	0.489	0.555	0.691	0.787	South Korea	0.676	0.787	0.860	0.862
Bahrain	0.574	0.643	0.654	0.758	Hong Kong	0.640	0.686	0.808	0.855
UAE	0.484	0.609	0.703	0.738	Japan	0.691	0.754	0.802	0.848
Jordan	0.496	0.671	0.685	0.711	Singapore	0.487	0.649	0.795	0.832
Oman		0.475	0.635	0.706	Mongolia	0.539	0.534	0.721	0.766
Brunei	0.588	0.647	0.685	0.704	Malaysia	0.488	0.619	0.687	0.719
Qatar	0.507	0.613	0.637	0.698	Philippines	0.519	0.568	0.622	0.661
Algeria	0.385	0.500	0.626	0.664	Thailand	0.387	0.517	0.624	0.661
Palestine		0.655	0.660		China	0.405	0.481	0.602	0.644
Tunisia	0.406	0.526	0.625	0.659	Vietnam	0.348	0.474	0.583	0.626
Lebanon			0.631	0.637	Indonesia	0.389	0.518	0.586	0.622
Kuwait	0.476	0.595	0.598	0.620	Timor-Leste		0.364	0.493	0.505
Libya	0.516	0.621	0.634	0.616	Cambodia	0.276	0.319	0.450	0.487
Egypt	0.389	0.468	0.551	0.604	Laos	0.288	0.352	0.429	0.484
Morocco	0.254	0.348	0.449	0.529	Myanmar	0.251	0.319	0.392	0.443
Syria	0.417	0.433	0.537	0.412					
Yemen	0.219	0.258	0.326	0.349					

Note: a. No Education Index data available for Taiwan, but the World Bank Knowledge Economy Index, 1995–2012 (now discontinued), shows Taiwan's Education Index (calculated under a different methodology from the current Education Index) ranking third in this sample in 1995, first in 2000, and first again in 2012 with a score of 0.886.

developed long before 1990. Singapore, which takes the top slot, is the only exception, as its education development did not accelerate until the late 1970s.[14] That is, although Singapore's education system was highly advanced by 1990, its older population had received fewer years of schooling than counterparts in Hong Kong, Taiwan, Japan, and South Korea, bringing down its composite score.

While the Education Index shows that Arab states have been increasing education access, PISA and TIMSS scores paint a bleaker picture of what schools are actually delivering, although the sample size for both assessments is small, as only the more economically developed states typically participate. This is because costs are borne principally by the participants; hence poorer states, which might be expected to perform below their better-off counterparts in both regions, do not normally submit for assessment.[15] Among those that do, East Asian states take many of the top slots while Arab states bring up the rear. In the 2015 PISA test, East Asian states and territories took eight of the top eleven spots in science, four of twelve in reading, and the top seven spots in mathematics, while the best-performing Arab state, the UAE, ranked no higher than forty-six in any of the three assessments. The remaining Arab state participants, all of which have "very high" or "high" HDI scores, were near or at the bottom of the

Table 10.2   Global HDI vs. Education Index Rankings, 2017 (Gain Since 1990/2000)

Country	HDI	Education Index	Gain	Country	HDI	Education Index	Gain
Singapore	9	33	0.345	Cambodia	146	152	0.211
Saudi Arabia	40	49	0.298	Laos	139	153	0.196
Algeria	85	100	0.279	Myanmar	148	162	0.192
Morocco	123	137	0.275	Hong Kong	7	24	0.191
Thailand	84	102	0.274	Qatar	37	85	0.191
Vietnam	117	115	0.258	South Korea	23	23	0.186
UAE	34	65	0.254	Bahrain	43	58	0.184
Tunisia	96	106	0.253	Kuwait	56	118	0.176
China	86	108	0.239	Japan	19	26	0.157
Indonesia	116	116	0.233	Philippines	113	101	0.142
Malaysia	57	74	0.231	Timor-Leste	132	145	0.141
Oman	48	82	0.231	Yemen	178	178	0.130
Mongolia	93	55	0.227	Brunei	39	84	0.116
Jordan	95	78	0.215	Libya	108	119	0.100
Egypt	115	121	0.215				

Note: States missing data for 1990, 2000, and/or 2017 are excluded (Palestine, Lebanon, Syria, and Taiwan).

table, alongside and in some cases even below Indonesia and far below Vietnam, both developing countries ranking only as "medium" on the HDI. PISA 2018 results indicate that recent reforms, in both Arab and lower-performing East Asian countries, have yet to bear fruit, with similar disparities repeated (see Figure 10.2). TIMSS results have likewise been gloomy (see Figure 10.3), and although most Arab states show improvements between fourth and eighth grades, this is likely because of dropout between grades or low transition rates (from primary to secondary), meaning that only the better-performing pupils make it to eighth grade at all.[16]

Despite generally high literacy rates among young people (ages fifteen to twenty-four) in both East Asia and the Arab world (above 90 percent for both genders in most cases, even among the poorer performers),[17] assessments of minimum proficiency levels attained in reading and mathematics by primary and junior secondary school leavers reaffirm the disparities between East Asia and Arab states with similar HDI rankings. As with PISA and TIMSS, cross-country comparisons are hampered by small sample sizes, since many countries covered in this chapter have not undertaken the assessments or consistently reported results to the United Nations Educational, Scientific, and Cultural Organization (UNESCO), which tracks these outcomes as part of the Sustainable Development Goal 4 (SDG4), "Quality Education." Nevertheless, the statistics available indicate that while many children are not reaching

Figure 10.2 PISA 2018 by Rank

Reading	Mathematics	Science
1 China[a]	1 China[a]	1 China[a]
2 Singapore	2 Singapore	2 Singapore
3 Macau	3 Macau	3 Macau
4 Hong Kong	4 Hong Kong	4 Vietnam
9 South Korea	5 Taiwan	6 Japan
13 Vietnam	6 Japan	8 South Korea
16 Japan	7 South Korea	10 Hong Kong
18 Taiwan	24 Vietnam	11 Taiwan
47 United Arab Emirates	48 Malaysia	49 Malaysia
56 Jordan	51 United Arab Emirates	50 United Arab Emirates
57 Malaysia	52 Brunei	51 Brunei
60 Brunei	58 Thailand	52 Jordan
61 Qatar	61 Qatar	54 Thailand
66 Saudi Arabia	66 Jordan	59 Qatar
67 Thailand	69 Lebanon	71 Indonesia
73 Indonesia	73 Indonesia	72 Saudi Arabia
74 Morocco	74 Saudi Arabia	73 Lebanon
75 Lebanon	75 Morocco	75 Morocco
78 Philippines	78 Philippines	78 Philippines

Notes: Total of seventy-nine participants in mathematics and science, seventy-eight in reading.
a. Beijing, Shanghai, Jiangsu, and Zhejiang only.

Figure 10.3 TIMSS 2015 by Rank

Mathematics Grade 4	Science Grade 4	Mathematics Grade 8	Science Grade 8
1 Singapore	1 Singapore	1 Singapore	1 Singapore
2 Hong Kong	2 South Korea	2 South Korea	2 Japan
3 South Korea	3 Japan	3 Taiwan	3 Taiwan
4 Taiwan	5 Hong Kong	4 Hong Kong	4 South Korea
5 Japan	6 Taiwan	5 Japan	6 Hong Kong
40 United Arab Emirates	39 Bahrain	23 Malaysia	24 United Arab Emirates
41 Bahrain	41 United Arab Emirates	24 United Arab Emirates	25 Malaysia
42 Qatar	42 Qatar	26 Bahrain	26 Bahrain
44 Oman	43 Oman	28 Lebanon	27 Qatar
45 Indonesia	45 Indonesia	29 Qatar	29 Thailand
46 Jordan	46 Saudi Arabia	31 Thailand	30 Oman
47 Saudi Arabia	47 Morocco	33 Oman	33 Jordan
48 Morocco	48 Kuwait	34 Kuwait	34 Kuwait
49 Kuwait		35 Egypt	35 Lebanon
		37 Jordan	36 Saudi Arabia
		38 Morocco	37 Morocco
		39 Saudi Arabia	39 Egypt

Notes: Total participants, mathematics grade 4, forty-nine; science grade 4, forty-eight; mathematics grade 8, thirty-nine; and science grade 8, thirty-nine.

basic proficiency in parts of East Asia, especially in the poorest countries, and that there is significant room for improvement in a number of middle-income states, such insufficiencies plague even the best performers in the Arab world (see Table 10.3).[18]

As Grindle demonstrates in Chapter 9, implementing the kind of "quality reforms" necessary to redress such failings is a great deal more difficult than expanding access to schooling. Yet clearly, much of East Asia has managed to do this, starting from often low baselines and overcoming many of the same systemic obstacles Arab states face. The remainder of this chapter accordingly focuses on three key areas—education spending, the evolving political/economic and social/cultural value of education in East Asia, and the capacity of the state to implement education policies—in an effort to isolate some of the factors contributing to success and failure of education and learning outcomes.

Education Spending

The first and ostensibly simplest question to ask is whether East Asia performs better than Arab states because it spends more. At first glance the answer is no; spending on education is higher in some instances and lower in others, and has been so since statistics for large numbers of countries began to be regularly reported by UNESCO and the World

Table 10.3 Percentage of Pupils Reaching Minimum Proficiency in Mathematics and Reading at Completion of Junior Secondary School, Listed by Mathematics Score (Highest to Lowest)

Country	Mathematics	Reading	Country	Mathematics	Reading
Macau	95.0	88.3	Lebanon	34.8	29.6
Singapore	93.5	88.9	Jordan	32.5	53.7
Hong Kong	91.0	90.7	Indonesia	31.4	44.6
South Korea	84.5	86.3	Tunisia	25.2	28.4
Vietnam	80.9	86.2	Oman	23.4	—
China	78.9	79.6	Egypt	21.3	—
Malaysia	58.5	54.2	Algeria	19.0	21.0
UAE	46.4	59.6	Kuwait	18.3	48.5
Thailand	46.2	50.0	Morocco	14.6	26.9
Bahrain	39.5	—	Cambodia	9.9	7.5
Qatar	36.0	48.4			

Source: Data compiled from UNESCO Institute of Statistics, *SDG 4* ("Proficiency" dataset), http://data.uis.unesco.org.

Note: Scores reported in 2015 except Macau and Malaysia, 2018; Kuwait (reading), 2017; Morocco (reading), 2018.

Bank in the 1990s. Prior to this, internationally available records are incomplete at best, for many states nonexistent, and a close look at domestically maintained statistics would be necessary to provide more details of spending over time. Additionally, without education sector–specific pricing data, government spending levels do not demonstrate purchasing power. Nevertheless, a few snapshots of spending as percentages of GDP and government expenditure, as well as per pupil spending, included in UNESCO, UNDP, and World Bank databases indicate that there are relatively high and low spenders in both the Arab world and East Asia, with mixed educational outcomes.

Tunisia has been the highest spender by percentage of GDP and public expenditure over the longest period, beginning with its first reported statistics in 1980, its lowest education spending in any reported year, standing at 4.9 percent of GDP. Since 1991 it has invested over 6 percent of GDP and 20 percent of public expenditure in education for all reported years. For the limited period Thailand has reported, it has spent the same or even more, never below 7 percent of GDP and in some years over 18 percent. More comprehensive government expenditure statistics range from a low of 16.2 percent to a high of 28.4 percent, confirming Thailand's commitment. These are the only two countries in either region consistently meeting the goals set by UNESCO's Global Education First Initiative (GEFI),[19] although Malaysia, Mongolia, Palestine, and Saudi Arabia have not lagged far behind, a group joined more recently by South Korea, Vietnam, and Oman. Spending less by percentage of GDP, but likewise investing a high proportion of government expenditure, the high-spending ranks expand to include Hong Kong (average greater than 20 percent), Morocco (greater than 20 percent), Singapore (greater than 19 percent), Jordan (greater than 18 percent), and, until the past few conflict years, Syria (greater than 18 percent). Formerly low-spending middle-income countries China and Indonesia have recently begun to invest more heavily in education, while in the poorest countries (Cambodia, Laos, Myanmar, and Timor-Leste) education spending remains low by both GDP and government expenditure.[20]

It is immediately apparent from these statistics that government spending does not correspond neatly to any of the previously described measures of education performance, although increasing investment from low baselines does correlate to gains in access and generally also in outcomes. Morocco, Vietnam, and Indonesia, for example, have all increased spending in recent years, and although Indonesia and Morocco still have a long way to go by quality measures, they have both significantly increased access, while Vietnam is already a star performer in both access and attainment. Thailand and Malaysia appear to tell the same story. Although their performances are currently mediocre on quality metrics, this seems to be a case of recent stagnation rather than failure to spend effectively at the outset; both countries have long invested heavily in education, expanding access and steadily improving learning outcomes, and both performed quite well relative to GNI when they first began to participate in TIMSS and PISA, but while GNI has risen significantly since 2000 (almost certainly attributable in part to more educated populations), test scores have remained stagnant or even fallen.[21] Research suggests that education reform rather than increased spending is thus needed, something both countries have recently acknowledged in planning large-scale education reform programs.[22]

If overall government spending does not predict education outcomes beyond initial development of basic education infrastructure and systems, spending per pupil (PPP dollars) tracks more closely, with the best-performing East Asian states also being the highest per pupil spenders in their region. Although data are incomplete, available figures unsurprisingly show that high per pupil spending correlates roughly to GNI, regardless of how much the country invests as a percentage of GDP or public expenditure. Singapore, among the region's richest states, is the highest spender, with per pupil spending (greater than $16,000) almost as high as Japan and Hong Kong combined. South Korea spends almost 20 percent more than either Japan or Hong Kong, although its GNI is slightly lower, while Taiwan spends approximately 20 percent less.[23]

In the Arab world, Qatar, Oman, and Kuwait (plus the UAE and Saudi Arabia) spend the most,[24] all investing more per pupil than any East Asian state except Singapore.[25] However, while Japan, Taiwan, and Hong Kong appear to be getting good value for their money, South Korea may be approaching and Singapore is likely past the point of diminishing returns. Clearly the return on investment in rich Arab states is low given that they perform no better, and in some cases worse, than their less wealthy neighbors, as well as behind even some of the poorer states in East Asia. Vegas and Coffin confirm this, demonstrating a statistically significant correlation between per pupil spending and PISA results, with approximately fourteen points gained for each additional PPP $1,000 spent, but only up to a cutoff point of less than $8,000, after which the return on investment diminishes.[26] Hence, low spenders who increase their education investment may make quality as well as access gains, while underperforming high spenders may need to reassess their allocative priorities.

Total spending is not only what central governments invest, but also what local authorities, families, and other community entities contribute. As several scholars have demonstrated, much of this spending, and household spending in particular, is not captured in statistics maintained by supranational institutions such as the World Bank and UNESCO or even, in many instances, domestic government agencies.[27] Nevertheless, drawing on limited data from multiple sources, a more complex picture of East Asia's education spending emerges. While South Korea, for example, has only quite recently invested large amounts of public money in education, Seth shows that spending has actually been high for many decades, with the brunt of costs borne by local authorities and families.[28] Kipnis and Li reach similar conclusions about China, challenging the established orthodoxy that China is a low spender.[29] Sparse data available from UNESCO statistics likewise show significant household spending in several countries (e.g., Japan, South Korea, and Indonesia) where compulsory education (typically primary and lower secondary) has ostensibly been free for many years.[30]

Where is all this money going? Although high household spending on education is common around the world, it is usually to compensate for lack of government spending and under-resourced schools, but this is clearly not the case in most of contemporary East Asia. Textbook costs are often regulated or subsidized for poorer students, and although tuition fees are commonly charged for upper secondary schools (not compulsory in most countries), these are not particularly high and, in the wealthiest states, such as Japan, Taiwan, and South Korea, appear to have deterred only the poorest families from educating their offspring beyond junior secondary. Tuition fees were recently waived for low-income families or abolished altogether in all three countries, as well as in Hong Kong, Malaysia, Thailand, and Indonesia, yet this has not dented household spending on education. On the contrary, it is trending upward, primarily a result of the widespread development of "shadow education"—namely, cram schools and other providers of extracurricular learning, including both legitimate and legal (though often poorly regulated) supplementary tuition, and murkier practices amounting to extortion or bribery in the form of "gifts" demanded of or offered by parents to schools and teachers.[31]

The answer to the initial question, "Is East Asia performing better because it is spending more?" may thus turn out to be yes, and regardless of whether the region spends more money than Arab states, the top performers undoubtedly spend more in terms of enormous time investments from children and parents. Not only do children in many of these countries typically spend more hours in school per day than their counterparts elsewhere, but even primary-schoolers often attend crammers several times a week, and many secondary school pupils daily.[32] This phenomenon goes back to the 1980s and earlier in the most developed parts of the region, but has been growing fast, particularly in China, not only in the wealthy first-tier cities of Shanghai, Beijing, Tianjin, and Guangzhou, but also in the second- and third-tier cities in the interior. Indeed, pupils in Shanghai spend more time on homework than their counterparts anywhere in the world.[33] Cram schools in Indonesia, Vietnam, and even in Cambodia, one of the poorest states in this sample, are likewise booming.[34] Although there have been repeated efforts to regulate and curtail the shadow education industry and reduce children's study burden, they have been largely unsuccessful.[35]

It is hardly surprising that time spent correlates to test results, but as with money, there is undoubtedly a point beyond which the investment has diminishing returns. A recent Organization for Economic Cooperation and Development (OECD) study, for example, found that Hong Kong and Taiwan, among the top scorers in PISA-science, achieved only around the OECD mean in points per study-hour (in and outside school), while Singapore and Korea were well below it; indeed, only Japan ranked near the top on the points/study-hours ratio. Children in Qatar, Tunisia, Thailand, and the UAE, meanwhile, scored 25–50 percent fewer points per study-hour.[36] Evidently then, more is not always better, and improving performance will require reevaluating teacher training, curriculum content, and teaching and learning strategies. That many of the most successful states in East Asia are already doing this, rather than basking in their consistent international assessment glory, is another clear indicator of their commitment to education.[37]

The Value of Education

If willingness to invest money, time, and effort to increase educational access and attainment is an indicator of how much education is valued, then who values it (state, society, families, and individuals) and why it is prized more highly in some states and societies than in others must be ascertained. This requires understanding the ways in which education has been intertwined with the workings of the state, and with the mechanisms through which the political economy both constrains and enables the cultivation and retention of human capital. It is here where differences between the contexts in which education has developed in East Asia and the Arab world begin to become clearer.

One obvious motivation for state investment in education in East Asia, as elsewhere, has been nation-building, mobilizing often diverse peoples and interests behind a common objective or "national purpose."[38] This has been particularly prevalent in new and multiethnic states, as well as in states undergoing decolonization or other political transitions. In

Japan, these efforts began in the late nineteenth century as a means of mobilizing the population to "enrich and strengthen" the nation (*fukoku kyōhei*) to resist imperialist encroachment. Similar (though far less successful) attempts were likewise made in China and Korea. Malaysia and Singapore, with no history as unified states, made vigorous efforts to foster national unity after independence (Malaysia in 1957, Singapore in 1959) and their split from one another in 1965. With mixed populations of Malays, Chinese, and Tamils, and facing ethnic unrest, both adopted the "neutral" English language of their former colonizers as the medium of instruction in public schools, and emphasized ethnic unity in the curriculum and in government.[39] In Taiwan, meanwhile, the Kuomintang's policies of decolonization (or, in many locals' minds, "recolonization") following the island's handover in 1945 after fifty years of Japanese rule, were aimed at (re)making the Japanese-educated population Chinese. Similarly, since Hong Kong's retrocession to the People's Republic of China (PRC) in 1997, the state has sought to promote "national education" to turn Hongkongers into PRC patriots.

Another widespread objective, especially for the region's authoritarian regimes, has been legitimizing the polity, often through inculcating state-decreed ideologies, while directly or indirectly suppressing competing ideas and ideals, political, economic, or religious. After the establishment of the PRC, new curricula were devised, including heavy doses of political education focused on the "inevitability" and "moral superiority" of communism, the role of the Chinese Communist Party (CCP) as national savior, and the evils of "the West."[40] Similar approaches were taken in North Korea and Vietnam.[41] Meanwhile, Taiwan and South Korea infused their curricula with anticommunist rhetoric, justifying authoritarian rule as essential to combating the Red threat.[42] In Indonesia, Malaysia, and the Philippines too, autocratic governments, facing real challenges to their authority from left-wing social, political, and even paramilitary movements, adopted strong, and often brutal, anticommunist positions.

While ideology may have been important rhetorically, regime consolidation in most of the region has derived primarily from performance legitimacy through postwar (whether World War II or civil wars) reconstruction and economic stabilization and development. In 1945, Japan was the only East Asian state with a moderately educated population, with Mongolia, the Philippines, Taiwan, and Thailand having established education systems, but lagging some way behind. Neighboring states had only marginal literacy rates, and upskilling the prospective work force to support economic development was thus a priority, particularly in states or territories with few natural resources other than "human capital," requiring cultivation rather than extraction. This drove efforts to foster universal literacy and numeracy, as well as the prioritization of science and technology over humanities and social sciences to support industrial modernization.

The economic motive underlying state-led education expansion in most instances has been closely connected to the "developmental state," identified by Chalmers Johnson as a "model" for industrialization and economic growth, which was established in Japan before World War II, and consolidated and expanded during postwar reconstruction and development.[43] This interventionist approach, Johnson found, was characterized by top-down steering, focusing on industrial policies, targeted research and development, and strategic co-optation of private enterprise to meet national economic objectives, and was implemented by technocrats operating within relatively efficient and low-corruption bureaucracies coordinating with government. Similar developmentalist strategies were adopted by Singapore, Taiwan, and South Korea in the 1960s–1980s, and subsequently by others in the region, including Malaysia, Thailand, Indonesia, China, and Vietnam.[44]

Education, although typically administered separately from the bureaucracies overseeing industrial development,[45] was an integral part of growth strategies in states that could not survive purely on revenues from extractive industries. Primary education was made compulsory across most of the region in the 1940s–1960s, and junior secondary in many countries soon thereafter.[46] In this way, although economic growth was launched in many parts of East Asia on the back of low-cost manufacturing, the region's competitive edge over other low-wage countries was gained in no small part by offering a more educated, hence more productive, work force (and given that authoritarian regimes were running most of the countries in the region, by suppressing organized labor movements, commonly in the guise of fighting the communist threat). An increasingly educated work force in turn provided the foundation for transitions to higher-value manufacturing and capital goods, as well as raising living standards and leading the state to disburse at least some of its newfound wealth in increasing public goods and services provision.

Among these public goods was more education, delivered not because the state required its people to be more educated (senior secondary education is still not compulsory in most East Asian states, even in those that have almost universalized it, such as Japan, Singapore, and South Korea), but because it was demanded by a growing middle class. As Chen Jing's comparative analysis has shown, under nondemocratic rule, tertiary education was funded at the expense of basic education, hence a privilege accessible mainly to elites,[47] much as it continues to be in the Arab world.[48] The impetus for expanded access to secondary and tertiary education thus came mainly from below as a demand for more equitable distribution of public goods.[49]

For a society or individuals to demand education, and especially to invest resources to access it to the extent so many East Asian families do, it must, of course, offer access to something of value, particularly social or economic value; few can afford to spend on learning simply because they value being learned. Even in the wealthiest parts of the region, the main business of the shadow education industry is not fulfilling demands for cultural enrichment (e.g., art, sport, or music), which is provided only minimally or not at all by public education, but rather supplying coaching in core school subjects: language, mathematics, science, and English. Some of this is, of course, remedial education for pupils who struggle in school, but the majority is aimed at test preparation for university, senior secondary, and in some countries even junior secondary entrance examinations/assessments; not because education provided by the state is low quality, but because places at the highest-ranking institutions are so prized and extra tuition is regarded as the only way to compete. When everyone is studying so hard, it creates a virtuous—or vicious—cycle that brings test scores up, including those of the least–economically advantaged pupils,[50] but puts enormous financial and psychological pressure on families.

What do "the best" schools and universities offer that is worth so much, and why are the examinations so important? It is no surprise that the answer to the first question is opportunities for socioeconomic mobility, and to the second that they grant access to the first, but two things are distinctive about many East Asian societies, the top education performers in particular: graduation from the best universities has long been a reliable route to power and privilege in both nondemocratic and democratic states, and admission to the best universities (and to the best schools lower down the chain that increase chances of acceptance at top tertiary institutions) is determined almost exclusively by performance on standardized tests. In regard to the latter, the system is far from a level playing field. Living in a neighborhood with good local primary schools (where enrollment is usually set by catchment area) and sufficient disposable income to cover extra tuition greatly improve chances of examination success, but no one is systematically excluded from joining the education competition, and the championship match itself—the entrance examinations—is not rigged. Indeed, the state goes to great lengths to prevent cheating in examinations and corruption in admissions, and violations are a public scandal.[51]

The emphasis on meritocracy is not new in East Asia, and although this chapter has thus far argued strongly against cultural explanations of East Asia's success, there is one particular tradition—Confucianism—in which the meritocratic principle is central to its entire conceptual framework, and to the ways in which it historically shaped access to and legitimacy of political power. Unlike many other "great traditions" in Asia, Confucianism is not a religion, but a philosophy of government, social organization, and human relations that to varying degrees dominated political and social life in China for almost 1,500 years, Vietnam for 1,000, and Korea for more than 500, and at times had considerable influence among Japan's intellectual elites, including, during the Tokugawa era (1600–1868), the support of the state. The Confucian concept of government and society is hierarchical, but crucially the hierarchy (outside the family) is predicated on virtue, achievable not through birth but through education and self-cultivation. In this way, paupers could rise to the highest echelons of power, and the legitimacy of the ruler and the system over which he presided hinged on principles of benevolence, justice, and merit. Although reality lagged far behind the ideal, by the eighth century in China, the tenth in Korea, and the eleventh in Vietnam, this had led to the appointment of bureaucrats through formal examinations, which the state exerted enormous (though often unsuccessful) efforts to keep corruption-free.[52]

This system survived, modified but more or less intact, until the turn of the twentieth century, strongly influencing reforms to the British civil service qualification system in the nineteenth century: first for India, subsequently for Britain, later exported to Britain's East Asian colonies.[53] It also impacted the ways in which assessments, promotion, and qualifications were devised for modern education systems, as well as for civil service recruitment in postcolonial East Asia. To the extent that meritocracy and rule by wisdom and virtue are ideals inherent in Confucianism, that upward mobility has been historically attainable through education,[54] and that the best performers in East Asia have at least some legacy of Confucianism, a weak culturalist argument can be made for a "special value" attached to education in these societies. Other claims for the impact of Confucianism (respect for authority, reverence for and emphasis on rote memorization of canonical texts, discipline, work ethic, and so forth) are unconvincing; similar values and practices can be found in one form or another in Buddhism (the majority religion in Thailand, Cambodia, Laos, Myanmar, and Mongolia) and Islam (the majority religion of Indonesia, Malaysia, and Brunei), as well as in many other religious and philosophical traditions around the world.[55] Furthermore, none of the so-called Confucian societies was ever exclusively Confucian; they were shaped by diverse religious and philosophical traditions, as indeed was Confucianism itself.[56]

A path-dependence argument holds somewhat more water, but while Confucian ideals of meritocracy and historical experience of it in some East Asian states may have predisposed their modern-day successors to adopt examination-based systems of recruitment from educational to economic and political institutions, and inclined those seeking social mobility to demand such systems, most East Asians before and during the time when modern education and civil service systems were established in the late nineteenth to mid-twentieth centuries were illiterate subsistence farmers with little expectation of significant socioeconomic benefits from sending their children to school. Furthermore, periods of internal and external disruption, such as revolutions, colonial rule, and civil war, which drastically transformed the balance of power and upended social structures in many of these countries, no doubt negated much (though not all) of the historical-cultural legacy. A utilitarian political-economic explanation for education's "special value" in East Asian societies today is thus more plausible than a cultural one. East Asian families' huge investment in education only makes sense inasmuch as it directly impacts socioeconomic prospects. And for faith in these prospects to be sustained, access to opportunity, economic opportunity in particular, needs to be relatively free, fair, and based on merit proven by qualifications or other standardized measures of attainment.

Education Policymaking and Implementation

If, as described above, both the state and the populace have generally been desirous of education in East Asia in recent decades, it would suggest that implementing policies that provide "more" or "better" education has been mostly straightforward, and, to be sure, building high-performing education systems in East Asia appears to have proceeded more smoothly than it has in the Arab world. This does not mean, however, that education policies are never contested. In the early years of implementing modern mass education systems, for example, persuading rural families to release children from manual labor or duties of care for younger siblings was not easy. Similar problems recurred in the wake of market reforms in China and Vietnam during the 1970s–1980s, when rural children's labor value began again to exceed the economic returns to education. State-led curriculum content revisions, examination format adjustments, or shifting higher-education entrance requirements, meanwhile, are often resisted by diverse stakeholders (such as textbook writers, university and school administrators, teachers, parents, and students), and although these fights are usually more public in democratic states, it does not mean policies are unquestioningly accepted in non-democratic ones. Indeed, stakeholder struggles and even education-related protests have taken place in a number of nondemocratic states in the region, on occasion directly connected to social and political movements demanding a more equitable share of public goods or greater role in decisionmaking processes.[57]

Regardless of intermittent local opposition, East Asia's recent performances indicate that education policies have mostly been successful, and that this success is being achieved under both democratic and various shades of autocratic rule (see Figure 10.4).[58] One might at first glance assume, therefore, that Douglass North and his new institutional economics colleagues' access order framework,[59] proposed by Alaoui and Springborg in the introduction to this volume as a common feature in education policy failures across the Arab world, does not apply in the East Asian case. A closer look at East Asia's success stories, as well as its ongoing challenges, however, suggests otherwise.

In the access order schema, Arab states are largely classified as "fragile" or "basic" limited access orders (LAOs), in which, respectively, less or more stable coalitions of elites cooperate to reduce violence and create conditions under which to maximize rents. Access to political and economic participation is restricted and instability is a perpetual concern. The East Asian states discussed here, on the other hand, are mostly "mature" limited access orders, in many instances meeting the "doorstep conditions" North and his colleagues identified as preceding a (possible though not guaranteed) transition to an open access order (OAO), a system more or less synonymous, in their definition, with democratic capitalist systems mainly found in Western Europe and North America: rule of law for elites, public and private "perpetually lived" organizations, and political control over organizations and entities with the capacity for violence. Although North and his colleagues and successors have had little to say about the theory's applicability to East Asia,[60] by these criteria South Korea and Taiwan, full democracies since the early 1990s, can largely be considered OAOs alongside Japan, while contemporary Singapore, Hong Kong, Mongolia, Malaysia, China, and Vietnam (and more tenuously Indonesia and perhaps even some of the poorest, least-developed, or recently war-torn countries, such as Cambodia and Timor-Leste) are mature LAOs, some of them approaching or already on the doorstep. The Philippines, Thailand, and Brunei fit more closely the definition of basic LAOs, while Myanmar, despite its recent transition to electoral democracy, looks more like a fragile LAO.[61]

Figure 10.4 **Economist Intelligence Unit, 2018 Democracy Index, Regime Type, and Global Ranking**

Flawed Democracy	Hybrid Regime	Authoritarian Regime	
21 South Korea	100 Morocco	115 Jordan	148 Bahrain
23 Japan	106 Lebanon (tie)	116 Kuwait	151 Laos
32 Taiwan	106 Thailand (tie)	118 Myanmar	154 Libya
42 Timor-Leste	109 Palestine	125 Cambodia	158 Yemen
52 Malaysia		126 Algeria	159 Saudi Arabia
53 Philippines		127 Egypt	166 Syria
62 Mongolia		130 China	167 North Korea
63 Tunisia		133 Qatar	
65 Indonesia		139 Vietnam	
66 Singapore		140 Oman	
73 Hong Kong		147 United Arab Emirates	

It is evident at a glance from the access order taxonomy that neither democracy nor capitalism is a sufficient condition to define a state as an open access order. Mongolia, Indonesia, Malaysia, the Philippines, Timor-Leste, and Myanmar are all (currently) electoral democracies and capitalist economies (with varying degrees of state intervention, corruption, and cronyism), yet in many respects meet fewer of the "doorstep conditions" than Singapore, Hong Kong, and, on some metrics, even "communist" China, Vietnam, and Cambodia. It is also clear that most of the region's best education performers are limited access orders meeting doorstep conditions, or, in the case of South Korea and Taiwan, were LAOs on the doorstep at the time their education systems were developed. Even Japan could arguably be included in this category during its education expansion, not only during the pre–World War II imperial period, but also in the postwar "1955 system," which saw the Liberal Democratic Party (LDP) remain in office until 1993, a hold only breaking briefly in the wake of a series of scandals involving collusion between politicians and business to protect their rents. Indeed, the LDP has spent barely five of the past sixty-five years out of power, raising some questions about Japan's OAO status.

Is there something about the mature limited access order, or at least the mature LAO in these specific East Asian contexts, that has facilitated education success? Answering that question is far beyond the scope of the short overview offered here, but two factors already noted above are worth reiterating: the developmental state and meritocracy. To the extent that the developmental state has increased rents, as well as improved economic and social conditions for wage labor, it has maintained performance legitimacy. At the same time, ensuring that education remains a merit-based pathway for (almost) anyone to join the elite (at least to gain access, if not promotion) has meant that policies that enhance these opportunities are generally supported. Investing in science and technology research and development and providing economic space (and often protectionist legislation) for domestic innovation, meanwhile, incentivized populations to acquire relevant technical skills, knowing that jobs were waiting to be filled.

These twin features have almost certainly played a significant role in allowing states to amass both institutional and infrastructural power, regardless of regime type, and thereby to implement education policies effectively without resorting widely to coercion.[62] In this respect, the most (and even some of the less) successful East Asian states can be said to have high degrees of "stateness," commonly defined as a consensus on "state identity" (what is "our" territory and who "belongs"), absence of interference in state affairs by "religious dogma," and the operation of "basic administration," in addition to monopolizing the capacity for violence (see Figure 10.5).[63] That is, stateness provides not only a measure of stability, national cohesion, and the ability to withstand shocks without collapsing into disorder and conflict, but also an ability to penetrate and mobilize society.

This is not to discount other social, political, and economic indicators of state capacity and legitimacy, or community co-optation. High levels of ethnic and linguistic homogeneity are common in many of the more successful East Asian states (although this homogeneity has often been cultivated over time, or imposed by colonial and postcolonial regimes), and uncommon in the less successful ones: bottom-ranking PISA performers Indonesia and the Philippines, for example, have vast populations for whom the school medium of instruction is a second or third language.[64] Additionally, economic inequality is generally lower among the better performers, and, significantly, was much lower during the developmental-state peak years.[65] Gender inequality has also historically been lower in East Asia than it has in Arab states, and although girls in Arab states today often outperform boys academically by greater margins than their East Asian counterparts, literacy rates among older women are substantially higher in East Asia, even in the least-developed states.[66] Other political and economic features, however—such as rule of law, separation of powers, corruption control, policy prioritization and coordination, efficiency of resource use, civic participation, property rights, private-enterprise opportunity, and many more—appear, at least in disaggregated form, to be more weakly correlated to education outcomes.[67]

Figure 10.5   Bertelsmann Transformation Index 2018: Stateness

Taiwan	10.0	Kuwait	7.3
Singapore	10.0	Thailand	6.8
South Korea	10.0	Morocco	6.8
Mongolia	9.0	Jordan	6.5
North Korea	9.0	Indonesia	6.5
China	8.8	Philippines	6.5
Vietnam	8.8	Egypt	6.3
United Arab Emirates	8.5	Bahrain	6.3
Laos	8.3	Saudi Arabia	5.8
Qatar	8.0	Lebanon	5.5
Malaysia	8.0	Myanmar	4.0
Cambodia	7.8	Syria	2.5
Algeria	7.5	Yemen	2.0
Tunisia	7.5	Libya	1.8
Oman	7.5		

Note: Japan, as a member of the Organization for Economic Cooperation and Development (OECD) before 1989, is excluded from the index, as are the smallest East Asian states, Brunei and Timor-Leste, and both territories Hong Kong and Macau. All other East Asian and all Arab states discussed in the chapter are included.

A more reliable indicator of state capacity (and the likelihood of "good governance" and effective policy implementation) may be the existence of bureaucracies recruited through competitive examinations, alluded to earlier. Most of the best and many of the middling performers in East Asia have examination-based recruitment, with Singapore and Hong Kong in particular renowned for their clean and efficient bureaucracies; Singaporean civil servants are paid extraordinarily highly in order to reduce their susceptibility to bribery. Chalmers Johnson likewise found that a highly educated and efficient bureaucracy was central to implementing Japan's developmentalist policies.[68] Even in China, where at minimum toeing the party line (and almost always joining the CCP) are requirements for any aspiring government official, serious efforts to recruit highly skilled technocrats to government administration have been ongoing since the early 1980s. Although corruption remains endemic, periodic campaigns to eradicate it (albeit frequently doubling as an excuse to eliminate political opposition) help demonstrate to the public that central government "serves the people" (*wei renmin fuwu*), as the CCP slogan goes, a tactic that appears to be working; public trust in central government in China is extremely high (though extremely low in local government).[69]

Trust would appear to be a useful, though not the most important, condition for the kind of consensus-generation that might facilitate smooth implementation of education policies. Japan, South Korea, and

Indonesia, for example, score lower on trust than China, but much higher on consensus-building.[70] Although this likely has considerably less to do with commitments to collaborative policymaking and implementation than with electoral democracy in which policy actors must frequently compromise, the fact that China and Vietnam have been able to deliver thoroughgoing and broadly popular education reforms while scoring poorly on consensus-building and other governance indicators validates criticisms of many qualitatively derived, quantitatively represented indexes cited in this chapter and elsewhere. It is often alleged, for example, that liberal Western-centric biases apply inappropriate interpretative frameworks to rate nondemocracies and states outside Europe and North America, and that results are thus unfair or inaccurate.[71]

Whether this is the case or not, it is clear that many of the mature limited access orders "on the doorstep" in East Asia, now and in the past, have what Grindle terms "good enough governance."[72] Together with high degrees of infrastructural power, a feature shared by many mature limited access orders in East Asia, the state has been able to mobilize human and material resources behind an array of policy initiatives. It may even be the case that authoritarian rule, in—and only in—combination with high state capacity and infrastructural penetration, competent and largely meritocratic bureaucracies, and low levels of social conflict, accelerated the development process in some East Asian states because policies and policy implementation were less widely contested or easily resisted. Although there have been regime and political system changes in recent decades, sustained or improved living standards and economic growth and expanded provision of public goods have enabled many democratic and nondemocratic states to retain infrastructural power and public trust.

This has most recently been on display in the region's handling of the COVID-19 pandemic. As with education, "culture," "Confucianism," and "authoritarian" mindsets have duly been trotted out by the foreign press, and even by some scholars, to explain East Asia's success,[73] but rapid nationally coordinated responses, mobilization of state resources to provide testing, contact tracing and personal protective equipment, regular clear communication by experts and leaders, and widespread support for and compliance with containment measures appear more reflective of state capacity and public trust than of culture or political system. That the best performers with COVID-19 are also among the best performers in education lends further support to this hypothesis. In public health-crisis management as in public education, East Asia thus appears, by and large, to tell a convincing story of good enough governance.

Conclusion: Lessons for Arab States?

If there is no uniquely "cultural" basis for East Asia's educational attainment, as this chapter has argued, can the region's successes be replicated elsewhere? Clearly some policymakers hope so. In Australia, for example, declining PISA rankings led to policy recommendations based on the education systems of several high-performing East Asian states.[74] Lessons the United States might learn from these countries were similarly promoted by the OECD.[75] In the Arab world, meanwhile, there is also interest in learning from East Asia. As Springborg shows in Chapter 5, Egypt has recently looked to Japan's education system for inspiration, particularly to the "communal spirit" it endeavors to promote through the *tokkatsu* component of the primary and junior secondary curriculum.[76] The UAE, in particular, has undertaken a sweeping education reform program to foster patriotism and civic virtue, as well as implementing mandatory military service and building a swath of national monuments and museums. While Finland's military service was ultimately selected as the model on which the UAE developed its own system, South Korea and Singapore were examined closely during the preparatory stages, and insights from their experiences in nation-building and delivering high growth and high-level education taken on board. Saudi Arabia is likewise beginning to look East.[77]

It is not hard to see the appeal of East Asian "models" for many Arab states aiming to upskill their populations in anticipation of a post-oil future, with a preference for those East Asian states that are succeeding in economic and educational terms while remaining politically illiberal. Education, however, may have unintended consequences. Educated youth played an important role in the democratic movements that brought down the South Korean, Taiwanese, and Indonesian authoritarian regimes in the 1980s–1990s. They have also been at the center of numerous antigovernment protests, most recently in Hong Kong's 2019 summer of discontent, which challenged the legitimacy of the Special Administrative Region's government, in Indonesia's September 2019 protests against weakening of the country's independent anticorruption watchdog and proposed civil code revisions that would roll back democratic gains, and in Thailand's current youth-led anti-junta demonstrations, calling for the dissolution of parliament and a new constitution. Even China's notoriously iron grip, now enhanced by sophisticated digital surveillance technologies, and extended to Hong Kong via new national security laws, has not prevented protests altogether, although unlike in many neighboring states, the political returns on education have, as in the Arab world and Singapore, generally been in favor of the status quo.[78]

Arab states need not, therefore, necessarily worry about breeding a generation of revolutionaries should they draw on East Asian models to upgrade their education systems to be more competitive in a rapidly transforming global economy. More challenging will be educating policymakers themselves to look beyond East Asia's headline-grabbing successes—PISA scores and tremendous economic growth—to understand the political economies and social structures that have enabled so many parts of East Asia to achieve so much so fast. This involves addressing the challenges of inequality, ethnic diversity, and gender disparities noted earlier, as well as many other problems specific to individual Arab states.

Thus, while there are many lessons that Arab states might learn from diverse East Asian experiences, clearly there are no one-size-fits-all, off-the-rack solutions to reforming education systems, content, and practices that can be straightforwardly transferred to other political, economic, and cultural settings, let alone in short time spans. Transforming the way education administrators, teachers, pupils, and parents think and behave cannot simply be accomplished overnight by executive order, changing laws, or throwing money at new policy initiatives; after all, change, as Hall and Hord so succinctly put it, "is a process, not an event."[79] Education reformers across the Arab world would do well, therefore, to look inward toward their own resources and needs, as well as to the experiences of others, to develop evidence-based reform measures, and thence to proceed with patience.

Notes

1. For information on the content and outcomes of these assessments, see TIMSS, http://www.timss.org, and PISA: http://www.oecd.org/pisa.

2. This began when Germany implemented educational reforms following a poor performance in the first PISA tests in 2000. See OECD, *Germany: Once Weak International Standing Prompts Strong Nationwide Reforms for Rapid Improvement,* http://www.oecd.org/pisa/pisaproducts/46581323.pdf; and Davoli and Entorf, "The PISA Shock, Socioeconomic Inequality, and School Reforms in Germany."

3. This was not, however, the case elsewhere with Shanghai's success similarly generating further bouts of PISA shock in many developed countries. See Jensen, "Catching Up"; and Haugsbakk, "From Sputnik to PISA-Shock." China has since added several other highly developed cities and provinces to its roster, which led to somewhat more modest scores in 2015. An adjusted group of test-takers returned China to the top spot in 2018.

4. Stevenson, Lee, and Stigler, "Mathematics Achievement of Chinese, Japanese, and American Children"; Flynn, *Asian Americans;* and Jerrim, "Why Do East Asian Children Perform So Well in PISA?"

5. Fang, Xu, Grant, Stronge, and Ward, "National Culture, Creativity, and Productivity"; French, French, and Li, "The Relationship Among Cultural Dimensions, Education Expenditure, and PISA Performance"; and Jensen, "Catching Up."

6. World Bank, *The East Asian Miracle.*

7. Xi, "Secure a Decisive Victory in Securing a Moderately Prosperous Society in All Respects and Strive for the Great Success of Socialism with Chinese Characteristics for the New Era." Also, "Commentary: 'A Community with Shared Future for Mankind' Brings Chinese Solutions to Global Governance," *Xinhua,* November 15, 2017, http://www.xinhuanet.com//english/2017-11/15/c_136753896.htm.

8. Herrmann-Pillath, "Fei Xiaotong's Comparative Theory of Chinese Culture"; Hofstede and Bond, "The Confucius Connection"; Zakaria, "Culture Is Destiny"; and Mabhubani, *Can Asians Think?*

9. These tendencies relate to long-standing issues in area studies, as well as to culturalist—and, in the East Asian case, Sinocentric—understandings of "regions" that it is far beyond the scope of this chapter to address. Suffice it to say that I take here a strictly geographical definition, including most states that have their major population and cultural centers and/or most of their territory in the continent's eastern half. Lack of data means that North Korea is excluded. Russia is also excluded as its history and cultural traditions align more closely with Europe's. Mongolia is included, as it shares at least as much with its neighbors to the east and south (as well as Russia/USSR to the north) as with those to the west. States and territories covered here thus include Brunei, Cambodia, China, Hong Kong, Indonesia, Japan, Laos, Macau, Malaysia, Mongolia, Myanmar, Philippines, Singapore, South Korea, Taiwan, Thailand, Timor-Leste, and Vietnam. Taiwan and Macau are included inconsistently in comparative tables as data are not maintained by most multilateral organizations cited here (e.g., UNESCO, UNDP, World Bank). Arab states covered include most of North Africa, the Levant, and the Gulf: Algeria, Bahrain, Egypt, Jordan, Kuwait, Lebanon, Libya, Morocco, Oman, Qatar, Saudi Arabia, Tunisia, the United Arab Emirates, and Yemen. Syria and Palestine are intermittently included where data are available. Iraq is excluded because of extreme data shortage. Comoros, Djibouti, and Sudan are likewise excluded, partly for reasons of data shortage, but also because they compare (unfavorably) only to the very worst performing East Asian states, none of which is discussed in detail here since my focus is on explaining East Asia's successes rather than its failures.

10. UN Sustainable Development Goal 4 calls for the delivery of "Quality Education," which, though a laudable objective, is difficult to define in ways that apply uniformly to all states and societies. Ongoing efforts to measure and standardize quality have led to the development of tests such as TIMSS and PISA, and although UNESCO tracks a range of additional metrics (drop-out rates, repeaters, minimum proficiency levels in reading and writing, etc.), I am not convinced that any of these individual or even aggregated indicators is adequate to define the term *quality* across the board. I thus prefer educational "attainment," "achievement," and "performance" to refer to these outcomes. On HDI, see Anand and Sen, "Human Development Index."

11. Although both Macau and Hong Kong are Special Administrative Regions (SAR) of China, the United Nations provides indicators for Hong Kong, but not for Macau; hence Macau is not ranked on the HDI or EI.

12. World Bank. "GNI per Capita, PPP (current international $)," https://data .worldbank.org/indicator/NY.GNP.PCAP.PP.CD.

13. The two lowest-ranking states, Syria and Yemen, are both currently in conflict, and of the two, only Yemen has consistently had a low HDI and EI. Syria's extremely low ranking is almost entirely attributable to the ongoing conflict. As of 2007, for example, it ranked between Egypt and Indonesia.

14. Lee, Goh, Fredriksen, and Tan, *Toward a Better Future.*

15. UNDP and more recently the OECD provide some support to encourage participation. https://www.oecd.org/pisa/pisa-for-development.

16. UNESCO Institute of Statistics, "Education" ("Participation" and "Progression" datasets), http://data.uis.unesco.org.

17. UNESCO Institute of Statistics, "Education" ("Literacy" dataset), http://data.uis.unesco.org.

18. *State of Education Report,* ASEAN, Jakarta, 2013; UNESCO Institute of Statistics, Sustainable Development Goals, *SDG 4* ("Proficiency" dataset), http://data.uis.unesco.org.

19. http://www.unesco.org/new/en/gefi/home.

20. Thirty percent of Yemen's government expenditure was on education in 2000 and 2001, but these are the only years reported. Statistics are also lacking for many other Arab states not mentioned here. UNESCO Institute of Statistics, "Education" ("Financial Resources" dataset), http://data.uis.unesco.org; Institute for Management Development, *IMD World Talent Ranking,* 2019, https://www.imd.org/research-knowledge/reports/imd-world-talent-ranking-2019.

21. World Bank Data: https://data.worldbank.org/indicator/NY.GNP.PCAP.PP.CD?locations=MY-TH; TIMSS: https://timssandpirls.bc.edu/timss-landing.html; PISA: https://www.compareyourcountry.org/pisa/country/mys?lg=en; https://www.compareyourcountry.org/pisa/country/THA?lg=en.

22. ASEAN, *State of Education Report,* Jakarta, 2013; Ministry of Education, Malaysia, *Malaysia Education Blueprint 2013–2025: Preschool to Post-Secondary Education* (Putrajaya: Kementerian Pendidikan Malaysia); Malaysia Economic Monitor, *High-Performing Education* (Bangkok: World Bank, 2013); Michel, "Education in Thailand"; Wiyaporn and Raksapolmuang, "Education Reform in Thailand."

23. UNESCO Institute of Statistics, "Education" ("Financial Resources" dataset), http://data.uis.unesco.org; Taiwan Ministry of Education, Department of Statistics, https://depart.moe.edu.tw/ED4500.

24. Comparable per pupil data unavailable for UAE and Saudi Arabia, respectively third and fourth highest GNI in the region. Both countries, but particularly UAE with its recent reforms, including Vision 2021 and Education Strategy 2017–2021, likely match or exceed spending by their similarly wealthy neighbors.

25. UNESCO Institute of Statistics, "Education" ("Financial Resources" dataset), http://data.uis.unesco.org; Institute for Management Development, *IMD World Talent Ranking,* 2019, https://www.imd.org/research-knowledge/reports/imd-world-talent-ranking-2019.

26. Vegas and Coffin, "When Education Expenditure Matters."

27. Benstead, in Chapter 6 of this volume; Puryear, "International Education Statistics and Research"; Seth, *Education Fever.*

28. Seth, *Education Fever.*

29. Kipnis and Li, "Is Chinese Education Underfunded?"

30. UNESCO Institute of Statistics, "Education" ("Financial Resources" dataset), http://data.uis.unesco.org.

31. Ibid.; also Bray and Lykins, *Shadow Education;* Hammond, "Corruption in the Classroom"; Kim and Lee, "Private Tutoring and Demand for Education in Korea"; and Zeng, *Dragon Gate.*

32. Kwok, "A Cultural Analysis of Cram Schools in Hong Kong"; Roesgaard, *Japanese Education and the Cram School Business;* "Testing Times," *The Economist,* December 31, 2011, https://www.economist.com/science-and-technology/2006/06/08/testing-times; "Crème de la Cram," *The Economist,* February 19, 2015, https://www.economist.com/asia/2015/09/19/the-creme-de-la-cram.

33. Larmer, "China's Cram Schools"; Sharma, "Asian Parents Suffering 'Education Fever.'"

34. Hammond, "Corruption in the Classroom"; Prum, "Cramming into Extra Classes Ahead of Exams"; Tanamal, "Bimbel Blues."

35. Japan's cram school industry developed in the 1950s to help pupils compete for limited university places. In Korea and Taiwan, it took off during the 1980s, likewise because academic (as opposed to vocational-technical) senior secondary school and university places were limited. Although enrollments have recently slowed, both as a result of fertility declines and expansion of higher education, competition for the "best" schools and universities remains fierce and long study hours in cram schools the norm. Efforts to curb this include, for example, South Korea's curfew on *hagwon* operating hours (2009), and two 2014 laws: Act on the Normalization of Public Education Prohibiting Pre-Studying and Measures on the Reduction of Private Tutoring and Normalization of Public Education. In China, multiple regulations have been issued since the 1990s relating to supplementary tuition or coaching being "offered" to (or forced on) students by schools and teachers, while more recent regulations have targeted the supplementary education sector. Japan has also made efforts to curb sector excesses, in addition to flirting with a more relaxed school curriculum (*yutori*) with fewer study hours in the mid-1990s to early 2000s. However, declining PISA and TIMSS scores, especially in reading, led to this policy being abandoned in the 2008 revised curriculum.

36. OECD, *Education Policy Outlook 2018* (Paris: OECD Publishing, 2018).

37. OECD, *Lessons from PISA for the United States, Strong Performers and Successful Reformers in Education* (Paris: OECD Publishing, 2011), http://dx.doi.org/10.1787/9789264096660-en.

38. Chia, *Education, Culture and the Singapore Developmental State;* Green, *Education and State Formation;* Vickers and Jones, *History Education and National Identity in East Asia.*

39. In Singapore's case, this was also explicitly tied to a fundamental need for "national survival" (Lee, Goh, Fredriksen, and Tan, *Toward a Better Future*). Malaysia switched to a policy of preferential treatment for Malays and other indigenous peoples (Bumiputera) and to Bahasa Malaysia as the national language in the 1970s. Recent reforms have sought to revert to English MOI secondary and tertiary schooling to enhance the country's international competitiveness (Ministry of Education, Malaysia, 2016).

40. Hu, "Orthodoxy over Historicity"; Alisa Jones, "Changing the Past to Serve the Present."

41. Dror, "Education and Politics in Wartime"; Hart, "Creating the National Other."

42. Taiwan Ministry of Education, *Taiwansheng geji xuexiao jiaqiang minzu jingshen jiaoyu shishi gangyao,* 1952; Kim and Jung, "Ideology, Nationalism, and Education."

43. Johnson, *MITI and the Japanese Miracle.*

44. Amsden, *Asia's Next Giant;* Mo and Weingast, *Korean Political and Economic Development;* Wade, *Governing the Market.*

45. In China, for example, the Ministry of Education was for many years directly subordinate to the State Planning Commission and subject to the commission's five-year plans. Taiwan's and South Korea's education policies were also connected to multi-year economic plans.

46. Only Japan, Taiwan (under Japanese rule), the Philippines (under US colonial rule), Thailand, and Mongolia had compulsory primary (and Mongolia also compulsory junior secondary) education before the end of WWII, albeit with varying degrees of compliance. Primary education was technically compulsory in Korea (also a Japanese colony), but not effectively implemented.

47. Chen, "Democratization and Government Education Provision in East Asia."

48. Alaoui and Springborg in Chapter 11 of this volume.

49. More recent investments in public services, such as in expanded secondary and tertiary education access and national healthcare in Taiwan and South Korea, and free and compulsory education in Thailand, have been delivered under democratic rule.

50. PISA scores for pupils even in the bottom socioeconomic deciles of the top-performing East Asian states are close to the mean OECD score (for all students), with particularly strong performances from Hong Kong and Vietnam, and with Japan, Taiwan, and South Korea not far behind. Disparities are much greater in China, as well as among middling-poorer East Asian performers Malaysia, Thailand, and Indonesia. (*Education Policy Outlook 2018* [Paris: OECD Publishing, 2018]).

51. "12 Disqualified for Cheating on Japan's Snow-Delayed University Exams," *Japan Times,* January 16, 2017, https://www.japantimes.co.jp/news/2017/01/16 /national/12-found-cheating-japans-unified-snow-delayed-college-entrance-exams -disqualified; "Shameful Exam Cheating," *Korea Times,* November 12, 2018, https://www.koreatimes.co.kr/www/opinon/2018/11/202_258577.html; "9.4m Students Sit China's Entrance Exam," *Xinhua,* June 7, 2018, http://www.xinhuanet.com/english /2017-06/07/c_136347887.htm. Criminal law in China was revised in 2015 to increase penalties for exam cheating. In response to a recent scandal in Shandong province, the PRC Ministry of Education released a strongly worded statement warning of strict punishments for cheats ahead of the 2020 entrance examinations ("Zui gao biaozhun, zui yan jucuo, quanli yi pu zuohao 2020nian gaokao gongzuo," July 2, 2020, http://www.moe.gov.cn/jyb_xwfb/gzdt_gzdt/s5987/202007/t20200702_469848 .html). China's system is, however, one of the region's more unfair ones, as quotas heavily favoring local (in-province) candidates make entrance requirements higher for out-of-province pupils, limiting access to top institutions, which are overwhelmingly concentrated in a few major cities.

52. Elman, *Civil Examinations and Meritocracy in Late Imperial China;* Suen and Yu, "Chronic Consequences of High-Stakes Testing?"

53. Teng, "Chinese Influence on the Western Examination System."

54. In China, in particular, access to the ladder was open; almost any man able to access an education could take the examinations. Korea's hereditary nobility and rigid class system, by contrast, greatly limited who could sit for the examinations.

55. Weber's claims of a "Protestant work ethic" as the root of capitalism, juxtaposed to Catholic indolence are of this type (Weber, *The Protestant Work Ethic and the Spirit of Capitalism*). European colonialists, in turn, arrogated these virtues to themselves in contrast to "decadent" and "lazy" "Orientals."

56. Deuchler, *The Confucian Transformation of Korea;* Woodside, "Territorial Order and Collective-Identity Tensions in Confucian Asia."

57. Student-led protests helped bring down the Rhee regime in South Korea in 1961; a popular movement demanding education reform coincided with the democratization process in Taiwan in 1994; Hongkongers demonstrated in 2012 against Beijing's efforts to impose "national education"; and in China, parents protested against stricter invigilation of examinations in 2013, and against criminalization of examination cheating in 2016.

58. EIU classification of regime type has many flaws, not least of which is the small number of country specialist assessors involved, but it does not appear to be any less flawed than Polity IV, which in 2018 categorized Myanmar on par with South Korea and above Malaysia, Indonesia, and Tunisia.

59. North, Wallis, and Weingast, "A Conceptual Framework for Interpreting Recorded Human History"; North, Wallis, Webb, and Weingast, "Limited Access Orders"; North, Wallis, Webb, and Weingast, *In the Shadow of Violence.*

60. East Asia's experience does not appear to have been considered in formulating the theory, and few scholars have applied it to the region. Rare exceptions include two chapters in the above-cited volume by North et al., *In the Shadow of*

Violence; Montinola, "Change and Continuity in a Limited Access Order"; and You, "Transition from a Limited Access Order to an Open Access Order."

61. Lee Jones's 2014 analysis of Myanmar's transition makes only limited reference to LAO theory, but demonstrates clearly the ways in which coalitions of interests have formed between business and the military, as well as the potential for these coalitions to collapse. See Lee Jones, "The Political Economy of Myanmar's Transition."

62. Mann, "The Autonomous Power of the State"; also Alaoui and Springborg in Chapter 1 of this volume.

63. Bertelsmann Transformation Index, https://www.bti-project.org/en/data; Linz and Stepan, *Problems of Democratic Transition and Consolidation.*

64. More than 700 languages are recognized in Indonesia and more than 150 in the Philippines. Filipino students were PISA tested in English, which 94 percent of the test-takers do not speak at home (PISA, "Philippines: Country Note," 2018, https://www.oecd.org/pisa/publications/PISA2018_CN_PHL.pdf).

65. Birdsall, Ross, and Sabot, "Inequality and Growth Reconsidered." Income inequality has been trending upward in recent years, however, particularly in China, Hong Kong, Singapore, Malaysia, and the Philippines. It has been rising more slowly and remains at or slightly above average European levels in Japan, South Korea, Taiwan, Thailand, and Indonesia.

66. UNESCO Institute of Statistics, "Education" ("Literacy" dataset), http://data.uis.unesco.org.

67. Bertelsmann Transformation Index, https://www.bti-project.org/en/data.

68. Johnson, *MITI and the Japanese Miracle.*

69. Edelman Trust Barometer (2001–2019), https://www.edelman.com/research/edelman-trust-barometer-archive.

70. Ibid.; also Bertelsmann Transformation Index, https://www.bti-project.org/en/data.

71. A normative liberal democratic point of departure is explicitly acknowledged by the Bertelsmann Project itself (https://www.bti-project.org/en/about/project/faq). See Pickel, Stark, and Breustedt, "Assessing the Quality of Measures of Democracy"; Tasker, "The Flawed 'Science' Behind Democracy Rankings"; Völkel, "Complex Politics in Single Numbers?"

72. Grindle, "Good Enough Governance."

73. Han, "La emergencia viral y el mundo de mañana"; Tagliapietra, "What If the Rest of Europe Follows Italy's Coronavirus Fate?"

74. Jensen, "Catching Up."

75. *Lessons from PISA for the United States, Strong Performers and Successful Reformers in Education* (Paris: OECD Publishing, 2011), http://dx.doi.org/10.1787/9789264096660-en.

76. *Tokkatsu* is a contraction of *tokubetsu katsudo,* or "special activities," which include both communal tasks (cleaning classrooms and other school spaces) and student-organized activities, such as school clubs and newspapers (http://www.p.u-tokyo.ac.jp/~tsunelab/tokkatsu; http://www.p.u-tokyo.ac.jp/~tsunelab/tokkatsu/edwc). As Springborg shows, it is unlikely that the "holistic education" of which *tokkatsu* is intended to be a part has been the primary motivation for Sisi and his allies' interest in the "Japanese model."

77. CSIS, 2018, Citizens in Training (podcast series), https://www.csis.org/podcasts/citizens-training; Calvert W. Jones, "New Approaches to Citizen-Building."

78. Ishac Diwan in Chapter 2 of this volume.

79. Hall and Hord, *Implementing Change.*

11

The Challenges of Educational Reform in the Arab World

Hicham Alaoui and Robert Springborg

The question this volume has addressed is why Arab edu-cational quality remains low despite robust efforts by analysts, practitioners, and international organizations to comprehend the causes and address them. The answer in a nutshell is that suggested reforms have focused primarily on overcoming technical constraints and improving access and infrastructure, rather than on systemic problems rooted in the region's political economies. These more profound constraints are remarkably similar across Arab countries. They reflect the regionwide political economy stemming primarily from dependence on hydrocarbon exports and, to a lesser extent, foreign aid and other exogenous capital, resulting in what neoinstitutional economists call limited-access orders.

Limited-access orders are political economies structured to aggrandize political power and economic rewards to the benefit of "insider" elites, while denying them to everyone else, lumped together as "outsiders." Contemporary Arab insiders are of two types: successors to the military officers and monarchs who took power at independence; and their accomplices, key of whom are cronies with whom they share rents and specialists in coercion and manipulation of publics. The negative consequences of limited-access orders for economic growth have recently been subject to extensive empirical investigation, but this volume is the first to apply findings and methods from that literature specifically to the education component of the service sector of economies. In sum, if there is a solution to the chronic underperformance of Arab educational systems, that solution must engage underlying political and economic problems first—not simply technical or pedagogical issues regarding the practice of instruction.

The chapters illustrate in different Arab settings common impacts of limited-access orders at all educational levels. Before we review these consequences, however, the relative similarities of Arab educational systems should be emphasized. A strong indicator of the regionalized nature of Arab educational systems is that most have been swept by the same three waves since independence. The initial one, immediately following independence, reflected what Merilee Grindle has in this volume (Chapter 9) and elsewhere identified as "access" reform. This took the form of expansion of educational systems at all levels, the push factor being creation of new educational resources including buildings, instructors, and educational materials; the pull factor being public employment for graduates, initially even those from secondary schools. This wave was driven by both the political exuberance associated with independence and the relative abundance of resources, whether inherited from the colonial power or resulting from the first oil boom, which commenced in 1973.

The waning of exhilaration associated with independence was coterminous with the decline of oil prices from the mid-1980s, with these two trends contributing to a second educational wave in the form of a further dramatic increase in university student enrollments in both absolute numbers and proportions of age cohorts. While expanded university enrollments were driven in part by growth of student throughput from lower levels, they also resulted from regime strategies to appease potentially politically active youths for whom insufficient jobs were available. The links between university education and public, indeed virtually all types of employment, were weakened, so that education, especially at the tertiary level, became not a pathway to success, but for many if not most youths merely a holding pen into which regimes directed them to avert political mobilization. Access to primary, secondary, and university education was not seen primarily as a means to build human capital and a civic society, but more as a means to ensure acquiescence. The limits of that strategy were revealed throughout the region by uprisings that commenced in 2011 and have bubbled up in various Arab countries since.

A third wave of educational change and the focus of this volume is now sweeping through the region, driven primarily by the increased desperation, or what might also be described as the greater realism, of incumbent regimes. Under increased budgetary pressures resulting from the downturn of hydrocarbon prices since 2014 and the direct and indirect economic pressures this has put on all Arab countries, now exacerbated by the 2020 pandemic, most regimes are seeking to limit and channel expenditures on education. In the regionwide absence of effective political parties and the declining efficacy of personalized patronage networks resulting from expanding populations, regimes are also seeking to use education as a vehicle through which to recruit cadres of politically loyal administrators and technocrats.

Regimes are thus further stratifying educational systems, implicitly abandoning the aspiration to achieve reasonable-quality universal education. They are seeking to reinforce their limited-access orders with technically competent, politically loyal products of increasingly differentiated educational systems. The promise to create "knowledge economies" based on enhanced human resources is more political sloganeering than a carefully conceived strategy of economic growth, which would require more encompassing, meritocratic human resource development. Aware that unemployment or marginal (part-time or informal) employment is the fate awaiting significant proportions of graduates of secondary schools and universities, regimes are seeking educational cost savings coupled with political containment. The bright hopes for education of the immediate post-independence period have given way to what seems a callous, if realistic, calculation by Arab elites that they will be unable to fulfill the aspirations of significant proportions of youths. To preserve their limited-access orders they instead are quietly reconfiguring and further stratifying their educational systems.

Paradoxically, this last wave to sweep through Arab educational systems does not result from increased regionalism, if by that term is meant something analogous to say the European Union (EU) and its facilitation of cross-border movement of goods, services, capital, and people. Indeed, Arab unity in fact and even in sloganeering has steadily receded since reaching its zenith more than a generation ago. Not only is inter-Arab migration as a proportion of total populations substantially lower than it was from the mid-1970s to the 1990s, but so too has the proportion of Arab students who study in another Arab country declined. Academic import substitution has swept across the region, with virtually all countries having now established kindergarten through PhD educational institutions, with national universities increasingly complemented by branches of non-Arab universities.

Higher-education import substitution has in the case of Saudi Arabia, Algeria, and some other wealthy hydrocarbon exporters been further supplemented by generous governmental support for overseas study, overwhelmingly in the West, although increasingly also in Asia. The days when relatively large numbers of Yemenis, Sudanese, Libyans, and others went to Egypt for secondary school and university educations, or Syrians, Iraqis, Palestinians, and Arabs from the Gulf to Lebanon, are past. It is paradoxical, therefore, that ever-growing similarity of Arab educational systems as they have passed through these three waves results less from shared inter-Arab educational experiences of political and administrative elites than from common forces driving their political economies, and hence their educational systems. Those forces now propelling the third wave are the structural features of Arab political economies combined with the content of economic and educational policies as well as the processes by which those policies are made.

Structural Drivers of the Third Wave of Arab Education

Educational policies are influenced by four structural characteristics of Arab political economies—inadequate economic growth, rapidly expanding and youthful populations, inequality, and state capacities below levels predicted by gross domestic products (GDPs) per capita. The first two characteristics are closely interrelated, as rapidly expanding populations require high rates of aggregate economic growth to achieve competitive improvements in GDP per capita. As the World Bank noted in 2018, "growth forecasts of about 2 to 3 percent are well below the high rates that prevailed between 2005 and 2010," during which time "youth unemployment in the MENA [Middle East and North Africa] region . . . averaged 24 per cent."[1] Even those less-than-optimistic growth forecasts have not been realized. Indeed, the International Monetary Fund (IMF) reports that in 2019 real GDP growth in the Middle East was the world's lowest, at –1.2 percent.[2] By comparison, emerging-market and developing economies as a whole grew in 2019 at an average annual rate of 3.9 percent.[3] For MENA as a whole, aggregate GDP growth slid from 1.2 percent in 2018 to 0.6 percent in 2019.[4] GDP per capita in that region declined by 0.6 percent in 2018 and by 0.9 percent in 2019.[5] Forecast GDP per capita growth for the Middle East and North Africa through 2021 was predicted by the World Bank in late 2019 to recover to an average of 1.3 percent, but it cautioned that there are "considerable downside risks."[6] The risk not anticipated by the Bank was the pandemic that commenced in early 2020, causing it to revise its estimates for GDP downward into negative territory for almost all MENA countries. Particularly worrisome is that GDP per capita growth is inversely related to relative national income, as the richer economies stagnate even more than the poorer ones, suggesting that many MENA countries are caught in middle-income traps resulting from low productivity growth.[7] In sum, the Arab world and Iran—the countries other than

Djibouti that constitute the World Bank's MENA region—are economically stagnating, especially so if the measure is per capita rather than gross national income (GNI).

This is ominous. Despite declining fertility rates in the region, the momentum of population growth is accelerating such that MENA's total population by 2090 is forecast to be in excess of 1 billion, larger than China's or Europe's.[8] Demography and unemployment dovetail here in systematic ways. The median age of a MENA resident is twenty-five—the second-youngest in the world, behind only sub-Saharan Africa—and within the Arab countries, a third of the populace is fourteen years of age or younger, and nearly another third are between fifteen and twenty-nine. The regional youth unemployment rate of 27 percent not only is the highest figure in the world, but also has remained stable for nearly two decades, creating an entire generational experience defined by job scarcity and economic underachievement.[9] That youths' prospects are truly grim is further suggested by the fact that the Arab world's labor force participation rate of 50.9 percent is the lowest for any world region or category of states, such as middle-income.[10]

Downward economic coupled with upward demographic trends have profound implications for governments. Even ignoring those millennials who have graduated from school and are seeking work, policymakers with fewer per capita resources must cope with the next generation down—large and expanding school-age populations. In Egypt, for example, over 20 million young people—almost the country's entire population only two generations ago—are presently enrolled in schools or universities, with the number of new entrants exceeding 2 million annually. Expanding educational capacities to meet this rising demographic tide would be a challenge even in rapidly growing economies. In stagnating ones, responding to the growing proportions of the ever-larger number of those in age cohorts seeking rewarding primary, secondary, and post-secondary educations requires very skillful balancing of priorities coupled with effective resource allocations.

These profound challenges have only been partially met. The result, as noted by the World Bank, is that "youth in MENA have achieved much higher education levels than their parents, more than any region in the world." Access reforms have produced in MENA "the highest intergenerational mobility in education in the world." Unfortunately, however, "mobility in income is low," so "returns to education in the labor market are among the lowest in the world."[11] Part of the explanation of such low returns is due to the failure to implement quality reforms. Allocating more public resources to education would help, but it would not be a cure-all. At present, MENA countries spend 4 percent of national income on education, a reasonable proportion by global standards.[12] Much of that is misspent, but even discounting misallocation, the pressures of rapidly expanding populations coupled with low-growth economies that produce declining revenues per capita and generate too few jobs to absorb graduates, require overhaul of existing educational and broader economic policies rather than just more funding.

Further exacerbating the problems of declining resources per capita and their misallocation is the unequal distribution of those resources. Inequality is marked both within political economies as a whole and in educational sectors specifically, with profoundly negative consequences for the latter. Gini coefficients for the MENA region are much higher than those for East Asia and Latin America, and so the general context within which educational services are delivered is not conducive to balanced educational achievements as typically produced in more equitable political economies. Recent work on inequality in MENA, moreover, drawing on a wider range of data than that traditionally used to produce Gini coefficients, suggests that inequality is much greater than previously thought.[13] Research supported by the World Inequality Database reveals the dramatically rising share in Lebanon, for example, of national income captured by those in the top 10 percent—about 60 percent—coupled with the declining share of those in the bottom half—about 10 percent. Fully one-quarter of national income accrues to 1 percent of the Lebanese population, "placing Lebanon among the countries with the highest level of income inequality in the world."[14] Alvaredo and Piketty's recent work on Egypt has found similarly high levels of inequality.[15] In MENA as a whole, the top income decile captures just less than two-thirds of gross national income, as compared to 37 percent for Western Europe, 47 percent for the United States, and 55 percent for Brazil.[16]

Within the educational sector, inequality characterizes allocation of and access to governmental resources and so plays a crucial role in determining educational outcomes. Middle-income MENA countries spend approximately 50 percent more in terms of their GDPs per capita than extra-regional comparators on upper-secondary education, and double the proportion spent by Organization for Economic Cooperation and Development (OECD) countries on tertiary education.[17] MENA countries as a whole commit the lowest amount of public resources proportionately to educationally vital preschool education of any global region.[18] The general rule of thumb for educational expenditures, violated in every Arab country, is that the larger the proportion spent on lower levels of education, the greater the benefits for learning and for achieving broader educational equality.

The impacts of inequality on educational outcomes are profound and varied, as two chapters in this volume indicate. Ishac Diwan (Chapter 2) attributes some of the low political return to Arab education to it being conducted in highly unequal societies where "the more educated (and, therefore, richer) individuals may fear that they would be taxed more in a democratic regime." The beneficiaries of educational resources thus tend to resist reforms. Lindsay Benstead's Tunisian data (Chapter 6) suggest to her that school quality is accounted for by "the socioeconomic and educational level of the parent," as well as by "the funding and management of the school system itself at the local level," both factors in turn shaped by overall inequality. Assaad and Krafft's empirical investigations of inequality's impacts on primary education in Egypt report similar findings. They conclude that "free basic education in Egypt is failing Egyptian children," who have to cope with "a distorted system where there is substantial inequality in succeeding in basic education depending on a child's family circumstances."[19]

For its part, the World Bank's major 2019 study of education in MENA revealed its highly unequal outcomes, such that it "has the biggest gaps in student achievement between top and bottom performers" of any global region.[20] The Bank's previous study had noted that "the education Gini coefficients for the MENA region are much higher than those of East Asia and Latin America, indicating more inequality in education in MENA."[21] Partly as a result of persisting educational inequality in MENA, increasing access to it, unlike in Latin America and East Asia, "does not seem to have contributed much to greater income equality."[22] In the vernacular, inequality in, inequality within, and inequality out characterize the societal context and consequences of educational policies and their impacts on student achievements.

The final structural impediment to improved educational outcomes posed by Arab political economies is that state capacities are below levels predicted by per capita and gross national incomes. Even if educational policies were appropriate, the ability to implement them is not of the standard found in most comparator countries.

State capacities consist of two basic types—those relevant to managing populations or managing economies. The former type, of more direct relevance to education, refers both to inclusion—integrating citizens into public life—and to developing human resources through provision of educational and health services. Inclusion is typically measured by comparative institutional performances of bureaucracies and representative bodies. Arab administrations suffer from the maladies of over-centralization, absence of merit-based recruitment and promotion, excessive size, and stove-piping. On the most relevant global indexes of administrative performance, the Government Closeness Index and the World Bank's Global Indicators of Regulatory Governance, the MENA countries perform extremely poorly, suggesting that those administrations fail adequately to extend public services in effective, impersonal fashion. As for representative bodies, the Parliamentary Powers Index reveals MENA parliaments to be the world's weakest, while the Arab Democracy Index reports a profound gap between formal legal provisions and their implementation, reflecting the inability of MENA parliaments to compel implementation of the laws they enact.

Poor governmental provision of education and health services, as is reflected in outcomes measured by comparative evaluations, parallels and reinforces deficiencies in facilitating inclusion. The gap between actual years of school and learning-adjusted years, on average in the MENA just under three, is greater than that of any other region.[23] On the World Bank's Human Capital Index, educational attainment and personal health in all MENA countries fall below levels that should be attained based on their relative wealth. Unlike state capacities for both inclusion and economic management, however, standardized direct measures of education and health services, as opposed to indirect measures based on their consequences, have yet to be adequately developed.

It is nevertheless clear from available quantitative and qualitative evidence that Arab state capacities are remarkably weak in comparison to averages for other countries at similar levels of economic development.[24] At first glance this underperformance seems hard to explain. If it were just a matter of improving administrative performance, surely one or even a few of the more than twenty Arab countries would have accomplished this by now. Many Arab states, including Egypt, Morocco, and Tunisia, have reasonably impressive histories of "stateness" and the capacities allegedly associated with it, whereas others, most notably those in the Gulf Cooperation Council (GCC), have imported from the West administrative forms, processes, and even personnel.[25] So, the historical path-dependency of some Arab states and the financial and political abilities of some others to import administrative models should have led a few at least to develop better capacities.

The answer to the puzzle is that the limited-access orders at the heart of Arab political economies are inimical to the development of state capacities, especially those regarding inclusion of citizens and development of their human resources. These capacities depend heavily upon effective, extensive relations between citizens and government with both sides benefiting from those interactions—that is, upon Michael Mann's "infrastructural power." The very logic of limited-access orders, however, is "separate and unequal," with insiders having privileged access to political and economic power and outsiders receiving through grace and favor some material benefits on the understanding they will not demand political access. True citizenship, based on rights and responsibilities, is discouraged and indeed antithetical to limited-access orders, and so infrastructural power is inherently weak. The very low political returns to education reported in this volume by Diwan reflect the weakness of citizenship, as do the Egyptian, Moroccan, and Tunisian curricular materials reviewed by Roel Meijer (Chapter 3) that are used in secondary school "citizenship" courses, but what in reality are didactic presentations of national history intended to glorify regimes.

In sum, the toxic combination of inadequate economic resources with rapid demographic growth, of inequality, and of inadequate state capacities—all due largely to the shortcomings of Arab political systems—has propelled the third wave, battering Arab educational systems. Thus far policy responses have been inadequate both in content and in method of adoption.

Policy Drivers of the Third Wave of Arab Education

Contemporary Arab education policy reforms are analogous to previous neoliberal economic ones adopted to cope with various pressures resulting primarily from the rising wave of globalization in the 1990s. Those top-down reforms were intended by incumbent elites not to truly liberalize political economies, but to preserve limited-access orders by generating new resources for insiders, some of which would in turn provide patronage to service clientele networks and decaying social contracts. The net result was an economically stagnant crony capitalism sustaining authoritarianism rather than a dynamic, private sector–led economy driving political liberalization.

Just as the reformist purposes of economic privatization were subverted by cronies and their political patrons who cooperated to capture state resources and control markets, so too is privatization of education unlikely to be a textbook case of success. As Christopher Davidson has illustrated (Chapter 7), US university-branch campuses in Gulf Arab states are intended by their government sponsors to serve political more than educational purposes, key of the former being bolstering soft power. The Algerian and Saudi governments have sent vast numbers of students abroad for university educations, according to Adel Hamaizia and Andrew Leber (Chapter 8) more for the political reasons of providing patronage and deterring domestic radicalism than for skill enhancement relevant to their national economies. Among the evidence they proffer in support of their argument are low return rates for Algerian students and low economic absorption rates for Saudi returnees. Although not strictly privatization, educating students abroad absorbs public resources that otherwise could be invested in domestic public educational institutions. In poorer countries, such as Egypt, privatization is intended primarily to relieve budgetary burdens and to facilitate elite recruitment rather than to serve as a thin edge of the wedge of broad pedagogical reform. Indeed, as Robert Springborg argues (Chapter 5), the Egyptian regime is intensifying its surveillance of and direct control over private educational institutions, including their language of instruction, curricula, program offerings, and even their personnel, while also seeking to gain soft power and revenues from their presence, especially that of foreign universities. Privatization is more likely to exacerbate rather than resolve educational shortcomings resulting from inequality, while also shoring up limited-access orders by facilitating selective elite recruitment rather than by broadening minds and laying educational foundations for citizenship. Invoking the analogy to its economic counterpart, educational privatization is likely to create "crony students" dependent upon the state and its political and economic largesse rather than to encourage in students the norms and means of achieving true personal political and economic independence. This in fact is the central finding of Calvert Jones's investigation into the consequences of elite private education in the United Arab Emirates (UAE).[26]

Other policies are unlikely to convert educational systems into motor forces of knowledge economies or liberalized political orders. Attracting donor support for public education seems intended as much to gain resources to ameliorate public criticism of low and ineffective governmental expenditures on education as actually to improve educational performance. If it were the latter, then the canons of good educational policy, such as enabling stakeholder participation and granting increased autonomy to educational institutions and professionals, would be more manifest. Disinterest in facilitating professionalization of the norms, capabilities, and organizations of educators combined with efforts to subordinate them to ever-tighter central control suggests that regimes do not want to empower key stakeholders and certainly not to upgrade them to participate in policymaking. This is true not just of primary and secondary school teachers, but also, as Florian Kohstall's comparison shows (Chapter 4), of Moroccan and Egyptian university academic staff seeking to participate in efforts to reform and internationalize their respective country's tertiary educational systems—so too does it apply at that level, albeit more so in the case of Egypt. The greater autonomy of university presidents and their institutions in Morocco, combined with more engagement with EU educational institutions, to say nothing of the country's more open political system, creates space within which policy-focused professional interaction can occur. But even in the relatively conducive Moroccan educational environment, tentacles of central control limit the policy influence of professionals and their organizations.

Preoccupation with political control is ubiquitous and deleterious for both the content of educational policies and the means by which they are determined. The attraction of computer-based teaching and learning—so-called EdTech—is less the potential to upgrade student abilities and skills than to assert more effective, direct control over them and their instructors, as the Egyptian case reviewed by Springborg (Chapter 5) illustrates.[27] The curricular issue of how much importance to assign the teaching of religion and in many Arab countries the key pedagogical issue of the language(s) in which students should be taught remain very much alive.[28] That they are nowhere close to being resolved reflects governmental inability and unwillingness to address vital sociopolitical issues involved in education and inadequate participation in decisionmaking by relevant stakeholders. Positive reference to and utilization of putative Asian educational models, coupled with regime skepticism and outright criticism of traditional liberal ones, appears driven less by appreciation of possible pedagogical advantages than by the belief that the ideal-typical Asian model is more supportive of authoritarianism. Creation of elitist public and private educational institutions, such as those in Egypt and the UAE, appears to be driven more by regime desire to shape loyal, trained supporters and the channels for their recruitment than by purely educational considerations.

Like the content of educational policies, the process by which they are made is also flawed. Grindle's observation (Chapter 9) that not all stakeholders in education are decisionmakers highlights the overall weakness of infrastructural power of Arab states. Those within limited-access orders will not empower outsiders by including them in decisionmaking processes even if their participation would improve policy outputs. At the systemic level, Arab political economies have not generated the class bases upon which external pressures can be applied to government to improve educational policy. Crony capitalism has disempowered the private sector bourgeoisie, traditional advocates of quality education, while further weakening and subordinating public employees. Despairing of prospects to improve public education, those with adequate material resources vote with their children's feet, sending them to private schools, a move tacitly supported by policymakers seeking to husband public funds. Grindle also notes that change teams in Latin America have typically been based in educational bureaucracies. Kohstall's analysis of Moroccan university reforms (Chapter 4) points to at least this example of something similar in the Arab world. But in most of the Arab world the lack of meritocratic civil services and of reformers within them, as well as their marginalization from policymaking, preclude civil servant reformers from contributing effectively to education policy. Finally, as noted previously, the Arab world and education within it is "de-regionalizing," as proportionately ever fewer Arabs have living and educational experiences in other Arab countries. As nationalism supplants Arabism at this practical level, it militates against learning experiences in similar environments that might then be applied "back home." In East Asia the so-called flying geese model, in which first Japan, then others including China and South Korea, led the flock of states in their journey toward economic growth, was paralleled in education, as Alisa Jones notes (Chapter 10). There is no flying goose for other Arab states to follow in reforming economic or educational policies. In sum, neither structural features of Arab political economies nor the making or content of policies are conducive to educational reforms. This begs the questions of if and how reform might come about within existing orders.

What Is to Be Done?

Since the track record of reform of Arab education is so poor and the durability of at least the model if not necessarily the incumbents in limited-access orders so striking, it is hard to be optimistic about the prospects for substantial, incremental improvement of Arab educational systems. On the other hand, possibly the darkest hour is that just before dawn. And if one scans the contemporary horizon of Arab political economies, there are faint glimmers that a new day for Arab education could be dawning.

At the systemic level, the most obvious glimmer is the decade-long series of Arab uprisings. They reflect grave dissatisfaction with the status quo, including with the quality of public services, of which education together with its broken linkage to employment, according to the World Bank's investigation, is at the top of the list.[29] Regimes are under pressure to react to popular demand for educational reforms. Several have embarked on cautious reforms intended to square the circle of preserving insider privileges while reducing popular discontent by opening up access to and improving the quality of education and other public services. This is inherently a slippery slope down which limited reforms, once adopted, could gain momentum that ultimately penetrates the limited-access order's hegemonic position, at least in the field of education if not more broadly.

The "transitology" literature that arose some two decades ago to describe transitions to democracy, especially from military rule in Latin America, describes the political calculus responsible for such changes. The core idea is that reformers on the inside of regimes coalesce with those on the outside, thereby marginalizing hardliners and ultimately displacing them. Whether this model is applicable to the tougher Arab political world, and whether it could apply in a specific policy area such as education, are open questions. If one had to bet, it would be that one or more Arab regimes will implement substantial educational reforms, either because the "soft-liners" within them will begin to experiment more actively, including in coalition with those on the outside demanding reforms, or that reforms initiated even by hardliners will gather momentum more or less of their own accord, pushed along by the very currents now driving popular discontent.

Given this, at least in theory educational reform is possible within the existing order, but with a caveat. In studies of democratization, such political shifts are typically caused by a crisis or rupture, such as economic breakdown, defeats in foreign wars, or political scandals, that compel actors in power to creatively rethink their existing approaches. The Arab Spring, the latest wave of uprisings that began most notably in Algeria and Lebanon in 2019, and the 2020 pandemic have all revealed endemic shortcomings of governance, but neither singly nor collectively have they yet propelled systemic educational reforms. Their intensity and frequency, however, suggest capacity to do so. Arab uprisings have signaled profound dissatisfaction with the status quo especially with inadequate provision of public services. The 2020 pandemic has revealed the literally deadly consequences of neglect of many Arab healthcare systems, to which those regimes responded by suppression of relevant information and repression of critics. Inadequate provision of quality education and medical care at affordable prices is now a principal driver of mass discontent, to which the response has invariably been to securitize the issue rather than to seek effectively to resolve it, including most graphically in the case of COVID-19. Previously such inadequacies were subordinated by regimes and by their populaces to ideological concerns, such as nationalism, the struggle against Israel, or those arising out of religious commitment. This, coupled with what amounted to the rationing of public goods through patronage systems, was sufficient for deficiencies to be more acceptable. Now, however, as World Bank studies and relevant survey data reveal, to say nothing of the chants of protesters, demand for improved and equitable service delivery has largely supplanted more amorphous ideological concerns. This push for reform of public-service delivery, including of education, is likely to continue, even intensify. It is driven by economic and demographic fundamentals including those just discussed as well as by urbanization, increased competition for formal private sector employment, greater gender equality, and spillover effects from inter-Arab social media that are to some extent replacing firsthand inter-Arab experiences for youths.

A related awareness factor might become that of cognizance of comparative performance. Heretofore the various standardized, global measures of societal-wide educational achievement, such as PISA, TIMSS, or the various rankings of the world's top 300 or 500 universities, have largely passed unnoticed by Arab publics, partly because regimes have not wanted this information to be disseminated. But that is changing as a result of these rankings appearing more frequently in global media, as well as because Arab leaders, including Egypt's President Sisi, are making ever more reference to them in attempts to proclaim national educational successes, presumably because they are aware of public dissatisfaction with the general absence of such. Globalization, in other words, creates demands for improved performance. At some stage at least some of those within limited-access orders may decide that reform is a more effective response than repression to ever-growing pressure for change, thus opening the door to insider-outsider reform coalitions.

Developments already under way may also contribute momentum to educational reform. As Kohstall has pointed out (Chapter 4) with regard to Egypt and Morocco, bilateral and multilateral donors can and do foster change teams within recipient educational systems. These teams might be deemed analogous to Arab human rights organizations also supported by external actors, something typically seized upon by repressive regimes to discredit those organizations. There are echoes of this in the politics of education in the Arab world, suggesting that regimes are aware of the reform leverage that external actors can apply. It is possible such leverage will be intensified as donors become more dissatisfied with the recalcitrance of recipients, or that those recipient regimes, more aware and fearful of public demands for quality-enhancing reforms, will grant donors greater leeway. Donors, moreover, are not just behemoths like the World Bank, the European Union, or the United States. They also include a host of smaller, typically private organizations that sponsor relatively small, unobtrusive projects, such as Tamam, but whose demonstration effects may in the aggregate not only contribute to demands for reform, but also provide appropriate models for it.[30] The Soros Foundation's support for tertiary education in Eastern Europe and regime reactions against it, however, illustrate the potential for backlash against such undertakings.

Educational innovations typically introduced by external actors but embraced by Arab governments may have unpredicted, unintended consequences. EdTech has been widely embraced in the Arab world, primarily because it seems to offer regimes enhanced control over all participants in educational systems as well as possible cost savings. Yet if the internet is a precedent, providing the basis for social media as it has, computerization of education might also have liberating side effects for students and their instructors. Among them could be reduced reliance on rote learning, on canonical texts, and on central authority sources in general. In their stead, more horizontal, user-guided learning techniques could flourish, thereby challenging vertically structured educational and political systems. Privatization might have a similar, equally unintended liberating effect. Arab regimes are seeking to square the circle of encouraging privatization while ensuring control of that sector, as the Egyptian case demonstrates. The methods of that control seem more obtrusive than those deployed in public education, where the whip-hand of control over salaries and other resources is paramount. So, it can be predicted with some confidence that those involved in private sector education will chafe at the bits governments seek to insert into their systems, among other things signaling to students that governments don't know best and that challenging their authority is acceptable, even preferable. In sum, a regime intent to improve at least some components of educational systems while maintaining, even enhancing, control over the sector and those in it, may prove to be a contradictory undertaking.

Conclusion

The points raised in this concluding chapter emerged from discussions among the contributors to the book and are illustrated in one or more previous chapters. They consist of diverse observations and even predictions, and so cannot be said to be firmly empirically grounded. That is consistent with the purpose of the volume, which was intended not to test hypotheses, but to speculate on various impacts Arab political economies have on their educational systems. This then is a tour of that horizon, not a definitive investigation of causes and consequences of specific such linkages. Its goal is to broaden perspectives on Arab education and factors shaping it so that efforts to improve it can include both fundamental and proximate technical causes. While important, donor and even analytical focus on the latter has left largely unaddressed the context within which specific educational problems arise and might best be addressed. Like all other aspects of public policy, that for education is driven by political concerns, which in Arab limited-access orders have been almost exclusively those of insiders seeking to preserve that status. Unless and until significant stakeholders in education are transformed into participants in decisionmaking about the sector, it will continue to underperform.

Notes

1. MENA Economic Monitor, Washington, World Bank, October 2018, p. 75. The only non-Arab countries included in the World Bank's MENA category are Iran, Djibouti, and Malta, the last of which is not included in this or the following data.

2. IMF Data Mapper, October 2019, https://www.imf.org/external/datamapper /NGDP_RPCH@WEO/OEMDC/ADVEC/WEOWORLD.

3. Ibid.

4. *Reaching New Heights,* MENA Economic Update, October 2019, http:// pubdocs.worldbank.org/en/660811570642119982/EN-MEM-ReachingNewHeights -OCT-19.pdf, p. 4.

5. Ibid.

6. Ibid., p. 6.

7. MENA Economic Monitor, October 2018, p. 30.

8. McKee et al., "Demographic and Economic Material Factors in the MENA Region."

9. Yom, "The Youth Generation," pp. 319–322.

10. https://data.worldbank.org/indicator/sl.tlf.acti.zs.

11. El-Kogali and Krafft, *Expectations and Aspirations,* p. 3.

12. Tunisia, for example, spends 20.6 percent of its national budget on education, almost double the OECD average. But while it is the case that the average proportion of state budgets allocated to education in MENA is relatively high, it has been declining for some two decades, "from a median level of 20.6 percent in 2000 (5.9 percent of GDP) to 13 percent in 2016 (4 percent of GDP)." Ibid., p. 51.

13. See, for example, Alvaredo and Piketty, "Measuring Top Income and Inequality in the Middle East."

14. https://wid.world/country/lebanon. See also Assouad, "Rethinking the Lebanese Economic Miracle."

15. Alvaredo and Thomas Piketty, "Measuring Top Income and Inequality in the Middle East."

16. Alvaredo, Assouad, and Piketty, "Measuring Inequality in the Middle East 1990–2016."

17. *The Road Not Travelled: Education Reform in the Middle East and North Africa* (Washington: World Bank, 2008), p. 61.

18. *Reaching New Heights,* MENA Economic Update, October 2019, http://pubdocs.worldbank.org/en/660811570642119982/EN-MEM-ReachingNewHeights-OCT-19.pdf.

19. Assaad and Krafft, "Is Free Basic Education in Egypt a Reality or a Myth?"

20. El-Kogali and Krafft, *Expectations and Aspirations,* p. 41.

21. *The Road Not Travelled*, p. 60.

22. Ibid., p. 72.

23. El-Kogali and Krafft, *Expectations and Aspirations,* p. xii.

24. For a review of this evidence, see Springborg, *Political Economies of the Middle East and North Africa.*

25. For a comparative analysis of the development of stateness in MENA, see ibid.

26. Calvert W. Jones, *Bedouins into Bourgeois.*

27. The World Bank's assessment of the benefits of "EdTech" in MENA and elsewhere suggests they may be more limited than claimed by their advocates and in any case require careful application to be useful. See El-Kogali and Krafft, *Expectations and Aspirations,* pp. 33–38.

28. For their negative implications for education, see ibid., p. 31.

29. *Inequality, Uprisings, and Conflict in the Arab World,* MENA Economic Monitor, Washington, World Bank, October 2015, http://documents.worldbank.org/curated/en/303441467992017147/pdf/Inequality-uprisings-and-conflict-in-the-Arab-World.pdf. A preparatory study for this report found that "the dissatisfaction with services is widespread. In the 2013 Gallup World Poll, on average about half of respondents in the MENA region, compared with about 30 percent in Asia and Latin America and the Caribbean, expressed their dissatisfaction with education services and health care in their country." See Brixi, Lust, and Woolcock, *Trust, Voice, and Incentives,* p. 1.

30. https://tamamproject.org.

Bibliography

Al-Abbas, Mutab bin Nasser. "Amerika: al-mulhaqiyya al-thaqafiyya tuhadhar al-mubta'ithin min al-mudhahirat al-silmiyya," *Al-Hayat,* March 20, 2011. https://www.sauress.com/alhayat/246446.

Abdel-Razek, Sherine. "Investing in Education," *Al-Ahram Weekly,* May 2, 2019.

Abdou, Ehaab D. "Copts in Egyptian History Textbooks: Towards an Integrated Framework for Analyzing Minority Representations," *Journal of Curriculum Studies* 50, no. 4 (2018): 476–507.

Abdou, Ehaab D. "'Confused Multiple Deities, Ancient Egyptians Embraced Monotheism': Analyzing Historical Thinking and Inclusion in Egyptian History Textbooks," *Journal of Curriculum Studies* 48, no. 2 (2016): 226–251.

Abdou, Ehaab D. "Construction(s) of the Nation in Egyptian Textbooks: Towards an Understanding of Societal Conflict," in *(Re)Constructing Memory: Education, Identity and Conflict,* edited by Michelle J. Bellino and James H. Williams. Rotterdam: Sense Publishers, 2017, pp. 75–98.

Abi-Mershed, Osama, ed. *Trajectories of Education in the Arab World: Legacies and Challenges.* London: Routledge, 2010.

Abramson, Larry. "Michigan State to Close Dubai Campus," NPR, July 6, 2010. https://www.npr.org/templates/story/story.php?storyId=128342097.

Abu Emiara, Mohamed Ashraf. "Carrots and Sticks: How Students Were Made into Poster Children for the Constitutional Amendments Referendum," *Mada Masr,* May 10, 2019. https://madamasr.com/en/2019/05/10/feature/politics/carrots-and-sticks-how-students-were-made-into-poster-children-for-the-constitutional-amendments-referendum.

Acemoglu, Daron, and James A. Robinson. *Economic Origins of Dictatorship and Democracy.* Cambridge: Cambridge University Press, 2005.

Afify, Heba. "The International School of Egypt's Military," *Mada Masr,* September 15, 2016. https://madamasr.com/en/2016/09/15/feature/society/the-international-school-of-egypts-military.

Akhtarkhavari, Nasreen Badi. "The Perceptions of Education and Satisfaction of Saudi Graduates: A Comparative Study of Saudi Graduates from American and Saudi Universities." Unpublished dissertation, Florida State University, 1994.

Akkary, Rima Karami. "Facing the Challenges of Educational Reform in the Arab World," *Journal of Educational Change* 15, no. 2 (2014): 179–202.

Aktouf, Omar. "La Décision de Bouteflika D'Interrompre les Bourses L'Etranger a Eté une Catastrophe," *Le Quotidien Algerie,* July 3, 2013. http://lequotidienalgerie .org/2013/07/03/la-decision-de-bouteflika-dinterrompre-les-bourses-a-letranger -a-ete-une-catastrophe-pr-omar-aktouf.

Alawi, Hussein. "The Effectiveness of Scholarship Education Abroad: Obstacles and Means of Development," 1979. In Arabic. A field study conducted by the Bureau of Civil Service, Kingdom of Saudi Arabia, quoted in Khaled Ahmad Alyahya, "Constructing a Comprehensive Orientation Program for Saudi Arabian Students in the United States." Unpublished dissertation, University of Pittsburgh, 1981.

Alayan, Samira. *Education in East Jerusalem: Occupation, Political Power, and Struggle.* New York: Routledge, 2019.

Alayan, Samira. "History Curricula and Textbooks in Palestine: Between Nation Building and Quality Education," in *The Politics of Education Reform in the Middle East: Self and Other in Textbooks and Curricula,* edited by Samira Alayan, Achim Rohde, and Sarhan Dhoub. New York: Berghahn Books, 2012.

Alayan, Samira, Achim Rohde, and Sarhan Dhoub, eds. *The Politics of Education Reform in the Middle East: Self and Other in Textbooks and Curricula.* New York: Berghahn Books, 2012.

Alberto, Alesina, and Nicola Fuchs-Schündeln. "Goodbye Lenin (or Not?): The Effect of Communism on People's Preferences," *American Economic Review* 97, no. 4 (September 2007): 1507–1528.

Alfaleh, Matrook. "The Impact of the Processes of Modernization and Social Mobilization on the Social and Political Structures of the Arab Countries with Special Reference to Saudi Arabia." Unpublished dissertation, University of Kansas, 1987.

Alfauzan, Abdallah M. "The Impact of American Culture on the Attitudes of Saudi Arabian Students in the United States Toward Women's Participation in the Labor Force in Saudi Arabia." Unpublished dissertation, Mississippi State University, 1992.

Alraddadi, Abdulaziz. "The Changing Socio-Political Attitudes of Saudi Students Studying Overseas," *Gulf Centre for Policy Studies,* 2014. https://www.gulfpolicies .com/attachments/article/2135/The%20Changing%20Sociopolitical%20Attitudes %20of%20Saudi%20Students.pdf.

Alsalaam, Saad Yasmine. "American Educated Saudi Technocrats: Agents of Change?" Unpublished dissertation, Tufts University, 2000.

Altbach, Philipp G., and Jane Knight. "Internationalization in Higher Education: Motivations and Realities," *Journal of Studies in International Education* 11 (2007): 290–307.

Alvaredo, Facundo, L. Assouad, and T. Piketty. "Measuring Inequality in the Middle East, 1990–2016: The World's Most Unequal Region?" World Inequality Database, 2018.

Alvaredo, Facundo, and Thomas Piketty. "Measuring Top Income and Inequality in the Middle East: Data Limitations and Illustration with the Case of Egypt," Working Paper 832. Cairo: Economic Research Forum, May 2014. https://wid .world/country/lebanon.

Alyahya, Khaled Ahmad. "Constructing a Comprehensive Orientation Program for Saudi Arabian Students in the United States." Unpublished dissertation, University of Pittsburgh, 1981.

El Amine, Adnan, ed. *Reform of General Education in the Arab World.* Beirut: UNESCO, 2005.

Amsden, Alice. *Asia's Next Giant: South Korea and Late Industrialization.* New York: Oxford University Press, 1989.

Anand, Sudhir, and Amartya Sen. "Human Development Index: Methodology and Measurement," Occasional Papers. New York: Human Development Report Office, 1994.

Anderson, Nick. "Can U.S. Universities Thrive in the Persian Gulf? These Scholars Say Yes," *Washington Post,* December 17, 2015. https://www.washingtonpost .com/news/grade-point/wp/2015/12/17/can-u-s-universities-thrive-in-the-persian -gulf-these-scholars-say-yes.

Anderson, Nick. "In Qatar's Education City, US Colleges Are Building an Academic Ooasis," *Washington Post,* December 6, 2015. https://www.washington post.com/local/education/in-qatars-education-city-us-colleges-are-building-an -academic-oasis/2015/12/06.

Anderson, Nick. "Northwestern Professor Raises Questions About Its Branch in Qatar," *Washington Post,* December 17, 2015. https://www.washingtonpost.com /news/grade-point/wp/2015/12/17/northwestern-professor-raises-questions -about-its-branch-in-qatar.

Anderson, Nick. "Texas University Gets $76 Million Each Year to Operate in Qatar, Contract Says," *Washington Post,* March 8, 2016. https://www.washingtonpost .com/news/grade-point/wp/2016/03/08/texas-university-gets-76-million-each -year-to-operate-in-qatar-contract-says.

Antwi-Boateng, Osman. "The Rise of Qatar as a Soft Power and the Challenges," *European Scientific Journal* 2, no. 4 (December 2013): 41–42.

Al-Ashkar, Nehal. "Rebuilding Education in Egypt," *Ahramonline,* July 19, 2018. http: //english.ahram.org.eg/NewsContent/1/151/308247/Egypt/Features/Rebuilding -education-in-Egypt-.aspx.

Askari, Hossein G., and John Thomas Cummings. "The Middle East and the United States: A Problem of 'Brain Drain,'" *International Journal of Middle East Studies* 8, no. 1 (1977): 65–90.

Assaad, Ragui. "Making Sense of Arab Labor Markets: The Enduring Legacy of Dualism." *IZA Journal of Labor and Development* 3, no. 1 (2014): 1–25.

Assaad, Ragui, and Caroline Krafft. "Is Free Basic Education in Egypt a Reality or a Myth?" Summary of Working Paper No. 179. Cairo: Egyptian Center for Economic Studies, 2015.

Assouad, Lydia. "Rethinking the Lebanese Economic Miracle: The Extreme Concentration of Income and Wealth in Lebanon 2005–2014." World Inequality Lab, Working Paper 2017/13.

Attalah, Motaz, and Farida Makar. *Nationalism and Homogeneity in Contemporary Curricula.* Cairo: Egyptian Initiative for Personal Freedom, 2014.

Austin, Simon. "Hughes to Hold City Owner Talks," BBC, November 11, 2008. http://news.bbc.co.uk/sport2/hi/football/teams/m/man_city/7722345.stm.

Al-Badah, Abdulaziz bin Ahmed. *Al-'ibti'ath: tarikuh wa atharuh.* Bila Nashir, 2010.

Baker, Raymond W. *Islam Without Fear: Egypt and the New Islamists.* Cambridge, MA: Harvard University Press, 2003.

El-Banyan, Abdullah. "Cross-Cultural Education and Attitude Change: A Study of Saudi Arabian Students in the United States." Unpublished dissertation, North Carolina State University at Raleigh, 1974.

El Baradei, Laila. *The Case for Decentralization as a Tool for Improving Quality in Egyptian Basic Education.* Cairo: Egyptian Center for Economic Studies, 2015.

El Baradei, Laila. "Decentralization of Pre-University Education in Egypt," in *Decentralization and Local Administration Issues Program #4.* Cairo: Public Administration Research and Consultation Center, 2015.

Barbuscia, Davide. "Qatar Sells Triple-Tranche Jumbo Bond to Raise $12 Billion," *Reuters,* March 6, 2019. https://www.reuters.com/article/us-qatar-bonds/qatar -sells-triple-tranche-jumbo-bond-to-raise-12-billion-idUSKCN1QN26L.

Barsoum, Marina. "Sisi Discusses Developing Education in Egypt with Minister," *Ahramonline,* December 24, 2018. http://english.ahram.org.eg/NewsContent /1/64/320624/Egypt/Politics-/Sisi-discusses-developing-education-in-Egypt -with-.aspx.

Beinin, Joel, and Zachary Lockman. *Workers on the Nile: Nationalism, Communism, Islam, and the Egyptian Working Class, 1882–1954.* London: I. B. Tauris, 1988.

Bellin, Eva. "The Robustness of Authoritarianism in the Middle East: Exceptionalism in Comparative Perspective," *Comparative Politics* 36, no. 2 (2004): 139–157.

Benchemsi, Ahmed. "Feb20's Rise and Fall: A Moroccan Story," July 17, 2012. http://ahmedbenchemsi.com/feb20s-rise-and-fall-a-moroccan-story.

Benchenna, Abdelfettah. "L'appui de la France à la Réforme de l'Enseignement Supérieur au Maroc: Quelles Finalités et Quels Enjeux?," *Journal of Higher Education in Africa/Revue de l'enseignement supérieur en Afrique* 7 (2009): 121–140.

Ben Hamadi, Monia. "Au Cœur de l'IVD: 60 Ans D'Histoire à Reconstituer," *Inkyfada,* November 17, 2016. https://inkyfada.com/fr/2016/11/17/ivd-auditions-data -histoire-tunisie.

Ben Hédi, Raouf. "Tunisie—Les fuyards tentent de réécrire l'Histoire," *Business News,* May, 15, 2019. https://www.businessnews.com.tn/tunisie-les-fuyards-tentent -de-reecrire-lhistoire,519,87846,3.

Bennoune, Mahfoud. *The Making of Contemporary Algeria.* Cambridge: Cambridge University Press, 1988.

Bensouiah, Azzedine. "HE System Under Pressure as Student Numbers Mount," *University World News,* September 7, 2018. https://www.universityworldnews .com/post.php?story=20180906124649727.

Benstead, Lindsay J. "Tunisia," in *The Government and Politics of the Middle East and North Africa: Development, Democracy, and Dictatorship,* 9th ed., edited by Sean Yom. Boulder: Westview Press, 2020, pp. 149–180.

Benstead, Lindsay J. "Tunisia," in *Palgrave Handbook of Women's Rights,* edited by Susan Franceschet, Mona Lena Krook, and Netina Tan. London: Palgrave Macmillan, 2018, pp. 517–530.

Benstead, Lindsay J., and Megan Reif. "Polarization or Pluralism? Language, Identity, and Attitudes Toward American Culture Among Algeria's Youth," *Middle East Journal of Culture and Communication* 6, no. 1 (2013): 75–106.

Benziane, Abdelbaki. "Economic Reforms in Algeria and Their Impact on Higher Education and Student Benefits," *The Journal of North African Studies* 9, no. 2 (2004): 106.

Bessis, Sophie, and Souhayr Belhassan. *Bourguiba,* 2nd ed. Paris: Elyzad, 2012.

Birdsall, Nancy, David Ross, and Richard Sabot. "Inequality and Growth Reconsidered: Lessons from East Asia," *World Bank Economic Review* 9, no. 3 (1994): 477–508.

Bisin, Alberto, and Thierry Verdier. "A Model of Cultural Transmission, Voting and Political Ideology," *European Journal of Political Economy* 16, no. 1 (March 2000): 5–29.

Blanchard, Christopher. "Saudi Arabia: Background and U.S. Relations." Washington: Congressional Research Service, 2009.

Blanchard, Christopher. "Saudi Arabia: Background and U.S. Relations." Washington: Congressional Research Service, 2019.

Blaydes, Lisa. *Elections and Distributive Politics in Mubarak's Egypt.* New York: Cambridge University Press, 2011.

Blaydes, Lisa. "Who Votes in Authoritarian Elections and Why? Determinants of Voter Turnout in Contemporary Egypt." Paper presented at the Annual Meeting of the American Political Science Association, August 31–September 3, 2006, Philadelphia, PA.

Boeren, Ad. "Relationships Between Scholarship Program and Institutional Capacity Development Initiatives," in *International Scholarships in Higher Education: Pathways to Social Change,* edited by Joan R. Dassin, Robin R. Marsh, and Matt Mawer. New York: Springer, 2017, pp. 59–60.

Borsali, Noura. *Bourguiba à l'Épreuve de la Démocratie, 1956–1963,* 2nd ed. Tunis: Imprimerie Tunis Carthage, 2012.

Boukhars, Anouar. "The Lesson from Morocco and Jordan: Reform or Perish." Middle East Institute, September 1, 2011. http://www.mei.edu/content/lesson-morocco-and-jordan-reform-or-perish.

Bourdieu, Pierre. *Homo Academicus,* translated by Peter Collier. Cambridge: Polity Press, 1988.

Boutieri, Charis. *Learning in Morocco: Language Politics and the Abandoned Educational Dream.* Bloomington: Indiana University Press, 2016.

Bray, Mark, and Chad Lykins. *Shadow Education: Private Supplementary Tutoring and Its Implications for Policy Makers in Asia.* Manilla: Asian Development Bank, 2012.

Brixi, Hana, Ellen Lust, and Michael Woolcock. *Trust, Voice, and Incentives: Learning from Local Success Stories in Service Delivery in the Middle East and North Africa.* Washington: World Bank, 2015.

Brock, Colin, and Lila Zia Levers, eds. *Aspects of Education in the Middle East and North Africa.* Oxford: Symposium Books, 2007.

Bruns, Barbara, and Ben Ross Schneider. "Managing the Politics of Quality Reforms in Education: Policy Lessons from Global Experience." International Commission on Financing Educational Opportunity, 2016.

Bsheer, Rosie. "A Counter-Revolutionary State: Popular Movements and the Making of Saudi Arabia," *Past and Present* 238, no. 1 (2018): 233–277.

Buckner, Elizabeth. "Access to Higher Education in Egypt: Examining Trends by University Sector," *Comparative Education Review* 57, no. 3 (August 2013): 527–552.

Burke, Peter J., and Jan E. Stets. *Identity Theory.* New York: Oxford University Press, 2009.

Butenschøn, Nils, and Roel Meijer, eds. *The Middle East in Transition: The Centrality of Citizenship.* Cheltenham: Edward Elgar, 2018.

Byrne, Jeffrey James. "Our Own Special Brand of Socialism: Algeria and the Contest of Modernities in the 1960s," *Diplomatic History* 33, no. 3 (June 2009): 427–447.

Camau, Michel, and Vincet Geisser, eds. *Habib Bourguiba: La trace et l'héritage.* Paris: Karthala, 2004.

Campante, Filipe R., and Davin Chor. "Why Was the Arab World Poised for Revolution? Schooling, Economic Opportunities, and the Arab Spring," *Journal of Economic Perspectives* 26, no. 2 (2012): 167–188.

Campos, Michelle U. *Ottoman Brothers: Muslims, Christians, and Jews in Early Twentieth-Century Palestine.* Stanford: Stanford University Press, 2011.

Cantini, Daniele. *Youth and Education in the Middle East: Shaping Identity and Politics in Jordan.* London: I. B. Tauris, 2016.

Cantoni, David, Yuyu Chen, David Y. Yang, Noam Yuchtman, and Y. Jane Zhang. "Curriculum and Ideology," *Journal of Political Economy* 125, no. 2 (April 2017): 338–392.

Chapman, David W., and Suzanne L. Miric. "Education Quality in the Middle East," *International Review of Education* 55, no. 4 (2009): 331–337.

Chen, David W. "N.Y.U. Promised Reforms in Abu Dhabi. Report Says It Has Reneged," *New York Times,* May 10, 2018.

Chen, Jing. "Democratization and Government Education Provision in East Asia," *Journal of East Asian Studies* 8, no. 2 (2008): 175–209.

Chia, Yeow-Tong. *Education, Culture and the Singapore Developmental State: "World-Soul" Lost and Regained?* Houndmills: Palgrave Macmillan, 2015.

Clark, Janine. *Local Politics in Jordan and Morocco: Strategies of Centralization and Decentralization.* New York: Columbia University Press, 2018.

Clark, Janine, Emanuela Dalmasso, and Ellen Lust. "Not the Only Game in Town: Local-Level Representation in Transitions." Program on Governance and Local Development, University of Gothenberg, Working Paper 15, 2017. http://gld .gu.se/media/1325/lust-dalmasso-clark-final.pdf.

Cochran, Judith. *Democracy in the Middle East: The Impact of Religion and Education.* Lanham, MD: Lexington Books, 2011.

Cohen, Joshua. "Deliberation and Democratic Legitimacy," in *Debates in Contemporary Political Philosophy,* edited by Derek Matravers, Jonathan Warburton, and Nigel Warburton. Abingdon: Taylor and Francis, 2005.

Cohen, Julia Phillips. *Becoming Ottomans: Sephardi Jews and Imperial Citizenship in the Modern Era.* Oxford: Oxford University Press, 2014.

Cole, Juan R. I. *Colonialism and Revolution in the Middle East: Social and Cultural Origins of Egypt's 'Urabi Movement.* Cairo: American University in Cairo Press, 1999.

Constant, Louay, Gabriella Gonzalez, Lynn Karoly, Charles Goldman, and Hanine Salem, eds. *Facing Human Capital Challenges in the 21st Century.* Santa Monica: RAND, 2008.

Cook, Bradley. "Egypt's National Education Debate," *Comparative Education* 36, no. 4 (2000): 477–490.

Cook, Bradley J., and Engy El Refaee. "Egypt: A Perpetual Reform Agenda," in *Education in the Arab World,* edited by Serra Kirdar. London: Bloomsbury Academic, 2019.

Crandal, Jonathan. "U.S. and Algeria: Uneasy Partners in Gas Market," *Washington Post,* November 4, 1977. https://www.washingtonpost.com/archive/politics/1977 /11/04/us-and-algeria-uneasy-partners-in-gas-market/83adfafb-799b-40e7-9989 -0599533ee995.

Croke, Kevin, Guy Grossman, Horacio A. Larreguy, and John Marshall. "Deliberate Disengagement: How Education Can Decrease Political Participation in Electoral Authoritarian Regimes," *American Political Science Review* 110, no. 3 (August 2016): 579–600.

Cronin, Stephanie. *Armies and State-Building in the Modern Middle East: Politics, Nationalism and Military Reform.* London: I. B.Tauris, 2014.

Crooks, Ed. "The US Shale Revolution: How It Changed the World (and Why Nothing Will Ever Be the Same Again)," *Financial Times,* April 24, 2015. https://www .ft.com/content/2ded7416-e930-11e4-a71a-00144feab7de#slide0.

Culbertson, Shelly. *Education of Syrian Refugee Children: Managing the Crisis in Turkey, Lebanon, and Jordan.* Santa Monica: RAND, 2015.

Dahl, Robert. "What Political Institutions Does Large-Scale Democracy Require?," *Political Science Quarterly* 120, no. 2 (2005): 187–197.

Dahmani, Frida. "Tahar Ben Ammar: l'autre père de l'indépendance," *Jeune Afrique,* July 30, 2015. https://www.jeuneafrique.com/mag/250303/culture /tunisie-tahar-ben-ammar-lautre-pere-de-lindependance.

Dalay, Galip. "Why the Middle East Is Betting on China." Project Syndicate, August 22, 2019. https://www.project-syndicate.org/commentary/china-middle -east-closer-economic-ties-by-galip-dalay-2019-08.

Daley, Suzanne. "N.Y.U. in the U.A.E.," *New York Times,* April 15, 2011. https:// www.nytimes.com/2011/04/17/education/edlife/edl-17abudhabi-t.html.

Dang, Thang. "Quasi-Experimental Evidence on the Political Impacts of Education in Vietnam," *Journal of Education Economics* 23, no. 2 (2019): 207–221.

Davidson, Christopher. *After the Sheikhs: The Coming Collapse of the Gulf Monarchies.* New York: Oxford University Press, 2013.

Davidson, Christopher. *Dubai: The Vulnerability of Success.* New York: Columbia University Press, 2008.

Davidson, Christopher. "Up for Debate: GCC Crisis." Middle East Institute, May 29, 2019. https://www.mei.edu/publications/debate-gcc-crisis.

Davoli, Maddalena, and Horst Entorf. "The PISA Shock, Socioeconomic Inequality, and School Reforms in Germany." IZA Policy Papers 140, Institute of Labor Economics, 2018.

Dawisha, Adeed. *Iraq: A Political History.* Princeton: Princeton University Press, 2009.

Dee, Thomas. "Are There Civic Returns to Education?," *Journal of Public Economics* 88, no. 9–10 (August 2004): 1697–1720.

Degorge, Barbara. "The Modernization of Education: A Case Study of Tunisia and Morocco," *The European Legacy* 7, no. 5 (2002): 579–596.

Dennehy, John. "British Museum Renames Gallery After Sheikh Zayed," *The National,* June 20, 2018. https://www.thenational.ae/uae/heritage/british-museum -renames-gallery-after-sheikh-zayed-1.742467#.

De Onis, Juan. "Faisal's Killer Is Put to Death," *New York Times,* June 19, 1975. https://www.nytimes.com/1975/06/19/archives/faisals-killer-is-put-to-death -prince-is-beheaded-before-a-crowd-of.html.

Desai, Raj M., Anders Olofsgård, and Tarik M. Yousef. "The Logic of Authoritarian Bargains," *Economics & Politics* 21, no. 1 (February 2019): 93–125.

Deuchler, Martina. *The Confucian Transformation of Korea: A Study of Society and Ideology.* Cambridge, MA: Harvard University Press, 1992.

Diamond, Larry. "Why Are There No Arab Democracies?," *Journal of Democracy* 21, no. 1 (January 2010): 93–104.

Di-Capua, Yoav. *Gatekeepers of the Arab Past: Historians and History Writing in Twentieth-Century Egypt.* Berkeley: University of California Press, 2009.

Dickinson, Elizabeth. "Exporting the Gulf Crisis." War on the Rocks, May 28, 2019. https://warontherocks.com/2019/05/exporting-the-gulf-crisis.

Diwan, Ishac. "Understanding Revolution in the Middle East: The Central Role of the Middle Class," *Middle East Development Journal* 5, no. 1 (March 2013): 1–30.

Diwan, Ishac, Adeel Malik, and Izak Atiyas, eds. *Crony Capitalism in the Middle East: Business and Politics from Liberalization to the Arab Spring.* Oxford: Oxford University Press, 2019.

Diwan, Ishac, and Irina Vartanova. "Does Education Indoctrinate?," *International Journal of Educational Development* 78 (October 2020).

Doumato, Eleanor Abdella, and Gregory Starrett, eds. *Teaching Islam: Textbooks and Religion in the Middle East.* Boulder: Lynne Rienner, 2007.

Draege, Jonas Bergan, and Martin Lestra. "Gulf-Funding of British Universities and the Focus on Human Development," *Middle East Law and Governance* 7, no. 1 (2015): 25–49.

Dror, Olga. "Education and Politics in Wartime: School Systems in North and South Vietnam, 1965–1975," *Journal of Cold War Studies* 20, no. 3 (2018): 57–113.

Eibl, Ferdinand. *Social Dictatorships: The Political Economy of the Welfare State in the Middle East and North Africa.* Oxford University Press, 2020.

Elbadawy, Asmaa. "Education in Egypt," in *The Egyptian Labor Market in an Era of Revolution,* edited by Ragui Assaad and Caroline Krafft. Oxford: Oxford University Press, 2015.

Elman, Benjamin. *Civil Examinations and Meritocracy in Late Imperial China.* Cambridge, MA: Harvard University Press, 2013.

Eltohamy, Amr. "Sisi Keeps Watchful Eye on Al-Azhar's Growing Role Abroad," *Al-Monitor,* April 7, 2019. https://www.al-monitor.com/pulse/originals/2019/04 /azhar-grand-imam-moderate-islam-terrorism-organizaitons.html.

Ennaji, Moha. "Multiculturalism, Citizenship, and Education in Morocco," *Mediterranean Journal of Educational Studies* 14, no. 1 (2009): 5–26.

Ennaji, Moha, *Multilingualism, Cultural Identity, and Education in Morocco.* New York: Springer Science, 2005.

Erdag, Ramazan. "Review of *Military Responses to the Arab Uprisings and the Future of Civil-Military Relations in the Middle East,* by William Taylor," *International Affairs* 91, no. 2 (2015): 434–435.

Essam El-Din, Gamal. "Budgetary Woes: Cabinet Ministers Complain of Inadequate Funding," *Al-Ahram Weekly,* May 16, 2019.

Fahmy, Ziad. *Ordinary Egyptians: Creating the Modern Nation Through Popular Culture.* Stanford: Stanford University Press, 2011.

Fang, Zheng, Xianxuan Xu, Leslie W. Grant, James H. Stronge, and Thomas J. Ward. "National Culture, Creativity, and Productivity: What's the Relationship with Student Achievement?," *Creativity Research Journal* 28, no. 4 (2016): 395–406.

Faour, Muhammad, and Marwan Muasher. *Education for Citizenship in the Arab World: Key to the Future.* Washington: Carnegie Endowment, October 2011. https://carnegieendowment.org/files/citizenship_education.pdf.

Fattah, Zainab, and Yousef Gamal El-Din. "U.A.E. Federal Bank to Sell Bond Following Passage of Debt Law," Bloomberg, February 9, 2019. https://gulfnews .com/business/markets/uae-federal-bank-to-sell-bond-following-passage-of -debt-law-1.61985403#.

Fearon, James D. "Ethnic and Cultural Diversity by Country," *Journal of Economic Growth* 8, no. 2 (June 2003): 195–222.

Feng, Yi, and Paul J. Zak. "The Determinants of Democratic Transitions," *Journal of Conflict Resolution* 43 (1999): 162–177.

Ferranti, David, Guillermo Perry, Francisco Ferreira, and Michael Walton. *Inequality in Latin America: Breaking with History?* Washington: World Bank, 2004.

Fish, M. Steven. "Islam and Authoritarianism," *World Politics* 55, no. 1 (October 2002): 4–37.

Flynn, James R. *Asian Americans: Achievement Beyond IQ.* Hillsdale, NJ: L. Erlbaum, 1991.

Forster, Nick. "Why Are There So Few World-Class Universities in the Middle East and North Africa?," *Journal of Further and Higher Education* 42, no. 8 (2018): 1025–1039.

French, Joseph, Atchaporn French, and Wei-Xuan Li. "The Relationship Among Cultural Dimensions, Education Expenditure, and PISA Performance," *International Journal of Educational Development* 44 (2015): 25–34.

Freund, Caroline, and Mélise Jaud. "On the Determinants of Democratic Transitions," *Middle East Development Journal* 5, no. 1 (2013): 1350005-1–1350005-30.

Friedman, Willa, Michael Kremer, Edward Miguel, and Rebecca Thornton. "Education as Liberation?" National Bureau of Economic Research, 2011. http://www .nber.org/papers/w16939.

Frosch, Dan. "Chaos at Home Stalls Tuition Aid for Libyan Students in U.S.," *New York Times,* May 10, 2011. https://www.nytimes.com/2011/05/11/education/11 students.html.

Fukurai, Hiroshi, and Kataoka Yusuke. "American Universities in Japan: Success or Failure? A Case Study of Texas A & M University-Koriyama," *Current Politics and Economics of Japan* 2, no. 2 (1993): 85–102.

Gambrell, Jon. "U.A.E. Cyber Firm DarkMatter Slowly Steps Out of the Shadows." Associated Press, February 1, 2018. https://apnews.com/e6c2cb4445b5464b8b 9548f7d314e9b8/UAE-cyber-firm-DarkMatter-slowly-steps-out-of-the-shadows#.

Gargash, Anwar. "Amid Challenges, UAE Policies Engage Gradual Reforms," *The National,* August 26, 2012. https://www.thenational.ae/amid-challenges-uae -policies-engage-gradual-reforms-1.409084.

Gause, Gregory F. "Kings for All Seasons: How the Middle East's Monarchies Survived the Arab Spring." Brookings Institution, September 24, 2013. https:// www.brookings.edu/research/kings-for-all-seasons-how-the-middle-easts -monarchies-survived-the-arab-spring.

Geddes, Barbara. *Politician's Dilemma: Building State Capacity in Latin America.* Berkeley: University of California Press, 1994.

Gehlbach, Scott, and Philip Keefer. "Private Investment and the Institutionalization of Collective Action in Autocracies: Ruling Parties and Legislatures," *Journal of Politics* 74, no. 2 (2012): 621–635.

Gengler, Justin, and Majed Al Ansari. "Qatar's First Elections Since 2017 Reveal Unexpected Impact of GCC Crisis," *Al-Monitor,* April 25, 2019. https://www .al-monitor.com/pulse/originals/2019/04/qatar-first-elections-reveal-unexpected -impact-gcc-crisis.html.

Ghamrawy, Muhammad. "Egypt Looks to Foreign University Campuses to Boost Education," *Al-Monitor,* September 25, 2018. https://www.al-monitor.com /pulse/originals/2018/08/egypt-law-foreign-universities-education.html.

Ghanmy, Monya. "Row over Algerian Education Minister's Nobel Prize Comments," *Al Arabiya,* August 10, 2018. http://english.alarabiya.net/en/News/north-africa /2018/08/10/Algerian-minister-s-says-Nobel-Prize-won-t-add-to-education -sparks-anger.html.

Ghettas, Mohammed Lakhdar. *Algeria and the Cold War: International Relations and the Struggle for Autonomy.* London: I.B. Tauris, 2017.

Ghorbal, Samy. *Orphelins de Bourguiba et héritier du prophète.* Tunis: Cérès éditions, 2012.

Ghosn, Emma. "Lebanese Teacher Unions in Turbulent Times: Their Challenges and Resistance." Paper presented at the CIES Education for Sustainability Conference, San Francisco, 2019.

Ghouati, Ahmed. "Réforme LMD au Maghreb: éléments pour un premier bilan politique et pédagogique," *Journal of Higher Education in Africa/Revue de l'enseignement supérieur en Afrique* 7, no. 1–2 (2009): 61–77.

Gift, Thomas, and Daniel Krcmaric. "Who Democratizes? Western-Educated Leaders and Regime Transitions," *Journal of Conflict Resolution* 61, no. 3 (2017): 671–701.

Gillies, John. *The Power of Persistence—Education System Reform and Aid Effectiveness: Case Studies in Long-Term Education Reform.* Washington: USAID, 2010.

Ginsburg, Mark, Nagwa Megahed, Mohammed Elmeski, and Nobuyuki Tanaka. "Reforming Educational Governance and Management in Egypt: National and International Actors and Dynamics," *Education Policy Analysis Archives* 18, no. 5 (2010): 1–54.

Gorman, Anthony. *Historians, State and Politics in Twentieth Century Egypt: Contesting the Nation.* Abingdon: RoutledgeCurzon, 2003.

Green, Andy. *Education and State Formation: The Rise of Education Systems in England, France, and the USA.* New York: St. Martin's Press, 1990.

Gregory, Joseph. "Ahmed Ben Bella, Revolutionary Who Led Algeria After Independence, Dies at 93," *New York Times,* April 12, 2012. https://www.nytimes.com/2012/04/12/world/africa/ahmed-ben-bella-algerias-first-president-dies-at-93.html.

Greif, Avner, and Steven Tadelis. "A Theory of Moral Persistence: Crypto-Morality and Political Legitimacy," *Journal of Comparative Economics* 38, no. 3 (September 2010): 229–244.

Grindle, Merilee S. *Despite the Odds: The Contentious Politics of Education Reform.* Princeton: Princeton University Press, 2004.

Grindle, Merilee. "Good Enough Governance: Poverty Reduction and Reform in Developing Countries," *Governance* 17, no. 4 (2004): 525–548.

Gross, Zehavit, and Lynn Davies, eds. *The Contested Role of Education in Conflict and Fragility.* Rotterdam: SensePublishers, 2015.

Guo, Quanzhi. "Top U.S. Colleges with Branches Overseas," *Forbes,* August 21, 2018. https://www.forbes.com/sites/quanzhiguo/2018/08/21/top-u-s-colleges-with-branches-overseas/#4.

Hakim, Ashraf. "Sacking TV Presenter Osama Kamal," *Madamasr,* September 5, 2019. https://madamasr.com/en/2019/09/05/feature/politics/sacking-tv-presenter-osama-kamal-how-graduates-of-the-presidential-leadership-program-manage-egypts-tv-channels.

Hall, Gene, and Shirley Hord. *Implementing Change: Patterns, Principles, and Potholes.* Boston: Allyn and Bacon, 2006.

Hall, Terry Ryan. "Saudi Male Perceptions of Study in the United States: An Analysis of King Abdullah Scholarship Program Participants." Unpublished dissertation, Western Kentucky University, 2013.

Hammond, Christopher. "Corruption in the Classroom: The Dilemma of Public School Teachers in Cambodia Providing Private Tutoring to Their Own Students," 2018. https://www.researchgate.net/publication/327971826_Corruption_in_the_Classroom_The_Dilemma_of_Public_School_Teachers_in_Cambodia_Providing_Private_Tutoring_to_Their_Own_Students.

Han, Byung-Chul. "La Emergencia Viral y el Mundo de Mañana," *El Pais,* March 22, 2020.

Al-Harbi, Muhammad. "Al-Harbish: 18 dawla tustaqbil mubta'ithiy al-sa'udiyya fi kanada," *Al-Arabiya,* August 7, 2018. https://www.alarabiya.net/ar/saudi-today/2018/08/07.

Hart, Dennis. "Creating the National Other: Opposing Images of Nationalism in South and North Korean Education," *Korean Studies* 23 (1999): 68–93.

Hassani-Idrissi, Mostafa. "Manuels D'Histoire et Identité au Maroc," *Revue internationale d'éducation de Sèvres* 69 (2015): 53–64.

Hassani-Idrissi, Mostafa. "Pour une Autre Réforme de l'Enseignement de L'Histoire au Maroc," *Revue Attadriss* 4 (2008): 72–81.

Haugsbakk, Geir. "From Sputnik to PISA-Shock—New Technology and Educational Reform in Norway and Sweden," *Education Inquiry* 4, no. 4 (2013): 607–628.

Hefner, Robert W., and Muhammad Qasim Zaman. *Schooling Islam: The Culture and Politics of Modern Muslim Education.* Princeton: Princeton University Press, 2007.

Henry, Clement M., and Robert Springborg. *Globalization and the Politics of Development in the Middle East.* Cambridge: Cambridge University Press, 2001.

Herb, Michael. *The Wages of Oil: Parliaments and Economic Development in Kuwait and the UAE.* Ithaca: Cornell University Press, 2014.

Herrmann-Pillath, Carsten. "Fei Xiaotong's Comparative Theory of Chinese Culture: Its Relevance for Contemporary Cross-Disciplinary Research on Chinese 'Collectivism,'" *Copenhagen Journal of Asian Studies* 34, no. 1 (2016): 25–57.

Hertog, Steffen. *Princes, Brokers, and Bureaucrats: Oil and the State in Saudi Arabia.* Ithaca: Cornell University Press, 2011.

Hertog, Steffen. "The Role of Cronyism in Arab Capitalism," in *Crony Capitalism in the Middle East: Business and Politics from Liberalization to the Arab Spring,* edited by Ishac Diwan, Adeel Malik, and Izak Atiyas. Oxford: Oxford University Press, 2019, pp. 39–66.

Hess, Steve. "From the Arab Spring to the Chinese Winter: The Institutional Sources of Authoritarian Vulnerability and Resilience in Egypt, Tunisia, and China," *International Political Science Review* 34, no. 3 (Feb. 2013): 254–272.

Hinnebusch, Raymond. "Liberalization Without Democratization in 'Post-Populist' Authoritarian States: Evidence from Syria and Egypt," in *Citizenship and the State in the Middle East: Approaches and Applications,* edited by Nils Butenschon, Uri Davis, and Manuel Hassassian. Syracuse: Syracuse University Press, pp. 123–145.

Hofstede, Geert, and Michael H. Bond. "The Confucius Connection: From Cultural Roots to Economic Growth," *Organizational Dynamics* 16, no. 4 (1988): 5–21.

Holmes, Amy Austin. "Egypt's Lost Academic Freedom," *Sada,* January 24, 2019. https://carnegieendowment.org/sada/78210.

Hounsell, Kayla. "Thousands of Saudi Students Remain in Canada, Despite Riyadh's Pledge to Axe Scholarships." CBC News, May 21, 2019. https://www.cbc.ca /news/canada/nova-scotia/saudi-arabia-students-remain-canadian-universities -healthcare-1.5141470.

Hovsepian, Nubar. *Palestinian State Formation: Education and the Construction of National Identity.* Newcastle: Cambridge Scholars, 2008.

Hu, C. T. "Orthodoxy over Historicity: The Teaching of History in Communist China," *Comparative Education Review* 13, no. 1 (1969): 2–19.

Huang, Futao. "Building the World-Class Research Universities: A Case Study of China," *Higher Education* 70, no. 2 (March 2015): 203–215.

Huntington, Samuel. *Political Order in Changing Societies.* New Haven: Yale University Press, 1968.

Inglehart, Ronald, and Pippa Norris. "Islamic Culture and Democracy: Testing the 'Clash of Civilizations' Thesis," *Comparative Sociology* 1, no. 3–4 (January 2002): 235–263.

Inglehart, Ronald, and Christian Welzel. "Changing Mass Priorities: The Link Between Modernization and Democracy," *Perspectives on Politics* 8, no. 2 (June 2010): 551–567.

Inglehart, Ronald, and Christian Welzel. *Modernization, Cultural Change, and Democracy: The Human Development Sequence.* New York: Cambridge University Press, 2005.

Ismail, Salwa. *Political Life in Cairo's New Quarters: Encountering the Everyday State.* Minneapolis: University of Minnesota Press, 2006.

Al-Ississ, Mohammed, and Ishac Diwan. "Preference for Democracy in the Arab World," *Politics and Governance* 4, no. 4 (December 2016): 16–26.

Jackson, Jamie. "Qatar Wins 2022 World Cup Bid," *The Guardian,* December 2, 2010. https://www.theguardian.com/football/2010/dec/02/qatar-win-2022 -world-cup-bid.

Jamal, Amaney A. "Reassessing Support for Islam and Democracy in the Arab World? Evidence from Egypt and Jordan," *World Affairs* 169, no. 2 (2006): 51–63.

Jayachandran, S. "Incentives to Teach Badly: After-School Tutoring in Developing Countries," *Journal of Development Economics* 108 (2014): 190–205.

Jensen, Ben. "Catching Up: Learning from the Best School Systems in East Asia." Grattan Institute, 2012. https://grattan.edu.au/wp-content/uploads/2014/04/130 _report_learning_from_the_best_detail.pdf.

Jerrim, John. "Why Do East Asian Children Perform So Well in PISA? An Investigation of Western-Born Children of East Asian Descent," *Oxford Review of Education* 41, no. 3 (2015): 310–333.

Johnson, Chalmers. *MITI and the Japanese Miracle: The Growth of Industrial Policy, 1925–1975.* Stanford: Stanford University Press, 1982.

Jones, Alisa. "Changing the Past to Serve the Present: History Education in Mainland China," in *History Education and National Identity in East Asia,* edited by Edward Vickers and Alisa Jones. New York: Routledge, 2005, pp. 65–100.

Jones, Calvert W. *Bedouins into Bourgeois: Remaking Citizens for Globalization.* New York: Cambridge University Press, 2017.

Jones, Calvert W. "New Approaches to Citizen-Building: Shifting Needs, Goals, and Outcomes," *Comparative Political Studies* 51, no. 2 (2018): 165–196.

Jones, Calvert W. "Saudi Arabia's Crown Prince Wants to Reengineer His Country. Is That Even Possible?," *Washington Post,* November 30, 2017. https://www .washingtonpost.com/outlook/saudi-arabias-crown-prince-wants-to-reengineer -his-country-is-that-even-possible/2017/11/30/514c8e94-d4bd-11e7-95bf-df7c 19270879_story.html.

Jones, Calvert W. "Seeing Like an Autocrat: Liberal Social Engineering in an Illiberal State," *Perspectives on Politics* 13, no. 1 (2015): 24–41.

Jones, Lee. "The Political Economy of Myanmar's Transition," *Journal of Contemporary Asia* 44, no. 1 (2014): 144–170.

Jones, Marie Thourson. "Regional Disparities and Public Policy in Tunisian Education," *Comparative Education* 22, no. 3 (1986): 201–220.

Jones, Toby Craig. *Desert Kingdom.* Cambridge, MA: Harvard University Press, 2010.

Kadi, Wadad, and Victor Billeh. *Islam and Education: Myths and Truth.* Chicago: University of Chicago Press, 2007.

Kadri, Aïssa. "La Formation à L'Étranger des Étudiants Algériens les Limites d'une Politique Rentière (1962–1995)," in *Diplômés Maghrébin d'ici et d'Ailleurs.* Paris: CNRS Editions, 1997.

Kanine, Sarah. "GUC: Studieren in Ägypten—nach deutschem Vorbild." DAAD, December 5, 2017. https://www2.daad.de/der-daad/daad-aktuell/de/59919-guc -studieren-in-aegypten—nach-deutschem-vorbild.

Kavanaugh, Shane Dixon. "He Was Accused of Killing a Portland Teen. Feds Believe the Saudis Helped Him Escape," *The Oregonian,* December 24, 2018. https:// expo.oregonlive.com/news/erry-2018/12/9b5b1eff724150/he-was-accused-of -killing-a-po.html.

Ketchley, Neil, and Michael Biggs. "The Educational Contexts of Islamist Activism: Elite Students and Religious Institutions in Egypt," *Mobilization* 22, no. 1 (2017): 58–61.

Khaled, Karim. "Politique de Formation à L'Étranger et l'Émigration Intellectuelle Algérienne," *Les cahiers du Cread,* 2014: 121–151.

Khelfaoui, Hocine. "Le Champ Universitaire Algérien Entre Pouvoirs Politiques et Champ Économique," *Actes de la Recherche en Science Sociales* (2003): 34–46.

Kim, Sun, and Dong-Joon Jung, DJ. "Ideology, Nationalism, and Education: The Case of Education Reforms in the Two Koreas." *Asia Pacific Education Review* 20 (2019): 295–304. https://doi.org/10.1007/s12564-019-09592-2.

Kim, Sunwoong, and Ju-Ho Lee. "Private Tutoring and Demand for Education in Korea," *Economic Development and Cultural Change* 58, no. 2 (2010): 259–296.

Kingdon, Geeta Gandhi, Angela Little, Monazza Aslam, Shenila Rawal, Terry Moe, Harry Patrinos, and Tara Beteille. *A Rigorous Review of the Political Economy of Education Systems in Developing Countries.* London: Department for International Development, 2014.

Kinninmont, Jane. "The Gulf Divided: The Impact of the Qatar Crisis." Chatham House Middle East and North Africa Research Programme, May 2019. https://www.chathamhouse.org/sites/default/files/publications/research/2019-05-30-Gulf%20Crisis_0.pdf.

Kipnis, Andrew, and Shanfeng Li. "Is Chinese Education Underfunded?," *China Quarterly* 202 (2010): 327–343.

Kirdar, Erra. *Education in the Arab World.* London: Bloomsbury Academic, 2017.

Klasen, Stephan. "Low Schooling for Girls: Slower Growth for All Cross-Country Evidence on the Effect of Gender Inequality in Education on Economic Development," *The World Bank Economic Review* 16, no. 3 (2002): 345–373.

Knipp, Kersten, and Imane Mellouk. "Qatar Boycott Three Years On: Everyone Loses." Deutsche Welle, June 5, 2020. https://www.dw.com/en/qatar-boycott-three-years-on-everyone-loses/a-5369028.

El-Kogali, Safaa El Tayeb, and Caroline Krafft. *Expectations and Aspirations: A New Framework for Education in the Middle East and North Africa.* Washington: World Bank, 2020.

Kohstall, Florian. "Die ägyptische Revolution als Generationenkonflikt: Studierende und Professoren auf dem Tahrir-Platz und in den Universitäten," in *Revolution und Regimewandel in Ägypten,* edited by Holger Albrecht and Thomas Demmelhuber. Baden-Baden: NOMOS, 2013, pp. 185–208.

Kohstall, Florian. "From Reform to Resistance: Universities and Student Mobilisation in Egypt and Morocco Before and After the Arab Uprisings," *British Journal of Middle Eastern Studies* 42 (Dec. 2015): 59–73.

Kremer, Michael, and Andrei Sarychev. "Why Do Governments Operate Schools?" Working Paper. Cambridge, MA: Harvard University, 2000. https://www.pinterest.ca/pin/299489443969488624/.

Kriener, Jonathan. *Lebanese, but How? Secular and Religious Conceptions of State and Society at Lebanese Schools.* Wurzburg: Ergon Verlag, 2011.

Kwok, Percy. "A Cultural Analysis of Cram Schools in Hong Kong: Impact on Youth Values and Implications," *Journal of Youth Studies* 12, no. 1 (2009): 104–114.

Labdelaoui, Hocine. "La migration des étudiants algériens vers l'étranger: les effets pervers d'une gestion étatique," *Les Cahiers du SOLIIS,* no. 2–3 (1997): 107–124. https://doi.org/10.4000/urmis.424.

Lajal, Mohammed Lamine. "La Migration des Compétences Arabes, les Causes et les Propositions, le Cas de l'Algérie." Master's thesis, Sciences Politiques, 1990. Quoted in Hocine Labdelaoui, "La Migration des Étudiants Algériens vers l'Étranger: Les Effets Pervers d'Une Gestion Étatique," *Les Cahiers du SOLIIS,* no. 2–3 (1997): 107–124. https://doi.org/10.4000/urmis.424.

Lakhal, Malek. "Interview avec Sghaier Salhi: Les non-dits de la Tunisie post-indépendance," Nawaat, April 5, 2018. https://nawaat.org/portail/2018/04/05/interview-avec-sghaier-salhi-les-non-dits-de-la-tunisie-postindependance.

Lane, Jason. "Importing Private Higher Education: International Branch Campuses," *Journal of Comparative Policy Analysis: Research and Practice* 13, no. 4 (2011): 367–381.

Langton, James. "Emmanuel Macron and UAE Leaders Formally Open Louvre Abu Dhabi," *The National,* November 8, 2017. https://www.thenational.ae/uae/emmanuel-macron-and-uae-leaders-formally-open-louvre-abu-dhabi-1.674159.

Larmer, Brook. "China's Cram Schools," *New York Times, Upfront Magazine,* March 30, 2015.

Larreguy, Horacio, and John Marshall. "The Effect of Education on Civic and Political Engagement in Non-Consolidated Democracies: Evidence from Nigeria," *Review of Economics and Statistics* 99, no. 3 (2017): 387–401.

Lee, Sing Kong, Chor Boon Goh, Birger Fredriksen, and Jee Peng Tan. *Toward a Better Future: Education and Training for Economic Development in Singapore Since 1965.*" Washington: World Bank, 2008.

Lefevre, Raphael. "The Coming of North Africa's 'Language Wars,'" *Journal of North African Studies* 20, no. 4 (2015): 499–502.

Levitsky, Steven R., and Lucan A. Way. "Beyond Patronage: Violent Struggle, Ruling Party Cohesion, and Authoritarian Durability," *Perspectives on Politics* 10, no. 4 (2012): 869–889.

Lewin, Tamar. "University Branches in Dubai Are Struggling," *New York Times,* December 27, 2009. https://www.nytimes.com/2009/12/28/education/28dubai .html.

Lin, Ann Chih. *Reform in the Making: The Implementation of Social Policy in Prison.* Princeton: Princeton University Press, 2000.

Lindsey, Ursula. "NYU-Abu Dhabi Behaves Like a Careful Guest in Foreign Land," *Chronicle of Higher Education,* June 3, 2012.

Linz, Juan, and Alfred Stepan. *Problems of Democratic Transition and Consolidation: Southern Europe, South America, and Post-Communist Europe.* Baltimore: Johns Hopkins University Press, 1996.

Lipton, Eric, Brooke Williams, and Nicholas Confessore. "Foreign Powers Buy Influence at Think Tanks," *New York Times,* September 6, 2014. https://www .nytimes.com/2014/09/07/us/politics/foreign-powers-buy-influence-at-think -tanks.html.

Lott, John R., Jr. "Public Schooling, Indoctrination, and Totalitarianism," *Journal of Political Economy* 107, no. S6 (December 1999): S127–S157.

Lucenti, Maria. "La Nouvelle Réforme Scolaire en Tunisie: Le Défi Démocratique entre Analyse des Manuels et Didactique," *Foro de Educación* 15, no. 23 (2017): 219–242.

Luciani, Giacomo. "Introduction: In Search of Economic Policies to Stabilise Democratic Transitions," in *Combining Economic and Political Development: The Experience of MENA,* edited by Giacomo Luciani. Leiden: Brill Nijhoff, 2017, pp. 1–21.

Lust, Ellen. "Democratization by Elections? Competitive Clientelism in the Middle East," *Journal of Democracy* 20, no. 3 (2009): 122–135.

Lust, Ellen. "Missing the Third Wave: Islam, Institutions, and Democracy in the Middle East," *Studies in Comparative International Development* 46 (April 2011): 163–190.

Lust, Ellen, Pierre Landry, Lindsay Benstead, and Dhafer Malouche. "The Tunisian Local Governance Performance Index (LGPI)." 2015. http://gld.gu.se/en /research-projects/lgpi.

Maadad, Nina. *Schooling and Education in Lebanon: Syrian and Syrian Palestinian Refugees Inside and Outside the Camps.* Bern: Peter Lang, 2017.

Maassen, Peter, and Christine Musselin. "European Integration and the Europeanisation of Higher Education," in *European Integration and the Governance of Higher Education and Research,* edited by Alberto Amaral, Guy Neave, Christine Musselin, and Peter Maassen. Heidleberg: Springer, 2009, pp. 3–14.

Mabhubani, Kishore. *Can Asians Think? Understanding the Divide Between East and West.* New York: Times Books International, 1998.

MacKinzie-Smith, Peter. "Introduction," in *Higher Education in Gulf States: Shaping Economies, Politics, and Culture,* edited by Christopher Davidson and Peter MacKenzie-Smith. London: Saqi Books, 2008.

Maddy-Weitzman, Bruce. "Women, Islam, and the Moroccan State: The Struggle over the Personal Status Law," *Middle East Journal* 59, no. 3 (2005): 394–410.

Maghraoui, Abdeslam M. *Liberalism Without Democracy: Nationhood and Citizenship in Egypt, 1922–1936.* Durham: Duke University Press, 2006.

Makdisi, Ussama. "After 1860: Debating Religion, Reform and Nationalism in the Ottoman Empire," *International Journal of Middle East Studies* 34 (2002): 601–617.

Al-Manee'a, Hayya bin 'Abd al-'Aziz. "Al-taghrib fi al-inghilaq," *Al-Riyadh,* February 13, 2013. http://www.alriyadh.com/812391.

Mann, Michael. "The Autonomous Power of the State: Its Origins, Mechanisms, and Results," *European Journal of Sociology* 25, no. 2 (1984): 185–213.

Mann, Michael. *The Sources of Social Power: A History of Power from the Beginning to AD 1760,* Volume 1. Cambridge: Cambridge University Press, 1986.

Manning, Robert A. "The Shale Revolution and the New Geopolitics of Energy." Atlantic Council, October 31, 2014. https://www.atlanticcouncil.org/in-depth -research-reports/report/the-shale-revolution-and-the-new-geopolitics-of -energy.

Marcoux, Jacques, and Caroline Bargout. "How Events Unfolded After Foreign Affairs Minister Sent Tweet Rebuking Saudi Arabia." CBC News, December 7, 2018. https://www.cbc.ca/news/canada/how-events-unfolded-after-foreign-affairs -minister-sent-tweet-rebuking-saudi-arabia-1.4935735.

Martel, Mika. "Tracing the Spark That Lights a Flame: A Review of Methodologies to Measure the Outcomes of International Scholarships," in *International Scholarships in Higher Education: Pathways to Social Change,* edited by Joan R. Dassin, Robin R. Marsh, and Matt Mawer. New York: Springer, 2017, pp. 281–304.

Masri, Safwan M. *Tunisia: An Arab Anomaly.* New York: Columbia University Press, 2017.

Matthiesen, Toby. *The Other Saudis: Shiism, Dissent and Sectarianism.* New York: Cambridge University Press, 2015.

Mazawi, André Elias. "Contrasting Perspectives on Higher Education in Arab States," in *Higher Education: Handbook of Theory and Research,* Volume 20, edited by J. C. Smart. Heidleberg: Springer, 2005, pp. 133–189.

Mazawi, Andre Elias. "Schooling and Curricular Reforms in Arab and Muslim Societies," *Middle East Journal* 62, no. 2 (2008): 329–337.

McKee, Musa, Martin Keulertz, Negar Habibi, Mark Mulligan, and Eckart Woertz. "Demographic and Economic Material Factors in the MENA Region," Working Papers 3 (October 2017). MENARA Project of the EU Horizon 2020 Research and Innovation Program. http://www.iai.it/sites/default/files/menara_wp_3.pdf.

Mehri, Darius B. "Pockets of Efficiency and the Rise of Iran Auto: Implications for Theories of the Developmental State," *Studies in Comparative International Development* 50, no. 3 (2015): 408–432.

Meijer, Roel. "Economic Deprivation, Political Corruption and the Rise of New Citizen Movements in the MENA Region," *Orient* 59, no. 4 (October 2018): 49–58.

Meijer, Roel. "From Colonial to Authoritarian Pact," in *The Routledge Handbook of Citizenship in the Middle East and North Africa,* edited by Roel Meijer, James N. Sater, and Zahra Babar. London: Routledge, 2021.

Meijer, Roel. *The Quest for Modernity: Secular Liberal and Left-Wing Political Thought in Egypt, 1945–1958.* London: RoutledgeCurzon, 2002.

Meijer, Roel, and Nils Butenschøn, eds. *The Crisis of Citizenship in the Arab World.* Leiden: Brill, 2017.

Meijer, Roel, James N. Sater, and Zahra R. Babar, eds. *The Routledge Handbook of Citizenship in the Middle East and North Africa.* London: Routledge, 2021.

Menaldo, Victor. "The Middle East and North Africa's Resilient Monarchs," *Journal of Politics* 74, no. 3 (2012): 707–722.

Merrouche, Ouarda. "The Long-Term Impact of French Settlement on Education in Algeria." Working Paper 2, Uppsala University Department of Economics, 2007.

Michel, Sandrine. "Education in Thailand: When Economic Growth Is No Longer Enough," *London Review of Education* 13, no. 3 (2015): 79–82.

Miller, Marine, and Camille Stromboni. "Sorbonne Abou Dhabi: Soupçons de Censure Envers une Universitaire," *Le Monde,* October 4, 2018. https://www.lemonde.fr/education/article/2018/10/04/sorbonne-abou-dhabi-soupcons-de-censure-envers-une-universitaire_5364667_1473685.html.

Milovanovitch, Mihaylo. "Trust and Institutional Corruption: The Case of Education in Tunisia." Edmond J. Safra Working Papers, No. 44, May 22, 2014.

Mo, Jongryn, and Barry Weingast. *Korean Political and Economic Development: Crisis, Security, and Institutional Rebalancing.* Cambridge, MA: Harvard University Press, 2013.

Mohamed, Eid, Hannah R. Gerber, and Slimane Aboulkacem, eds. *Education and the Arab Spring.* Rotterdam: SensePublishers, 2016.

Montinola, Gabriella. "Change and Continuity in a Limited Access Order: The Philippines," in *In the Shadow of Violence: Politics, Economics, and the Problems of Development,* edited by Douglass North, John Wallis, Steve Webb, and Barry Weingast. Cambridge: Cambridge University Press, 2012, pp. 149–197.

Mostafa, Amr. "Egyptian Public Universities Seeking to Make Profits," *Al-Monitor,* March 7, 2019. https://www.al-monitor.com/pulse/originals/2019/03/egypt-free-education-non-profit-universities-law-controversy.html.

Mostafa, Randa. "Judicial Candidates Forced to Undergo Unprecedented Evaluations as Presidency Exerts Further Control," *Mada Masr,* February 13, 2019. https://madamasr.com/en/2019/02/13/feature/politics/judicial-candidates-forced-to-undergo-unprecedented-evaluations-as-presidency-exerts-further-control.

Muasher, Marwan, and Nathan J. Brown. *Engaging Society to Reform Arab Education: From Schooling to Learning.* Washington: Carnegie Endowment for International Peace, 2018.

Murphy, Lawrence. *The American University in Cairo, 1919–1987.* Cairo: American University in Cairo Press, 1987.

Nagle, John. "Academic Freedom: I Spent Four Months at UAE's National University—This Is What I Found." The Conversation, October 22, 2018. https://theconversation.com/academic-freedom-i-spent-four-months-at-uaes-national-university-this-is-what-i-found-105254.

Al-Nassar, Fahd Mohammed. "Saudi Arabian Educational Mission to the United States: Assessing Perceptions of Student Satisfaction with Services Rendered." Unpublished dissertation, University of Oklahoma, 1982.

Nasser, Ramzi. "Qatar's Educational Reform Past and Future: Challenges in Teacher Development," *Open Review of Educational Research* 4, no. 1 (2017): 1–19.

Naviwala, Nadia. "Why Can't Pakistani Children Read? The Inside Story of Education Reform Efforts Gone Wrong." The Wilson Center, July 2019. https://www.wilsoncenter.org/publication/why-cant-pakistani-children-read-the-inside-story-education-reform-efforts-gone-wrong.

Nir, Sarah Maslin. "N.Y.U. Journalism Faculty Boycotts Abu Dhabi Campus," *New York Times,* November 7, 2017. https://www.nytimes.com/2017/11/07/nyregion /nyu-journalism-professors-abu-dhabi-campus.html.

Noland, Marcus. "Explaining Middle Eastern Authoritarianism." Working Paper 05-5, Institute for International Economics, June 2005.

Norris, Pippa. *Democratic Deficit: Critical Citizens Revisited.* Cambridge, MA: Cambridge University Press, 2011.

North, Douglass C., John Joseph Wallis, Steven B. Webb, and Barry R. Weingast, eds. *In the Shadow of Violence: Politics, Economics, and the Problems of Development.* Cambridge: Cambridge University Press, 2013.

North, Douglass C., John Joseph Wallis, Steven B. Webb, and Barry Weingast. "Limited Access Orders in the Developing World: A New Approach to the Problems of Development." Policy Research Working Paper WPS4359, World Bank, 2007.

North, Douglass C., John Joseph Wallis, Steven B. Webb, and Barry R. Weingast. "Limited Access Orders: Rethinking the Problems of Development and Violence." Stanford University, January 25, 2011. https://web.stanford.edu/group /mcnollgast/cgi-bin/wordpress/wp-content/uploads/2013/10/Limited _Access_Orders_in_DW_-II_-2011.0125.submission-version.pdf.

North, Douglass, John Joseph Wallis, and Barry Weingast. "A Conceptual Framework for Interpreting Recorded Human History." Working Paper 75, Mercatus Center, George Mason University, 2009.

Nye, Joseph. *Soft Power: The Means to Success in World Politics.* New York: Public Affairs, 2004.

O'Donnell, Guillermo A., Philippe C. Schmitter, and Laurence Whitehead. *Transitions from Authoritarian Rule: Comparative Perspectives.* Baltimore: Johns Hopkins University Press, 1986.

Ottaway, David. "Saudi Arabia's Race Against Time." Occasional Papers Series, Woodrow Wilson Center Middle East Program, Washington, 2012.

Paul, Katie. "Saudi Tightens Rules for Scholarships to Study Abroad," February 1, 2016. https://www.reuters.com/article/us-saudi-education/saudi-tightens-rules -for-scholarships-to-study-abroad-idUSKCN0VA35R.

Pennell, C. R. *Morocco Since 1830: A History.* New York: New York University Press, 2000.

Perkins, Kenneth J. *A History of Modern Tunisia.* New York: Cambridge University Press, 2004.

Pickel, Susanne, Toralf Stark, and Wiebke Breustedt. "Assessing the Quality of Measures of Democracy: A Theoretical Framework and Its Empirical Application," *European Political Science* 14 (2015): 496–520.

Pritchett, Lant. "'When Will They Ever Learn?' Why All Governments Produce Schooling." BREAD Working Paper 31, June 2003.

Prum, Seila. "Cramming into Extra Classes Ahead of Exams," *Phnom Penh Post,* October 21, 2009. https://www.phnompenhpost.com/post-plus/cramming-extra -classes-ahead-exams.

Przeworski, Adam. *Democracy and the Limits of Self-Government.* New York: Cambridge University Press, 2010.

Puryear, Jeffrey M. "International Education Statistics and Research: Status and Problems," *International Journal of Educational Development* 15, no. 1 (1995): 79–91.

Quran, Layla. "Saudi Students in U.S. Say Their Government Watches Their Every Move." PBS, March 19, 2019. https://www.pbs.org/newshour/world/saudi-students -in-u-s-say-their-government-watches-their-every-move.

Raghavan, Sudarsan. "In New Egyptian Textbooks, 'It's Like the Revolution Didn't Happen,'" *Washington Post,* April 23, 2016. https://www.washingtonpost.com /world/middle_east/in-new-egyptian-textbooks-its-like-the-revolution-didnt -happen/2016/04/23/846ab2f0-f82e-11e5-958d-d038dac6e718_story.html.

Rajakumar, Mohanalakshmi. *Love Comes Later.* Self-published, 2013.

Reda, Lolwa. "New Cumulative Secondary System to Be Applied 2018/19," *Egypt Today,* September 9, 2018. https://www.egypttoday.com/Article/1/57333/New -Cumulative-Secondary-School-System-to-be-applied-2018-19.

Redden, Elizabeth. "The Doha Experiment," *Inside Higher Ed,* November 2, 2017. https://www.insidehighered.com/news/2017/11/02/new-book-former-professor -looks-georgetowns-campus-qatar-warts-and-all.

Redden, Elizabeth. "Persona Non Grata," *Inside Higher Ed,* March 18, 2015. https:// www.insidehighered.com/news/2015/03/18/nyu-professor-denied-entry-uae -where-university-has-campus.

Redden, Elizabeth. "University College London to Close Qatar Campus," *Inside Higher Ed,* January 4, 2019. https://www.insidehighered.com/quicktakes/2019 /01/04/university-college-london-close-qatar-campus.

Redden, Elizabeth. "Visa Denied," *Inside Higher Ed,* January 9, 2017. https://www .insidehighered.com/news/2017/01/09/georgetown-student-denied-visa-study -universitys-qatar-campus.

Reid, Donald Malcom. *Cairo University and the Making of Modern Egypt.* Cambridge: Cambridge University Press, 1990.

Robson, Laura. *States of Separation: Transfer, Partition and the Making of the Modern Middle East.* Berkeley: University of California Press, 2017.

Roesgaard, Marie H. *Japanese Education and the Cram School Business: Functions, Challenges and Perspectives of the Juku.* Copenhagen: NIAS Press, 2006.

Romani, Vincent. "The Politics of Higher Education in the Middle East: Problems and Prospects." Middle East Brief 36, Crown Center for Middle East Studies, Brandeis University, May 2009.

Rosenstone, Steven J., and John Mark Hansen. *Mobilization, Participation and Democracy in America.* New York: Macmillan, 1993.

Ross, Michael L. "Does Oil Hinder Democracy?," *World Politics* 53, no. 3 (April 2001): 325–361.

Rouag, Abdelwalid, and Jan Stejskal. "Assessing the Performance of the Public Sector in North African and Middle East Countries," *International Journal of Public Sector Performance Management* 3, no. 3 (2017): 279–296.

Rugh, William A. "Arab Education: Tradition, Growth and Reform," *Middle East Journal* 56, no. 3 (2002): 396–414.

Al-Sabbagh, Mohammed. *Al-ibti'ath wa makhatiruh.* Ri'asat Idarat al-Buhuth al-'ilmiyya wal ifta wal da'wah wal irshad (Saudi Arabia), 1977.

Sa'di, Ibrahim, and Marwan al-Harbi. "Al-taghayur al-qimi lada al-'aideen min al-ibti'ath al-khariji fi daw ba'th al-mutaghayirat al-nafsiyya wal dimographiyya." Kursi al-amir naif bin abdulaziz lil qiyam al-aklaqiyya, King Abdulaziz University, 2017, pp. 40–46.

Salehi-Isfahani, Djavad. "Education, Jobs, and Equity in the Middle East and North Africa," *Comparative Economic Studies* 54, no. 4 (2012): 843–861.

Salehi-Isfahani, Djavad, Nadia Belhaj Hassine, and Ragui Assaad. "Equality of Opportunity in Educational Achievement in the Middle East and North Africa," *Journal of Economic Inequality* 12 (2014): 489–515.

Salmi, Jamil. *The Challenge of Establishing World Class Universities.* Washington: World Bank, 2009.

Salmi, Jamil. *Crise de L'Enseignement et Reproduction Sociale au Maroc.* Casablanca: Éditions Maghrébines, 1985.

Sanborn, Howard, and Clayton L. Thyne. "Learning Democracy: Education and the Fall of Authoritarian Regimes," *British Journal of Political Science* 44, no. 4 (2014): 773–797.

Sasnal, Patricja. *Myths and Legends: Modern History and Nationalist Propaganda in Egyptian Textbooks.* Warsaw: The Polish Institute of International Affairs, 2014. https://www.files.ethz.ch/isn/180939/Myths%20and%20Legends_%20 Modern%20History%20and%20Nationalistic%20Propaganda%20in%20Egyptian %20Textbooks.pdf.

Schaefer, Isabel. *Political Revolt and Youth Unemployment in Tunisia: Exploring the Education-Employment Mismatch.* London: Palgrave Macmillan, 2018.

Schectman, Joel, and Christopher Bing. "Exclusive: UAE Used Cyber Super-Weapon to Spy on iPhones of Foes." Reuters, January 30, 2019. https://www .reuters.com/article/us-usa-spying-karma-exclusive/exclusive-uae-used-cyber -super-weapon-to-spy-on-iphones-of-foes-idUSKCN1PO1AN.

Schneider, Suzanne. *Mandatory Separation: Religion, Education, and Mass Politics in Palestine.* Stanford: Stanford University Press, 2018.

Schwab, Klaus. "The Global Competitive Report 2017–2018." World Economic Forum. http://www3.weforum.org/docs/GCR2017-2018/05FullReport/TheGlobal CompetitivenessReport2017%E2%80%932018.pdf.

Schwartzstein, Peter. "How Saddam and ISIS Killed Iraqi Science," *Smithsonian Magazine,* May 29, 2018. https://www.smithsonianmag.com/history/how-saddam -and-isis-killed-iraqi-science-180969097.

Sebat, George. "Mon Souhait: L'Enseignement du Judaïsme Marocaine," *Juif du Maroc,* July 25, 2018. http://juifdumaroc.over-blog.com/mon-souhait-l-enseignement -du-judaisme-marocain.html.

Seth, Michael J. *Education Fever: Society, Politics, and the Pursuit of Schooling in South Korea.* Honolulu: University of Hawaii Press, 2002.

Seurat, Michel. *L'Etat de Barbarie.* Paris: Editions du Seuil, 1989.

Shannon, Matthew K. *Losing Hearts and Minds: American-Iranian Relations and International Education During the Cold War.* Ithaca: Cornell University Press, 2017.

Al-Shaqawi, Ameen bin Abdullah. "Makhatir al-ibti'ath wa dhawabitihi." Alukah, February 8, 2015. https://www.alukah.net/social/0/82284.

Sharkey, Heather J. *A History of Muslims, Christians and Jews in the Middle East.* Cambridge: Cambridge University Press, 2017.

Sharkey, Heather J. *American Evangelicals in Egypt.* Princeton: Princeton University Press, 2008.

Sharma, Yojana. "Asian Parents Suffering 'Education Fever.'" BBC, October 22, 2013. https://www.bbc.com/news/business-24537487.

Al-Shedokhi, Saad Abdul-Karim. "An Investigation of the Problems Experienced by Saudi Students While Enrolled in Institutions of Higher Education in the United States." Unpublished dissertation, Oregon State University, 1986.

Siddhanta, Suddhasil, and Debasish Nandy. "Gender Gap in Education: A Fresh Exploration," *SSRN,* 2003. https://www.researchgate.net/publication/255569854 _Gender_Gap_in_Education_A_Fresh_Exploration.

Sobhy, Hania, Nayera Abdel Rahman, Omnia Khalil, Reem Abdelhaliem, and Sarah Anne Rennick. "Civil Society and Public Policy Formation: Strategies from Morocco and Egypt." Arab Reform Initiative, 2017. https://www.arab-reform.net /en/node/1077.

Soussi, Mouez, and Donia Smaali Bouhlila. "Child Labor and Schooling," in *The Tunisian Labor Market in an Era of Transition,* edited by Ragui Assaad and Mongi Boughzala. Oxford: Oxford University Press, 2018.

Spilimbergo, Antonio. "Democracy and Foreign Education," *American Economic Review* 99, no. 1 (2009): 528–543.

Springborg, Robert. "The Effects of Patronage Systems and Clientelism on Citizenship in the Middle East," in *The Crisis of Citizenship in the Arab World,* edited by Roel Meijer and Nils Butenschøn. Leiden: Brill, 2017, pp. 407–434.

Springborg, Robert. "An Egyptian Education: Militarizing Schoolchildren to Serve Sisi's Regime," *The New Arab,* October 29, 2018. https://english.alaraby .co.uk/english/comment/2018/10/29/an-egyptian-education-militarising-school children-to-serve-sisis-regime.

Springborg, Robert. *Political Economies of the Middle East and North Africa.* Cambridge: Polity Press, 2020.

Staniland, Paul. "Militias, Ideology, and the State," *Journal of Conflict Resolution* 59, no. 5 (2015): 778–781.

Stepan, Alfred C., and Graeme B. Robertson. "An 'Arab' More Than a 'Muslim' Democracy Gap," *Journal of Democracy* 14, no. 3 (July 2003): 30–44.

Stevenson, Harold W., Shin-ying Lee, and James W. Stigler. "Mathematics Achievement of Chinese, Japanese, and American Children," *Science* 231 (1986): 693–699.

Strzyżyńska, Weronika. "Sheikh It Off: Inside UCL's Decision to Leave Qatar." The Cheese Grater, October 23, 2017. https://cheesegratermagazine.org/2017/10/23 /sheikh-off-inside-ucls-decision-leave-gulf.

Al-Subaiey, Maryam. "Qatarization Policy: Implementation Challenges." Brookings Doha Center, June 7, 2016. https://www.brookings.edu/wp-content/uploads /2016/07/06_bdc_essay_winner.pdf.

Sudairi, Muhammad. "Fighting the Smokeless War: A Comparative Study on the Origins, Conceptualizations and Practices of Cultural Security in China and Saudi Arabia." PhD dissertation, University of Hong Kong, 2019.

Suen, Hoi K., and Lan Yu. "Chronic Consequences of High-Stakes Testing? Lessons from the Chinese Civil Service Exam," *Comparative Education Review* 50, no. (2006) 1: 46–65.

Tagliapietra, Simone. "What If the Rest of Europe Follows Italy's Coronavirus Fate?," *The Guardian,* March 10, 2020.

Taha, Rana, and Martin Morgan. "Mickey Mouse Expelled from Egypt Schools." BBC, September 28, 2018. https://www.bbc.com/news/blogs-news-from-elsewhere -45671180.

Al-Tahtawi, Rifa'a Rifa'I. *An Imam in Paris: Al-Tahtawi's Visit to France 1826– 1831,* edited and translated by Daniel Newman. London: Saqi Books, 2004.

Tanamal, Yvette. "Bimbel Blues: How After-School Cram Sessions Became Necessary in Indonesia." Vice Media Group, August 14, 2018. https://www.vice.com /en_asia/article/gy3k87/bimbel-blues-how-after-school-cram-sessions-became -necessary-in-indonesia.

Tasker, Peter. "The Flawed 'Science' Behind Democracy Rankings," *Nikkei Asian Review,* February 25, 2016.

Taylor, Charles, and Wasmiah Albasri. "The Impact of Saudi Arabia King Abdullah's Scholarship Program in the U.S.," *Open Journal of Social Science*s 2 (2014): 109–118.

Teng, Ssu-yu. "Chinese Influence on the Western Examination System," *Harvard Journal of Asiatic Studies* 7 (1942): 267–312.

Tessler, Mark. "Islam and Democracy in the Middle East: The Impact of Religious Orientations on Attitudes Towards Democracy in Four Arab Countries," *Comparative Politics* 34, no. 3 (April 2002): 337–354.

Thabet, Alaa. "Journey to the Future on Board the NTA," *Ahramonline,* September 9, 2019. http://english.ahram.org.eg/News/346329.aspx.

Thelen, Kathleen, and James Mahoney. "Comparative-Historical Analysis in Contemporary Political Science," in *Advances in Comparative-Historical Analysis,* edited by James Mahoney and Kathleen Thelen. Cambridge: Cambridge University Press, 2015, pp. 3–36.

Thompson, Elizabeth. *Colonial Citizens: Republican Rights, Paternal Privilege, and Gender in French Syria and Lebanon.* New York: Columbia University Press, 2000.

Tok, M. Evren, Lolwah Alkhater, and Leslie Pal, eds. *Policy-Making in a Transformative State: The Case of Qatar.* London: Palgrave Macmillan, 2016.

Toumi, Abdennour. "Is Algeria Facing a Brain Drain?," *Arab Daily News,* May 20, 2019. https://thearabdailynews.com/2019/05/20/is-algeria-facing-a-brain-drain.

Trabelsi, Salwa. "Regional Inequality of Education in Tunisia: An Evaluation by the Gini Index," *Région et Développement* 37 (2013). https://pdfs.semanticscholar.org/72e0/2238149c40f39c777351109da54ee4948b6c.pdf.

Travers, Eileen. "University Initiatives Melt Borders with Brazil," *University World News,* March 18, 2012. https://www.universityworldnews.com/post.php?story=2012031523350556.

Troianovski, Anton, and Nakashima, Ellen. "How Russia's Military Intelligence Agency Became the Covert Muscle in Putin's Duels with the West," *Washington Post,* December 28, 2018. https://www.washingtonpost.com/world/europe/how-russias-military-intelligence-agency-became-the-covert-muscle-in-putins-duels-with-the-west/2018/12/27/2736bbe2-fb2d-11e8-8c9a-860ce2a8148f_story.html.

Ulrichsen, Kristian Coates. "Academic Freedom and UAE Funding," *Foreign Policy,* February 25, 2013. https://foreignpolicy.com/2013/02/25/academic-freedom-and-uae-funding.

Ulrichsen, Kristian Coates. *The Gulf States in International Political Economy.* New York: Palgrave Macmillan, 2016.

US Department of State. "Tunisia," March 9, 2012. https://web.archive.org/web/20121013143542/http://www.state.gov/outofdate/bgn/tunisia/196390.htm.

Vairel, Frédéric. "'Qu'avez-vous fait de vos vingt ans?' Militantismes marocains du 23 mars (1965) au 20 février (2011)," *L'Année du Maghreb* 8 (2012): 219–238.

Vassiliev, Alexei. *The History of Saudi Arabia.* London: Saqi Books, 1998.

Vavrus, Frances, and Lesley Bartlett. *Critical Approaches to Comparative Education: Vertical Case Studies from Africa, Europe, the Middle East, and the Americas.* New York: Palgrave Macmillan, 2009.

Vegas, Emiliana, and Chelsea Coffin. "When Education Expenditure Matters: An Empirical Analysis of Recent International Data," *Comparative Education Review* 59, no. 2 (2013): 289–305.

Verba, Sidney, Kay Lehman Schlozman, and Henry E. Brady. *Voice and Equality: Civic Voluntarism in American Politics.* Cambridge, MA: Harvard University Press, 1995.

Verdier, Marie. "Il Faudrait un Audit pour Sauver la Justice Transitionnelle en Tunisie," *La Croix,* March 27, 2018. https://www.la-croix.com/Monde/Afrique/Il-faudrait-audit-sauver-justice-transitionnelle-Tunisie-2018-03-27-1200927155.

Vickers, Edward, and Alisa Jones. *History Education and National Identity in East Asia.* London: Routledge, 2005.

Vidano, Adriana. "Dans les Manuels Scolaires, l'Histoire de la Tunisie S'Arrête en 1964." Nawaat, September 21, 2018. https://nawaat.org/portail/2018/09/21/dans-les-manuels-scolaires-lhistoire-de-la-tunisie-sarrete-en-1964.

Viet, Vincent. *La France Immigrée. Construction d'une Politique 1914–1997.* Paris: Fayard, 1998.

Völkel, Jan C. "Complex Politics in Single Numbers? The Problem of Defining and Measuring Democracy," *Middle East Critique* 24, no. 1 (2015): 67–81.

Voreacos, David, and Michael Riley. "Trump Fundraiser Claims Qatar Used U.S. Firm in Hacking." Bloomberg, May 24, 2018. https://www.bloomberg.com /news/articles/2018-05-24/broidy-s-expanded-hack-allegations-fault-ex-spy -emir-s-brother.

Wade, Robert. *Governing the Market: Economic Theory and the Role of Government in East Asian Industrialization.* Princeton: Princeton University Press, 1990.

Wail, Benaabdelaali, Said Hanchane, and Abdelhak Kamal. "A New Data Set of Educational Inequality in the World, 1950–2010: Gini Index of Education by Age Group." Association Marocaine de Sciences Economiques, October 2011. http://www.amse.ma/doc/WP_2012_09.pdf.

Waldner, David. *State Building and Late Development.* Ithaca: Cornell University Press, 1999.

Wang, Yuhua. "Are College Graduates Agents of Change? Education and Political Participation in China," *SSRN,* February 2018. https://ssrn-com.proxy.lib.pdx .edu/abstract=2905288.

Wasserman, Gary. *The Doha Experiment: Arab Kingdom, Catholic College, Jewish Teacher.* New York: Skyhorse, 2017.

Weber, Max. *The Protestant Work Ethic and the Spirit of Capitalism.* 1950 [1905]. https://www.marxists.org/reference/archive/weber/protestant-ethic/.

Wedeen, Lisa. *Ambiguities of Domination: Politics, Rhetoric, and Symbols in Contemporary Syria.* Chicago: University of Chicago Press, 2005.

Werenfels, Isabelle. *Managing Instability in Algeria: Elites and Political Change Since 1995.* New York: Routledge, 2007.

Wickham, Carrie Rosefsky. *Mobilizing Islam: Religion, Activism, and Political Change in Egypt.* New York: Columbia University Press, 2002.

Williams, Brooke, Eric Lipton, and Alicia Parlapiano. "Foreign Government Contributions to Nine Think Tanks," *New York Times,* September 7, 2014. https:// www.nytimes.com/interactive/2014/09/07/us/politics/foreign-government -contributions-to-nine-think-tanks.html?mtrref=goodtimesweb.org&assetType =REGIWALL.

Wiseman, Alexander W., Naif H. Alromi, and Saleh Alshumrani, eds. *Education for a Knowledge Society in Arabian Gulf Countries.* Bingley: Emerald Group Publishing, 2014.

Wiyaporn, Patchanee, and Pathomporn Raksapolmuang. "Education Reform in Thailand: The Case of Basic Education Quality Improvement for Raising the National Competitiveness of Thailand Among ASEAN Member Countries." Parliamentary Institute of Cambodia, 2017. https://www.pic.org.kh/images /2017Research/20170523%20Education_Reform_Thailand_%20Eng.pdf.

Wolfinger, Raymond E., and Steven J. Rosenstone. *Who Votes? Storrs Lectures on Jurisprudence.* New Haven: Yale University Press, 1980.

Woodside, Alexander. "Territorial Order and Collective-Identity Tensions in Confucian Asia: China, Vietnam, Korea," *Daedalus* 127, no. 3 (1998): 191–220.

World Bank. *World Development Report 2018: Learning to Realize Education's Promise.* Washington: World Bank, 2018.

World Bank. *The East Asian Miracle: Economic Growth and Public Policy.* Oxford: Oxford University Press, 1993.

Wright, Joseph, Erica Frantz, and Barbara Geddes. "Oil and Autocratic Regime Survival," *British Journal of Political Science* 45, no. 2 (2015): 287–306.

Xi, Jinping. "Secure a Decisive Victory in Securing a Moderately Prosperous Society in All Respects and Strive for the Great Success of Socialism with Chinese

Characteristics for the New Era." Speech delivered at the Nineteenth Party Congress, October 18, 2017.

Yates, Miranda, and James Youniss, eds. *Roots of Civic Identity: International Perspectives on Community Service and Activism in Youth.* New York: Cambridge University Press, 1998.

Yerkes, Sarah, and Muasher Marwan. "Decentralization in Tunisia: Empowering Towns, Engaging People." Carnegie Endowment for International Peace, May 17, 2018. https://carnegieendowment.org/2018/05/17/decentralization-in-tunisia -empowering-towns-engaging-people-pub-76376.

Yom, Sean. "The Youth Generation: Education and Transition," in *The Societies of the Middle East and North Africa: Structures, Vulnerabilities, and Forces,* edited by Sean Yom. London: Routledge, 2019, pp. 319–322.

Yom, Sean L., and F. Gregory Gause III. "Resilient Royals: How Arab Monarchies Hang On," *Journal of Democracy* 23, no. 4 (2012): 74–88.

You, Jong-Sung. "Transition from a Limited Access Order to an Open Access Order: The Case of South Korea," in *In the Shadow of Violence: Politics, Economics, and the Problems of Development,* edited by Douglass C. North, John Wallis, Steven Webb, and Barry Weingast. Cambridge: Cambridge University Press, 2012, pp. 293–327.

Younes, Rasha. "Northwestern University's Precarious Role Under Qatar's Repressive Laws." Human Rights Watch, February 6, 2020. https://www.hrw.org/news /2020/02/06/northwestern-universitys-precarious-role-under-qatars-repressive -laws.

Youness, Ahmed. "University Staff in Egypt Receive Military Training," *Al-Monitor,* July 26, 2019. https://www.al-monitor.com/pulse/originals/2019/07/egypt -universities-military-sessions-army-role.html.

Yousef, Abdullah A. "Drug Problem and Social Change in Saudi Arabia: A Study of the Attitude of Saudi Students Studying in the United States of America Towards Drug Use in Saudi Arabia." Unpublished dissertation, Western Michigan University, 1991.

Zakaria, Fareed. "Culture Is Destiny: A Conversation with Lee Kuan Yew," *Foreign Affairs* 73, no. 2 (1994): 109–126.

Zalata, Shady. "Interview: Head of Egypt's New State Academy to Train Future Leaders," *Ahramonline,* November 2, 2018. http://english.ahram.org.eg/News Content/1/64/315566/Egypt/Politics-/Interview-Head-of-Egypts-new-state -academy-to-trai.aspx.

Zeng, Kangmin. *Dragon Gate: Competitive Examinations and Their Consequences.* London: Cassell, 1999.

The Contributors

Hicham Alaoui is a research associate at the Weatherhead Center for International Affairs at Harvard University. He has served on the board of the Freeman Spogli Institute at Stanford University, the MENA Advisory Committee for Human Rights Watch, and the Advisory Board of the Carnegie Middle East Center. His academic research has been published in journals such as *Politique Internationale, Le Debat, Pouvoirs, Le Monde Diplomatique,* and *Journal of Democracy.* He has also contributed to periodicals such as the *New York Times, Le Monde, La Nouvelle Observateur, El Pais,* and *Al-Quds.* His memoir, *Journal d'un Prince Banni,* was published in 2014 by Éditions Grasset, and has since been translated into several languages.

Lindsay J. Benstead is associate professor of political science in the Mark O. Hatfield School of Government and director of the Middle East Studies Center at Portland State University. Previously, she served as fellow in the Middle East Program and the Women's Global Leadership Initiative at the Woodrow Wilson International Center for Scholars and Kuwait Visiting Professor at Sciences Po in Paris. Her research on women and politics, public opinion, and survey methodology has appeared in *Perspectives on Politics, International Journal of Public Opinion Research, Governance,* and *Foreign Affairs.*

Christopher M. Davidson is associate fellow of the Royal United Services Institute and a fellow of the European Centre for International Affairs. Previously a reader in Middle East politics at Durham

University and assistant professor at Zayed University in the United Arab Emirates, he has a long-standing interest in the politics and political economy of the Arab Gulf states. His publications include *Dubai: The Vulnerability of Success; Abu Dhabi: Oil and Beyond;* and *Higher Education in the Gulf: Building Economies, Politics, and Culture* (as coeditor).

Ishac Diwan is professor of economics at Paris Sciences et Lettres where he holds the chair of the Economy of the Arab World. He currently teaches at the Ecole Normale Superieure in Paris, and has previously held teaching positions at Columbia University, School for International Public Affairs, and at the Harvard Kennedy School. His recent (co-authored) books include *A Political Economy of the Middle East* and *Crony Capitalism in the Middle East* (Oxford University Press, 2019). He is also widely published on issues of global finance, macroeconomics, and development strategies.

Merilee S. Grindle is Edward S. Mason Professor of International Development, emerita, at the Harvard Kennedy School. She has also served as director of the David Rockefeller Center for Latin American Studies at Harvard University and as president of the Latin American Studies Association. She is author of several books and numerous articles on the comparative politics of policymaking and policy implementation.

Adel Hamaizia is a PhD candidate at the University of Oxford, where he focuses on the political economy of informality in Algeria. He is committee vice chair of the Oxford Gulf and Arabian Peninsula Studies Forum and associate fellow at the Chatham House MENA program.

Alisa Jones is senior lecturer in the Asian and Oriental Studies Institute at the University of Tübingen and research development manager for the university's China Centre. Her principal research interests lie in the history and politics of education and concepts and practices of citizenship in China and Taiwan. She is editor of *History Education and National Identity in East Asia* (with Edward Vickers) and author of *History and Citizenship Education in Post-Mao China: Politics, Policy, Praxis.*

Florian Kohstall is in charge of university cooperation with the Middle East and North Africa at the Center for International Cooperation at Freie Universität Berlin. He is head of the Welcome Initiative and founder of Academics in Solidarity, a transnational mentoring program for displaced scholars. Until 2015 he was the director of the Freie Universität Berlin Cairo Office. He has also been a research fellow at the French research center CEDEJ and taught political science in Aix-en-Provence, Lyon, and Cairo.

Andrew Leber is a PhD candidate at Harvard University's Department of Government. He studies the politics of policymaking under authoritarianism, with a particular focus on Saudi Arabia and the Arab Gulf monarchies. His work has appeared in the *Review of Middle East Studies, British Journal of Middle East Studies, Mediterranean Studies,* and *MERIP.*

Roel Meijer is associate professor, teaching Middle Eastern history, at Radboud University, Nijmegen, Netherlands. He has coedited three volumes on citizenship in MENA: *The Crisis of Citizenship in the Arab World* (with Nils A. Butenschøn); *The Middle East in Transition: The Centrality of Citizenship* (with Nils A. Butenschøn); and *The Routledge Handbook of Citizenship in the Middle East and North Africa* (with James Sater and Zahra Babar).

Robert Springborg is a nonresident research fellow of the Italian Institute of International Affairs, Rome, and adjunct professor, Simon Fraser University. Formerly he was professor of national security affairs at the Naval Postgraduate School, Monterey, and program manager for the Middle East for the Center for Civil-Military Relations; holder of the MBI Al Jaber Chair in Middle East Studies at the School of Oriental and African Studies in London, where he also served as director of the London Middle East Institute; director of the American Research Center in Egypt; and university professor of Middle East politics at Macquarie University in Sydney, Australia. He has also taught at the University of California, Berkeley; the University of Pennsylvania; the College of Europe, Warsaw; the Paris School of International Affairs of Sciences Po; and the University of Sydney. In 2016 he was Kuwait Foundation Visiting Scholar, Middle East Initiative, Kennedy School, Harvard University. His most recent books are *Egypt* and *Political Economies of the Middle East and North Africa.*

Index

About the Book

Despite substantial spending on education and robust support for reform both internally and by external donors, the quality of education in many, if not most, Arab countries remains low. Which raises the question: Why?

The authors of *The Political Economy of Education in the Arab World* find answers in the authoritarian political economies that shape the architecture of national governance across the region. Presenting studies from North Africa and the Gulf region, as well as comparative perspectives from Asia and Latin America, they show clearly that efforts to improve education—and thereby enhance economic development and broaden the base of citizenship on which more stable and effective systems of governance can be built—will fail until ruling elites are no longer able to increase their political and economic power at the expense of the greater good.

Hicham Alaoui is research associate at the Weatherhead Center for International Affairs, Harvard University. **Robert Springborg** is a nonresident research fellow of the Italian Institute of International Affairs and adjunct professor in the School of International Studies at Simon Fraser University.